Leading Socially Just Schools

Equity and social justice have become central to the work of schools. Teachers and leaders are at the forefront of building socially just schools. Issues related to equity and social justice in education, however, are complex and deeply contested. Professional learning is critical to enable teachers and school leaders to develop the understandings, skills, and confidence to grapple with often challenging issues. This book brings together a range of contributions from different systems. The contributors to this book explore ways in which professional learning can support efforts to bring about socially just schools. The authors adopt a variety of perspectives, with some looking at professional learning around a broad concept of social justice and the task of addressing the gap between advantaged and disadvantaged learners. Other contributors explore the question of professional learning in relation to a specific issue or area of practice to raise awareness and deepen knowledge and skills. Barring one, all the chapters in this book were originally published as a special issue in the journal *Professional Development in Education*.

Christine Forde is Emeritus Professor at the University of Glasgow. Current research includes social justice leadership, middle leadership in schools, life histories and headship, and governance. She is a Fellow of the International Professional Development Association and received the Robert Owen Award for services to Scottish education in 2019.

Deirdre Torrance is Senior Research Fellow in Educational and School Leadership in the School of Education, University of Glasgow. Deirdre leads the Future of Headship Research Team and is engaged in numerous collaborative research and writing projects around policy, leadership preparation, school leadership and management, and social justice leadership.

Leading Socially Just Schools
The Role of Professional Learning and Growth

Edited by
Christine Forde and Deirdre Torrance

LONDON AND NEW YORK

First published 2024
by Routledge
4 Park Square, Milton Park, Abingdon, Oxon OX14 4RN

and by Routledge
605 Third Avenue, New York, NY 10158

Routledge is an imprint of the Taylor & Francis Group, an informa business

Chapter 1 © 2024 Christine Forde and Deirdre Torrance
Foreword, Chapters 2–15 and Afterword © 2024 International Professional Development Association

All rights reserved. No part of this book may be reprinted or reproduced or utilised in any form or by any electronic, mechanical, or other means, now known or hereafter invented, including photocopying and recording, or in any information storage or retrieval system, without permission in writing from the publishers.

Trademark notice: Product or corporate names may be trademarks or registered trademarks, and are used only for identification and explanation without intent to infringe.

British Library Cataloguing in Publication Data
A catalogue record for this book is available from the British Library

ISBN13: 978-1-032-41349-5 (hbk)
ISBN13: 978-1-032-41350-1 (pbk)
ISBN13: 978-1-003-35766-7 (ebk)

DOI: 10.4324/9781003357667

Typeset in Minion Pro
by Newgen Publishing UK

Publisher's Note
The publisher accepts responsibility for any inconsistencies that may have arisen during the conversion of this book from journal articles to book chapters, namely the inclusion of journal terminology.

Disclaimer
Every effort has been made to contact copyright holders for their permission to reprint material in this book. The publishers would be grateful to hear from any copyright holder who is not here acknowledged and will undertake to rectify any errors or omissions in future editions of this book.

Contents

Citation Information vii
Notes on Contributors x
Foreword xii
Fiona King

1 Introduction 1
  Christine Forde and Deirdre Torrance

Leadership development and leading socially just schools

2 Anti-racist school leadership: making 'race' count in leadership preparation
  and development 9
  Paul Miller

3 What is the problem? A critical review of social justice leadership preparation
  and development 24
  Deirdre Torrance, Christine Forde, Fiona King and Jamila Razzaq

4 Learning to lead socially just schools: an exploration of candidate readiness
  for equity-focused principal preparation in the United States 38
  Corrie Stone-Johnson, Corey Gray and Casandra Wright

5 The need for career-long professional learning for social justice leaders in affluent
  school contexts 52
  Karen Huchting and Jill Bickett

6 Professional development for school leaders in England: decision-making
  for social justice 65
  Ian Potter and Stephanie Chitpin

Leading in socially just schools

7 Promoting socially just schools through professional learning: lessons from four US
  principals in rural contexts 79
  Pamela S. Angelle, Mary Lynne Derrington and Alex N. Oldham

8 Critical professional development and the racial justice leadership possibilities of teachers of colour in K-12 schools 93
Rita Kohli, Marcos Pizarro, Luis-Genaro Garcia, Lisa Kelly, Michael Espinoza and Juan Córdova

9 The role of trade union provision for critical professional learning in supporting member teachers' social justice leadership practice 106
Halil Buyruk

Teacher development to build practice in socially just schools

10 Promoting professional growth to build a socially just school through participation in ethnographic research 121
Begoña Vigo-Arrazola and Dennis Beach

11 'Every single student counts': leadership of professional development underpinned by social justice for sessional staff in a South Australian university 134
Sarah K. Hattam and Tanya Weiler

12 A cross-school PLC: how could teacher professional development of robot-based pedagogies for all students build a social-justice school? 147
Elson Szeto, Kenneth Sin and George Leung

13 Supporting gender-inclusive schools: educators' beliefs about gender diversity training and implementation plans 162
Mollie T. McQuillan and Jennifer Leininger

14 Learning about culture together: enhancing educators cultural competence through collaborative teacher study groups 183
Chrystal S. Johnson, Jennifer Sdunzik, Cornelius Bynum, Nicole Kong and Xiaoyue Qin

15 The professional development needs of primary teachers in special classes for children with autism in the Republic of Ireland 197
Caitríona Finlay, William Kinsella and Paula Prendeville

Afterword: inserting social justice into professional development 218
Ira Bogotch

Index 224

Citation Information

The following chapters, except for Chapter 15, were originally published in the journal *Professional Development in Education*, volume 47, issue 1 (2021). Chapter 15 was originally published in volume 48, issue 2 (2022) of the same journal. When citing this material, please use the original page numbering for each article, as follows:

Foreword
Fiona King
Professional Development in Education, volume 47, issue 1 (2021), pp. 1–2

Chapter 2
Anti-racist school leadership: making 'race' count in leadership preparation and development
Paul Miller
Professional Development in Education, volume 47, issue 1 (2021), pp. 7–21

Chapter 3
What is the problem? A critical review of social justice leadership preparation and development
Deirdre Torrance, Christine Forde, Fiona King and Jamila Razzaq
Professional Development in Education, volume 47, issue 1 (2021), pp. 22–35

Chapter 4
Learning to lead socially just schools: an exploration of candidate readiness for equity-focused principal preparation in the United States
Corrie Stone-Johnson, Corey Gray and Casandra Wright
Professional Development in Education, volume 47, issue 1 (2021), pp. 36–49

Chapter 5
The need for career-long professional learning for social justice leaders in affluent school contexts
Karen Huchting and Jill Bickett
Professional Development in Education, volume 47, issue 1 (2021), pp. 50–62

Chapter 6
Professional development for school leaders in England: decision-making for social justice
Ian Potter and Stephanie Chitpin
Professional Development in Education, volume 47, issue 1 (2021), pp. 63–74

Chapter 7
Promoting socially just schools through professional learning: lessons from four US principals in rural contexts
Pamela S. Angelle, Mary Lynne Derrington and Alex N. Oldham
Professional Development in Education, volume 47, issue 1 (2021), pp. 75–88

Chapter 8
Critical professional development and the racial justice leadership possibilities of teachers of colour in K-12 schools
Rita Kohli, Marcos Pizarro, Luis-Genaro Garcia, Lisa Kelly, Michael Espinoza and Juan Córdova
Professional Development in Education, volume 47, issue 1 (2021), pp. 89–101

Chapter 9
The role of trade union provision for critical professional learning in supporting member teachers' social justice leadership practice
Halil Buyruk
Professional Development in Education, volume 47, issue 1 (2021), pp. 102–114

Chapter 10
Promoting professional growth to build a socially just school through participation in ethnographic research
Begoña Vigo-Arrazola and Dennis Beach
Professional Development in Education, volume 47, issue 1 (2021), pp. 115–127

Chapter 11
'Every single student counts': leadership of professional development underpinned by social justice for sessional staff in a South Australian university
Sarah K Hattam and Tanya Weiler
Professional Development in Education, volume 47, issue 1 (2021), pp. 128–140

Chapter 12
A cross-school PLC: how could teacher professional development of robot-based pedagogies for all students build a social-justice school?
Elson Szeto, Kenneth Sin and George Leung
Professional Development in Education, volume 47, issue 1 (2021), pp. 141–155

Chapter 13
Supporting gender-inclusive schools: educators' beliefs about gender diversity training and implementation plans
Mollie T. McQuillan and Jennifer Leininger
Professional Development in Education, volume 47, issue 1 (2021), pp. 156–176

Chapter 14
Learning about culture together: enhancing educators cultural competence through collaborative teacher study groups
Chrystal S. Johnson, Jennifer Sdunzik, Cornelius Bynum, Nicole Kong and Xiaoyue Qin
Professional Development in Education, volume 47, issue 1 (2021), pp. 177–190

Chapter 15
The professional development needs of primary teachers in special classes for children with autism in the Republic of Ireland
Caitríona Finlay, William Kinsella and Paula Prendeville
Professional Development in Education, volume 48, issue 2 (2022), pp. 233–253

Afterword
Afterword: inserting social justice into professional development
Ira Bogotch
Professional Development in Education, volume 47, issue 1 (2021), pp. 191–196

For any permission-related enquiries please visit:
www.tandfonline.com/page/help/permissions

Notes on Contributors

Pamela S. Angelle, The University of Tennessee, Department of Educational Leadership and Policy Studies, Knoxville, TN, USA.

Dennis Beach, Department of Educational Research and Development, University of Borås, Borås, Sweden; Department of Education and Special Education, University of Gothenburg, Gothenburg, Sweden.

Jill Bickett, Department of Educational Leadership, Loyola Marymount University, Los Angeles, CA, USA.

Ira Bogotch, Department of Educational Leadership and Research Methods, Florida Atlantic University, Boca Raton, FL, USA.

Halil Buyruk, Department of Educational Sciences, Ankara University, Ankara, Turkey.

Cornelius Bynum, Department of History, Purdue University, West Lafayette, IN, USA.

Stephanie Chitpin, Ottawa University, Canada.

Juan Córdova, Highline Public Schools, WA, USA.

Mary Lynne Derrington, The University of Tennessee, Department of Educational Leadership and Policy Studies, Knoxville, TN, USA.

Michael Espinoza, Campbell Union High School District, Campbell, CA, USA.

Caitríona Finlay, School of Education, University College Dublin, Dublin, Ireland.

Christine Forde, School of Education, University of Glasgow, Glasgow, UK.

Luis-Genaro Garcia, Sacramento State University, Sacramento, CA, USA.

Corey Gray, Department of Educational Leadership and Policy, University at Buffalo, NY, USA.

Sarah K. Hattam, UniSA College Education Futures, University of South Australia, Australia.

Karen Huchting, Department of Educational Leadership, Loyola Marymount University, Los Angeles, CA, USA.

Chrystal S. Johnson, Department of Curriculum and Instruction, Purdue University, West Lafayette, IN, USA.

Lisa Kelly, Oakland Unified School District, Oakland, CA, USA

Fiona King, School of Inclusive and Special Education, Dublin City University, Dublin, Ireland.

William Kinsella, School of Education, University College Dublin, Dublin, Ireland.

Rita Kohli, University of California, Riverside, CA, USA.

Nicole Kong, Department of Library Sciences, Purdue University, West Lafayette, IN, USA.

Jennifer Leininger, Lurie Children's Hospital's Gender & Sex Development Program, Chicago, IL, USA.

George Leung, TWGHs Kwan Fong Kai Chi School, Hong Kong SAR, China.

Mollie T. McQuillan, Department of Educational Leadership and Policy Analysis, University of Wisconsin Madison, Madison, WI, USA.

Paul Miller, University of Greenwich, London, UK.

Alex N. Oldham, The University of Tennessee, Department of Educational Leadership and Policy Studies, Knoxville, TN, USA

Marcos Pizarro, San José State University, San José, CA, USA.

Ian Potter, GFM Education Ltd.

Paula Prendeville, School of Education, University College Dublin, Dublin, Ireland.

Xiaoyue Qin, Department of Curriculum and Instruction, Purdue University, West Lafayette, IN, USA.

Jamila Razzaq, Board Director Aappa Aziz Trust, Rawalpindi, Pakistan.

Jennifer Sdunzik, Department of Curriculum and Instruction, Purdue University, West Lafayette, IN, USA.

Kenneth Sin, Department of Special Education and Counselling, Centre for Special Educational Needs and Inclusive Education, The Education University of Hong Kong, Hong Kong SAR, China.

Corrie Stone-Johnson, Department of Educational Leadership and Policy, University at Buffalo, NY, USA.

Elson Szeto, Department of Education Policy and Leadership, Centre for Special Educational Needs and Inclusive Education, Hong Kong SAR, China.

Deirdre Torrance, School of Education, University of Glasgow, Glasgow, UK.

Begoña Vigo-Arrazola, Department of Educational Sciences, University of Zaragoza, Zaragoza, Spain.

Tanya Weiler, UniSA College Education Futures, University of South Australia, Australia.

Casandra Wright, Department of Educational Leadership and Policy, University at Buffalo, NY, USA.

Foreword

Fiona King

In my last editorial in Professional Development in Education (Vol 45.2 2019), I wrote about professional learning empowering teachers to stay close to their moral purpose, which for me as an educator is about inclusion. Accordingly, I was delighted to be asked to write the Foreword for this special issue on *The place of professional growth and professional learning in leading socially just schools*. It has afforded me another opportunity to reflect on my moral purpose and my work within the International School Leadership Development Network (King and Travers 2017), exploring the perspectives and practices of leaders who advocate for social justice. As an Associate Editor of PDiE, it allows me to answer the call of the editorial board to reflect on a wider set of questions and perspectives around the possibilities of professional learning, in this instance, specifically related to leading socially just schools.

One of the key issues raised throughout the special issue is centred around how we use terms interchangeably (inclusion, equity, equality, diversity) when researching, writing and in the practice of social justice. Acknowledging there is no universally agreed definition of these terms brings with it the concern of making meanings clear, within an endeavour to build understandings of the challenges involved. Further, we know that context is key in framing such concepts and practices. Therefore, within our own professional learning contexts, it is important to articulate what we mean by social justice. Reflecting on my own work, I am always drawn back to this definition of inclusion, 'the careful and thoughtful marriage of educational excellence, equity and social justice' (Pelletier et al. 2011, p. 6).

The focus on social justice in this special issue is timely against the backdrop of Education 2030 (UNESCO 2015) Sustainable Goal 4, which places inclusion and equity centre stage for enhanced economic, social and political development. It also builds nicely on a recent paper in PDiE by Poekert et al. (2020) who highlighted the 'critical framing of issues towards social justice' as a key principle in leadership for professional learning towards educational equity. All of the articles in this special issue highlight the importance of professional learning that focuses on critical thinking, critical reflection and social justice. But what does this mean for us as professional educators and researchers? At its core, this involves critical self-reflection or reflexivity where we articulate our own assumptions and biases. For example, Stone-Johnson, Gray & Wright in their article in this special issue (p. 38) call for those operating from a deficit perspective to develop an ability to critically question inequities in schools. Accordingly, we ought to think critically about our own context and how inequities and marginalisation are created and reproduced, not just at an individual level but also systemically. To illustrate further, Ira Bogotch in his afterword (p. 218) suggests '*the first critical reflective practice in any PD [professional development] would be to ask participants to turn to the person sitting next to them (at the appropriate social distances) and discuss how the pandemic has revealed truths [inequities] that are becoming evident to parents, teachers, administrators, and staff*' (p. 220). He adds that this must include a focus on the structural and systemic barriers students and staff face. Professional learning that involves critical reflection on the influences that shape our beliefs and practices as educators are equally important, for example, social, economic, political, personal influences.

Professional learning that creates awareness is just a first step. It needs to go beyond this as Christa Boske advocates in her recent book, 'Standing still is not an option' (Boske 2019). Key in this is the teachers' role which is a political and agentive one. We need to ACT together and reflect on action, in order to transform inequitable practices. A number of the articles in this special issue argue for professional learning that is collaborative and focuses on methodologies, to elicit and learn from the voices of those marginalised. Vigo-Arrazola and Beach, in their article, clearly promote the 'political act of giving voice as political agency' (p. 115). Many authors believe this act will facilitate our professional learning and critical self-reflection in terms of the repositioning of beliefs and values, along with the fostering of an openness to act against inequitable and marginalising practices and processes. Highlighted also is the need for continuing professional learning to support staff in these ongoing actions towards the advancement of socially just schools.

Professional Development in Education would like to thank the two Guest Editors of this special issue, Christine Forde and Deirdre Torrance, for the amazing job they have done in selecting, co-ordinating and developing this publication. In particular, the organisation of the articles into three themes – Leadership development and leading socially just schools; Leading in socially just schools and Teacher development to build practice in socially just schools – makes it easily accessible for readers to engage with and reflect on the theme or themes of particular interest to them in their context at this time. The afterword by leading expert in the field Ira Bogotch does a remarkable job of reflecting on the articles, posing key questions and challenges for us to engage with as readers. Social justice is of utmost importance in education, with intrinsic inequities having been highlighted further by the global pandemic. This special issue invites professional educators, researchers and policymakers alike to reflect critically on the inequities in our various contexts, to look beyond the boundaries of within-school practices to identify the barriers and then collaboratively problem-solve. Standing by and doing nothing is not an option. Social justice leadership involves us all through an activist transformative stance suggesting leadership learning ought to be part of all professional learning and development. We are being challenged to work together to hear the voices of those being marginalised, in a bid to act and transform schools and society. The potential of ongoing job-embedded professional learning to empower us to stay close to this moral purpose is evident across these articles, as they challenge us to develop approaches and methodologies to enhance awareness and act in a socially just way.

ORCID

Fiona King http://orcid.org/0000-0001-5749-1435

References

Boske, C., 2019. *Standing still is not an option: school children using art for social change*. Charlotte, NC: Information Age Publishing.

King, F. and Travers, J., 2017. Social justice leadership through the lens of ecological systems theory. In: *Global perspective of social justice leadership for school principals*. Charlotte: Information Age Publishing-IAP.

Pelletier, K., et al., 2011. *The next frontier: inclusion in international schools; a practical guide for school leaders*. Available from: http://www.nextfrontierinclusion.org/wp-content/uploads/2014/10/NFI-Practical-Guide-2nd-Edition.pdf [Accessed 4 Nov 2020].

Poekert, P., et al., 2020. Leadership for professional learning towards educational equity: a systematic literature review. *Professional development in education*, 46 (4), 541–562. doi:10.1080/19415257.2020.1787209

UNESCO, 2015. *Education 2030: incheon declaration and framework for action*. Available from: http://www.uis.unesco.org/Education/Documents/incheon-framework-for-action-en.pdf [Accessed 4 Nov 2020].

Introduction

Christine Forde and Deirdre Torrance

The special issue of *Professional Development in Education* (*PDiE*), 'The Place of Professional Growth and Professional Learning in Leading Socially Just Schools', came together at unique point in history. The backdrop of the global Covid-19 pandemic and the growth in the Black Lives Matter Movement, highlighted the significant divide between advantaged and disadvantaged communities and the urgent need to address issues of inequality, marginalisation and discrimination. Two years on, and against the current global context of economic challenges, of diminishing energy resources, climate change and conflict, these issues remain highly relevant in education. This backdrop underlines the significance of schools not only for their communities but also for civic society more broadly. Policy imperatives such as the OECD's twofold aim of 'Excellence and Equity', look to schools to work for overall improvements of achievement alongside, in a context of increasing diversity, ensuring the needs of all learners are addressed. Issues related to achievement of diverse groups of learners are central to the work of leading socially just schools. However, we need also to be mindful of the vital role schools and other education establishments play in building wider participation and the inclusion of all young people in society to foster greater social cohesion. The articles collected in this book edition explore the issues related to professional learning as school leaders look to lead socially just school.

In meeting the range of expectations, both educational and societal, leaders and teachers in schools are faced with many challenges, and to addresses these they need to engender greater understanding and practice to build equity of outcome rather than just equality of opportunity. There is then, an important question about how school leaders are prepared for and prepare others in school to bring about and sustain the changes necessary to build socially just schools. A significant literature exists on the issues of social justice and education and within this body of work, a growing recognition of the role of school leaders in advocating for social justice. However, knowledge and understanding of the issues around the professional growth and development to support and sustain such practices is far less extensive. The purpose of this collection is to contribute to the development of knowledge and practice around the role of professional learning and growth in leading and sustaining socially just schools.

The special issue, 'The Place of Professional Growth and Professional Learning in Leading Socially Just Schools,' built on the previous special issue of *PDiE* on 'Leadership for Professional Learning', by exploring the role and contribution of professional learning for leaders in the leading of socially just schools. Leadership learning in the development of social justice leadership – of school leaders and of teachers – is one dimension of this theme. Another dimension is the pivotal role that school leaders and others play in providing professional learning opportunities for teachers to enable them to address issues of inequity in school.

The starting point for the special issue was the work of the International School Leadership Development Network (ISLDN), a collaborative project established in 2010 between the British Educational Leadership, Management and Administration Society (BELMAS) and the University Council for Education Administration (UCEA) in the USA. The purpose of this Network has been to build a comparative study examining the development and practice of social justice school leaders. In its first decade, the ISLDN developed two research strands: the practice and development of (1) leaders in high need, low performing schools and (2) leaders who advocate for social justice. Members of the ISLDN have produced case studies in their own system and collaborated through joint conference papers and publications, including articles and edited volumes. The work contributed from members of the Network in the special issue constituted a further development for ISLDN, examining the issue of professional learning in social justice outcomes. The ISLDN continues to evolve with current work exploring the role of school leaders through the Covid-19 pandemic and beyond; the contribution of other leaders in school to social justice leadership; and the development of comparative studies exploring context, policy and practice in social justice leadership.

A number of chapters are from members of the ISLDN network (Miller; Torrance et al.; Potter and Chitpin; Angelle et al. and Szeto et al.). Other chapters have come from authors who responded to the international call for papers (Huchting and Bickett; Stone-Johnson et al.; Kohli et al.; Buyruk; Vigo-Arrazola and Beach; Hattam and Weiler). Two final chapters were submitted independently to *PDiE* and, as these addressed issues relevant to the theme of this special issue, were included. This collection comprises largely of empirical studies undertaken in different contexts, examining different dimensions of social justice and equity in education. The issue also includes a critical review of the literature (Torrance et al.) and two conceptual papers (Miller; Vigo-Arrazola and Beach). For the book edition of this collection, a further chapter has been included to provide an additional perspective to the question of the significance of professional learning in addressing the needs of diverse groups of learners (Finlay et al.).

The ISLDN research has identified that context is a critical dimension in the building of socially just schools (Angelle and Torrance 2019). Our intention, therefore, as editors of the special issue of *PDiE* was to advance thinking in the areas of professional learning and development, leadership development and social justice through a variety of perspectives across different education systems and this broad perspective has been replicated in this edited book. Much of the substantive literature is concerned with the development of social justice leadership practices in circumstances where learners experience significant marginalisation and disadvantage, archetypically the inner city school serving minority communities. Although this is a critical dimension, this collection of chapters underlines the necessity and challenges of building socially just schools regardless of school location, in affluent or impoverished communities, rural or urban settings, in public education or market-driven contexts. This collection of chapters is diverse, drawing from different education systems globally, providing myriad perspectives in critical reflecting on issues of social justice and professional learning across different contexts.

Much of the focus of current literature is on formal leadership preparation programmes and so in the special issue, we looked to present different perspectives, to map out various strategies, approaches and pedagogies in professional learning and development, to explore ways of building social justice praxis across schools and within classrooms. Accordingly, the chapters in this book are organised around three broad themes:

(1) Leadership development and leading socially just schools
(2) Leading in socially just schools
(3) Teacher development to build practice in socially just schools.

In the first theme, 'Leadership development and leading socially just schools', the chapters focus on leadership development for aspiring and serving school leaders. We use the conceptual paper by Miller and the critical review by Torrance et al. to frame this theme. Miller's critical essay underlines the role of leadership development preparing school leaders for anti-racist leadership. Miller puts forward a useful ecological model to underpin anti-racist leadership development, a model that could potentially be adapted to examine different dimensions of social justice leadership. Miller also provides a valuable outline of relevant areas that should be included in all leadership development programmes. In their critical review, Torrance et al. adapted a framework from political theory to interrogate the expanding body of literature on social justice leadership preparation, identifying the implications for the pedagogies of professional learning as well as issues for future research. Stone-Johnson et al. continue the focus on leadership preparation, examining the question of candidate readiness for professional learning that is orientated towards issues of social justice and equity. This is an exploratory study that considers the question of the selection of candidates on the basis of their preparedness to engage with social justice issues, an 'equity mind set' that others have advocated. Huchting and Bickett investigate an area where there has been little research to date – social justice leadership in affluent contexts and highlight the importance of leadership development in raising awareness and building skills and resilience to sustain this focus in a context where there can be limited obvious concern. This article also signals the importance of career-long leadership development, an issue echoed in the final study in this theme by Potter and Chitpin. They explore the professional learning of serving school leaders as they grapple with issues of social justice and equity in their school, including data-driven decision-making. While data-driven decision making might be conceived as a technical skill in a performance policy agenda, Potter and Chitpin argue that professional learning should foster a position that places values at the heart of decision-making in schools.

The second theme, 'Leading in socially just schools', focuses on the role of professional learning to enable leaders at all levels in a school to contribute to socially just schools. Ready access to meaningful external development opportunities for leaders is not always available, and so these chapters provide valuable in-house examples of professional learning in contexts where there may be limited alternatives. Angelle et al. present a case study of four school principals serving rural communities in the USA where there is limited access to professional development. A key feature of the leadership of these principals is the shaping of professional learning opportunities in the day-to-day work of the school to enable teachers to address the learning needs of increasingly diverse groups of learners. Kohli et al.'s study examines the experiences and impact of the Racial Justice Institute, a tailored professional development programme for teachers of Colour. The authors explore the way in which this programme is both affirming of teachers of Colour and also strengthens the 'leadership-efficacies' of these teachers to support their work in school. Buyruk also raises the question of how teachers can access professional learning on issues related to social justice where there is little available support. The chapter discusses the role of a teacher union in Turkey in providing professional development opportunities central to the fostering of a critical consciousness.

The final theme, 'Teacher development to build practice in socially just schools' turns to the issue of the development of teachers and their practice. These chapters reflect the diversity of approaches to teacher development, including the use of collaborative learning. Vigo-Arrazola and Beach provide insight into the developmental opportunities for teachers involved in an ethnographic study on family participation, itself an important concern in socially just schools. Through a meta-analysis of previous ethnographic studies, the authors highlight the way in which the co-production of a research project between researchers and teachers brings awareness and opportunities for dialogue and indeed, can contribute to more democratic schools. The title of the next article by Hattam and

Weiler, 'Every Single Student Counts' is a theme underpinning this collection. This chapter examines a professional learning programme for sessional tutors in an Australian university to develop more inclusive pedagogic practices, with many resonances for the development of pedagogic practice in different education sectors. Szeto et al.'s article provides a different perspective, developing pedagogic practice to address the needs of diverse learners through collaborative professional learning. The chapter examines the professional development of teachers through a cross-school learning community where the focus is on robot-based pedagogies to address the needs of learners with diverse special educational needs. McQuillan and Leininger also look at the contribution of professional development in building inclusive education, here specifically gender-inclusive schools. They investigate the impact of gender-diversity training, looking at participants' beliefs and how this training supports educators in the task of creating 'a safe, educational environment for students'. The finding highlights positive outcomes from the training but also the need for ongoing professional growth and learning, a theme echoed in many of the chapters. The next chapter from Johnson et al. returns to the process of collaborative professional learning in the form of an African American history-centred collaborative teacher study group. The purpose of the study group was to build the cultural competence of educators and the outcomes point to the work of the group influencing practice in school. The final chapter in this section is an additional article published in *PDiE* subsequent to the special issue. The study by Finlay et al. has been included as it makes the important link between special educational provision, addressing the needs of diverse groups of learners and the importance of teacher learning to enable them to work productively with young people with specific learning needs. Finlay et al. report on a study conducted in the Republic of Ireland, where a policy strategy has been to establish special classes for learners with Autism Spectrum Disorder (ASD) in mainstream primary schools. The authors highlight the necessity of professional learning for teachers teaching in these classes to enable them to provide appropriate educational experiences. This study, like the other chapters, reveals the power of different forms of professional learning in firstly, raising the awareness of school leaders and teachers around issues of social justice; and secondly, through engendering the self-efficacy necessary to bring about change in schools.

For the special issue we were pleased that Ira Bogotch accepted the invitation to write an Afterword. In this Bogotch highlights several themes enhancing understandings of the issues raised but also challenging the contributing authors and the field to think beyond the boundaries of the established programmes. These challenges remain relevant and critical. Bogotch urges change: "With respect to leadership for social justice, we educators have to be more political, more critical in analyzing our own terminology, concepts and action inside contexts of professional development, professional learning and professional growth" before proposing that, "The open-ended question is how do we as researchers participate in making social justice a reality [for practitioners] sooner rather than later?"

In the special issue we were interested in presenting different approaches to professional development in different contexts and the contribution of professional learning to bringing about change. Leading and teaching are deeply contextualised practices and the studies in this collection reveal how school leaders and teachers grapple with specific challenges within their setting. However, there are many common threads and so there is much to learn from these chapters from different systems across the world about how professional learning can enable school leaders and teachers to contribute to the creation and sustaining of socially just schools. As the impact of Covid-19 pandemic and other global events rumble on, we live in a context of uncertainty on many fronts. Schools and other educational establishments are part of the infrastructure of civic society and remain central to daily life. In the context of the Covid-19 pandemic, educational establishments continued to play a significant role in sustaining learners, their families and communities and continue to grapple with the psychological, social and economic consequences of the pandemic. Now against a backdrop of conflict alongside global economic and environmental issues, the role of schools and education remains critical. These chapters highlight the importance of professional learning in fostering the understandings, skills and commitment of educators to build practice in teaching and in leadership that recognises and respects the identities of all learners and enables all learners to flourish and lead schools to contribute to the building of resilient communities.

Reference

Angelle, P. S., and Torrance, D. (Eds.). (2019). *Cultures of Social Justice Leadership: An Intercultural Context of Schools.* Cham, Switzerland: Springer.

Leadership development and leading socially just schools

Anti-racist school leadership: making 'race' count in leadership preparation and development

Paul Miller

ABSTRACT
School leaders in England have a huge task to mediate factors in a school's environment (regulatory/legal and institutional). Rapid and sometimes conflicting policy agendas for improved performance have become a main preoccupation of school leaders as they jostle to keep their jobs as they wrestle to implement the latest government mandate. As a result, many school leaders ignore, at best, or are unprepared for, at worse, how to deal with institutional impacts and challenges associated with unprecedented levels of migration, and race discrimination. This is compounded by school leaders' lack of understanding of, for example, personal and structural racism, and how these collude against attempts to build racially inclusive school environments. Through an ecological model this paper argues that in spite of performativity pressures, school leaders should develop skills, attributes and knowledge in areas of curriculum diversity, recruitment and career progression, leading change for race diversity that (i) reflects the contexts within which they live and work, and that (ii) empowers them to more effectively serve their institutions. The paper asserts that 'anti-racist' training for school leaders should be central to ongoing professional development efforts, especially in multi-cultural, multi-racial and multi-ethnic societies/educational environments.

Race, ethnicity and school leadership: a historical and emergent context

Many schools and school leaders in England, and elsewhere, are confronted, almost daily, with issues to do with 'race' involving their staff and students. Unfortunately, many of these school leaders, both those who are very experienced and others less experienced, struggle to adequately and successfully address and engage with the range of race-related concerns they/their schools face. In increasingly polarised global and British societies, racism and race discrimination have nearly become normalised – leaving educational institutions, and many of those who study and work in them, exposed to the rhetoric and practice of racism. Anzaldua (1990) notes that 'racism is a slippery subject, one which evades confrontation, yet one which overshadows every aspect of our lives' (Anzaldua 1990, p. xix). This observation points to the pervasive nature of racism, and its near inescapable characteristic and presence. Nevertheless, 'what has emerged over the last decade or so is an acknowledgment of the complexities of racism' (Aveling 2007, p. 69); and the realisation that racism is 'not a static, fixed, or coherent set of beliefs that uniformly influences the way individuals think and behave regardless of context' (Connolly 1996, p. 174). Notwithstanding, Macpherson (1999) in the 'Stephen Lawrence Inquiry Report' provides that, racism is, 'Conduct or words or practices which advantage or disadvantage people because of their colour, culture or ethnic origin. In its more subtle form, it is as damaging as in its overt form' (p. 41). Consistent with the pervasive and near inescapable character of racism,

> [I]t will therefore be important that all staff, including recently recruited staff, are aware of procedures to deal with racist incidents and support to tackle racial bias and stereotyping. Strong leadership from the school's governors and the school's senior management team on the unacceptability of racism will give staff the confidence to manage incidents well. (Lancashire County Council 2007, p. 6)

Racism extends beyond individual expressions of prejudice and 'includes systematic, structural, unequal relations of power' (Raby 2004, p. 380); and could also be viewed as

> the result of a complex interplay of individual attitudes, social values and institutional practices. It is expressed in the actions of individuals and institutions and is promoted in the ideology of popular culture. It changes its form in response to social change .(Australia – Department of Education and Training n.d., p. 1)

Thus, 'it is no longer useful ... to speak of racism as if it were a homogeneous phenomenon' (Castles 1996, p. 18) and an understanding of its complexities becomes essential to recognising and tackling it in its various guises. Conceptual differences around racism aside, a racist is typically seen as someone who discriminates based on 'race' or skin colour; or someone who, according to 'common sense,' is 'bad, mad or misinformed, or even stupid' (Pettman 1992, p. 56).

Racism can take many forms. For example:

- Personal: related to private beliefs, prejudices, and ideas that individuals have about the superiority of whites and the inferiority of non-whites.
- Interpersonal: occurring between individuals. It occurs when the private beliefs of individuals affect or influence their interactions with others.
- Institutional: related to unfair treatment, policies and practices, inequitable opportunities and impacts within organisations and institutions, based on race, which routinely produce unequal outcomes for whites and non-whites.
- Structural: related to a system in which policies, institutional practices, cultural representations, and other norms work in various, often reinforcing ways to perpetuate racial group inequality. It involves the cumulative and compounding effects of several factors including the history, culture, ideology, and interactions of institutions and policies that systematically privilege white people over non-whites.

This paper acknowledges the different levels of racism, although its main focus will be on upskilling and educating school leaders to tackle institutional racism. This is not to say however that school leaders do not have a duty of care to tackle all forms of racism, including personal racism. As noted by Yamato (1990), 'racism is pervasive to the point that we take many of its manifestations for granted, believing "that's life"' (p.20), and leaving many of its assumptions and manifestations unchecked or unquestioned (Hollinsworth 1998). This paper is based on three main questions: (i) Why does "race" matter in leadership preparation and development? (ii) What content on "race" could be included in leadership preparation and development? (iii) How could "race" be included in leadership preparation and development? Before I attempt to answer these questions, I will provide an introduction to the context of race/racism and educational leadership in England.

Race, ethnicity and school leadership in England

There is a dearth of literature on what educational and/or other institutions do to tackle institutionalised racism – with much of the available literature focused on structural and other factors that both foster and embed race discrimination/racism (Miller 2019a). In its simplest sense, an educational institution is a microcosm of society, not only reflecting its diversity of peoples but also its diversity of values and epistemologies. Consequently, the routinisation of practices and the development of cultures therein are crucial to how individuals and groups inhabit and experience these institutions. In the main, England (and by extension the UK) can be considered an inclusive country. However, beneath the surface, the practices and cultures of many institutions, within and outside education, are anything but inclusive. What goes on in educational institutions is important for several reasons, not least because educational institutions are melting pots of diversity and difference, and thus mirrors of society, but because many of society's values are simultaneously tested out, challenged, shaped, re-affirmed and embedded through and within the social discourses and practices occurring within these (and other) institutions. Consequently, educational institutions have a significant role and responsibility to tackle all forms of prejudice through its curricular, human resource policies and other operational practices and systems.

Bell (2004) notes that racism is a reality. Miller (2019b, p. 2) also notes that 'racism in England's education system is a reality – a reality played out in different ways, affecting students and staff in multiple ways and influencing their experience of, and interaction with/in the education system' (p. 2). This reality is juxtaposed against England's '... deep sensitivity to ... ethnic and cultural difference' (Phillips 2016, p. 1), which arguably provides fertile ground for augmenting racist attitudes and cultures, aided by leadership inaction (Miller 2019c); lack of monitoring of institutional practices by government (Miller 2016), and a weak legislative framework (Miller 2019a). Thus, England's (and by extension the UK's) deep sensitivity to ethnic and cultural difference underpins and reifies deep levels of mistrust for 'the other', often manifested in how 'the other' is treated, and what opportunities are available to 'the other'. Put differently, despite espoused values of equality, diversity and inclusion, many of England's educational institutions, have created, fostered and/or reinforced systems of 'in group' and 'out group' along racial lines; systems which privilege the experience and worth of some over others (Miller 2019b).

On their own, staff of BAME heritage are incapable of successfully resolving these tensions due to resistance (McNamara et al. 2009) or suspicion (Bhopal and Jackson 2013) or both, and due to the restrictive nature of BAME capital (Miller 2016). Notwithstanding these tensions, it should be emphasised that educational leaders wield significant power, and are

> ... uniquely placed to influence staff, students and other stakeholders in ways that help raise their awareness of and attention to issues of racism/race discrimination, and to helping and enabling them to tackle race and other forms of discrimination, and to promoting, building and sustaining educational institutions in ways that positively influence all who study and work therein. (Miller 2019b, p. 2)

Since 'leaders/leadership can be a powerful antidote to race inequality and discrimination in organisations' (Miller 2019b, p. 2), it is appropriate that professional development efforts focus attention on an area that so far has not been satisfactorily addressed, and an area not systematically built into training and/or development activities. This paper contends that school leaders in England need to develop an 'anti-racist' language and practice, based on appropriate skills, attributes and knowledge geared towards enabling and empowering them to (better) tackle institutional racism/race discrimination.

Students and teachers of BAME heritage in England

As of January 2017, there were 8.67 million pupils enrolled in state-funded and independent schools in England. Of the 4,689,660 at primary schools, circa 32.1% (1,505,381) are of BAME heritage; and of the 3,223,090 at secondary schools, circa 29.1% (937,919) are of BAME heritage (DfE, 2017). Patterns of variation exist within the overall data, with some schools in London, for example, having up to 70% BME students enrolled, although staffing profiles do not always reflect the ethnic diversity of the student body. Furthermore, the proportion of students of BAME heritage has risen steadily since 2006, and account for circa 66.3% of the increase in primary school students between 2016 and 2017.

According to the latest school workforce data available from the Department for Education (DfE, 2020), as at January 2020, there were approximately 453,000 teachers in the state sector in England. This number is broken down as follows: White: 85.9% (or 399,300) are White-British, 3.9% (or 18,000) are from 'Other White' backgrounds, 1.6% (or 7,300) are White-Irish; Asian: 1.9% (or 8,900) are Indian, 1.2% (or 5,500) are Pakistani, 0.6 (or 2,700) are Bangladeshi, 0.7 (or 3,100) are 'Asian other'; Black: 1.0% (or 4,800) Black Caribbean, 0.9% (or 4,000) are Black African, 0.3% (1,500) are 'Black other'; Mixed: Mixed White/Asian (0.3% or 1,600), Mixed Black/African (0.1% or 600), Mixed Black/Caribbean (0.4% or 1,700), Mixed Other (0.5% or 2.400); Chinese: 0.2 (or 800), 'Any other' (0.6% or 2,700); Unknown: 7.79% (or 35,300). Put differently, there are approximately White-British 399,300 teachers (85.9%), 35,000 teachers (7.79%) whose ethnicity is unknown, and 18,400 teachers (6.31%) of BAME heritage. Furthermore, there are approximately 22,400 principals or headteachers: 92.9% (or 20,809) are White-British, 1,200 (or 5.3%) whose ethnicity is unknown, and 391 (or 1.7%) of BAME heritage (DfE, 2020).

Institutional interaction and students and staff of BAME heritage

From the data in the previous section, there are millions of students and thousands of teachers of BAME heritage within England's education system. For many of these students and staff however, their experience of their institution is highly fraught. Camacho Felix (2019) found that the experience of students of BAME heritage can be described as one of, 'A Lack of Belonging; A Loss of Confidence and A Feeling of Neglect' (p. 5). Demie (2003) also found four main school-related factors that contribute to how students of BAME heritage experience their school organisations: "… stereotyping; teachers' low expectations; exclusions and Headteachers' poor leadership on equality issues" (p. 243). Low teacher expectation is strongly correlated to low attainment amongst students of BAME heritage (Gillborn 1995, Curtis 2008). Low teacher expectation is believed to be influenced by racism (Gillborn 1996, Gillborn and Youdell 2000, Strand 2015). Strand (2012) found students of BAME heritage were systematically 'encouraged' to take foundation courses, which has contributed to achievement gaps. He concluded that institutional racism and low teacher expectations are two reasons why they were not entered for top-tier exams.

Another factor influencing the attainment of students of BAME heritage is their exclusion from learning opportunities and from school. For example, students of BAME heritage are most likely to be excluded from school (DfE, 2016) and represent the most excluded group of pupils (Gillborn and Youdell 2000, DfE 2016). Furthermore, they have rates of permanent exclusion nearly three times that of the student population (DfE 2016). The failure of the curriculum to adequately cater to the needs of students from minority ethnic backgrounds (Macpherson 1999, Strand 2015) has also been cited as a factor in their overall educational experience. Furthermore, students of BAME heritage are subjected to institutional racism in British schools through, inter alia, teachers' 'conscious or unconscious stereotypes and assumptions about minority groups [which] can impact negatively on pupils' achievements' (Maylor et al. 2009, p. 25); which can dramatically undermine their chances of academic success (Curtis 2008, Demie and Mclean 2017). On their own, or together, these factors can perpetuate low attainment and engagement. Importantly, they provide us an insight into the experience of students of BAME heritage educational institutions.

Overall, the experiences of teachers of BAME heritage in their institutions are broadly consistent with how students of BAME heritage experience their institutions. Although possessing similar career aspirations, ambitions and qualifications as White teachers, it has been found that they are far more likely to be disciplined; to face criticism from colleagues and parents (McNamara et al. 2009); to experience occupational segregation (Miller 2019a); and be passed over for promotion (SecEd, 2015, Miller 2016). Furthermore, trainee teachers of BAME heritage are least likely to complete their training (Pells 2017), due to lack of support (Lander 2011); racism (Callender 2019) and feelings of ethnic and cultural isolation (Miller 2020). The experience of teachers of BAME heritage in educational institutions is thus a deeply fraught issue – which has implications for their recruitment, development, retention and progression.

Despite the existence of equality legislation, and despite campaigns in the public domain, many educational institutions have done very little to improve the experience of students and staff of BAME heritage. Miller (2018) observes a zero-sum game where, instead of facing up to racism within their institutions, some educational leaders opt to prioritise performance agendas at the expense of enforcing the 'race' equity agenda, often seeing one thing as being incompatible with the other. Furthermore, the Equality Challenge Unit (2011) reported that where some institutions have embarked on initiatives with race, where these have not been led and managed from the top, either directly or indirectly, they have experienced very little to no positive result. Accordingly, the effort and response of educational institutions to tackling race discrimination in their midst have been seen as 'lacking commitment to change' (Ahmed 2007, p. 236); 'light touch' (Miller 2016, p. 218); and not having '… the … resources and authority for the initiative …' (ECU 2011, pp. 46–47).

Why does 'race' matter in leadership preparation and development?

Tackling racism/race discrimination in schools and other educational institutions is not a quick fix; nor is it a single linear process. With increased globalisation and migration, the job of tackling racism/race discrimination is one that educational leaders, irrespective of school location and size, and irrespective of country, can expect to grapple with. For the most part, school leaders are unprepared for the challenges of tackling and achieving racial equity, and are uncomfortable with calling out racism (Aveling 2007, McMahon 2007, Ryan 2012); this, because, school leadership preparation and development programmes have traditionally focused on management skills (Fullan 1999) and have not given adequate attention either to the need for or skills to mediate the increasing diversity that has come to characterise many schools/modern day schooling (Henze 2000). Thus, Greene (2007) notes, 'Addressing structural racism is one of the toughest jobs that any leader can face ….' (p. 10). The tension among individual leaders and educational systems and educational institutions that place a subordinate value on tackling racism/race discrimination presents a real and certain threat to achieving race equality. As Greene (2007) notes,

> In institutions where there is little or no consciousness of racial bias, the social culture of unconscious racism will influence basic policies and practices. Unfortunately, even in institutions that have a fairly high degree of awareness of race bias, unconscious or unexamined aspects of the institution's social culture can unintentionally reinforce dynamics that continue to privilege people with white skin. (p.11)

Accordingly, ensuring school leaders have the appropriate language, skills and knowledge to push back against and successfully tackle racism/race discrimination is important and beneficial to the individual leader, the institutions they lead, and the education system and to society in which they live and work. The Coalition for Equity and Rights (n.d.), found that:

> [T]raining opportunities are a great way to build the capacity of the school to address incidents of racist bullying and create inclusive learning environments. This creates a consistency in approach and improves competence and confidence in this area. (CRER/respectme, nd, p.11)

Drawing on Henze (2000), Gooden (2012); Brooks (2012); Brooks and Jean-Marie (2007); Theoharis and Brooks (2012); Brooks and Watson (2018), and Miller (2019a), several reasons underpinning the importance of school leaders understanding of racism, and developing a language and practice of 'anti-racism' are suggested below:

(1) **School leaders have the power to influence race relations positively**: Schools and other educational institutions play a complex and uneasy role in changing race relations, sometimes hindering and fostering positive relations, often at the same time (Henze 2000).

Despite performativity constraints and other barriers, committed school leaders find ways to make race central to the work of their personal practice and the life of their schools (Miller 2019b).

(2) **School leaders have the power to establish and influence cultures**: Each school organisation is unique, but what the school becomes noted and known for is largely down to the ability of the leader to set goals and parameters and work towards them. As noted by Miller (2018), leadership shapes culture, and culture shapes leadership. This truism is important, but given the uniqueness of each institution, helping school and other educational leaders develop their ability to read their institution is a crucial element of influencing and leading change.

(3) **School leaders can help reframe problems, ameliorate conflicts and inform strategies**: Issues to do with 'race' tend to evoke and provoke a plethora of emotions and responses. When leaders understand what racism is, and its effects, they are in a much better position to directly and indirectly mediate, tackle race related infractions, and resource, lead, support and demand actions. Furthermore, being knowledgeable about racism and its effects enable the leader to 'reframe the problem, recognising overt conflict as a "symptom" and underlying tensions and root causes as the "illness"' (Henze 2000, p. 2).

(4) **School leaders can secure buy-in and create an institutional multiplier effect**: Many people are concerned about racism in educational institutions. Some do nothing about it because they do not see it as their job; and others want to do something but are not sure what they can do. On the back of highlighting the extent of the problem or issue, the school/ educational leader can cascade the knowledge of what's required and how this could be approach to others (teachers, parents, students, community members, school boards, etc.). This inclusive and collective approach to tackling the difficult issue of institutional racism/ race discrimination provides opportunities for teachers, students and others to 'own the issue', thereby creating a greater likelihood of interventions being successful and sustained (Miller 2019b).

(5) **School leaders can more easily influence practice outside their institutions**: It is easy to pretend that a problem does not exist, or to allow it to slip down the priority list, when one does not know how to tackle it. When school leaders understand racism, and its effects; many will want to attempt to tackle this, not only within their organisation but also beyond recognising the interlocking relationship between what happens in educational institutions and what happens in society. School leaders learning together, reflecting together, strategising together to tackle racism/race discrimination can improve the quality of institutional interventions well beyond their own institutions and they can support each other (which can lead) to greater levels of accountability.

Successfully tackling institutional racism/race discrimination requires huge investments in time, the personal commitment of leaders, and human and financial resources. The Dismantling Racism project (2019) notes,

> The process of Dismantling Racism is not just about individuals changing our behaviour and ways of thinking. This important work must in turn trigger a commitment to dismantling racism in organizations in order to provide us to move effective and accountable racial justice organizing. (p.56)

Likewise, Miller (2019b) asserted,

> [D]oing race equality is serious business, and doing race equality in schools or educational institutions is serious business that requires courage and the moral use of power that extends beyond sympathising to taking actions. (p. 17)

For school leaders and educational institutions to dismantle institutional racism, a pre-requisite is developing the courage to tackle it, which itself follows from an understanding of the nature of racism and its effects.

What content on 'race' could be included in leadership preparation and development?

There is no one size fits all to tackling institutional racism and attempts to tackle racism must acknowledge contextual and other complexities. This was clearly articulated by the Dismantling Racism project (2019) which proposed,

> There is no cookie cutter approach to anti-racist organizational development. The road to anti-racist organizational development is necessarily impacted by the size, structure, mission, constituency and geographic location of an organization. (p. 56)

Nevertheless, and despite the unavailability of a one size fits all approach to tackling institutional racism, and despite contextual differences, it is crucial all school leaders are provided with appropriate and adequate content knowledge that will enable them to (i) talk confidently about race/racism; (ii) respond to changing student and teacher demographics; (iii) cater adequately to the learning and development needs of students; (iv) tackle discrimination in the recruitment, development and progression of staff; and (v) build racially inclusive institutional processes, structures and cultures. These five areas are by no means exhaustive, and each area has potential to be a separate module. These are summarised below:

(i) **Learning to talk confidently about race/racism**: This important area acknowledges that to tackle racism in any form, people need to get comfortable talking about it – drawing on a language register that is shared and/or understood by all. Understanding racism, 'moves beyond a focus on the symptoms of racism to an understanding of what racism is, where it comes from, how it functions, why it persists, and how it can be undone' (Greene 2007, p. 10). Furthermore, understanding racism provides opportunities to develop a language around it and its effects (e.g. discrimination, micro-aggression etc.). With this knowledge, school leaders are in a better position to recognise individual acts of racism/race discrimination, institutional racism and structural racism, and are in a much better position to share their knowledge with others around them (students, staff, governors, donors, benefactors) in order to create institutional-wide awareness and to define the parameters of institutional-wide practice.

(ii) **Who is in my school? Respond to changing student and teacher demographics**: This area reflects the fact that globalisation and migration are recalibrating the physical, psychological and cultural aspects of school/education. Far from leaders simply knowing that their institutions are changing, they need to know the students and staff make up, so their school is representative of its local community and of society. Accordingly, leaders need to immerse themselves in data concerning staff and students. For example, they should know the ethnic make-up of staff and students, the languages spoken by staff and students, the gender balance among staff and students, and their cultural references. In particular to students, they need to also know their socio-economic profile, and in particular to staff, they also need to know paygrade, job role, years in job role and contract type. Importantly, school/educational leaders need to know why it is important for them to know these things, and how this knowledge can assist their decision-making. In the context of debates on racism/race discrimination, not only is this area of knowledge common-sense, it is also about recognition, which can be an enabling factor in how students learn and in how staff and students make sense of and respond to their school environment. Miller (2019b) provides examples of school leaders proactively working with professional teaching associations to (i) recruit teachers of BAME heritage to better reflect and serve the needs of their student population, and, (ii) actively work with teachers and local school community organisations to embrace and demonstrate an awareness and appreciation for the traditions and cultures that reflect the lived experience of staff and students present at school.

(iii) **Whose curriculum? Catering to the learning and development needs of all students**: This important area has been the subject of much discussion in the last decade. Although a school's ability to do this is complicated by several constraints within (staffing, time available, etc.) and outside a school (pre-set national curriculum, government policy, etc.), delivering a curriculum that caters to the learning and developmental needs of all students is crucial to their development and thriving as independent human beings. Providing a 'qualitatively different educational experience' (Miller 2012, p. 9) to students of BAME heritage, that reflects their needs, histories, cultures is not merely about representation and recognition, but also about respect. School/educational leaders need to understand what respect means in this context. That is, respect for their cultures, ethnicities, their right to be seen and heard in everyday educational discourses. Where this kind of educational experience is not available to students of minority ethnic backgrounds, educational institutions risk alienating students and staff from these backgrounds, which in turn can lead to resentment which, by extension can undermine the confidence of staff and students in their institutions and in the ability of its leaders to deliver inclusive educational content for all and to demonstrate inclusive curriculum leadership.

(iv) **Tackling discrimination in the recruitment, development, retention and progression of staff**: This crucial area acknowledges the complexities of talent management in general (Lewis and Heckman 2006, Christensen and Rog 2008) and in education in particular (Haque and Elliott 2016). By understanding the value of staff of minority ethnic heritage in their schools, leaders can address gaps in their recruitment, development, retention and progression. They learn about bias, and how this manifest in everyday decision-making around staff; and about how to limit bias infiltrating decisions about staffing, etc. Furthermore, supporting educational leaders to work effectively with 'others' to improve BAME teacher recruitment will help them develop essential skills and networks, including working with a school's local community to boost recruitment from that community, and with teacher networks (e.g. BAME teacher networks), teaching organisations, teaching unions, ITE providers, etc., to improve teacher recruitment. Development, retention and progression are at the heart of debates on talent management. In the context of institutional racism/race discrimination, these are at the heart of an 'ongoing struggle' for 'legitimacy' and 'enabling' among teachers of BAME heritage (Miller 2016, p. 1). School/educational leaders need support in thinking through institutional factors, personal conundrums, as well as administrative roles and responsibilities in creating an enabling environment for all staff – regardless of race/ethnicity.

(v) **Building racially inclusive institutional processes, structures and cultures**: This important area revolves around 'creating change', and 'making change sustainable'. This includes looking at existing processes, for example in the: (i) attraction, recruitment and selection of staff; (ii) reward, recognition, professional development and progression of staff; (iii) tracking of complaints against staff and students of BAME heritage; (iv) tracking of disciplinary measures taken against staff and students of BAME heritage; (v) development and/or review of policy around inclusion/anti-racism; (vi) institution-wide action-planning and monitoring of BAME student attainment; (vii) annual monitoring of agreed actions and targets related to staff and students of BAME heritage. This also involves working with a range of stakeholders, both internal and external to the institution, and including staff and students of BAME heritage to contribute to the development, implementation, monitoring and evaluation of interventions.

As mentioned above, these five areas in no way reflect an exhaustive and/or comprehensive body of knowledge for what could be involved in developing 'race conscious' or anti-racist leaders. However, they provide a starting point, since undoing racism requires working to a 'common language' with an 'anti-racist organizational plan' (Greene 2007, p. 10); and the development of a '... comprehensive understanding of how racism and oppression operate within an organization's own walls' (Dismantling Racism project, p. 56). Since, institutions, like individuals can evolve to become antiracist, successful institutional change must, simultaneously, include individual and institutional components, working together and in sync.

How could 'race' be included in leadership preparation and development?

Tackling institutional racism/race discrimination is not an easy task, and requires courageous leadership (Soyei 2011, Miller 2019b). Nevertheless, to improve the likelihood of success, courageous leadership itself should manifest from a set of *a priori* knowledge and skills. In other words, in the same way school leaders need to know about curriculum and instruction, they also need to know about racism and how this impacts staff, students and the institution as a whole. Accordingly, they must also be in a position to work with staff, students and others within and outside a school, to create the conditions for improvement. School leaders set the tone for their schools, and they can therefore influence, if not define its overarching ethos. Put differently, it is virtually impossible to (re)-culture a school without first, equipping the leaders to see that tackling institutional and other forms of racism is not an 'add on' but part of its 'core business', and second, assisting them in combining their skills and knowledge to work with, and motivate others in building and ensuring cultures of equity for all.

However, there is no single way to equip school leaders with the knowledge and skills needed to tackle institutional and other forms of racism which may manifest at school. Darling-Hammond et al. (2007), and Soyei (2011) found that although in-service programmes catered to the curriculum and instructional needs of school leaders, this did not include content on understanding racism and/or how to tackle racism. Furthermore, a Public Agenda Report (2008) reported that principals suggested their colleagues were more helpful in their preparation for administration than graduate courses (NEA Policy Brief 2008). These findings would suggest the preparation and development of school leaders' 'race consciousness' are neglected. Although not discounting university training in educational administration and/or leadership, 'equally important is the training and support school leaders receive after they're hired' (Mitgang and Gill 2012, p. 24). From a survey of almost 1,000 principals, Whitmire (2012) found that over half feel they would be more effective with ongoing development. Fullan (2009) reasons that leaders will need job-embedded learning, system-embedded learning, and organisationally-embedded learning which focuses on 'shared learning' in the context in which they work. Furthermore, Allio (2006) also acknowledges,

> Men and women become leaders by practice, by performing deliberate acts of leadership. Evidence suggests that the most effective leadership programs will focus on building self-knowledge and skills in rhetoric and critical thinking.

Specifically, regarding content on 'race', Greene (2007) found that 'workshops offered opportunities for managers to practice race dialogues, learn new techniques, and ask questions as well as learn from each other' (Greene, p.11). Greene also observed, 'it became clear that our managers needed specialized training in order to be able to fully integrate anti-racist principles into the core of their management' (p.11). The illustrations above are a timely reminder that there can be no one size fits all approach to the preparation and development of school leaders, and there can certainly be no one size fits all approach in helping them to develop as anti-racist leaders. Accordingly, and drawing on the range of professional development approaches highlighted above, this paper suggests that an ecological model of professional development is needed for school leaders to support them in developing a language and practice of race consciousness. This is presented below.

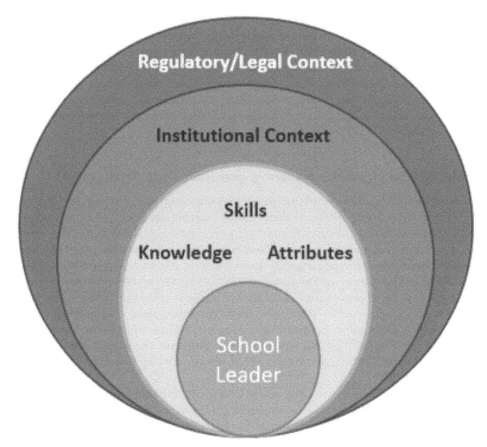

Figure 1. Ecological Model of Professional Development.

Attributes (be): These are related to an individual's core self: personality, values and beliefs. Professional development opportunities should get school leaders to reflect on who they are as individuals, as leaders, and on what matters to them as individuals and as leaders. There may be times when these may be out of sync, and it is important that school leaders not only reflect on why aspects of their core selves may be out of sync but also how to get them back in sync. For example, is institutional racism an important issue or concern for school leaders? How is this concern manifested? Do they as leaders see it as their duty/responsibility to tackle institutional racism? How do they go about tackling institutional racism/race discrimination? Underlying these tensions is the question of a leader's willingness to tackle problems, exert their influence, and advance the overall human good and value of the organisation.

Skills (do): Helping school leaders to undertake a skills audit is as important as unearthing aspects that need development. School leaders need several key skills to effectively manage the complexity of their roles. For example: (i) problem-solving skills; are school leaders equipped to solve complex institutional problems such as institutional racism and race discrimination? How can they develop these skills? Are they prepared to seek out and develop these skills? (ii) social judgement skills; are school leaders sufficiently equipped to read individuals and institutions? Being able to read the individuals within an organisation, and the mood of the organisation is key to tackling institutional and other forms of racism. (iii) professional skills; are school leaders sufficiently networked within and outside their institution? Can they leverage support and respect for change initiatives within and outside their institution? How can they increase their visibility on an issue without undermining their position?

Knowledge (know): Are school leaders sufficiently aware of the extent and forms of race discrimination (and other challenges) faced by staff and students within the institution? Are they aware of how widespread the issues are? Do they know the impact of these challenges on individuals, groups, families?

Have they considered the impact of these challenges/occurrences on the school's reputation, sustainability, etc.? What accountability mechanisms are in place for those in breach of rules and regulations? What support or redress is available for victims of race discrimination? These provide an illustrative list of questions representing the complexity of problem-solving around institutional racism.

Context (where, when): Are there issues, processes and people in a school's context that promote institutional racism? Are these issues historical or contemporary? How can these issues be tackled? What resource (financial, human, etc.) is required and can these be found internally? What would it mean for the institution if these issues were not tackled? Do schools have legal and regulatory duties for tackling institutional racism/race discrimination? What are these duties? Is there a monitoring, reporting and public accountability duty? Do schools face consequences when legal duties are not enforced?

This ecological model is concerned with equipping school leaders with job-embedded learning, system-embedded learning, and organisationally embedded learning (Fullan 2009) which recognises the uniqueness of context, and how school leaders engage with that context. As provided by Greene (2007),

> The core of anti-racist work is to seek to recognize institutional bias and to make structural changes that are supported by policies and procedures that are accountable with outcomes of equity. Leaders, managers and supervisors must be taught to recognize that contemporary forms of racism exist and become familiar with the various forms that it takes in the lives of all staff and clients. They must become vigilant in learning and identifying what those issues are and how they are perpetuated in the organization's policies, practices and procedures. The goal of anti-racist work is to widen the circle of power and opportunity. The leadership must be taught how to help white staff as well as staff of color to better understand how systemic racism works and impacts all staff and clients and be prepared to offer strategies and support for systemic change. (p. 11)

Taking these observations into account, it is acknowledged that this ecological model is contingent upon the individual school leader making a commitment, and acting on/out this commitment to tackling institutional racism/race discrimination; and in doing so, they will devise ways to lead and support their school towards a language and a practice of anti-racism; a language and a practice that starts with and embodies their personal values and beliefs but also draws from a wider set of values and beliefs as applicable.

Resolving the future? Tackling the challenges to building a race equity culture

Whilst several educational leaders across the sector, from nursery to university, express a desire to build a culture of race equity within their institutions, several often face challenges in how to go about this. Suarez (2018, p. 2) provides examples of three common challenges:

- Uncertainty on where and how to start: White leaders may fear saying or doing the wrong thing, or being perceived as blind towards the experiences of staff of BAME heritage. Similarly, leaders of BAME heritage, who have otherwise succeeded within white dominant cultures, may fear being ignored or dismissed for being too 'passionate' if they raise concerns about inequity.
- Lack of awareness of personal biases: Leaders of organisations seeking to close the wealth gap or otherwise 'level the playing field' may naturally view themselves as anti-racist. Even committed leaders (including those of BAME heritage) can be unaware of the ways they contribute to or perpetuate structural racism.
- Impatience with the work required to build a culture of race equity. Race equity work is serious business and it needs to go beyond the transactional, e.g.: increased representation and developing institutional policies around race diversity and inclusion, shifts in institutional practices and cultures. This requires accepting that this work and process takes time, is not straightforward, and requires embracing the challenges and tensions associated with this work. To compound the three challenges identified by Suarez above, I argue here that there are three categories (five types) of leaders, and their position on this typology is a response to tackling racism in their institutions, and an indication of the levels and types of support they may require. See Table 1: Types of (educational) leaders

Table 1. Descriptive statistics.

Indifferent	'Racism/ race discrimination is not a problem in our school'; prioritise performativity agendas; tackling racism not important enough to be a KPI
Sympathisers	
Passive sympathisers	They acknowledge there is a problem, but do nothing to address it, and/or argue that they do not know what to do or how to tackle it; they do not seek help to tackle it; racism not important enough to be a KPI
Performative sympathisers	They acknowledge racism is a problem; commit to help but invest only minimally; intervention usually derived from own interest; tackling racism not important enough to be a KPI
Activists	
Accidental activists	They acknowledge racism is a problem; they are committed to making some form of intervention to tackling it; they may not know the outcome; or the plan may not be clear, but their commitment is clear; tackling racism important, could be treated as a KPI
Deliberate activists	They acknowledge racism is a problem; there is a personal commitment to change; resources – financial, human and time, are provided to devise planned interventions which are monitored and accounted for; tacking racism is a KPI

Bell (2004) notes that racism is a reality. Miller (2019b) also notes racism in education in England is a reality. Brooks and Jean-Marie (2007) further note that school leaders both influence and are influenced by racism. Thus, to stand a chance of creating and sustaining an antiracist institution, school leaders first comprehend the levels of racism in society and how these influence them; second, they need to understand their own roles in perpetuating structural and interpersonal racism; and third, they need to identify and commit resources to addressing these. As provided by Greene (2007) highlights, 'Structural racism requires institutional support and cultural nurturing' (p. 11) – and school leaders should not be complicit in this, nor can they appear or afford to be. Drawing on Suarez (2018, p. 203), and to increase the likelihood of being successful in tackling institutional and other forms of racism/race discrimination, school leaders should:

- Learn the history and context of structural racism in England, and how it has affected people of BAME heritage;
- Listen to the lived experiences of people of BAME heritage within their institutions, without placing the emotional burden of justifying the validity of those experiences on them;
- Reflect on the role that leaders and their institutions play in perpetuating structural racism and dominant culture, which is an organisational culture influenced by the leadership, management, and development of white men and women;
- Examine the effects of implicit bias on disciplinary or related activities, recruitment and promotion, professional development, team power dynamics, and other critical programmes, management, funding, and operation decisions;
- Consider the messages, both implicit and explicit, that leaders and leadership styles shaped by dominant culture send to staff, communities, and stakeholders;
- Define roles and goals around race equity;
- Fund race equity initiatives so that resources, including consultants, training, and one-on-one coaching, are available to grow staff capacity.

Anti-racist school leadership requires a nuanced approach grounded in an understanding of the history and context of structural racism, of personal racism and of the peoples affected by and those perpetrating acts of racism. Although each institution's journey is unique, Suarez (2018, p. 4) propose that each must undergo three stages of change, collectively described as the Race Equity Cycle:

- Awake: increased race diversity in organisations; focused on representation;
- Woke: internal change in behaviours, policies, and practices; equipping people to talk about race; focus on deeper inclusion and creating space so that everyone is comfortable sharing their experiences;
- Work: unstinting application of a race equity lens to examine an institution's programmes, practices and processes.

Crucial to creating an institution that is 'woke' or demonstrably race-conscious in language and practice are leaders who commit to their development in words and deeds and in the development of staff and students and everyone in the school community.

Conclusions

Anti-racist school leadership starts with making 'race' count in leadership preparation and development. Developing a race-conscious language and practice as a leader is not a linear activity, nor is it a one size fits all activity. The uniqueness of context: environmental and institutional must be recognised as a lever in a leader's ability to influence change and the pace at which change occurs. Through an ecological model, each leader develops an appropriate set of attributes, skills and knowledge which, although influenced by the particularities of each school's context, are enacted through a sense of personal agency. Thus, developing a language of race consciousness will not itself lead to a practice of race consciousness and inclusion if the school leader does not want to, or otherwise feels incapable of enacting such a practice. Despite the approach to preparation and/or professional development, developing a language and a practice of race consciousness or race equity culture therefore starts with and relies upon the individual school leader for its viability and sustainability.

Disclosure statement

No potential conflict of interest was reported by the author.

References

Ahmed, S., 2007. You end up doing the document rather than doing the doing: *diversity, race equality and the politics of documentation*. Ethnic and racial studies, 30 (4), 590–609. doi:10.1080/01419870701356015.
Allio, R.J., 2006. *Leadership development: teaching versus learning*. Emerald Group Publishing Limited.
Anzaldua, G., Ed., 1990. *Making face, making soul, Haciendo Caras: creative and critical perspectives by women of colour*. San Francisco: Aunt Lute Foundation Books.
Aveling, N., 2007. Anti-racism in schools: a question of leadership? *Discourse: studies in the cultural politics of education*, 28 (1), 69–85. doi:10.1080/01596300601073630.
Bell, D., 2004. *Silent covenants: brown v. board of education and the unfulfilled hopes for racial reform*. Oxford: Oxford University Press.
Bhopal, K. and Jackson, J., 2013. *The experiences of Black and minority ethnic academics: multiple identities and career progression*. Southampton: University of Southampton.
Brooks, J. and Watson, T., 2018. School leadership and racism: an ecological perspective. *Urban education*, 54 (5), 1–25.
Brooks, J.S., 2012. *Black school, White school: racism and educational (mis)leadership*. New York, NY: Teachers College Press.
Brooks, J.S. and Jean-Marie, G., 2007. Black leadership, White leadership: race and race relations in an urban high school. *Journal of educational administration*, 45 (6), 756–768. doi:10.1108/09578230710829928.
Callender, C.C., 2019. Race and race equality: whiteness in initial teacher education. In: P. Miller and C. Callender, eds. *Race, education and educational leadership: an integrated analysis*. London: Bloomsbury.
Camacho Felix, S., 2019. *Addressing attainment gaps: BAME students experiences and recommendations for LSE*. London School of Economics: Learning and Teaching Centre.

Castles, S., 1996. The racism of globalisation. *In*: E. Vasta and S. Castles, eds. *The teeth are smiling: the persistence of racism in multicultural Australia*. Sydney, Australia: Allen & Unwin.

Christensen, J. and Rog, H.E., 2008. Talent management: A strategy for improving employee recruitment, retention and engagement within hospitality organizations. *International journal of contemporary hospitality management*, 20 (7), 743–757. doi:10.1108/09596110810899086.

Connolly, P., 1996. Seen but never heard: rethinking approached to researching racism and young children. *Discourse*, 17 (2), 171–183.

CRER/Respectme, n.d.. *Addressing inclusion: effectively challenging racism in schools*. Edinburgh: The Scottish Government.

Curtis, P., 2008. *Education: black caribbean children held back by institutional racism in schools*, Guardian, September.

Darling-Hammond, L., et al., 2007. *Preparing school leaders for a changing world: lessons from exemplary leadership development programs*. Stanford, CA: Stanford University, Stanford Educational Leadership Institute.

Demie, F., 2003. Raising the Achievement of Black Caribbean pupils in British schools: unacknowledged problems and challenges for policy makers. *London review of education*, 1 (3), 229–248. doi:10.1080/1474846032000146785.

Demie, F. and Mclean, C., 2017. *Black caribbean underachievement in schools in England*. London: Research and Statistics Unit, Lambeth Education and Learning.

Department for Education, 2016. *Permanent and fixed-period exclusions in England: 2014 to 2015*, DfE SFR26/2016.

Department for Education, 2020. *School workforce in England: november 2018*. Available from: https://www.ethnicity-facts-figures.service.gov.uk/workforce-and-business/workforce-diversity/school-teacher-workforce/latest [Accessed March 2020].

Department of Education and Training, n.d.. *Racism no way, fact sheets*. Available from: www.racismnoway.com.au/library/understanding/index-What.html [Accessed February 2020]

Dismantling Racism, 2019. *Anti-racist organizational development, catholic volunteer network*. Available from: https://catholicvolunteernetwork.org/wp-content/uploads/2019/02/Anti-Racist-Organizational-Development-and-Assesment-Tool-Western-States-Center.pdf

Equality Challenge Unit, 2011. *The experience of Black and minority ethnic staff in higher education in England*. London: Equality Challenge Unit.

Fullan, M., 1999. *Change forces: the sequel*. London: Taylor & Francis/Falmer.

Fullan, M., 2009. *The challenge of change: start school improvement now*. Thousand Oaks, CA: Corwin Press.

Gillborn, D., 1995. *Racism and anti-racism in real schools*. Buckingham, UK: Open University Press.

Gillborn, D., 1996. Student roles and perspectives in antiracist education: A crisis of white ethnicity. *British educational research journal*, 22 (2), 165–179. doi:10.1080/0141192960220202.

Gillborn, D. and Youdell, D., 2000. *Rationing education: policy, practice, reform and equity*. Buckingham: Open University Press.

Gooden, M.A., 2012. What does racism have to do with leadership? Countering the idea of color-blind leadership: a reflection on race and the growing pressures of the urban principalship. *Educational foundations*, 67–84. Winter-Spring.

Greene, M.P., 2007. Beyond diversity and multiculturalism: towards the development of anti-racist institutions and leaders. *Journal for non-profit management*, 9–17.

Haque, Z. and Elliott, S., 2016. *Visible and invisible barriers: the impact of racism on BME teachers*. London: National Education Union/Runnymede Trust.

Henze, R.C., 2000. *Leading for diversity: how school leaders achieve racial and ethnic harmony*. University of California: Center for Research on Education, Diversity and Excellence, Research Brief 6.

Hollinsworth, D., 1998. *Race and racism in Australia*. 2nd ed. Katoomba, Australia: Social Science Press.

Lancashire County Council, 2007. *Guidelines and procedures for dealing with and reporting racist incidents in schools*. Lancs: Directorate for Children and Young People, School Effectiveness Service.

Lander, V., 2011. Race, culture and all that: an exploration of the perspectives of White secondary student teachers about race equality issues in their initial teacher education. *British educational research journal*, 43 (1), 29–48.

Lewis, R.E. and Heckman, R.J., 2006. Talent management: a critical review. *Human resources management review*, 16 (2), 139–154. doi:10.1016/j.hrmr.2006.03.001.

Macpherson, W., 1999.*The Stephen Lawrence inquiry*. London, The Stationery Office, CM 4262-I.

Maylor, U., et al., 2009. *Black childrens' achievement programme evaluation - Report [Report commissioned by the DCSF]*. London, DCSF.

McMahon, B., 2007. Educational administrators' conceptions of whiteness, anti-racism and social justice. *Journal of educational administration*, 45 (6), 684–696. doi:10.1108/09578230710829874.

McNamara, O., et al., 2009. *The leadership aspirations and careers of Black and minority ethnic teachers*. London: NASUWT and National College for Leadership of Schools and Children's Services.

Miller, P., 2012. Editorial: educational leadership in the caribbean & beyond. *Journal of the university college of the Cayman Islands*, 6, 9–10.

Miller, P., 2016. 'White sanction', institutional, group and individual interaction in the promotion and progression of black and minority ethnic academics and teachers in England. *Power & education*, 8 (3), 205–221. doi:10.1177/1757743816672880.
Miller, P., 2018. Race discrimination, cultural inequality, and the politics of knowledge in England. *University of Northumbria, British Educational Research Association - Annual Conference Keynote*, 11 – 13 September.
Miller, P., 2019a. Race and ethnicity in educational leadership. *In*: T. Bush, L. Bell, and D. Middlewood, eds. *Principles of educational leadership & management*. 3rd ed. London: SAGE.
Miller, P., 2019b. 'Tackling' race inequality in school leadership: positive actions in BAME teacher progression – evidence from three English schools. *Educational management administration & leadership*, 174114321987309. OnlineFirst. doi:10.1177/1741143219873098.
Miller, P., 2019c. Race discrimination, cultural inequality, and the politics of knowledge in England. *In*: R. Papa, ed. *Springer handbook on promoting social justice in education*. Netherlands: Springer.
Miller, P., 2020. Race/ethnicity, identity and co-identification in higher education: are we there yet? *Conference Keynote: University of Greenwich's SHIFT Conference*, January London, UK.
Mitgang, L. and Gill, J., 2012. *The making of the principal: five lessons in leadership training. Perspective*. Wallace Foundation.
NEA Policy Brief, 2008. *Changing role of school leadership*. Available from: http://www.nea.org/assets/docs/PB09_Leadership08.pdf
Pells, R., 2017. *Black and minority teachers face 'inherent racism' in UK schools, report warns*. The Independent Online. Available from: https://www.independent.co.uk/news/education/education-news/bme-teachers-racism-uk-schools-black-minority-ethnic-education-nasuwt-runneymede-trust-a7827131.html
Pettman, J., 1992. *Living in the margins: racism, sexism and feminism in Australia*. Sydney, Australia: Allen and Unwin.
Phillips, T., 2016. *Race & faith: the deafening silence*. London, Civitas: Institute for the Study of Civil Society. Available from: http://www.civitas.org.uk/content/files/Race-and-Faith.pdf [Accessed April 2020].
Raby, R., 2004. There's no racism at my school, it's just joking around': ramifications for anti-racist education. *Race, ethnicity and education*, 7 (4), 367–383. doi:10.1080/1361332042000303388.
Ryan, J., 2012. *Struggling for inclusion educational leadership in a Neoliberal World: issues in the research, theory, policy, and practice of urban education*. Charlotte, NC: Information Age Publishers.
SecEd, 2015. *Improving diversity among leaders*. Available from: www.sec-ed.co.uk/best-practice/improvingdiversity-among-leaders [Accessed March 2020].
Soyei, S., 2011. *The barriers to challenging racism and promoting race equality in England's schools*. Tyne & Wear: Show Racism the Red Card.
Strand, S., 2012. The White British-Black caribbean achievement gap: tests, tiers and teacher expectations. *British educational research journal*, 38 (1), 75–101. doi:10.1080/01411926.2010.526702.
Strand, S., 2015. *Ethnicity, deprivation and educational achievement at age 16 in England: trends over time*. University of Oxford. Available from: https://www.gov.uk/government/uploads/system/uploads/attachment_data/file/439867/RR439B-Ethnic_minorities_and_attainment_the_effects_of_poverty_annex.pdf.pdf
Suarez, K., 2018. *The role of senior leaders in building a race equity culture*. Boston: The Bridgespan Group.
Theoharis, G. and Brooks, J.S., Eds., 2012. *What every principal needs to know to create equitable and excellent schools*. New York: Teachers College Press.
Whitmire, T., 2012. *Strengthening school leadership*. Portland, Oregon: Stand for Children Leadership Center, June.
Yamato, G., 1990. Something about the subject makes it hard to name. *In*: G. Anzuldua, ed. *Making face, making soul*. San Francisco: Aunt Lute Foundation Books.

What is the problem? A critical review of social justice leadership preparation and development

Deirdre Torrance, Christine Forde, Fiona King and Jamila Razzaq

ABSTRACT
Despite growing interest in social justice leadership and awareness of the need to include this focus in leadership preparation and development, little is understood of practices used to support such commitment. In this article, Bacchi's (2012a) Foucaldian approach is drawn from, to provide a specific means of critically analysing what problem(s) social justice leadership preparation/development is intended to address. Through critical reflexivity, the political dimensions of policy and practice are surfaced. Through this process, key influences of regimes of power are identified, within which leadership development programmes are situated. Considerations for leadership development and school practices foreground the identification of next steps for research.

Introduction

Bogotch (2008) highlights debates about definitions of social justice and suggests that education can provide a testbed for the development of social justice practice. Recently social justice has become a key policy concern gaining traction in different systems leading to an increasing focus on social justice leadership. In this article, we draw from Theoharis' (2007) definition with social justice leadership exercised by headteachers who 'make issues of race, class, gender, disability, sexual orientation, and other historically and currently marginalizing conditions […] central to their advocacy, leadership practice, and vision' (p. 223). The concern for social justice leadership has led to 'a paradigmatic shift in leadership development from indifference or ignorance toward issues of social justice by practitioners and scholars to an embracement of said issues' (Jean-Marie et al. 2009, p. 5). Consequently, social justice leadership development is an area for scholarly enquiry where there is a small but expanding literature. There remains limited clarity either about the practices that constitute social justice leadership development or the issues it is intended to address.

This article examines critically the scholarly literature on social justice leadership development through formal programmes. This review is underpinned by Bacchi's (2012a) Foucaldian approach to examine the problem(s) social justice leadership development is intended to address. In doing so, we open up to critical scrutiny the purposes and practices of social justice leadership development and understand the regimes of power – political and professional – within which such programmes are situated. This article begins with Bacchi's process of problem analysis followed by an outline of the methods used to gather and analyse the literature on social justice leadership development. The findings are presented, followed by a discussion of next steps in research.

'What's the problem': overview of Bacchi's approach

There have been previous reviews of the literature on the subject of social justice leadership development such as Jean-Marie et al. (2009) which used a systematic content analysis. Building on this we are interested in exploring critically the unquestioned assumptions underpinning the purposes and practices of social justice leadership development. Bacchi (2012a), drawing on Foucault's (1977) argument about the significance of exploring why and how things become named as problems, provides an approach to the critical reading of key texts. Bacchi (2012a) describes her approach as 'what's the problem represented' to be (WPR), providing a means of 'disrupting taken-for-granted truth' (p.4). She coins the term 'problem representation' explaining 'the WPR approach rests on a basic premise – that what we say we want to do about something indicates what we think needs to change and hence, how we constitute the "problem"' (p.4) That is, how the problem is identified, classified, and regulated. She argues that

> the practice of studying problematizations encourages exactly this form of critical reflexivity. Such a practice prompts researchers to keep a critical eye to their own analyses, which can only ever be part of a problematization (p.7).

Part of the purpose of using Bacchi as a tool for analysis is her focus on the political dimensions of policy and practice. 'Bacchi considers the role played by academic researchers in the processes of knowledge production and governing, and the relationship between researchers and policymakers. She makes a strong case for researchers to pay greater critical attention to the effects of the evidence-based policy paradigm' (Partridge 2010, p. 12). We would extend this to argue that as researchers and teacher educators we need to examine critically the assumptions underpinning practice in leadership development including headship preparation where many such programmes are part of policy and regulation. Bacchi (2012b) builds into WPR self-problematisation, an undertaking to apply these questions to one's own presuppositions and assumptions. Leadership development is well established in various systems and, following Bacchi's (2012a) argument, we need to consider the complex relations that produce social justice as an essential policy problem within the discourse and the effects this has on the operation of professional learning. Bacchi's approach enables us to surface both the unquestioned assumptions and the regimes of power embedded in the processes of social justice leadership development.

Focus, literature search and analysis

There are two interconnected sets of practices in social justice leadership development, the practice of headteachers in school and that of teacher educators providing leadership development which is intended to either prepare teachers for headship or provide ongoing professional development for serving headteachers. In this article, we examine the practice of teacher educators. From a host of common terms for describing the various roles, we use the following: headteacher for principal; teacher educators for educational administration professors and learners for pupils/students. The literature on social justice leadership development is diverse covering questions of the curriculum, pedagogy, and learning in formal programmes as well as issues related to inequality and discrimination. For this review, articles examining teacher professional development and social justice and informal leadership development were excluded. A systematic search was conducted using combinations of key terms (Table 1) to identify a diverse set of materials: policy critiques, scholarly discussions, and empirical studies.

Table 1. Search terms.

Leadership	Social justice
Development	Equity, equitable
Preparation	Equality, inequality
Professional learning	Race/ethnicity
Principal	Black
Headteacher	Gender
	Inclusive
	LGBTQI; sexual orientation
	Disability

There were three stages of the analysis of the literature. The first stage consisted of reading through the identified articles and generating broad themes to sort items into clusters (Table 2).

Table 2. Broad themes in the literature.

Advocacy and purposes
Curricular frameworks
Practice: pedagogies, selection, assessment
Course dynamics
Specific dimensions: race/ethnicity, gender, disability, SEN, ASN, LGBTQI, poverty
Practice in school
Capacities, competencies and skills

The second stage consisted of reviewing these clusters using four key questions:

- Why is social justice leadership development deemed necessary?
- What are the stated purposes of these programmes?
- What sets of practices comprise the processes of social justice leadership development?
- How is social justice constructed?

The third stage was our adaption of Bacchi's (2012b) WPR questions to analyse the data and prepare a critical commentary on this body of scholarship. Bacchi's original questions and our adaptations are set out in Table 3.

Table 3. Critical questions.

Bacchi's questions	Adapted questions
What is the problem represented to be in a specific policy?	What is the problem represented to be in this body of work?
What presuppositions or assumptions underlie this representation of the problem?	What presuppositions or assumptions underlie the advocacy for social justice leadership development?
How has this representation of the problem come about?	What are the issues with extant provision that lead to this focus on social justice leadership development?
What is left unproblematic in this problem representation? Where are the silences? Can the problem be thought about differently?	What are the underpinning assumptions in the construction of this form of leadership development? Are there missing areas, are there alternative approaches?
What effects are produced by this representation of the problem?	How is leadership development to go forward?
How/where has this representation of the problem been produced, disseminated and defended? How could it be questioned, disrupted and replaced?"	As a body of knowledge how has this developed and what areas need to be further examined?

Using Bacchi's questions: a critical commentary

We now use the adapted questions to provide a critical commentary of the literature on social justice leadership development. In this, we are not simply looking at aspects that have been identified as problematic. Rather, we are exploring the process of problematisation which enables us to critically scrutinise this literature and to identify 'possible deleterious effects they set in operation' (Bacchi 2012a, p. 7). Framing the analysis in this way enables us to consider critically the purposes and practices of social justice leadership development and the underpinning power regimes.

What is the problem represented to be in this body of work?

The key problem represented in this literature concerns the limitations of conventional leadership development. There are several facets to the problem with issues relating to societal trends, policy drivers, and school-level practices. The wider sociopolitical context is identified as a significant issue with Karanxha et al. (2014) highlighting the 'persistence of social inequities (reflected for instance as classism, racism, sexism, heterosexism and ablism)' (p.1187), arguing for a form of leadership development that enables 'educators to respond to the call for equity'. This approach is necessary because of both historical and current patterns of marginalisation and prejudice. Demographic changes in the US (Young and Brooks 2008) are raising questions about diversity and achievement:

> schools in the United States are becoming more ethnically and linguistically diverse, while the White population is decreasing [...] the achievement gap [...] between affluent students and poor students and between White students and students of color continues (Hernandez and Marshall 2017, p. 203).

In other systems too increasing diversity, alongside an achievement gap is evident in the problem represented: 'London is a city of vast disparities between rich and poor and a growing racial achievement gap' (Johnson and Campbell-Stephens 2010, p. 845). Conventional leadership development programmes are not deemed to adequately support the endeavours of headteachers looking to address the learning needs of all learners.

The complex relationship between these wider socio-political issues and education policy is brought into sharp focus in the American literature (Marshall and Oliva 2006). Policy is deemed a useful tool leveraging change. In the USA, for example, *No Child Left Behind* (NCLB) (DE, 2001) has led to every school being 'held publicly accountable for the success of all children' (Hernandez and Marshall 2017, p. 203). Similar opportunities have been provided by explicit statements in policy and professional standards in the UK. However, policy can have unintended consequences (Woods et al. 2020). A driving policy force remains the improvement of attainment (Gerstl-Pepin et al. 2006) but professional standards that underpin leadership development programmes do not necessarily surface issues related to equity and fairness (Celoria 2016).

In the representation of the problem, social justice leadership development is deemed essential because the tensions around high stakes accountability, performance, and ensuring the progress of all learners come into play in shaping the day-to-day practice of headteachers. The achievement gap points to the marginalisation of different groups of learners: 'the evidence is clear and alarming that various segments of our public-school population experience negative and inequitable treatment on a daily basis' (Brown 2006, p. 702). These 'disparities in achievement across racial groups' (Hernandez and Marshall 2009, p. 318) remain continuing patterns. Consequently, 'a commitment to fight for the success of all students rather than accept their failure is inevitable' (Jean-Marie 2010, p. 110) and therefore is central in social justice leadership development. Such a commitment extends beyond simply addressing the achievement gap to a concern with wider school transformation, creating inclusive schools reflecting the lived experiences of learners. Boske (2011, p. 84) argues that in American public schools 'children are exposed to the effects of these inequities through the perpetuation of hegemonic school practices, which reproduce and reinforce cultural and educational traditions of White, middle-class, English-speaking, Christian, heterosexual communities'. There is a perceived need to work towards the 'desired future of education' (Feldman and Tyson 2014, p. 1112). Social justice leadership development, then, is about creating 'counternarratives' which 'reinvent democratic processes' (Foster 2004 cited Cambron-McCabe and McCarthy 2005 p. 208) and enable headteachers to understand and dismantle barriers to learning to address the two goals of academic achievement and preparing students to live as critical citizens (McKenzie et al. 2008).

What presuppositions or assumptions underlie the advocacy for social justice leadership development?

Bacchi's (2012b) second question invites us to critically appraise the assumptions underpinning the representation of the problem and its proposed solution. In the literature, there are two intertwined assumptions about firstly, new forms of leadership and secondly, the role of social justice leadership development in fostering these. Theoharis' (2007) definition providing a broad-based construction of social justice leadership around 'issues of race, class, gender, disability, sexual orientation, and other historically and current marginalising conditions' is drawn on frequently. This new form of leadership is variously described with the emphasis on values, action, and change: for López et al. (2006, p. 14) it is 'leadership for equity'; for Bertrand and Rodela (2018) a participative approach with leadership opportunities for learners, parents, and the community. Change is central to these new forms of leadership with headteachers described as 'agents of cultural transformation' (Johnson et al. 2011, p. 159), 'moral stewards' (Brown 2005, p. 155) 'revolutionary educational leaders' (Jean-Marie et al. 2009, p. 7), 'conscionable citizens in a global context' (Huchting and Bickett 2012, p. 82) and 'antiracist leaders' (Young and Laible 2000, p. 3). Leadership development is perceived as the means to reshape leadership: 'new leaders who have the knowledge, skills and dispositions to close the achievement gap and who are capable of leading successful efforts to meet the challenges in today's schools' (López et al. 2006, p. 12).

The assumption underlying these programmes of social justice leadership development is that headteachers will be able to realise change using the knowledge developed through these programmes, 'we propose that unless school leaders develop coherent conceptualisations of social justice, they will be unlikely to fashion their leadership accordingly' (Feldman and Tyson 2014, p. 1106). Policies such as, for example, NCLB (DE, 2001), mark a move from providing equal opportunities for all 'to school systems producing equal educational outcomes for all their students' (Feldman and Tyson 2014, p. 1105). Within this literature there are repeated references to the development of headteachers to 'act equitably on behalf of all of their students and staff' (Marshall and Hernandez 2012, p. 458), to create 'rigorous high-quality learning opportunities for all students' (Trujillo and Cooper 2014, p. 157) and 'contribute to the learning for all' (Johnson et al. 2011, p. 153–4). The focus on all learners is a consistent theme throughout the literature. Miller and Martin (2015) seek to enable leaders to build 'various proactive systems of support … focused on student learning needs in specific areas' (p.143). Thus, Hernandez and McKenzie (2010) look for programmes to enable leaders 'to understand their service to their community … [and] … the difference they could make in their own communities' (p.54). However, there is little to indicate the complex nature of this work, notably in balancing the range of (often conflicting) needs for increasingly diverse groups of learners.

What are the issues with extant provision that lead to this focus on social justice leadership development?

Bacchi's third question is concerned with tracing the ways in which the representation of a problem has come about. In this literature, this representation has come about partly through the critique of extant leadership development programmes and partly from committed teacher educators who have highlighted the gaps and tensions in relation to neutral, especially colour-blind forms of leadership development. The literature is highly critical of conventional practice which does not take cognisance of wider societal change, diversity, and the lived experiences of marginalised groups: 'What some preparation programs have found is that too often our students have been ill-prepared to engage the multiple layers of social and cultural realities within which students and school communities live everyday' (Gooden and Dantley 2012, p. 238). Similarly, until very recently leadership development programmes contained 'only an implicit, rather than an overt, commitment to the enhancement of social justice through the management of the English state school system' (Brundrett and de Cuevas 2007, p. 44). The concern relates to a perceived lack of skill and understanding on the part of headteachers which may exacerbate existing social inequalities either through ignorance of social justice issues from the lived perspective of school community members, or through structural barriers and elitist constructions of leadership (Bertrand and Rodela 2018).

The issues raised in the literature concern the content, pedagogies, and other practices notably a selection of programme participants. Teaching strategies to build knowledge and skill relating to existing paradigms of instructional leadership are deemed insufficient (McKenzie et al. 2008). The content of conventional programmes does not deal with social justice: for example, 'issues of racism continue to be neglected within most educational leadership preparation programs' (Diem and Carpenter 2013, p. 59), often guised as treating everyone the same (Blackmore 2010). Conventional programmes repeat ingrained school perceptions, behaviours, and systemic barriers such as colour-blindness and the pedagogy of these is also perceived as problematic:

> Much professional development has been modelled on the transmission model – assuming that passing on information and exchanging ideas will change practice – with little attention paid to the needs, fears and desires, or lack of motivation and incentives, amongst recipients to change their practices (Blackmore 2010, p. 56).

Although issues of social justice and equality may be dealt with in conventional programmes these issues are often offered as a single course. This is deemed problematic, 'leadership preparation faculty will need to push for more than one diversity course as having only one or none can have the effect of marginalizing content that should be integrated within our preparation programs' (Gooden and Dantley 2012, p. 245). Social justice should be a defining feature of leadership development.

Miller and Martin (2015), therefore, argue that 'the social justice leadership discourse calls for preparation experiences that are very different from the theory and research that the academic disciplines provide' (p.131). Further, a hidden curriculum in conventional programmes ignores social justice and operates to discriminate against minority groups. Practice related to the selection of programme participants provides an example. Selection is pivotal in shaping the composition of a programme's cohort, valuing diverse participants who have demonstrated social justice in their professional experience (Rodríguez et al. 2010). In addition, selection onto licensure programmes which are part of headteacher pipelines, impact on the future profile of headship (Agosto et al. 2015). Karanxha et al. (2014) and Boske and Elue (2018) provide thought-provoking case studies where projects to increase student diversity are resisted by some teacher educators. Even where the evidence demonstrates a disproportionate rejection of candidates of colour – notably Black African American women – some teacher educators continue to minimise racial and ethnic diversity (Karanxha et al. 2014).

The issues related to conventional leadership programmes raise questions about the power and position of teacher educators: 'Problem definition, a core activity that drives ameliorative [social problem] program development, is often a dominant culture's interpretation of reality' (SenGupta et al. 2004, p. 8). Faculty attitudes are identified as a block:

> despite some promising work and compelling recommendations by particularly committed individual scholars, a vast majority of educational administration faculty members remain silent on issues of race, making unclear the scope of the field's commitment to diversity (Young and Brooks 2008, p. 393).

This reluctance is sometimes construed as a concern about dealing with difficult issues on the programme but equally influential is the fear of being marginalised by other teacher educators: 'it's not simply a fear of discomfort, but may actually reflect a fear of rocking the boat so much that one is dumped out' (Killingsworth et al. 2010, p. 534). Boske and Elue (2018) and Karanxha et al. (2014) illustrate graphically the range of behaviours some teacher educators engage in to resist change within leadership development programmes.

Advocacy and the development of a different approach to leadership development is often progressed by committed individual teacher educators. Jean-Marie (2010) describes this as 'fire in the belly' with teacher educators, sometimes in the face of considerable resistance from colleagues, seeking to expose discriminatory practices and build more equitable practices:

> In essence, my classroom community is a nurturing place for educational leaders to explore and begin to deepen their commitment to social justice. I view this kind of work as political activism to move the discourse of social justice to deeply embedded practices." (p.111).

Whereas Bacchi's third question helped identify the 'problem' of conventional leadership development programmes, the next question enables us to critically appraise new forms of social justice leadership development presented in this literature.

What are the underpinning assumptions in the construction of this form of leadership development? Are there missing areas, are there alternative approaches?

In advocating for and investigating social justice leadership development, some studies are more descriptive and evaluative, setting out different areas of the curriculum, techniques to be used and participants' responses to this. However, other studies draw more substantially from theoretical discussions to illuminate different issues related to social justice in education and to frame pedagogy in these programmes.

Theoretical insights drawn from a wider literature relating to, for example, critical race theory, feminist theory, queer theory which, as Blackmore (2010) argues, enables participants to address issues of power and exclusion, are only rarely included in leadership development: 'the complexity of the social and structural inequalities, how difference works through power relations, and positions them as leaders in and from dominant cultures' (p.55). These theories provide 'alternative social justice perspectives', exploring dimensions such as 'multicultural leadership, feminist leadership, critical African American and Latino leadership traditions' (Cambron-McCabe and McCarthy 2005, p.203). Given the US origin of most of this literature, it is not surprising that critical race theory (Ladson-Billings 2009) is a central tool associated with theoretical constructs such as racial identity development (Hernandez 2012), whiteness, and privilege (Agosto et al. 2015, Zarate and Mendoza 2018). These theoretical insights enable participants to examine their unquestioned beliefs and provide tools for leading to action (Forde 2014).

Feldman and Tyson (2014) draw on four theoretical frameworks which provide 'the backbone for conceptualising and doing the work of preparing leaders' (p.1112) to become change agents. These frameworks are:

> antibias education (combines racial identity development theory with progressive grassroots activism); critical pedagogy (based on critical social theory, conceptualising teaching and learning as a form of social activism); multicultural education (the idea of social transformation through cognition); whiteness studies (locating race as the central structure of oppression operating in society) (Feldman and Tyson 2014, p. 1112).

Several detailed frameworks are presented in the literature. Hernandez and McKenzie (2010) provide a set of five questions relating to social justice practice, theoretical perspectives and tensions and dilemmas that guides each class in their programme. The purpose of this focus is to build as Capper et al. (2006) propose, a critical consciousness, knowledge, and practical skills focused on social justice. Diem and Carpenter (2012) propose five elements related to race: 'color-blind ideologies, misconceptions of human difference, merit-based achievement, critical self-reflection, and issues of silence' (p.107). Theoharis and Causton-Theoharis (2008) outline different facets that foster the critical dispositions for headteachers through developing theoretical perspectives, building a vision and sense of agency.

Less theorised are issues related to pedagogic practice and learning. Brown (2005) proposes alternative instructional approaches combining 'critical reflection, rational discourse, and policy praxis' (p.157). This approach is built on three theoretical frameworks, Adult Learning Theory, Transformative Learning Theory, and Critical Social Theory, thereby enabling headteachers to grow in 'awareness, acknowledgement and action!' (Brown 2006, p. 731). Furman (2012) proposes another theoretical framework where social justice is constructed as praxis. Praxis has 'the potential to be a powerful, unifying concept in regard to leadership for social justice, because it captures both the reflection and action needed for such work' and to enable the development of innovative approaches. For Furman (2012) 'Praxis involves the continual, dynamic interaction among knowledge acquisition, deep reflection, and action at two levels – the intrapersonal and the extrapersonal – with the purpose of transformation and liberation (p.203). Within this, there are five 'arenas: the personal, interpersonal, communal, systemic, and ecological' (p.204).

Jean-Marie et al. (2009) argue that leadership development needs to move in 'the direction of a social constructivist approach to teaching and learning involving critical dialogue and pedagogy, and a concentrated effort to understand knowledge construction and social development' (p.11--12). The overarching approach is that of 'critical pedagogy' (Guillaume et al. 2019). This is constructed in different ways including critical reflection on practice, on participants' lived experiences and on beliefs and values. In constructing the problem of a lack of understanding and lived experiences of the participants, awareness raising is central to the development of a critical consciousness. McKenzie et al. (2008) describe this as an ongoing developmental journey which is modelled on the programme by teacher educators: changing minds by interrogating established thinking patterns, uncontested beliefs, and values. McKenzie and Scheurich (2004) propose 'equity traps' as a teaching tool to surface unquestioned beliefs. Equity traps are defined as 'dysconsciousness' [that] prevents us from seeing and believing in the possibility that all students of colour can achieve and that we can have the ability and the will to make this happen (p.603). The intention is to 'prepare new leaders to critically inquire into the taken-for-granted structures and norms that often pose insurmountable barriers for many students' academic success'. (Cambron-McCabe and McCarthy 2005, p.204) and to enable the participants to understand the consequences of their actions on the whole school community.

In this, critical reflection is a central concern with a range of approaches drawn from different theoretical understandings. Hernandez and Marshall (2009) advocate multifaceted approaches where through reading, discussions, experiential learning, and reflection, participants develop greater self-awareness of their own cultural identity and the unquestioned assumptions underpinning this. Here, transformational learning experiences include 'cultural plunges, reflective writing, neighbourhood walks, home visits and equity audits' (p.204). For Feldman and Tyson (2014), Brown (2006) and Furman (2012) pedagogy is not about a set of techniques. Instead, these practices represent an exercise of power to effect personal and professional change in participants.

Fostering a critical consciousness is complex: 'social justice leadership was implied in students' work but the program struggled at times in pushing students to become more critically conscious'. (Hernandez and McKenzie 2010, p. 57–58). This is a searching reflection on 'practices, experiences and beliefs' (Gooden and Dantley 2012, p. 239). Huchting and Bickett (2012) in this endeavour stress the importance of supportive structures on an individual basis. Mullen et al. (2014) advocate cultural dialogues which explore meanings along with practising interchanges in safe contexts. The power relations that exist in leadership development classrooms are only limitedly acknowledged. Constructivist principles allow opportunities for co-construction of courses with participants (Hernandez and McKenzie 2010, Rodríguez et al. 2010). Nevertheless, these are 'pedagogies of discomfort' (Boler and Zembylas 2003, p. 131) in which critical pedagogy is balanced with creating a safe space (Diem et al. 2013) in which to confront issues. However, leadership development classrooms are not necessarily always a safe space. Boske and Elue (2018) and Diem et al. (2013) explore course dynamics which operate to marginalise and exclude groups of participants from minority backgrounds.

One area which is central to award-bearing leadership development programmes is assessment, a powerful tool for either reinforcing existing paradigms and practices or realising change. The literature provides examples of the challenges in developing a critical consciousness, which is 'far beyond knowledge acquisition at the formal cognitive level' (Brown 2004, p. 81). Young and Laible (2000) assert that: 'Future school leaders should not be granted licensure or graduate from their preparation programs without an understanding of racism, racial identity issues, racial oppression, and how to work against racism in schools' (p.21). This has implications for the type of assessment tasks required of participants designed to disrupt existing power relationships. Zarate and Mendoza (2018) propose that weekly peer reflection 'displaced the instructor's position of authority' (p.7). However, there is little consideration of the assessment process, either of valid means to assess this learning or of the power relationships that underpin such processes.

How is leadership development to go forward?

We have examined previously the critique of conventional leadership development and alternative approaches to curriculum, pedagogy, and the theoretical underpinning of these programmes. Bacchi's question now leads us to consider the effects of these representations of the problem and the future direction of social justice leadership development. Jean-Marie et al. (2009) argue that 'social justice as an educational intervention is a continuously relevant topic that should be infused into every aspect of leadership preparation' (p.1). However, we need to appreciate the power regimes underpinning leadership development programmes. Thus, Rusch (2004) argues that 'the power structure of the field of educational administration can serve as a barrier to engaging in a discourse about complex issues' because 'those in privileged positions – no matter how well intended – are not likely to willingly make changes that result in the loss of privilege' (p.31–32). The pivotal role of committed individual teacher educators provides a foundation but this is insufficient and there is a need to broaden this base. The concerns expressed by teacher educators about confrontation and lack of support for a social justice perspective need to be addressed. This can be achieved at least in part by teacher educators becoming more knowledgeable about issues related to social justice and equity as well as becoming more skilled in constructivist pedagogic practices to foster a critical consciousness.

There is also an additional dimension surfaced in only a limited number of studies. Constructions of social justice leadership in this literature emphasise an activist orientation, where headteachers act to bring about significant change. There is little to be found in the literature in terms of developing sets of practices through which headteachers can bring about the transformational change in school (Miller and Martin 2015). Brown's (2006) discussion is an example of the listing of programme activities such as 'cultural biographical life histories, prejudice reduction workshops, reflective analysis journals, cross-cultural interviews, educational plunges, diversity panels' (p.204). It is in only the last example that there is an explicit link to practice in school, 'activist action plans' (p.204). As headteachers are described as 'agents of change' bringing about transformative practice in school, a crucial aspect of concern involves the development of skills to enable headteachers to bring about change beyond school structures, to impact on the day-to-day practice of teachers in schools. Here we need to develop understandings of the processes of developing leadership practice to transform both school leadership practice and the pedagogic practice of classroom teachers. Part of the future direction of social justice leadership development would be to connect with this literature on social justice leadership practice. Research conducted in over 20 education systems by the International School Leadership Development Network (ISLDN) (Angelle, 2017) could contribute to developing the practice of social justice leadership through leadership development programmes.

As a body of knowledge how has this developed and what areas need to be further examined?

Rodríguez et al. (2010) caution that 'developing social justice university programs in a country of great inequities and injustice is difficult' (p.152) but nevertheless essential 'in a democracy whose rhetoric commits itself to social justice and equity for everyone' (p.153). Leadership development programmes are important in enabling headteachers' social justice leadership practice. As societies become more diverse there is the danger of increasing fragmentation and sectionalism. Public schooling systems are seen as potentially contributing significantly to social cohesion providing opportunities for marginalised groups. There is a strong imperative for action and change across this body of work, with much of the focus on building the commitment of headteachers to achieve this. The perception is that schools and more specifically headteachers are best placed to ameliorate social justice issues and address the 'attainment gap' rather than politicians, social policy, or society as a whole. However, while the important contribution of social justice leadership development is underlined in this literature, there is less focus on the significant constraints that existing regimes of power place on those delivering leadership development and on programme participants in realising the ambitions of this approach. As the field evolves one of the tensions to be grappled with is the complex nature of social justice, socio-politically and culturally beyond education.

McKenzie et al. (2008) put forward a proposal for programmes to tackle inequalities and injustices on a broad base: 'racism, sexism, classism, homophobia, and all other abuses of power (p.13)'. One of the challenges is to balance this broad-based approach to social justice leadership, with building a deep understanding and skill in addressing issues of marginalisation and discrimination experienced by particular groups. There is a tendency in this body of scholarship for educators to focus on some marginalised groups, raising issues around an overloaded curriculum and the expertise of teacher educators. There is a strong emphasis on issues related to race (Gooden and Dantley 2012, Diem and Carpenter 2012, Zarate and Mendoza 2018), challenging colour-blindness (Gerstl-Pepin et al. 2006) and raising issues related to racial identity (Hernandez 2012) and White privilege (Young and Laible 2000). The concern raised by Marshall and Hernandez (2012) and O'Malley and Capper (2015) is that LGBTQI issues are not included in social justice leadership development which is reflected in our review of this literature which identified only two articles. The inclusion of LGBTQI 'is determined by [an] individual professor teaching the course than any articulated curricular priority associated with the course' (O'Malley and Capper 2015, p. 313). Further, of the reviewed articles, two dealt specifically with the issue of gender (Rusch 2004, Killingsworth et al. 2010) and two dealt with issues related to disability. Pazey and Cole (2013) look for the inclusion of special educational needs in a 'culturally responsive pedagogy' (p.261). Although it might be argued that implicitly the intersection of various factors is appreciated, this does leave significant gaps.

Brundrett and de Cuevas (2008, p. 248) note with the increased focus on social justice leadership development in the literature: 'a powerful and persuasive academic discourse has begun to emerge that emphasises the importance of headship in assisting in the construction of a more just society'. However, a key issue is the use of the literature in shaping policy and practice to realise the radical reforms being advocated firstly, around the design and practice of such programmes and then secondly, around the impact of these programmes on participants' practice in school with the goal of building more equitable school practice. Much of the literature tends to be drawn from small-scale studies of an individual programme in one institution. There is a small number of larger-scale work notably McKenzie et al.'s (2008) collaborative proposal for a curriculum or theoretically informed investigations of issues related to social justice (Blackmore 2010, Hernandez 2012) and to pedagogy (Brown 2004, Furman 2012). The case studies often explore complex issues around power and privilege, predominantly in relation to race. They are also illuminative of different pedagogic practices and learning tools. In this body of work, however, evaluation is confined largely to participants' responses to different pedagogic practices rather than exploring longer-term impact. The impact of social justice leadership development on participants' practice in school and the outcomes of this need to be investigated empirically.

The other aspect needing further examination is the role of teacher educators teaching on educational leadership programmes, who presumably form a significant audience for this body of work. There is evidence of resistance (Boske and Elue 2018) by teacher educators who either prioritise the improvement agenda or see issues of social justice leadership being well served by a single course within the programme. A further issue identified is the lack of skill and confidence on the part of teacher educators in dealing with complex issues related to the education of marginalised groups where teacher educators tend to be from privileged groups, White and middle class (Rusch 2004).

Summary: Setting a research agenda

A number of issues have been highlighted through this critical literature review both within the current body of work, and with the identified gaps and silences (Bacchi, 2012a) in the literature. The vast majority of studies report on work in the USA with only four studies from the UK and one comparative study. Part of this reflects the longstanding place of principal preparation in the USA, where there has been significant attention to historical and contemporary issues of diversity, discrimination and education. However, as leadership development becomes part of policy in different systems, and headteachers grapple with the demands of raising attainment and increasingly diverse pupil populations, there is a need to build research on social justice leadership development for aspiring and serving headteachers contextualised in different systems.

The ISLDN research has highlighted the work of social justice leaders across the world, often working in extreme circumstances (Barnett and Woods forthcoming). Personal commitment and personal experiences of headteachers are important drivers in the development of social justice leadership. However, this is not sufficient in itself. If we are to look for systemic change, it seems important that headteachers have access to leadership development that provides underpinning conceptualisations to inform their practice in taking forward social justice leadership. The issue of learner diversity and the implications for schools remain much contested, with a need to build on the American scholarship in this area by considering the implications for both leadership development programmes and research within systems globally. Different systems are grappling in different ways with increasingly diverse learner populations. Given the deeply contextualised nature of social justice practice, there is a need for comparative work across different systems, comparing the purposes and practices around the advancement of social justice leadership development. The extant body of work sets out the purposes, content, and pedagogic practices used in the programmes studied but these are often small scale. Larger scale possibly comparative studies on questions related to why social justice leadership development is necessary, the purposes and practices of such programmes, the constructions of social justice underpinning these programmes and the relationship between social justice leadership and practice in school would extend the field considerably.

Disclosure statement

No potential conflict of interest was reported by the authors.

ORCID

Christine Forde http://orcid.org/0000-0001-6484-1704
Fiona King http://orcid.org/0000-0001-5749-1435

References

Agosto, V., Karanxha, Z., and Bellara, A., 2015. Battling inertia in educational leadership: CRT Praxis for race conscious dialogue. *Race, ethnicity and education*, 18 (6), 785–812. doi:10.1080/13613324.2014.885420.

Angelle, P.S., ed. 2017. *A global perspective of social justice leadership for school principals*. Charlotte, NC: IAP.

Bacchi, C., 2012a. Why study problematizations? Making politics visible. *Open journal of political science*, 2 (1), 1–8. doi:10.4236/ojps.2012.21001.

Bacchi, C., 2012b. Introducing the 'what's the problem represented to be?' approach. *In*: A. Bletsas and C. Beasley, eds. *Engaging with Carol Bacchi: strategic interventions & exchanges*. Adelaide: University of Adelaide Press, 21–24.

Barnett, B. and Woods, P., forthcoming. *Educational leadership for social justice and improving high-needs schools: findings from 10 years of international collaboration*.

Bertrand, M. and Rodela, K.C., 2018. A framework for rethinking educational leadership in the margins: implications for social justice leadership preparation. *Journal of research on leadership education*, 13 (1), 10–37. doi:10.1177/1942775117739414.

Blackmore, J., 2010. 'The other within': race/gender disruptions to the professional learning of white educational leaders. *International journal of leadership in education*, 13 (1), 45–61. doi:10.1080/13603120903242931.

Bogotch, I., 2008. Social justice as an educational construct: problems and possibilities. *In*: I. Bogotch, et al., eds. *Radicalizing educational leadership: dimensions of social justice*. Rotterdam: Sense, 79–112.

Boler, M. and Zembylas, M., 2003. Discomforting truths: the emotional terrain of understanding difference. *In*: P. P. Trifonas, ed. *Pedagogies of difference*. New York: RoutledgeFalmer, 115–138.

Boske, C., 2011. Using the senses in reflective practice: preparing school leaders for non-text-based understandings. *Journal of curriculum theorising*, 27 (2), 82–100.

Boske, C. and Elue, C., 2018. "Hold on! I'll just google it!": critical conversations regarding dimensions of diversity in a school leadership preparation program. *Journal of cases in educational leadership*, 21 (1), 78–99. doi:10.1177/1555458917712547.

Brown, K.M., 2004. Leadership for social justice and equity: weaving a transformative framework and pedagogy. *Educational administration quarterly*, 40 (1), 77–108. doi:10.1177/0013161X03259147.

Brown, K.M., 2005. Social justice education for preservice leaders: evaluating transformative learning strategies. *Equity & excellence in education*, 38 (2), 155–167. doi:10.1080/10665680590935133.

Brown, K.M., 2006. Leadership for social justice and equity: evaluating a transformative framework and andragogy. *Educational administration quarterly*, 42 (5), 700–745. doi:10.1177/0013161X06290650.

Brundrett, M. and de Cuevas, R., 2007. Setting an agenda for social justice through leadership development. *Management in education*, 21 (4), 44–48. doi:10.1177/0892020607082676.

Brundrett, M. and de Cuevas, R.A., 2008. Setting an agenda for the development of the next generation of school leaders: a commitment to social justice or simply making up the numbers? *School leadership and management*, 28 (3), 247–260. doi:10.1080/13632430802145852.

Cambron-McCabe, N., and McCarthy, M. M., 2005. Educating school leaders for social justice. *Educational Policy*, 19 (1), 201–222.

Capper, C.A., Theoharis, G., and Sebastian, J., 2006. Toward a framework for preparing leaders for social justice. *Journal of educational administration*, 44 (3), 209–224. doi:10.1108/09578230610664814.

Celoria, D., 2016. The preparation of inclusive social justice education leaders. *Educational leadership and administration: teaching and program development*, 27, 199–219.

Department of Education, 2001. *No child left behind*. Washington: US Government.

Diem, S., Ali, N., and Carpenter, B.W., 2013. "If I don't use the word, i shouldn't have to hear it": the surfacing of racial tensions in a leadership preparation classroom. *Journal of cases in educational leadership*, 16 (4), 3–12. doi:10.1177/1555458913515989.

Diem, S. and Carpenter, B.W., 2012. Social justice and leadership preparation: developing a transformative curriculum. *Planning and changing*, 43, 96–112.

Diem, S. and Carpenter, B.W., 2013. Examining race-related silences: interrogating the education of tomorrow's educational leaders. *Journal of research on leadership education*, 8 (1), 56–76. doi:10.1177/1942775112464962.

Feldman, S.B. and Tyson, K., 2014. Clarifying conceptual foundations for social justice in education. *In*: I. Bogotch and C. Shields, eds.. *International handbook of educational leadership and social (in)justice*. Dordrecht: Springer, 1105–1124.

Forde, C. (2014). Issues of Social Justice and Fairness in the Development of Aspiring Head Teachers. In I.Bogotch and C. Shields International Handbook of educational leadership and social (In) justice (pp. 1125-1143). Springer, Dordrecht.

Foster, W., 2004. The decline of the local: A challenge to educational leadership. *Educational administration quarterly*, 40 (2), 176–191. doi:10.1177/0013161X03260360.

Foucault, M., 1977. In: D.F. Bouchard and S. Simon, trans. *Language, counter-memory, Practice: selected essays and interviews*. Ithaca, New York: Cornell University Press.

Furman, G., 2012. Social justice leadership as praxis: developing capacities through preparation programs. *Educational administration quarterly*, 48 (2), 191–229. doi:10.1177/0013161X11427394.

Gerstl-Pepin, C., Killeen, K., and Hasazi, S., 2006. Utilizing an "ethic of care" in leadership preparation: uncovering the complexity of colorblind social justice. *Journal of educational administration*, 44 (3), 250–263. doi:10.1108/09578230610664841.

Gooden, M.A. and Dantley, M., 2012. Centering race in a framework for leadership preparation. *Journal of research on leadership education*, 7 (2), 237–253. doi:10.1177/1942775112455266.

Guillaume, R.O., Saiz, M.S., and Amador, A.G., 2019. Prepared to lead: educational leadership graduates as catalysts for social justice praxis. *Journal of research on leadership education*, 1–20. doi:10.1177/1942775119829887.

Hernandez, F., 2012. Racial identity development in principal preparation programs: linking theory to practice. *In*: C. Boske and S. Diem, eds. *Global leadership for social justice: taking it from the field to practice*. Bingley, UK: Emerald, 103–118.

Hernandez, F. and Marshall, J., 2017. Auditing inequity. *Education and urban society*, 49 (2), 203–228. doi:10.1177/0013124516630598.

Hernandez, F. and Marshall, J.M., 2009. "Where I came from, where i am now, and where i'd like to be": aspiring administrators reflect on issues related to equity, diversity, and social justice. *Journal of school leadership*, 19 (3), 299–333. doi:10.1177/105268460901900303.

Hernandez, F. and McKenzie, K.B., 2010. Resisting social justice in leadership preparation programs: mechanisms that subvert. *Journal of research on leadership education*, 5 (3), 48–72. doi:10.1177/194277511000500302.

Huchting, K. and Bickett, J., 2012. Preparing school leaders for social justice: examining the efficacy of program preparation. *In*: C. Boske and S. Diem, eds. *Global leadership for social justice: taking it from the field to practice*. Bingley, UK: Emerald, 79–101.

Jean-Marie, G., 2010. "Fire in the belly" igniting a social justice discourse in learning environments of leadership Preparation. *In*: A.K. Tooms and C. Boske, eds. *Bridge leadership: connecting educational leadership and social justice to improve schools*. North Carolina: IAP, 97–124.

Jean-Marie, G., Normore, A.H., and Brooks, J.S., 2009. Leadership for social justice: preparing 21st century school leaders for a new social order. *Journal of research on leadership education*, 4 (1), 1–31. doi:10.1177/194277510900400102.

Johnson, L., et al., 2011. Leadership preparation for culturally diverse schools in Cyprus, Norway, and the United States. *In*: R.M. Ylimaki and S.L. Jacobson, eds. *US and cross-national policies, practices, and preparation*. Dordrecht: Springer, 153–177.

Johnson, L. and Campbell-Stephens, R., 2010. Investing in diversity in London schools: leadership preparation for Black and global majority educators. *Urban education*, 45 (6), 840–870. doi:10.1177/0042085910384353.

Karanxha, Z., Agosto, V., and Bellara, A., 2014. Modeling social justice educational leadership. *In*: I. Bogotch and C. Shields, eds. *International handbook of educational leadership and social (in) justice*. Dordrecht: Springer, 1187–1206.

Killingsworth, M.F., et al., 2010. The gender dynamics of educational leadership preparation: A feminist postmodern critique of the cohort experience. *Journal of research on leadership education*, 5 (12), 531–567. doi:10.1177/194277511000501209.

Ladson-Billings, G., 2009. Critical race theory in education. *In*: M.W. Apple, W. Au, and L.A. Gandin, eds. *The routledge international handbook of critical education*. New York: Taylor & Francis, 110–122.

López, J.A., Magdaleno, K.R., and Reis, N.M., 2006. Developing leadership for equity: what is the role of leadership preparation programs? *Educational leadership and administration: teaching and program development*, 18, 11–19.

Marshall, C. and Oliva, M., 2006. Building the capacities of social justice leaders. *In*: C. Marshall and M. Oliva, eds. *Leadership for social justice*. Boston: Pearson, 1–15.

Marshall, J.M. and Hernandez, F., 2012. "I would not consider myself a homophobe": learning and teaching about sexual orientation in a principal preparation program. *Educational administration quarterly*, 49 (3), 451–488. doi:10.1177/0013161X12463231.

McKenzie, K.B., et al., 2008. From the field: A proposal for educating leaders for social justice. *Educational administration quarterly*, 44 (1), 111–138. doi:10.1177/0013161X07309470.

McKenzie, K.B. and Scheurich, J.J., 2004. Equity traps: A useful construct for preparing principals to lead schools that are successful with racially diverse students. *Educational administration quarterly*, 40 (5), 601–632. doi:10.1177/0013161X04268839.

Miller, C.M. and Martin, B., 2015. Principal preparedness for leading in demographically changing schools: where is social justice training? *Educational management, administration and leadership*, 43 (1), 129–151. doi:10.1177/1741143213513185.

Mullen, C.A., Young, J.K., and Harris, S., 2014. Cultural dialogue as social justice advocacy within and beyond university classrooms. *In*: I. Bogotch and C. Shields, eds. *International handbook of educational leadership and social (in) justice*. Dordrecht: Springer, 1145–1168.

O'Malley, M.P. and Capper, C.A., 2015. A measure of the quality of educational leadership programs for social justice: integrating LGBTIQ identities into principal preparation. *Educational administration quarterly*, 51 (2), 290–330. doi:10.1177/0013161X14532468.

Partridge, E., 2010. *Analysing policy: what's the problem represented to be? Carol Bacchi*. Book Review. Australia: Pearson Education, French Forest. No. 106.

Pazey, B.L. and Cole, H.A., 2013. The role of special education training in the development of socially just leaders: building an equity consciousness in educational leadership programs. *Educational administration quarterly*, 49 (2), 243–271. doi:10.1177/0013161X12463934.

Rodríguez, M.A., et al., 2010. A cross-case analysis of three social justice-oriented education programs. *Journal of research on leadership education*, 5 (3), 138–153. doi:10.1177/194277511000500305.

Rusch, E.A., 2004. Gender and race in leadership preparation: a constrained discourse. *Educational administration quarterly*, 40 (1), 14–46. doi:10.1177/0013161X03259110.

SenGupta, S., Hopson, R., and Thompson-Robinson, M., 2004. Cultural competence in evaluation: an overview. *New directions for evaluation*, 2004 (102), 5–19. doi:10.1002/ev.112.

Theoharis, G., 2007. Social justice educational leaders and resistance: toward a theory of social justice leadership. *Educational administration quarterly*, 43 (2), 221–258. doi:10.1177/0013161X06293717.

Theoharis, G. and Causton-Theoharis, J.N., 2008. Oppressors or emancipators: critical dispositions for preparing inclusive school leaders. *Equity & excellence in education*, 41 (2), 230–246. doi:10.1080/10665680801973714.

Trujillo, T. and Cooper, R., 2014. Framing social justice leadership in a university-based preparation program. *Journal of research on leadership education*, 9 (2), 142–167. doi:10.1177/1942775114525046.

Woods, P.A., et al., 2020. *Educational leadership, management and administration in the United Kingdom: a comparative review*. Sheffield: British Educational Leadership, Management and Administration Society.

Young, M.D. and Brooks, J.S., 2008. Supporting graduate students of color in educational administration preparation programs: faculty perspectives on best practices, possibilities, and problems. *Educational administration quarterly*, 44 (3), 391–423. doi:10.1177/0013161X08315270.

Young, M.D. and Laible, J., 2000. White racism, antiracism, and school leadership preparation. *Journal of school leadership*, 10 (5), 374–415. doi:10.1177/105268460001000501.

Zarate, M.E. and Mendoza, Y., 2018. Reflections on race and privilege in an educational leadership course. *Journal of research on leadership education*, 15 (1), 56–80. doi:10.1177/1942775118771666.

Zembylas, M., 2010. The emotional aspects of leadership for social justice: implications for leadership preparation programs. *Journal of educational administration*, 48 (5), 611–625. doi:10.1108/09578231011067767.

Learning to lead socially just schools: an exploration of candidate readiness for equity-focused principal preparation in the United States

Corrie Stone-Johnson, Corey Gray and Casandra Wright

ABSTRACT
In spite of concerted improvement efforts to improve curricula, many university-based principal preparation programmes in the United States do not explicitly attend to issues of equity or social justice in a thorough way. While curricular efforts are important, they are not enough on their own; a working theory in the field of educational leadership is that an equity-mindset is also needed and that social justice-oriented principal preparation programs should select individuals who already 'have a propensity, at a minimum, to critically question the inequities found in schools' for admission into programs. Generally speaking, however, there is a dearth of literature on both candidate selection for preparation programs and equity beliefs of current and pre-service school leaders. In this paper, we explore how potential candidates for a principal preparation program in an urban school district view equity and the vexing question of how to prepare socially just leaders.

Introduction

As schools become increasingly diverse and as differences in achievement are connected to demographic differences (Reardon *et al.* 2019), it is critical that programs that prepare school leaders address equity and social justice issues in coursework and fieldwork experiences. Increasingly, principal preparation programs in the United States are responding to this concern with curricular changes such as powerful learning experiences, which are 'adult learning experiences that reflect a set of nine andragogical practices that individually, or in combination, have been shown to help broaden and shift leadership candidates' mindsets' (Cunningham *et al.* 2019, p. 75) and a tighter alignment with equity-focused leadership standards (National Policy Board for Educational Administration 2015). While curricular efforts are important, though, they are not enough on their own; a working theory in the field of educational leadership is that an equity-mindset is also needed and that social justice-oriented principal preparation programs should select for admission into programs individuals who already 'have a propensity, at a minimum, to critically question the inequities found in schools' (McKenzie and Scheurich 2004, p. 118). However, little research describes the beliefs of practicing educators generally (Browne-Ferrigno and Muth 2009, Nelson and Guerra 2014, Hernandez and Marshall 2017), and even less describes pre-service leaders' beliefs specifically. What does exist, particularly in the US, suggests that many school leaders operate from a deficit perspective, holding negative beliefs about students and families from diverse backgrounds that lead to lower expectations (Flessa 2009, Nelson and Guerra 2014). It is not known if most or even many candidates for admission have an equity mindset. Thus, more research is needed to understand the beliefs of aspiring leaders who could enter preparation programs in order to 1) begin to add to the knowledge base of leaders' beliefs generally, and 2) inform decisions specifically about the kinds of curricular experiences that would be needed to advance such individuals' decision-making, as beliefs can change as a result of practice (Brown 2004).

Our exploratory study responds to the first research need by asking: How do potential leadership preparation candidates describe their beliefs about equity? To address this question, we rely on data from a survey of one urban district's coaches which asked them to consider a series of questions about their beliefs about equity. In this district, coaches are in a quasi-leadership role; they do not have formal leadership credentials (and hence would be potential candidates for a leadership preparation program) yet they are identified as teacher leaders within their schools. Briefly, we found that while nearly all coaches indicated that addressing issues of inequity within the school environment is important, issues such as systemic racism and beliefs in meritocratic achievement surfaced in coaches' responses to questions about equity. For example, more than half of the coaches surveyed said they believed that everyone is equal in the United States and that if a person works hard, they will be successful. These beliefs indicate deficit thinking, which may result in lower expectations for students, particularly those from linguistically and racially diverse backgrounds (Nelson and Guerra 2014).

Responses such as these add urgency to the need to learn more about potential candidates' beliefs about equity in considering program admission to principal preparation programs. If many or most of the potential candidates to a program operate from a deficit perspective, we must learn more about if such individuals can develop the propensity to critically question the inequities found in schools and what experiences would help them do so. As pressures grow to add more and more features to preparation programs in line with the skills that are needed for equity-focused leadership (Anderson et al. 2018, Barakat et al. 2019), questions of where such coursework or experiences will occur and how loom large. The findings of this study will contribute to both policy and practice discourses in educational leadership and principal preparation.

Review of the literature

This study seeks to begin to build a knowledge base on pre-service leaders' beliefs about equity, as little is known about this topic. Such knowledge is essential for multiple reasons. First, deficit thinking can hinder the success of the very types of change efforts that are aimed at increasing educational outcomes for students from diverse backgrounds (Flessa 2009). Second, beliefs can change (Brown 2004), and preparation programs could be a vehicle for such change. Third, it is suggested that social justice-oriented principal preparation programs should select individuals for admission those who already 'have a propensity, at a minimum, to critically question the inequities found in schools' (McKenzie et al. 2008, p. 118). Yet, as described above, little is known about the beliefs of the pool of educators who could apply to preparation programs in general, and equally little is known about those who do apply.

In this section, we first present the concept of deficit thinking as a lens by which to understand the beliefs of school leaders. We then review the literature on social justice leadership and social justice leadership preparation, educators' beliefs about equity, and the selection processes used for admission into leadership preparation programs.

Deficit thinking

Broadly speaking, deficit thinking as it relates to schooling is the theory that student failure is the result of perceived student deficits, such as language ability, motivation, or behaviour (Valencia 2010). Essential to the concept of deficit thinking is the notion of victim blaming, or the idea that students are themselves responsible for poor school performance rather than institutional or systemic inequality. Deficit beliefs create a disincentive for educators to engage in reform (Garcia and Guerra 2004); if educators do not identify as part of the problem there is little motivation to change their own behaviour (Nelson and Guerra 2014).

McKenzie and Scheurich (2004, p. 601–602) call deficit thinking an equity trap, or 'ways of thinking or assumptions that prevent educators from believing that their students of color can be successful learners.' As such, these beliefs pose multiple challenges. First, they are, as Weiner (2006) suggests, both deeply embedded and unspoken within educational systems. That is to say, they exist without people knowing fully that they hold them. Second, deficit beliefs are pervasive. In Nelson and Guerra (2014) qualitative study of educators in two states, 72% of participant educators exhibited one or more deficit beliefs about students and families of diverse backgrounds. Third, they are a prerequisite for educational change; without changing the beliefs about how students can succeed, other efforts such as curriculum or staffing changes are likely to fail (Flessa 2009).

In spite of the deleterious effects of deficit thinking, surprisingly little research explores the deficit thinking characteristics of educators (Flessa 2009, Walker 2011, Nelson and Guerra 2014). Equally surprising, little research explores how preparation programs work to remediate deficit beliefs. Research in the field of educational administration and leadership has begun to consider this work vis-à-vis the development of social justice leadership.

Social justice leadership and leadership preparation

The inequitable contexts and consequences of schooling gives rise to what many in the field of educational administration and leadership call social justice leadership (Stone-Johnson and Wright 2019). Theoharis (2007, p. 223) defines social justice leadership as principals who 'make issues of race, class, gender, disability, sexual orientation, and other historically and currently marginalized conditions in the United States central to their advocacy, leadership practice, and vision.' Social justice leadership requires ongoing interrogation of the assumptions that undergird inequitable school policies and practices (Cambron-McCabe and McCarthy 2005). Leadership for social justice involves identifying these inequitable opportunities and outcomes and actively working to replace them with more equitable ones (Furman 2012).

While there is a strong suggestion that social justice leadership is important for students and schools, there is not definitive agreement on what a preparation curriculum focused on social justice leadership would look like; indeed, the research that specifically attends to leadership preparation for social justice remains limited (Capper et al. 2006, Furman 2012) Diem and Carpenter (2012) reviewed the literature from the top journals in educational research and found surprisingly little coverage of the topic. The literature does not address the details of what a program centred around social justice would look like (McKenzie et al. 2008) and is primarily small qualitative case studies that focus on specific individual programs or a set of theoretical frameworks without an action plan to prepare leaders for the work (Furman 2012). A more recent review of the literature conducted by two of this study's authors found that even less attention has been paid to the topic in the ensuing years (Stone-Johnson and Wright 2019).

In spite of a limited research base, calls to orient programs to be social-justice focused continue. Research suggests that traditional preparation programs give only minimal consideration to social justice concerns (Brown 2004, Cambron-McCabe and McCarthy 2005). Few programs assess their students' cultural competence (Barakat et al. 2019) and frequently issues of diversity are only taken up in a special course during the program (Hawley and James 2010). There is a deepening call from the field to support school leaders as they attempt to create equitable schools for their students (Cambron-McCabe and McCarthy 2005, Furman 2012) and to tighten the connection between what Trujillo and Cooper (2014, p. 143) say are 'rich descriptions of what it looks like when leadership preparation programs enact a social justice framework' and what researchers note is a focus on the capacities of social justice leadership, such as critical consciousness, and the actual skills required to do such work (Furman 2012). Doing this work requires knowing more about where students in preparation programs are before they enter.

Beliefs of applicants

As we have described throughout this paper, surprisingly little is known about the beliefs of school leaders in general and applicants to preparation programs in particular. There is limited conversation about dispositions (Allen *et al.* 2014), yet a review of programs found that 70% of programs reported having a formal procedure for assessing leadership dispositions, but that there was not agreement on how institutions defined dispositions (Melton *et al.* 2010). A study of student selection for admittance into UCEA principal preparation programs, a consortium of universities with preparation programs, indicates that most programs consider applicants' social justice dispositions, but again these are not well-defined (Anderson *et al.* 2018).

Nelson and Guerra (2014, p. 72) argue that 'few educator preparation programs adequately address the issue of deficit beliefs and cultural knowledge among pre-service educators.'

When attention is paid to applicants' beliefs, it tends to focus on their beliefs about themselves as leaders and the role of leadership more broadly. For example, Young *et al.* (2011) describe candidates' perspectives on a spectrum with leader-centric tendencies at one end and collaborative tendencies at the other. When it comes to beliefs about equity and justice, however, programs may fear contending with the difficult issues of social and political differences (Allen *et al.* 2014).

In spite of limited research on the topic of *pre-service* leaders' beliefs generally and about equity specifically, substantial research points to the importance of *sitting* leaders' beliefs about equity (Brown 2004, Theoharis 2007, Flessa 2009, Furman 2012, Gooden and Dantley 2012, Nelson and Guerra 2014). This gap in time poses an essential question: if it is known that leaders need strong beliefs about equity to make lasting change in schools, but little is known about the equity beliefs of people seeking to be prepared to be school leaders, what role could or should selection play in the process of program admission?

Selection

Researchers in the field of principal preparation and educational leadership continue to emphasise the importance of selection in principal preparation (Darling-Hammond *et al.* 2007, Anderson *et al.* 2018) yet few studies examine leadership preparation candidates as the unit of study (Browne-Ferrigno and Muth 2009). Browne-Ferrigno and Muth (2009) review of studies from 2001 to 2007 showed little evidence of study of program candidates, and the most recent *Handbook on the Education of School Leaders* (Fuller *et al.* 2016, p. 93) contends that the status of research on this topic has changed little and 'the underwhelming amount of research and comprehensive descriptions of selection processes are still a concern.' This lack of research suggests a dire need for a more robust knowledge base about selecting candidates for acceptance into preparation programs.

Winn *et al.* (2016) demonstrate that preparation programs rely heavily on objective forms of data about candidates such as transcripts, resumes, prior degrees, and leadership experience. Many also use subjective assessments such as personal statements and references. Interestingly, 81% of UCEA programs seek evidence of social justice dispositions in candidates, but to date there is little in the literature that catalogues these dispositions.

Thus, our exploratory study picks up where the current literature leaves off. Our purpose is to begin to catalogue potential applicants' beliefs about equity. These individuals, at the time of the study, had not applied to a program. Rather, we sought to understand the beliefs of the pool of potential applicants in our geographic area.

Methods

In this exploratory study, we aim to understand more about the beliefs of pre-service leadership candidates in order to consider how preparation might influence their beliefs in positive ways. The study takes place in a rapidly diversifying urban centre in New York State. The research team includes one faculty member from the neighbouring research university and two doctoral students, one who serves in a senior level position in the district in the study and the other who is a local school administrator in a suburban district. This particular district provides a unique context in which to explore socially just principal preparation. The city school district continues to struggle across the board with raising students achievement and even more so with achievement gaps between subgroups of students; district data indicate that in 2015–2016, 34% of White students in the district scored proficient (locally defined as scoring a 3 or 4 out of four on state tests) in grades 3-8 English Language Arts while only 11% of African-American students and 11% of Hispanic-Latino students did so. Similarly, in maths, 34% of White students scored proficient while 10% of African-American students and 10% of Hispanic-Latino students did so. The school district also has a very small population of teachers from minority background; only 8.5% of teachers are African-American, 1% are Asian, and 4% are Latino, in a district where more than 70% of students are African-American or Latino.

The survey was developed in part to understand the potential applicant pool for a newly developed preparation program at the University. It was created as part of an independent study that included all three authors. The survey was administered by the students in the independent study (two of the authors of this study) to understand equity perceptions of potential school leadership candidates and to understand what experiences students in a preparation program would need to feel successful. This new program was funded by the state; created specifically to attract and develop leaders from the district; and jointly developed by the university, the district, and an outside leadership development agency. Survey questions were designed by the students in the independent study based on their list of social justice leadership readings and focused on three areas: 1) program features that would attract or deter potential candidates from applying to the new program, such as course delivery mode, instructor, class meeting times; 2) potential candidates' beliefs about equity regarding understanding of student access to the curriculum, English language coursework, student effort, and the role of leaders in creating equitable school environments; and 3) demographic and experiential characteristics of potential candidates including gender, race, and years of experience in the field.

The survey was administered to all coaches in the district (n = 81) between September and November 2018. A total of 77 coaches responded to the survey. Of those who provided demographic information, nearly half (36, or 48%) were between the ages of 25–34, and 40% were between the ages of 45 and 54 (n = 30). Approximately 80% (n = 61) identified as White and 84% (n = 63) identified as female. More than 50% of participants had more than twenty years in the field (n = 39), and almost 90% (n = 67) had more than ten years in the field.

Slightly more than 80% of respondents said that if they were encouraged to participate in a preparation program by someone in their district they would be more likely to participate. About 65% said they would be likely to pursue an administrative position upon completion of a leadership program. While these are not applicants to a program (and several of the applicants have completed programs), these answers provide some insight into interest in leadership preparation.

For the purposes of this exploratory study, the primary method of analysis is descriptive statistics, including percentages of individuals who responded to questions in particular ways. Given the small number of participants, however, and the general lack of diversity of the participants, any claims about these findings must be tempered. The intent of this descriptive analysis is to begin to give shape a question about which, as described above, little is known: who is entering programs and in particular, what are their beliefs not only prior to entering the program but indeed before being eligible for an applicant pool.

While our hope with this exploratory study is to begin to develop an understanding of the candidate pool of potential principal preparation students, and to understand more about the process of selection generally and what should be considered as programs aim to develop more equitable and just leaders for their local schools, we recognise that this study has several limitations. First, the survey was developed from course readings from the independent study. The survey has not been determined to be valid or reliable; rather, it was designed to explore the beliefs of the potential candidate pool for the new program and was designed more to inform curriculum and program design. Second, the data reflect only one program; more study is needed to understand regional factors that may influence selection. More specifically, the study only reflects conceptions of equity leadership in the United States and within the state and city in which the study takes place. Finally, the respondents were not applicants to a principal preparation program at the time of the survey. Thus, it is not known if those who would put their names forward would be those individuals who express stronger beliefs about equity; following such a pool of potential applications through the application process itself would certainly shed more detailed light on the applicant pool overall. However, this introductory view into a potential pool of applicants offers important insight into the equity beliefs of potential pre-service school leaders.

Findings

This exploratory study considers how potential leadership preparation candidates describe their beliefs about equity in order to understand broadly the role of programs in addressing leaders' beliefs and in the immediate to understand more about the applicant pool of potential school leaders. In this section, we present the findings from a survey administered to all coaches in one urban school district. In this district, coaches are not considered administrators. Rather, coaches serve as instructional support in buildings in the subject areas of literacy and mathematics. While the survey covered questions about program design and candidate beliefs and readiness, in this paper we focus only on candidate beliefs and readiness. As described above, the questions can be divided into two categories: beliefs about equity/deficit thinking and readiness to lead. For the purposes of this article, we begin to define a new concept which we refer to as readiness for equity-focused leadership. Readiness for equity-focused leadership involves critical consciousness coupled with the will and skill to contest oppressive internal and external challenges within the context of the K-12 US educational system. Readiness to lead for equity can have a direct impact on the manner in which a candidate views curriculum design and implementation, parental engagement, and student behaviour management systems (Nelson and Guerra 2014). A candidate's ability to demonstrate readiness to lead for equity can function as a predictor of success in leadership preparation programs and the corresponding education of students in K-12 classrooms to effectively lead culturally responsive learning environments (Gordon and Ronder 2016).

Deficit thinking

Five questions addressed candidates' beliefs about equity. The first of these five questions asked respondents to identify the extent to which they believe that quality education will positively impact the lives of children from less abundant homes. Out of 77 possible respondents, 76 answered the questions. All respondents agreed to some extent; 70 strongly agreed and 6 agreed.

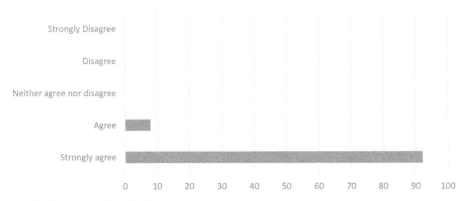

Figure 1. Positive impact of quality education.

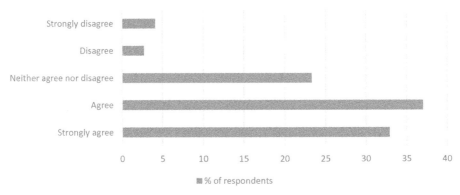

Figure 2. Inequitable structures and systems.

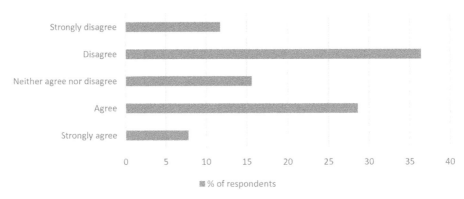

Figure 3. Everyone is equal.

The second question asked respondents to describe their beliefs about the extent to which they perceive there are systems and structures in place within American society that create inequality for some marginalised groups of people. All 77 respondents answered. These answers show more variation than the first question. While most participants (55) agreed to some level, 22 participants felt neutral or disagreed to some extent.

The third question asked respondents the extent to which they believe everyone is equal in the US; if a person works hard, they will be successful. All 77 respondents answered the questions.

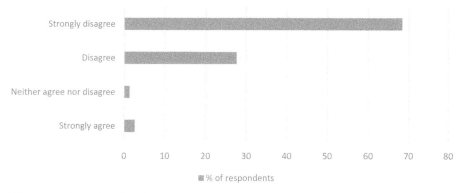

Figure 4. Expectations for students living in poverty.

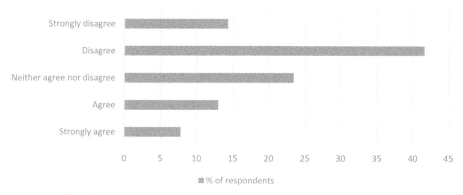

Figure 5. Expectation for student assimilation.

The fourth question focused on beliefs about school success. Respondents were asked the extent to which they believe that because Common Core standards are so rigorous, children from impoverished settings should not be expected to excel in school. Out of 77 possible respondents, 76 answered the question. Nearly all (n = 73) disagreed to some extent.

Finally, the last question in this section asked: It is important for people from other countries to completely assimilate into American culture. All 77 respondents answered the question.

Readiness to lead

The next series of questions focused on respondents' readiness to lead in diverse contexts. The first question asked respondents to assess the extent to which they believe that openly

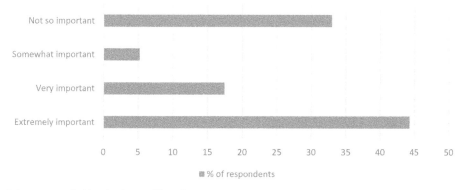

Figure 6. Importance of addressing issues of inequity.

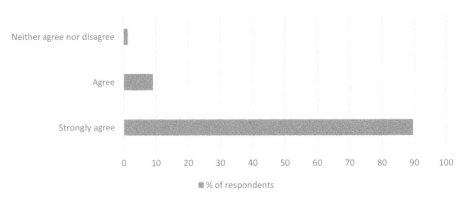

Figure 7. Enjoy working with diverse children.

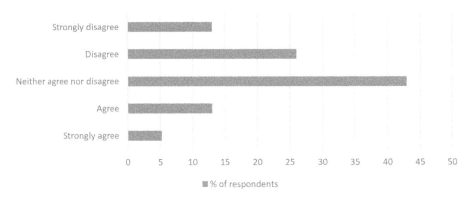

Figure 8. Enjoy working with people who are similar.

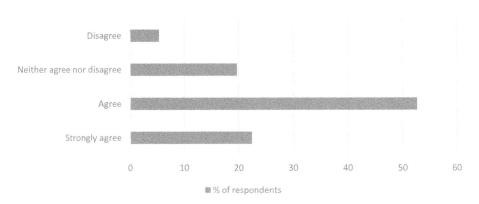

Figure 9. Confident to confront colleagues.

addressing issues of inequity within the school environment is important. All 77 respondents answered.

The second question asked the extent to which respondents enjoy working with children from diverse backgrounds. All 77 respondents answered.

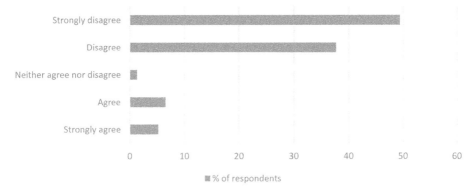

Figure 10. Culturally and linguistically relevant pedagogy *not* important.

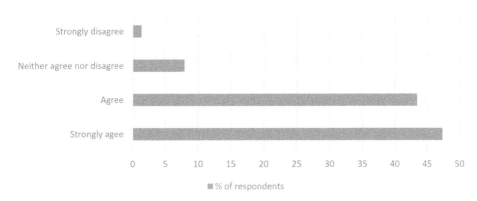

Figure 11. Value bilingual education.

The third question asked respondents the extent to which they enjoy working with people who are similar to them. All 77 respondents answered.

The fourth question asked respondents the extent to which they agree that they are able to confidently confront colleagues when they make a derogatory statement about people from historically marginalised background. All but one individual responded.

The fifth question in this section asked respondents the extent to which they agree that culturally and linguistically relevant pedagogy is *not* important. All respondents answered.

Finally, the sixth question in this section asked respondents to identify the extent to which they agree that they value bilingual education. All 77 respondents answered.

Discussion

In the field of educational leadership, and specifically in the area of principal preparation, research underscores the importance of certain programmatic features that are associated with success. These features include but are not limited to using a cohort model, partnering with districts, and providing powerful learning experiences that connect classroom learning with real-world experiences (Darling-Hammond *et al.* 2007, Anderson *et al.* 2018). Still, an essential piece of the leadership preparation puzzle – the students themselves – remains a surprisingly understudied area (Browne-Ferrigno and Muth 2009, Fuller *et al.* 2016). This gap in knowledge may be less of a focus because in many areas in the US programs may not have the luxury of considering who they admit due to either a general shortage of interested candidates or market saturation. Certainly, and to some extent problematically, university-based programs need to fill their seats. But, if the goal of principal preparation is to prepare leaders who are ready to lead schools across all contexts, and the selection process to admit candidates into such programs could be better informed, then much more information about the available pool of applicants is needed, specifically about their beliefs about the students and families who attend schools in diverse contexts.

Our findings indicate at least two important points to consider. First, many participants in this study demonstrate at least some level of deficit thinking. While nearly all believe that education can have a positive impact on students from what we termed 'less abundant' homes and nearly all (96%) *disagreed* that children from impoverished settings should not be expected to excel in school, less than half of respondents agreed that everyone is equal; approximately 30% felt neutrally or disagreed that systems are inequitable; and about 16% neither agreed nor disagreed and 36% agreed to some extent that working hard is the key to success. Returning to the concept of deficit thinking, school leaders who operate under deficit beliefs feel that students themselves are responsible for their lack of success rather than the structures and systems around them (Valencia 2010). The birds' eye view of data shared here suggests that many of the participants view individuals as responsible for their own success.

Second, deficit thinking itself is inherently problematic but becomes even more so if readiness to lead is a consideration. Again, we define readiness to lead equitably as a combination of will and skill. The second series of six questions moves beyond innate beliefs (measures of thinking) to actionable beliefs (measures of potential leadership). Actionable beliefs are those beliefs which can translate into discrete school leadership moves, such as confronting racism or supporting culturally relevant curriculum. Four of the questions considered address programmatic and curriculum issues that are essential pieces of a successful school. For example, the questions address beliefs about culturally relevant pedagogy, bilingual education, and working with diverse children and colleagues. The remaining two questions address tackling inequity (rather than merely believing it exists) and confronting colleagues who make derogatory statements about people from non-majority backgrounds.

On the positive side, nearly all respondents said they enjoy working with diverse children and most said they disagree that they enjoy working with people who are similar (implying, we hope, that this means they prefer working with people who are different). Problematically, however, more than 10% said they did not find culturally and linguistically relevant pedagogy to be important and nearly 8% said they neither agreed nor disagreed that bilingual education is important. Given that these individuals work in a highly diverse district, the implication of their beliefs about equitable educational offerings should they choose to move into leadership positions within their own district are concerning.

About 1 out of 3 respondents said that openly addressing issues of inequity in school was not so important and about 3 out of 4 said they feel confident confronting colleagues who make derogatory statements about others. These beliefs about leading for equity lie in direct opposition to the idea that school leaders should be social justice advocates (Theoharis 2007). At a minimum, they indicate that many people who could be in the pool of applicants for leadership preparation programs do not have an equity mindset. Of course, programs cannot expect students to enter the program fully prepared to lead for equity. Developing leadership skills is of course among the most essential aspect of leadership preparation. Yet questions of how much time to spend and even faculty readiness to do the work loom large. If students are entering programs without both leadership skills broadly and equity mindsets specifically, shifts must occur to attend to both.

This exploratory study cannot make sophisticated claims about applicants' equity beliefs; it is limited to one district and is a very small sample. However, the findings do begin to build a picture of the equity beliefs of people who would be potential applicants for a preparation program. The general picture painted is a mixed one. On the one hand, while some participants exhibited facets of deficit thinking, not all did. On the other hand, several participants indicated that they are not confident confronting colleagues with deficit thinking or tackling inequity in their schools. While a leadership preparation program could provide them with opportunities to learn these skills, it is clear that a high level of work would be required to prepare future leaders to engage in such activities.

It is at this juncture where the issue of selection becomes more important. If programs use a variety of measures to consider candidates for admission, where does the role of equity beliefs fit in? Should it, as McKenzie et al. (2008) suggest, be a delimiting factor and admission should only be for those who already have an equity-mindset? Certainly in markets where programs are competitive and where there are more applicants than there are seats, such a screen would be helpful. But if programs are less competitive or if there is market saturation such that individual programs have fewer candidates to choose from, then the data from this exploratory study suggest that applicants who would otherwise be strong (leadership experience as coaches, demonstrated success as coaches, etc.) could enter with some level of deficit thinking. It is then incumbent upon programs to consider how to address equity and social justice as part of their teaching. What remains unknown is whether programs could do enough to move deficit thinking in a positive direction if candidates enter without an equity mindset.

Importantly, they also point to the importance of considering more robust measures of equity dispositions or beliefs in general and specifically upon program entry. What is an equity belief and how can it be measured? As described earlier, there is a belief that social justice leadership preparation is needed, but there is not agreement on what a social justice disposition actually looks like. The findings from this small study show that it is highly complex. A very quick questionnaire might show that on the surface individuals have an equity mindset or a social justice disposition. For example, nearly all of the respondents to this survey said education is important for students living in poverty and that expectations for achievement should not be lowered for students living in poverty. Almost all said they enjoy working with diverse students. But when probed deeper, certain beliefs about systemic inequity surfaced, beliefs that expose deficit thinking even in light of positive sentiments about student diversity. Thus, caution must be exercised when considering social justice dispositions for program entry; what kinds of questions are being asked to elicit responses?

Questions about selection also arise when considering what happens to individuals with deficit thinking who apply to programs. If they apply to programs that screen for an equity mindset, will they apply to programs that do not? If so, what are the implications of bifurcated preparation? Relatedly, if programs who need applicants must admit students who express deficit thinking to some degree, what are the programmatic and curricular implications, especially given all of the other aspects of preparation that are required? This is perhaps the most vexing question. Are programs designed to provide the technical skills for leadership, and can addressing inequity be considered a technical skill? This is a question that the field of leadership preparation has not fully answered.

The findings from this study can serve as a first step in describing the beliefs of individuals who are interested in or capable of applying to preparation programs. The findings also suggest that more attention needs to be paid to the selection process in admissions, as well as the ongoing professional development needs beyond preparation. The findings call attention to the fact that applicants to preparation programs may need development towards an equity mindset, and that preparation programs should be more mindful of readiness to lead in considering the work needed to prepare leaders to lead equity-focused schools.

Disclosure statement

No potential conflict of interest was reported by the authors.

References

Allen, J.G., Wasicsko, M.M., and Chirichello, M., 2014. The missing link: teaching the dispositions to lead. *International journal of educational leadership preparation*, 9 (1), n1.

Anderson, E., et al., 2018. Examining university leadership preparation: an analysis of program attributes and practices. *Journal of research on leadership education*, 13 (4), 375–397. doi:10.1177/1942775117735873.

Barakat, M., Reames, E., and Kensler, L.A., 2019. Leadership preparation programs: preparing culturally competent educational leaders. *Journal of research on leadership education*, 14 (3), 212–235. doi:10.1177/1942775118759070.

Brown, K.M., 2004. Leadership for social justice and equity: weaving a transformative framework and pedagogy. *Educational administration quarterly*, 40 (1), 77–108. doi:10.1177/0013161X03259147.

Browne-Ferrigno, T. and Muth, R., 2009. Candidates in educational leadership graduate programs. *In*: M.D. Young and M.D. Young, eds.. *Handbook of research on the education of school leaders*. New York, NY.

Cambron-McCabe, N. and McCarthy, M.M., 2005. Educating school leaders for social justice. *Educational policy*, 19 (1), 201–222. doi:10.1177/0895904804271609.

Capper, C.A., Theoharis, G., and Sebastian, J., 2006. Toward a framework for preparing leaders for social justice. *Journal of educational administration*, 44 (3), 209–224. doi:10.1108/09578230610664814.

Cunningham, K.M., et al., 2019. Using powerful learning experiences to prepare school leaders. *Journal of research on leadership education*, 14 (1), 74–97. doi:10.1177/1942775118819672.

Darling-Hammond, L., et al., 2007. Preparing school leaders for a changing world: lessons from exemplary leadership development programs. School Leadership Study. Final Report. Stanford Educational Leadership Institute.

Diem, S. and Carpenter, B.W., 2012. Social justice and leadership preparation: developing a transformative curriculum. *Planning and changing*, 43, 96–112.

Flessa, J., 2009. Urban school principals, deficit frameworks, and implications for leadership. *Journal of school leadership*, 19 (3), 334–373. doi:10.1177/105268460901900304.

Fuller, E.J., Reynolds, A.L., and O'Doherty, A., 2016. Recruitment, selection, and placement of educational leadership students. *In*: *Handbook of research on the education of school leaders*. Routledge, 91–131.

Furman, G., 2012. Social justice leadership as praxis: developing capacities through preparation programs. *Educational administration quarterly*, 48 (2), 191–229. doi:10.1177/0013161X11427394.

Garcia, S.B. and Guerra, P.L., 2004. Deconstructing deficit thinking: working with educators to create more equitable learning environments. *Education and urban society*, 36 (2), 150–168. doi:10.1177/0013124503261322.

Gooden, M.A. and Dantley, M., 2012. Centering race in a framework for leadership preparation. *Journal of research on leadership education*, 7 (2), 237–253. doi:10.1177/1942775112455266.

Gordon, S.P. and Ronder, E.A., 2016. Perceptions of culturally responsive leadership inside and outside of a principal preparation program. *International journal of educational reform*, 25 (2), 125–153. doi:10.1177/105678791602500202.

Hawley, W. and James, R., 2010. Diversity-responsive school leadership. *UCEA review*, 51 (3), 1–5.

Hernandez, F. and Marshall, J., 2017. Auditing inequity: teaching aspiring administrators to be social justice leaders. *Education and urban society*, 49 (2), 203–228. doi:10.1177/0013124516630598.

McKenzie, K.B., et al., 2008. From the field: A proposal for educating leaders for social justice. *Educational administration quarterly*, 44 (1), 111–138. doi:10.1177/0013161X07309470.

McKenzie, K.B. and Scheurich, J.J., 2004. Equity traps: A useful construct for preparing principals to lead schools that are successful with racially diverse students. *Educational administration quarterly*, 40 (5), 601–632. doi:10.1177/0013161X04268839.

Melton, T., Mallory, B.J., and Green, J., 2010. Identifying and assessing dispositions of educational leadership candidates. *Educational leadership and administration: teaching and program development*, 22, 46–60.

National Policy Board for Educational Administration, 2015. *Professional standards for educational leaders*. Reston, VA: NPBEA.

Nelson, S.W. and Guerra, P.L., 2014. Educator beliefs and cultural knowledge: implications for school improvement efforts. *Educational administration quarterly*, 50 (1), 67–95. doi:10.1177/0013161X13488595.

Reardon, S.F., Kalogrides, D., and Shores, K., 2019. The geography of racial/ethnic test score gaps. *American journal of sociology*, 124 (4), 1164–1221. doi:10.1086/700678.

Stone-Johnson, C., & Wright, C. (2019). Leadership preparation for social justice in educational administration. In R. Wright (Ed.) Leadership Preparation for Social Justice in Educational Administration. Dordrecht, Netherlands: Springer Publishing doi:10.1007/978-3-319-74078-2

Theoharis, G., 2007. Social justice educational leaders and resistance: toward a theory of social justice leadership. *Educational administration quarterly*, 43 (2), 221–258. doi:10.1177/0013161X06293717.

Trujillo, T. and Cooper, R., 2014. Framing social justice leadership in a university-based preparation program: the university of California's principal leadership institute. *Journal of research on leadership education*, 9 (2), 142–167. doi:10.1177/1942775114525046.

Valencia, R.R., 2010. *Dismantling contemporary deficit thinking: educational thought and practice*. New York, NY: Routledge.

Walker, K.L., 2011. Deficit thinking and the effective teacher. *Education and urban society*, 43 (5), 576–597. doi:10.1177/0013124510380721.
Weiner, L., 2006. Challenging deficit thinking. *Educational leadership*, 64 (1), 42.
Winn, K. M, Anderson, E., Groth, C., Korach, S., Pounder, D., Rorrer, A, & Young, M.D. (2016). A deeper look: INSPIRE data demonstrates quality in educational leadership preparation. Charlottesville, VA: UCEA
Young, M.D., *et al.*, 2011. Measuring change in leadership identity and problem framing. *Journal of school leadership*, 21 (5), 704–734. doi:10.1177/105268461102100504.

The need for career-long professional learning for social justice leaders in affluent school contexts

Karen Huchting and Jill Bickett

ABSTRACT
School leaders, who subscribe to social justice leadership (SJL), are situated to combat inequitable outcomes inherently produced by educational contexts. For school leaders to transform inequitable systems, they must develop a broad and deep understanding of social justice in their leadership preparation programmes and beyond. Through qualitative interview data, we uncover the needs of graduates of an SJL doctoral preparation programme, who work in affluent school contexts in the USA. Affluent schools are defined as economically elite contexts, which ultimately can engender an 'economic elite domination' (Gilens and Page 2014, p. 566). SJL is needed in these contexts in order to dismantle the status quo and educate affluent students to work for and with others. Findings suggest that while graduates improved their *own* sense of leading for change, they often experienced tension attempting to overturn the status quo due to social and political pressures. Graduates often had different views than their colleagues, leading to alienation and burn-out. Insights from graduates about the implications for professional learning to lead socially just schools that touch upon the complex factors that impede aspirations for social justice, are highlighted in this manuscript.

Educational contexts continue to produce inherently unequal educational outcomes (Black and Murtadha 2007), disproportionately affecting historically marginalised communities. In the United States (U.S.), these inequitable outcomes are often found along racial and poverty lines. For example, according to the National Centre for Education Statistics (NCES 2017), White students continue to score higher than Black and Hispanic students on reading and mathematics achievement tests. In addition to test scores, school attendance and retention rates are higher among White students. Further, Advanced Placement and International Baccalaureate credits are higher among White and Asian students, while suspension rates are higher among Black students (NCES 2017). These school achievement indicators are set against the backdrop of socioeconomic status when we consider that the percentage of children living in poverty in the U.S. is highest among Black (37%) and Hispanic children (31%) (NCES 2017). With such inequity persisting in the field of education, there is clear need for school leaders committed to equity and access for all students (Bogotch 2002, Cambron-McCabe and McCarthy 2005, Marshall and Oliva 2006, Gorski 2017, Knight-Manuel and Marciano 2018).

While unequal educational outcomes occur across educational contexts, affluent schools, defined as economically elite contexts (Swalwell 1994), are often overlooked in the discussion about achievement differentials given their focus on 'college-preparatory' academics. There is an inherent assumption that high achievement occurs for all students at elite schools due to economic homogeneity of the student body. While academic achievement may be strong in such school contexts, ultimately, these contexts can engender an 'economic elite domination' (Gilens and Page 2014, p. 41), and not necessarily produce students inclined to work for the common good (Gilens and Page 2014). This is a critical context because those who are affluent wield a grossly disproportionate amount of power, and yet, a socially just society is structured with democratic principles and radical egalitarianism (Gilens and Page 2014). Additionally, the historical record indicates that some students are advantaged by their dominant place in society, and therefore experience a kind of privilege that allows them the 'ability to act without consequences and as if one had the right to set the rules' (Choules 2007, p. 472). Social justice leadership (SJL) assists affluent students to recognise and respond to the demands of redistribution as expressions of justice (Swalwell 1994). Goodman (2000) suggests that engaging dominant groups to explore issues of social justice and diversity is challenging but necessary in order to disrupt the status quo. Thus, the development of SJL is especially needed in affluent contexts in order to dismantle the status quo, and educate affluent students to work for and with others (Arrupe 1973).

Research indicates that school leaders are a critical component to student success, second only to good teaching (Louis et al. 2010). This is because school leaders are situated to combat inequitable outcomes inherently produced by educational contexts (Black and Murtadha 2007). Leaders are positioned to shape a vision of academic success for all students, create safe school climates for learning and positive interactions, and enable processes and people to function at their best (Louis et al. 2010). Yet, for school leaders to become the change agents necessary to transform inequitable systems, they must develop a broad and deep understanding of social justice in their leadership preparation programmes, which should continue to be professionally developed in their school contexts. Bogotch (2000) asserts that, 'educational leadership must continuously confront the issue of "social justice" in all its guises, and deliberately make social justice a central part of educational discourse and actions' (p.3). Thus, this paper explores issues related to social justice leadership (SJL) within affluent school contexts and the implications for career-long professional development (PD). To contextualise the experiences of socially just school leaders in affluent contexts, we begin with a review of the literature on professional learning to highlight key themes and effective qualities. Then, we frame the study through the lens of key components of SJL for career-long learning (Forde and Torrance 2016).

Review of key themes from literature about professional learning

Across the literature, there is a call for educators to engage in continual PD for career-long learning. Effective PD is characterised in the literature as aligned to the needs of the school community, focused on relevant information for the school context, and implemented in collaboration with the school community, supported by leadership (Bayar 2014, Louws et al. 2016, Darling-Hammond et al. 2017). Kennedy (2005) responded to the demand of practitioners wanting to know what effective PD should look like and offered a review of PD models. For example, some PD may be offered simply to train staff and faculty by transmitting information. Kennedy (2014) later addressed standards-based models of PD and their alignment to district or state standards and focus on accountability. A coaching and mentoring model of PD is aligned to the community of practice model (Wenger 1998). The transformative model of PD advocates for transformation of context, not just distribution of information. This collaborative professional inquiry model (Kennedy 2014), involves educators identifying problems of practice in their own contexts, and developing methods of assessing and remediating problems through recent scholarship and self-directed study, in cycles of data gathering and analysis, much like action research (Kennedy 2014).

While Guskey (2003) asserts that there is no consensus on PD design, many researchers have attempted to identify effective PD features. Teachers indicate that effective PD activities consist of an appropriate alignment to their needs and the school context, teacher involvement in the design and planning of the PD, active participation, long-term engagement, and highly qualified instructors (Bayar 2014). A recent study (Darling-Hammond et al. 2017) found seven common features of effective PD including: 1) a focus on content relevant to teachers' classroom contexts; 2) incorporating active learning, much like what teachers provide for their students; 3) supporting collaboration; 4) using modelling for effective practice; 5) providing coaching focused on teacher's individual needs; 6) offering both frequent feedback and reflection; and 7) providing adequate time for teachers to process and practice new strategies.

In order for PD to be truly effective, however, it must occur in contexts conducive for implementation. DuFour and Marzano (2011) highlighted that effective PD involves a school leader who works to create the culture of a professional learning community throughout the school. The effectiveness of PD suffers if the school leadership is hierarchical, and lacks the vision to support its implementation (Louws et al. 2016). And perhaps most importantly, leaders must consider the personal context of the teachers. PD must engage the 'initial conditions' of the educator (Keay et al. 2018) and 'teacher contexts [should be] considered as a source for learning' (Koffeman and Snoek 2018, p. 467). Further, leaders should empower teachers to contribute to the development and implementation of their own PD for optimum effectiveness (Zein 2015).

Review of key themes from literature about social justice leadership development

To create social justice leaders, leadership preparation programmes incorporate key elements to develop a SJL practice among their candidates. Such programmes incorporate rigorous curriculum, model appropriate pedagogy, and implement assessment practices to continuously improve their work (Capper et al. 2006). Moreover, preparation programmes must create the conditions where knowledge, skills, and dispositions of leaders are transformed to encourage SJL (Capper et al. 2006). At the core of this learning, leadership preparation programmes must create a climate of 'emotional safety for risk taking' (p. 212) because transformation requires leaders to be vulnerable as they challenge their own beliefs, biases, and privilege. Thus, programmatic features (i.e. curriculum, pedagogy, assessment) and person-centred characteristics (i.e. knowledge, skill, disposition) combine to assist leaders in transforming their leadership through the lens of social justice. However, developing a SJL practice is incomplete without the opportunity to implement the knowledge and skills developed during preparation programmes; content cannot be disconnected from practice. In fact, emphasis on knowledge alone has been criticised (Levine 2005), due to the risk of being reduced to 'cultural literacy' (Forde and Torrance 2016). And the development of SJL skills necessitates practice in school contexts, beyond academic simulations. Similarly, merely learning on the job without connection to a knowledge base and tested theory is inadequate (Forde and Torrance 2016). Murphy (2001) asserts that the field of education has focused on the development of knowledge in educational leadership programmes to the exclusion of a practice-based knowledge. Additionally, however, he maintains that making practice-based knowledge the gold standard is also a failed endeavour for successful professional learning. Thus, professional growth to lead socially just schools must continue to occur in the school site in order to sustain lessons learned during a preparation programme.

Framing the study

While the literature has outlined core components of leadership preparation programmes (Capper et al. 2006) and various models and design elements of effective PD (Kennedy 2014), this study is framed by literature specifically focused on leadership for social justice for career-long growth and learning. Forde and Torrance (2016) examined the core components of leadership development and social justice identified in the literature and assert three core components for professional growth, as follows: 1) the knowledge base; 2) identity and stance; and 3) political acumen and advocacy (p. 112–115).

The knowledge base

Forde and Torrance (2016) imply that the tension between the importance of knowledge-building and the value of practitioner experience at the intersection of school leadership and social justice, can be bridged by Boske's (2014) understanding of the significance of context. Boske asserts, 'Those who prepare school leaders will need to continuously negotiate and renegotiate, as well as construct and reconstruct ways of knowing about community, political ideals, history, leadership, and what is meant by "social justice" within specific contexts' (p. 294). Thus, Forde and Torrance (2016) assert that the knowledge base for developing social justice leadership cannot rely exclusively on relevant research or practitioner experience, but rather, must be a blend of both, with the acknowledgement of educator context as pivotal for successful uptake.

Identity and stance

Aspiring leaders should be encouraged to explore their identity and stance and to consider how this benefits or hinders their leadership positionality and decision making. Similar to the notion of disposition (Capper et al. 2006), educational leaders' different developmental orientations influence their thinking about, and practice of, SJL (Drago-Severson and Blum-DeStefano 2019). However, recent research suggests that education programmes often treat identity as a unidimensional construct, rather than acknowledging intersectionality (Pugach et al. 2018). Understanding the complexity of identity is critical for effective leadership training. Further, spaces for critical self-reflection in professional learning can help leaders to clarify and deepen their identity (Boske 2014). This critical self-reflection is especially important for leaders who are not from marginalised populations because their differing positionality can distance them from understanding students' gifts, talents, and needs (Khalifa 2015). Boske (2014) also suggests that the critical self-reflection of educators is necessary 'to *understand, to become,* and *to know* social justice work' (p. 304). Thus, understanding self can ultimately lead to what might be called 'educational activism,' where leaders work to disrupt the status quo and advocate for the needs of all students (Theoharis 2010).

Political acumen and advocacy

Leadership programmes must also prepare educators for the politics and perseverance that leading schools requires. Forde (2014) calls this the 'grit' of social justice (p. 1140), which is a necessary tool for implementing strategies for equity and access. Hynds (2010) affirms that resistance can occur when implementing reform initiatives using a social justice orientation. Hynds (2010) asserts that school leaders need further education about the complexity and challenge of social justice reform work. The work of social justice leaders is, according to Boske (2014), 'a highly emotional endeavor requiring courage, integrity, imaginative possibilities and self awareness' (p. 289). Therefore, PD for SJL must include the acknowledgement that while this work is critical, it is also difficult (Dimmock 2012), requiring leaders to go above and beyond their normal duties to navigate these contentious spaces. Additionally, the work of social justice activism, identity exploration, and the connection of theory to practice in schools requires time and focus. While this may not be as challenging in leadership preparation programmes, it is particularly challenging in schools. In fact, while PD is vital to school success (Guskey and Huberman 1995), research suggests that U.S. teachers generally spend less time in professional learning opportunities with their peers than teachers in top-performing countries (Darling-Hammond et al. 2009).

The current study

While unequal outcomes occur across educational contexts, little is known about the practice of SJL in affluent school contexts. Yet, these elite schools are critical contexts, given that the affluent wield a grossly disproportionate amount of power. Thus, SJL in such contexts may contribute to a more just future by assisting students to dismantle the status quo. However, little is known about the challenges and tensions of engaging in SJL in these contexts. To that end, this study was guided by the question: What are the unique challenges for educational leaders in practicing SJL in affluent contexts?

Method

The purpose of this study was to illuminate the voices of graduates from an educational leadership preparation programme, who practiced SJL in schools defined as affluent, or those that serve the economically elite (Swalwell 1994). We operationalised the definition of an affluent school context as a private, tuition-based, independent school. Based on this definition, some religious schools were also included because they met the criteria of being private and tuition-based. Through qualitative interview data, we uncover the commonalities of experiencing the phenomena of serving as a social justice leader in an affluent school context and illuminate the PD needs of these school leaders.

Context of study

Located in the diverse city of Los Angeles (LA), this study focused on school leaders of affluent, tuition-based schools, including private, independent, and religious school contexts. According to our participants, annual tuition costs ranged from 20 USD K-$65 K for the schools represented in the study, with religious schools charging lower amounts and boarding schools charging the most (see Table 1). Furthermore, participants indicated that their schools served a predominantly White student demographic and while some described financial aid initiatives, the majority of participants described their school communities as predominantly having 'full pay' families. Many discussed the commonality of having Diversity, Equity, and Inclusion initiatives at their schools and that students 'on scholarship' were few in number and frequently students of colour with financial needs. Furthermore, participants characterised the schools as marked by celebrity culture, including famous students and students with famous parents, ranging from professional athletes, to Hollywood actors and producers, to politicians.

Procedures

A qualitative phenomenological approach was used in this study to describe the meaning of a lived experience of a phenomenon for several individuals (Moustakas 1994, Creswell 2014). The phenomenon under study is the experience of working as a social justice leader in an affluent school in LA. Our social justice leaders share the commonality of having attended a doctoral programme in leadership for social justice grounded in Jesuit philosophy. In this manuscript, we critically examine

Table 1. Participant demographics.

Gender	Leadership position	Type of school	Tuition
Female	Vice President	Private, Independent, Religious Secondary	$21 K
Male	Maths Curriculum Coordinator	Independent TK-6	$40 K
Female	Assistant Head of School	Private, Independent, K-12	$40 K
Male	Science Department Chair	Private, Independent Secondary	$50 K-$65 K[a]
Male	Curriculum & Technology Coordinator	Private, Independent K-12	$40 K
Female	Assistant Principal	Private, Religious Secondary School	$20 K
Female	College Advisor	Private, Religious Secondary School	$25 K
Female	Lead Grade Teacher	Private, Independent K-12	$40 K
Female	Humanities Curriculum Coordinator	Private, Independent K-12	$40 K

[a]Tuition is at the higher amount for students who board at the school.

data from graduates of this educational leadership for social justice doctoral programme, housed at a Jesuit university, to illuminate the complex issues of social justice in affluent school communities. Jesuit institutions are explicit about their mission of social justice. The aim of a Jesuit education is to prepare leaders who become conscionable citizens in a global context (Kolvenbach 2000) and to form 'men and women for others' (Arrupe 1973). Arrupe's notion also encourages transformation through action. Social justice in the Jesuit tradition is a call to challenge the status quo, to provide a voice for the voiceless, and to walk humbly and collaboratively with the marginalised (Ellacuria 1982). Thus, we defined social justice leadership as challenging the status quo.

Measures

Data for this study were obtained from exit interviews that are conducted annually with graduates as they exit the Jesuit-informed leadership for social justice programme. During these audio-recorded semi-structured interviews, graduates were asked to reflect on their transformation during the leadership preparation programme, specifically related to how they lead their educational community through the lens of social justice. Leaders provided examples of their social justice practice as well as discussed areas of improvement and continuing areas of need. For this study, we analysed the interview data from select graduates who work in affluent contexts to describe the commonalities of this particular phenomenon.

Participants

To be eligible for participation in this study, participants needed to be a graduate of the educational leadership for social justice programme and hold a leadership role in an affluent school, defined as tuition-based and private/independent. Leadership roles were defined broadly in alignment with the educational leadership programme's criteria for admittance. For example, the programme requires at least two years of experience in educational leadership prior to beginning the three year program and defines leadership as 'leading from any chair' (Zander and Zander 2000). To that end, participants held a variety of roles in schools, ranging from a lead grade level teacher, to a Department Chair, to a Vice President. A total of nine graduates, who met the criteria of working in affluent contexts were interviewed.

Results

To analyse the data, we engaged in multiple cycles of coding and pattern analysis (Miles et al. 2014). First, interview data were coded inductively, allowing themes to emerge from the interviews to showcase commonalities in the lived experience of the participants related to the phenomenon of being a leader for social justice in an affluent school context. Then, we examined patterns among the codes using the analytical memos from the inductive cycle to eventually categorise themes. During this cycle, we deductively analysed themes by adapting the core components of leadership in social justice determined by Forde and Torrance (2016) and applying them to the data. Given the small sample size, comparisons by school context (i.e. religious versus secular) were not made. To that end, findings are derived from these core components, which require an understanding of the knowledge base, identity and stance, and political acumen and advocacy necessary for social justice leaders. This approach to qualitative data analysis allowed for a rich, in-depth description of the phenomenon.

The knowledge base: context matters

A common theme that emerged from the data was the notion that the dynamics within a school matter when attempting to engage in SJL. Graduates shared the commonality that their ability to engage in SJL greatly depended on whether there was support or pushback from the school administration (i.e. heads of school, school boards) and parents. For instance, a male graduate shared that his initiative to make changes to Honours and Advanced Placement course enrolment in order to allow greater access for underrespresented students was made possible, in part, by a strong school administration whose support allowed the change.

However, more often than not, graduates had the opposite experience. They shared that after they graduated, they were often thwarted by differing expectations of school leadership practices embraced by colleagues. There was a sense of dissonance expressed between graduates' beliefs about SJL and the norms, expectations, and practices accepted within their affluent school contexts. For instance, a graduate who identifies as Latina and works as the Assistant Principal of a predominantly White religious school, shared: 'I feel like the culture of the school has put a damper on the ideas and excitement I had during the [preparation] programme.' She commented on how teachers and administrators had 'attitudes of resistance to change' and she felt like her suggestions for improvement were 'disregarded' which made her 'frustrated.'

Meanwhile, the Science Department Chair at a private, independent (non-religious) school indicated that the biggest obstacle to his SJL practice was the pushback received from parents based on political and religious pressures. For example, he shared how the school had attempted to implement more culturally and religiously inclusive initiatives by bringing in guest speakers for student assemblies to address issues of racism and homophobia, by providing prayer rooms and accommodations during Ramadan for Muslim students, and by excusing Jewish students during the high holidays. But several White, conservative, Christian parents complained directly to the school board that these initiatives were actually excluding the dominant White majority students. Some parents claimed their 'legacy White son [felt] excluded' at the school because of the inclusivity initiatives. As a result, affluent parents pressured the school board to allow more conservative speakers to speak at assemblies, who agreed in order to 'maintain balance.' He shared how it felt like 'the parents pulled the rug out from under our work.'

Similarly, a female graduate shared how she was hired to create a humanities curriculum for the secondary level at an independent private school. She opted for the overarching learning outcome to develop a culture of leadership for social justice among the students where she was intentional about each academic experience in the curriculum to help students make meaning and co-construct knowledge about the world. However, she felt that as students adopted a more critical understanding of the world, parents began to work behind the scenes and went 'above her head to leaders and the school board.' When she was finally included in the conversation about the curriculum, she was accused of being anti-Semitic by parents, even though she, herself has Jewish heritage. The contentious experience and personal attacks undermined her attempts of engaging in SJL practice. In short, these examples indicate how the context of the school is a common aspect of experiencing the phenomenon of engaging in SJL in affluent schools. Awareness of the social, cultural, religious, and political landscape of the schools was a common response to the question of how to feel more prepared to engage in SJL in affluent schools.

Identity: reflection, activism, & magis

Understanding the ways in which intersecting identity markers contribute to one's positionality to engage in SJL is critical and factors related to race and gender were certainly revealed during the interviews. For example, a female Vice President shared that she was often 'fighting for her voice,' illuminating the struggle of being a female leader of an all-male, religious environment. She further shared how she had been asked by male colleagues to 'not be so confrontational' at times. Another female school leader, who identifies as Black, shared that she is the only elementary school leader with her doctorate of education and yet the school principal and some White parents refuse to use the title 'Dr.' when addressing her. However, she noted that they use the title to address the White secondary school principal with the same degree. These examples indicate how leaders who engage in SJL work are often confronted with issues of identity, especially in how others view them.

To bolster such attacks on identity, a key finding that emerged among leaders in affluent contexts was the need for self-awareness and critical reflection. Across all interviews, social justice leaders articulated that during their programme of study, they became more aware of issues of race, racism, economic power, and privilege – their own and within the structures of society. It was clear that leaders were constantly assessing their own positionality during their SJL, asking whether they 'were doing enough', and feeling frustrated that transformation towards equity was slow.

Awareness and reflection
Adopting a critical mindset about privilege in affluent contexts was a common feature among the leaders. These leaders clearly demonstrated how they engaged in critical reflection in their SJL practice. Several graduates called out the common experience of seeing an increase in Diversity, Equity, and Inclusion efforts in private, affluent schools. As one student shared, 'there has been a tremendous push in independent schools for Directors of Inclusion, Diversity, and Equity.' However, graduates were keenly aware of the tension between espousing a social justice mission, when the very existence of the school is to serve the needs of the elite.

One graduate, who worked as a curriculum coordinator at a private, independent (non-religious) school, noted that the school publicly espoused a mission of equity and attempted to create access to the school for those who could not afford the tuition but only offered limited financial aid. He shared that 'people don't like to think or talk about the financial part but [it can] undermine the mission' and be 'more on paper' than implemented. He shared, 'full-pay families in LA are mostly White.' In other words, he asserted that when a school claims a social justice mission but does not change financial policies, the student body remains rather homogenous, contradicting the mission and reinforcing privilege. Another graduate articulated this tension by sharing how the system of private, independent schooling 'capitalises on corporate money' by catering to the wealthy and how this contradiction ultimately influenced her decision to leave her role as a Curriculum Coordinator of an affluent school and return to teach in public education. Finally, a White male teacher and Curriculum Coordinator shared how he feels surrounded by leaders at his school, who have a difficult time confronting their own privilege and often complain that they feel 'like they are being attacked as a White man.' He said that publicly the leaders 'talk a really big game, but when it comes down to confronting bias and privilege, it becomes a different story.' In short, there was a commonality among graduates working in affluent school contexts – they were keenly aware of privilege and the tension of engaging in SJL in the elite context and they were willing to be self-aware and interrogate their own privilege, as well as the structures of privilege within their contexts.

Educational activist
The common practice of critical reflection often played out in an awareness of how students were interacting with the affluent culture of the school. Leaders shared many examples of student wealth, including expensive cars, name-brand purses, and high fashion. But these commonalities of the school context created the situation where students receiving scholarship support, who were often students of colour, did not feel as though they fit in because they had to take the bus or could not afford the latest trend. As such, leaders for social justice embraced the identity of an 'educational activist' to try and assist these students, relegated to the margins.

To fight for her students, a school leader discussed how she started an affinity group for students of African descent at her private, independent school because she noticed that there were very few Black students at the school and she wanted to provide cultural experiences for them. She shared that initially there was pushback from non-Black parents, who felt the affinity group was exclusive. Some parents even asked; 'If my kid's not Black, can my kid participate?' But, after many years of back and forth with the administration, the initiative generated enough interest that other cultural groups began asking for their own affinity groups, and now she has an annual budget of 1500 USD for cultural events. Yet, this work is in addition to her daily role as the Lead Grade Teacher, noting that often SJL practices require leaders to go above and beyond.

Another teacher shared how she also was committed to providing 'safe-spaces' for her predominantly White students to grapple with issues of race, especially in response to the Black Lives Matter movement, which had emerged as a sensitive topic at her school. Her work on restorative justice practices provided the tools for students 'to cultivate a critical self-reflective and consistent practice grounded in true solidarity work to begin to repair historical wrongdoing.' This work gained such popularity that she eventually started a similar group for faculty at the school. Yet, when she left the school, so too did the affinity groups. She shared that leaders of social justice often need to 'take the long view and practice lots of self-care' trusting that even when faced with resistance, 'to do what you can, when it is possible, knowing things change.'

This need for patience as an activist was a very common experience among leaders in affluent schools. A male Mathematics Curriculum Coordinator stressed, 'in this [affluent] context, change can be very slow, but that doesn't mean that things are not changing.' Another graduate discussed the need to have patience with others, especially when facing resistance regularly trying to make changes at the school. He shared that it can be very frustrating 'to get pushback, to be met with a lot of resistance, when something is clear to you that is happening, where there's a need for change, but others don't feel the same.'

Magis

It was evident from the examples given by graduates that their identity as an activist extended to their practice in that they worked harder as a leader for social justice. All of the graduates provided examples of their SJL practices, which showcased their hard work, persistence, and deep commitment to what the Jesuit's call the *magis* – the more. In the Jesuit sense, this concept describes the restlessness leaders experience knowing that more can be done to combat inequity (Kolvenbach 2000). For example, a graduate shared 'If you're going to be a social justice transformative leader, you need to be willing to actually do the work. Some people kind of just coast and feel like their presence there alone makes a difference. That's not enough.'

One graduate shared that after she created an affinity group for students of African descent, other cultural groups wanted to start their own affinity groups as well and turned to her for advice. This led her to develop trainings and workshops, attend countless meetings, write policies, and engage the administration for budget-related needs, etc. Her work did not stop with addressing the initial issue. Another student noted that when she created the humanities curriculum to focus on current events, it naturally led students to want to create affinity groups to discuss current events outside of class. This led to her becoming the faculty moderator of affinity groups, leading retreats for students, and starting groups for teachers to also discuss current events.

Graduates working in affluent contexts demonstrated a commitment to go above and beyond – the *magis*. While many expressed feelings of isolation, burnout, and exhaustion as a result, they also identified tools that assisted them to continue 'in the struggle' including dispositional characteristics such as charisma, intelligence, and authenticity. As one graduate shared, the leaders who were truly 'transformative and powerful … were scholars.' He shared how 'sometimes it feels like people in charge don't know how to raise the bar. Effective leaders not only had charisma, but they could talk to us about the ideas that were in research.' Another graduate shared the impact of being authentic by saying 'you have to be willing to show people your vulnerability.' His commitment to being authentic endeared him to his students. 'Children of privilege have the opportunity to change the world, that's why I work with them. I am under the assumption that these students need to be trained as allies.' His authenticity, credibility, and commitment to go above and beyond with his work allowed him to be successful.

Political acumen: being strategic

Findings suggest that while graduates improved their *own* awareness and deepened their *own* sense of leading for change, they often experienced tension attempting to overturn the status quo because of the social and political context of the school, which often led to feelings of isolation, alienation, and burn-out. One graduate shared the importance of knowing about the difficulty of transitioning out of doctoral work. 'When you come out of a [preparation] programme like this and you're so immersed in the [SJL] work, you're dropped into a different reality.' Such experiences meant leaders had to have 'thick skin.'

In addition to knowing the social and political landscape of the school and being aware of power dynamics, social justice leaders also shared that it was important to understand how to engage in change efforts. Graduates discussed common skills that were helpful in implementing their SJL, including a resounding need to 'find allies.' There was a common sentiment of 'knowing where to push'; 'knowing who will help'; and 'knowing which battles to fight.' Common skills included the ability to ask difficult questions, to have hard conversations, and to be strategic.

Asking difficult questions

A critical skill that emerged as a commonality among graduates was summarised by a graduate, who shared that to do SJL work in affluent schools, leaders must be able and know how to use their voice to advocate for students, 'to navigate and have conversations with those who are unlike you.' Asking difficult questions was a common experience among graduates. For instance, a graduate shared how after he recognised that students of colour were not enrolling in the advanced courses he was forced to 'take a hard look at all of our practices. Because I can say that it almost happened there, and I changed it, but where else is it happening on campus?' He indicated that engaging in SJL, forces leaders to dig deeper and truly analyse policies and practices and ask tough questions. Another graduate began to question school policies and procedures that did not align to her understanding of SJL. She shared the example of an upcoming schoolwide celebration where all of the students were required to bring in a monetary gift and she said, 'Have you thought about the fact that a few of these kids are not going to be able to bring in that 25.00 USD gift? Have you thought about how that is going to make them feel?' Her challenge to the administration was considered unwelcome but she felt she at least had the ability to ask the critical question. And another graduate shared, 'I feel like I'm at a school where there's not yet permission to talk about race so that's very difficult but at the same time, when it popped up, we talked about it. I didn't avoid it. I tried to work through some of this stuff at the administrative and pedagogical level.'

Picking your battles

In addition to the skillset of asking tough questions and having difficult conversations about school policies and practices, graduates also shared the commonality of needing to be strategic in their SJL practices. One graduate actually said that he actively considers, 'picking and choosing battles' when addressing issues at his school. For example, he implemented a new policy about admitting students of colour to an advanced mathematics course and said: 'Being strategic, I didn't tell my administration team that I made the change. I didn't have to, but I could have. I felt that if I did, I would have been opening a door to a conversation that they wouldn't have been ready to have.' He navigated the change in the policy by being strategic about not disclosing the changes he had made to other administrators whom he knew would not be supportive. The decision fell within his purview and he opted to not share his decision with other administrators because he believed they were not ready to engage deeply about the underlying issues of equity and access.

A Black female school leader shared a similar skill of deciding when to fight back and when to be patient. As one of only 5 Black faculty or staff members at her K-12 independent school, she shared that she chooses to not correct them when they call her 'Ms.' instead of 'Dr.' because she feels the energy to engage the school administration and parents is likely not going to change their behaviour.

Being strategic also took on a common occurrence of being 'undercover.' A college advisor at a private, religious school indicated that for a very long time, ethnic affinity groups simply operated outside the official approval of the school and were 'undercover.' She shared how sometimes in SJL, there is a need 'to go forward and get permission later.' Yet, such work was always anxiety-provoking because as she shared, the school was ever mindful to not 'upset alums and other stakeholders.' This sentiment that SJL work is an undercover enterprise was echoed by an Assistant Head of School, who said that so much of her SJL work is kept 'under the rug' because the school is constantly 'worried about constituents all of the time.' Political acumen was commonly displayed in strategic ways so as to not upset potential funders and key decision-makers.

Discussion

Insights from graduates about the implications for professional learning to lead socially just schools, touch upon the complex factors that impede aspirations for social justice. Based on the findings there are implications for professional learning in school contexts and educator preparation programmes as well. PD for leaders of social justice in education must be ongoing, both during their professional preparation programmes and within their school contexts, throughout their careers. In order for professional learning to be continually transformative, we recommend a parallel approach (Huchting et al. 2017) where school site PD programmes and professional preparation programmes inform each other and work in concert across content and time to create career-long social justice educators.

School site professional development programmes

From our review of the findings we assert that the PD programming best aligned to educators working in affluent contexts is the transformative PD model (Kennedy 2014). In this model, educators become change agents, both identifying the need for transformation, and being allowed the autonomy or agency to enact it. Professional learning for SJL must also be sustained over time, and depart from the 'one shot' guest speaker paradigm of the past. It requires visionary leadership, must provide collaboration for developing allies, be focused on content relevant to educator need, and target social justice issues based on school context (DuFour and Marzano 2011, Darling-Hammond et al. 2017). It must include safe spaces for self-reflection, an important aspect of self-care (Boske 2014). Identity work, including understanding both personal and professional contexts (Capper et al. 2006, Forde and Torrance 2016) and sustaining the disposition for educational activism (Theoharis 2010) is also critical for uncovering bias, and providing a foundation for resisting the status quo in affluent contexts. Additionally, schools should consider personal teacher contexts as a source for professional learning (Keay et al. 2018, Koffeman and Snoek 2018).

Professional preparation programmes

The findings related to professional preparation programmes suggest the need for a more careful consideration of context for the social justice educator, and a more thorough exposure to the knowledge, skills, and dispositions necessary to challenge the resistance to advocacy for access and equity (Capper et al. 2006, Forde and Torrance 2016). The complexities of the affluent school context are particularly confounding, which points to the need for preparation programmes to provide a broader exploration of the variety of contexts students encounter, and a further deepening of political acumen to negotiate the tensions within those spaces (Forde and Torrance 2016). Preparation programmes must consider meeting the needs of social justice leaders by helping educators deepen and enhance their own school site based professional learning. In this way the parallel approach to professional learning converges to meet the career-long needs of social justice educators.

This empirically grounded study is significant because the findings demonstrate that while graduates are transformed to lead their educational communities through a lens of social justice, their transformation is limited when affluent educational communities view leadership and issues of social justice differently. This study therefore informs ongoing and sustainable professional learning in schools from the perspective of the school leaders who experience the struggle every day. Providing a platform for real school leader experiences to be shared may begin to combat the feelings of isolation and alienation expressed by our graduates. Certainly, their recommendations shed light on needed changes to policy and practice. It is clear from the findings that ongoing PD, beyond SJL preparation degree programmes, is needed if social justice leaders are to address the inequitable outcomes inherent in the educational system.

Disclosure statement

No potential conflict of interest was reported by the authors.

References

Arrupe, P.S.J., 1973. Men for others. *In*: C.E. Meirose and S.J. compiler, eds. 1994. *Foundations*. Washington D.C.: Jesuit Secondary Education Association, 31–40.
Bayar, A., 2014., 'The components of effective professional development activities in terms of teachers' perspectives'. *International online journal of educational sciences*, 6 (2), 319–327.
Black, W.R. and Murtadha, K., 2007. Toward a signature pedagogy in educational leadership preparation and program assessment. *Journal of research on leadership education*, 2 (1), 1–29. doi:10.1177/194277510700200101.
Bogotch, I., 2002. Educational leadership and social justice: practice into theory. *Journal of school leadership*, 12(2), 138–156. doi:10.1177/105268460201200203.
Bogotch, IE. 2000., Educational leadership and social justice: Theory into practice. 17 November, University Council for Educational Administration, Albuquerque. Available from: https://files.eric.ed.gov/fulltext/ED452585.pdf
Boske, C. (2014). Critical reflective practices: Connecting to social justice. In Bogotch, I., & Shields, C. M. (Eds.). (2014). International handbook of educational leadership and social (in) justice (Vol. 29). (pp. 289-308). Dordrecht: Springer.
Cambron-McCabe, M. and McCarthy, M., 2005. Educating school leaders for social justice. *Educational policy*, 19(1), 201–222. doi:10.1177/0895904804271609.
Capper, C.A., Theoharis, G., and Sebastian, J., 2006. Toward a framework for preparing educational leaders for social justice. *International journal of educational administration*, 44 (3), 209–224. doi:10.1108/09578230610664814.
Choules, K., 2007. The shifting sands of social justice discourse: from situating the problem with "them" to situating it with "us. *Review of education/pedagogy/cultural studies*, 29(5), 461–481. doi:10.1080/10714410701566348.
Creswell, R., 2014. *Research design: qualitative, quantitative and mixed methods approaches*. Thousand Oaks, CA: Sage.
Darling-Hammond, L., et al., 2009. State of the profession: study measures status of professional development. *Journal of staff development*, 30 (2), 46–50.
Darling-Hammond, L., Hyler, M.E., and Gardner, M., 2017. *Effective teacher professional development*. Palo Alto, CA: Learning Policy Institute. Available from: https://learningpolicyinstitute.org/product/effective-teacher-professional-development-report
Dimmock, C., 2012. *Leadership: capacity building and school improvement*. London: Routeledge.
Drago-Severson, E. and Blum-DeStefano, J., 2019. A developmental lens on social justice leadership: exploring the connection between meaning making and practice. *Journal of Educational Leadership and Policy Studies, Special Issue #1on Educational Leadership and Social Justice*, 3 (1). Available from: https://files.eric.ed.gov/fulltext/EJ1226921.pdf
DuFour, R. and Marzano, R., 2011. *Leaders of learning: how district, school, and classroom leaders improve student achievement (bringing the professional learning community process to life)*. Bloomington, IN: Solution Tree Press.
Ellacuria, I.S.J., 1982. *The task of a Christian university*. Commencement address at Santa Clara University. 5 June, Santa Clara University, Santa Clara. Available from: www.scu.edu/jesuits/ellacura.html.
Forde, C., 2014. Issues of social justice and fairness in the development of aspiring head-teachers: I had not really thought about my values before. *In*: I. Bogotch and C.M. Shields, eds. *International handbook of educational leadership and social [in]justice*. Dordrecht: Springer, 1125–1143.

Forde, C. and Torrance, D., 2016. Social justice and leadership development. *Professional development in education*, 43 (1), 106–120. Available from: https://www.tandfonline.com/doi/full/10.1080/19415257.2015.1131733

Gilens, M & Page, BI., 2014. Testing Theories of American Politics: Elites, Interest Groups, and Average Citizens. *Perspectives on politics*, 12 (3), 564–581.

Goodman, D., 2000. Moving people from privileged groups to support social justice. *Teachers college record*, 106 (2), 1061–1085. Available from: https://www.vanderbilt.edu/wp-content/uploads/sites/149/Motivating-People-from-Privilege-to-Justice.pdf

Gorski, P., 2017. *Reaching and teaching students in poverty: strategies for erasing the opportunity gap*. 2nd ed. New York: Teachers College Press.

Guskey, T., 2003. What makes professional development effective? *Phi delta kappan*, 84(10), 748–750. doi:10.1177/003172170308401007.

Guskey, TR., & Huberman M., 1995. '*Professional development in education: New paradigms and practices*'. Teachers college press, 290.

Huchting, K., Bickett, J., and Fisher, E., 2017. Preparing social justice leaders to deconstruct heterosexual privilege. *In*: V. Stead, ed. *A guide to LGBTQ+ inclusion on campus post pulse*. New York: Peter Lang, 141–158.

Hynds, A., 2010. Unpacking resistance to change within-school reform programmes with a social justice orientation. *International journal of leadership in education*, 13(4), 377–392. doi:10.1080/13603124.2010.503282.

Keay, J.K., Carse, N., and Jess, M., 2018. Understanding teachers as complex professional learners. *Professional development in education*, 40 (5), 688–697. doi: 10.1080/19415257.2014.955122.

Kennedy, A., 2005. Models of continuing professional development: a framework for analysis. *Professional development in education*, 31 (2), 235–250. Available from: https://www.tandfonline.com/doi/pdf/10.1080/13674580500200277

Kennedy, A., 2014. Understanding continuing professional development: the need for theory to impact on policy and practice. *Professional development in education*, 45(3), 456–471. doi:10.1080/19415257.2018.1557239.

Khalifa, M., 2015. *Culturally responsive school leadership*. Cambridge, Mass: Harvard Education Press.

Knight-Manuel, M. and Marciano, J., 2018. *Classroom cultures: equitable schooling for racially diverse youth*. New York: Teachers College Press.

Koffeman, A. and Snoek, M., 2018. Identifying context factors as a source for teacher professional learning. *Professional development in education*, 45(1), 125–137. doi:10.1080/19415257.2018.1449004.

Kolvenbach, P.S.J., 2000. The service of faith and the promotion of justice in American Jesuit higher education. *Address presented at the Commitment to Justice in Jesuit higher education conference*. Santa Clara CA: Santa Clara University. Available from: http://www.sjweb.info/resources/searchList.cfm

Levine, A., 2005. *Educating school leaders: the Levine report. The education schools project*. Available from: http://edschools.org/pdf/Educating_Teachers_Report.pdf

Louis, K.S., et al., 2010. *Learning from leadership: investigating the links to improved student learning*. New York: The Wallace Foundation. Available from: http://www.wallacefoundation.org/knowledge-center/school-leadership/key-research/Documents/Investigating-the-Links-to-Improved-Student-Learning.pdf

Louws, M.L., et al., 2016. Exploring the relation between teachers' perceptions of workplace conditions and their professional learning goals. *Professional development in education*, 43(5), 770–788. doi:10.1080/19415257.2016.1251486.

Marshall, C. and Oliva, M., 2006. *Leadership for social justice: making revolutions in education*. Boston, MA: Pearson.

Miles, M., Huberman, M., and Saldana, J., 2014. *Qualitative data analysis: A methods sourcebook*. 3rd ed. Thousand Oaks, CA: Sage.

Moustakas, C., 1994. *Phenomenological research methods*. Thousand Oaks, CA: Sage.

Murphy, J., 2001. Re-culturing the profession of educational leadership: new blueprints. *Paper commissioned for the first meeting of the National Commission for the Advancement of Educational Leadership Preparation*, 19–21 September. Wisconsin. 10.1177/0013161X02382004

National Center for Education Statistics (NCES), 2017. *The condition of education*. Washington, D.C: NCES Publications. Available from: https://nces.ed.gov/pubs2017/2017144.pdf

Pugach, M., Gomez-Najarro, J., and Matewos, A., 2018. A review of identity in research on social justice in teacher education: what role for intersectionality? Available from. *Journal of teacher education*, 70 (3). doi:10.1177/0022487118760567.

Swalwell, K., 1994. Mind the civic empowerment gap: economically elite students and critical civic education. *Curriculum Inquiry*, 45(5), 491–512. doi:10.1080/03626784.2015.1095624.

Theoharis, G., 2010. Disrupting injustice; principals narrate the strategies they use to improve their schools and advance social justice. *Teachers college record*, 112 (1), 331–373. Available from: https://eric.ed.gov/?id=EJ888448

Wenger, E., 1998. *Communities of practice: learning, meaning and identity*. Cambridge: Cambridge University Press.

Zander, R.S. and Zander, B., 2000. *The art of possibility*. Boston, MA: Harvard Business School Press.

Zein, S., 2015. Factors affecting the professional development of elementary English teachers. *Professional development in education*, 42(3), 423–440. doi:10.1080/19415257.2015.1005243.

Professional development for school leaders in England: decision-making for social justice

Ian Potter and Stephanie Chitpin

ABSTRACT
A study of nine headteachers in England, using a research protocol developed and carried out in Ontario, finds implications for the professional development of school leaders with respect to their decision-making to achieve greater equity. The types of professional development that leaders found to be most effective within their particular contexts are identified. The challenges faced by school leaders are explored in relation to their efforts to reduce context-specific achievement gaps. The data generated from semi-structured interviews are examined within the context of the English school system, which is highly neoliberalised and has a performative driven policy landscape. The impact of this context on the practice of school leadership for social justice is discussed and, in particular, how data-based decision-making can be improved through professional development in order to achieve more equitable outcomes, especially for disadvantaged students. The paper has relevance for practitioners in how its findings illuminate professional development practices that school leaders might benefit from and from an argument that reflective and reflexive school leaders are more likely to make objective, critically informed decisions.

Introduction

England's education system requires that school leaders make use of data to analyse the achievements of their students and, from that analysis, make decisions relating to addressing gaps in attainment between different cohorts of learners. In many educational systems throughout the world, this has become expected practice, as schools are held more and more accountable for increasing not only the proportion of students who meet educational expectations but also reducing achievement gaps among subgroups of students within the public school system (Chitpin 2019). Thus, the educational landscape in England is no different than many other jurisdictions in demanding its leader-managers to develop greater proficiency in using data to inform their decision-making. Earl and Katz (2006) contend that school leaders are not always sufficiently prepared for such data analysis and Chitpin (2019) contends there is little in the literature related to the mental models that may be required in the decision-making processes of school administrators. Furthermore, there has been little research regarding the types of professional development school leaders desire in order to support their learning and development, as they strive to lead socially just schools in a data-based, data-driven and data-informed context. In fact, research by the International School Leader Development Network (ISLDN) has identified how school leaders find performance data both a support and a hindrance in their endeavours for school improvement (Angelle 2017).

Do school leaders consider these data-based, data-driven or data-informed contexts when making decisions? According to Chitpin (2019), 'data-driven' or 'data-informed' represent buzz-words that often become used interchangeably in referring to improved organisational decision-making. Chitpin explains that, although the terms are related, there are noteworthy differences, particularly since

> [D]ata-based decision-making refers to an ongoing process of collecting and analyzing different types of data (summative and formative) to help schools make informed decisions about student outcomes (Skalski and Romero 2011). Data-driven decision-making, on the other hand, refers to collection and analysis of data to make specific, often time-sensitive decisions. (p. 2)

Indeed, in England, schools use data from national test scores, particularly end-of-key-stage tests, to make decisions relating to explicit student needs and to differentiate curriculum provisions, as a consequence. This type of data is frequently linked with big data and data analytics, particularly quantitative/statistical analytics, and schools find themselves categorised according to algorithms determined externally. Chitpin (2019) further states;

> data-informed decision-making is a term used when data and facts are an influential factor, but not the only factor in decision-making. For example, school leaders may not base their decisions purely on the literacy and numeracy scores but on 'softer' data that may be more descriptive in nature. (p. 2)

This research illustrates how school leaders within a relatively defined geographical area in England differed in the extent to which they gave weight to the 'big-data' informing their decision-making.

The field for this research encompassed a number of schools in the South of England. Interviews were carried out among a range of state-funded schools, including primary, secondary and special provision schools. The interview protocol used was developed by the second author at the University of Ottawa and has been used in research studies with Canadian principals (Chitpin 2019).

The empirical evidence informing this research comes from those semi-structured interviews carried out with nine school leaders in England in order to investigate what influences them most in their operational decision-making when it comes to achieving equity in student outcomes. These school leaders were asked to identify any disadvantaged populations within their schools and were also requested to describe the various achievement gaps associated with these groups. They were also asked to elaborate on the types of professional development that they considered most effective with respect to achieving equity in student outcomes. Hence, in describing how school leaders make decisions to achieve greater equity, this paper identifies the types of professional development that school leaders found to be most effective, within their particular educational contexts. In concluding on the finding that school leaders benefit from particular types of professional development probably more than others, the paper identifies how important is support for how leaders frame their decision-making; it, therefore, proposes further research into a framework, known as the Objective Knowledge Growth Framework (OKGF) that is based on Popper's (1979) critical rationalism (Chitpin 2016), to support school leaders and their professional development.

The English context

Educational policy in England provides premium funding to schools for each student identified as 'economically' disadvantaged. As a result, school leaders are expected to account for how that 'premium' money is spent in closing gaps in achievement between the disadvantaged and the non- or less disadvantaged students. This policy transaction affords a lens regarding how these leaders address inequality through greater equity in outcomes. It represents a 'neoliberal' approach to addressing inequity, and one that school leaders in England have been working with for many years. Indeed, the regulator, Ofsted, has inspected schools on their expenditure of these 'additional' funds and evaluates the impact of that expenditure. There is contention in the field about how this money is being spent in socially just ways. To complicate matters, there is also contention surrounding exactly what constitutes disadvantage and injustice.

Neoliberalism can be defined as a resurgence of nineteenth-century ideas associated with *laissez-faire* economics and free-market capitalism (Smith 2019). Neoliberalism defines successful schools as those achieving high academic performance. The criteria for success are set by governance and the data is often used comparatively, in comparison with other countries using standardised and/or international tests (Ball 2012). This has created a regime where the performance of schools, whether 'strong' or 'poor,' is attributed to schools and individuals rather than to socio-political, economic or cultural factors (Angus 2012). As such, it produces a zeitgeist that Ball (2008) refers to as 'performativity.' Consequently, school leaders are increasingly being held responsible for their students' academic achievement and, so, a successful school leader is one whose school achieves high standardised test scores. In England, failure to produce elevated scores can lead to a school leader losing his/her job (Lynch *et al.* 2017), generally, after an Ofsted judgement deems the provision to be inadequate because the student outcomes are insufficient.

This notion of 'achievement gaps' aligns closely with the Organisation for Economic Co-operation and Development (OECD) indicators, which, in part, is due to the fact that the OECD is responsible for neoliberal policy initiatives, including the field of education. Despite this responsibility, Chitpin (2019) argues that 'equity claims relating to inclusion strategies and achievement gaps remain largely outside of neoliberal policy mandates' (p. 4), even while educational policy is being made by the OECD. This has created conditions in England whereby government rhetoric has constructed equity in a neoliberal way by labelling social mobility as a policy for social justice. This rhetoric is presumed to enable the disadvantaged to achieve equally, along with their non-disadvantaged peers, in order to meritocratically provide them the opportunity to join the 'privileged.' While this espousal seems like a manifesto for equity, it is seriously undermined by the ways in which the manipulation of big data regulates the numbers of students empowered to 'push through' the sluices to 'higher esteem.' This is because national standardised tests are 'fixed' in their distribution of outcomes to ensure they are comparable with what the same cohort attained, on aggregate, earlier in their school career. For example, in England, a year group taking their standardised national exams (GCSEs) at age 16 have their results determined by what the profile of attainment was when they were 11 years old, taking their Standard Assessment Tests (SATs) at the end of key stage two, which are taken in the final year of their education, known a primary schooling. Key stage two results are linked similarly to the end of key-stage-one results, taken when students are 7 years old. We contend that a criteria referenced approach would be ethically sounder if big data and standardised testing are to be employed for achieving (or regulating) greater equity.

Furthermore, the predilection in the English system to norm referenced standardised national testing has implications for notions of equity. Having to rank results according to a Bell Curve resonates with notions of constructing a norm that reinforces a perceived 'natural' order within a society (Herrnstein and Murray 1994). Achievement is not determined by what the learner has attained in absolute terms. They do not 'pass' because of how much they have learned and can do and know. Their level of success is determined by how well everyone else does. It is 'inequality by design (Fischer *et al.* 1996). The system of assessment becomes self-fulfiling and hegemonic in its outcomes. As Fischer et al. explain: 'The more institutions sort people by test scores, the better the test scores predict sorting' (p 44). Thus, policy determines where 'individuals end up on the ladder of inequality' (p 17). Criteria referenced approaches to testing would be less neoliberal and more socially just.

The shift towards adopting neoliberal attitudes in England can be traced to the early 1980 s (Ball 2008 &, 2012) and local management of schooling. Under neoliberalism, standardised tests are used to judge a school system's 'value for money' and to introduce competitiveness in the global marketplace. Control over curriculum is generally centralised in order to increase accountability. In England, this happened with the introduction of a National Curriculum in 1988 at about the same time as a school regulator, the Office of Standards in Education (Ofsted), the school inspectorate, was established (Twenty years later, with the advent of Academies, which are state-funded and state-regulated secondary schools, these schools were given the 'freedom' to not have to 'deliver' the National Curriculum; however, the specifications for standardised national testing are inextricably linked to the National Curriculum).

How can achievement gaps be managed?

Chitpin (2019) discusses three approaches to reducing the achievement gap and this paper adds a fourth, which is professional development strategies. In so doing, Chitpin refers to Thrupp (2007) and his 'calling-out' of the achievement gap as an 'inconvenient truth.'

> It has long been argued that inequality arises from an education system geared towards white, middle-class values (See Bourdieu and Passeron 1977). Educators, school leaders, policymakers, and social scientists have taken a number of approaches to address this achievement gap. However, so far, there is little consensus as how best to resolve such differences in educational outcomes (Jeynes 2015). (Chitpin 2019, p. 4)

Approach 1: economic/financial solutions

As Chitpin (2019) explains, if we believe these gaps in attainment generally stem from socio-economic phenomena, then it will require financial solutions to remedy that gap; a monetary solution is the logical approach. Drawing on the perspectives of several social scientists (Chideya 1995, Jeynes 1999, 2003, 2015, Rothstein 2004), Chitpin illuminates achievement gaps that persist over time in conjunction with a socio-economic gap and, hence, should one wish to bridge the gap, one necessarily must provide schools and families with the economic resources they need in order to perform at higher levels. 'The Ontario Ministry of Education website lists numerous funding initiatives that have already been completed to improve education funding, capital outlay, and other resources to advance student achievement' (See Chitpin 2019, p. 5), whereas, the English Department of Education employs a pupil premium funding initiative to compensate for inequities of life-chances.

Approach 2: differentiated learning strategies

Learning style theorists, according to Chitpin (2019, p. 5), posit that achievement gaps can exist because schools need to demonstrate a greater degree of cultural sensitivity and awareness of different students' distinct learning styles (Banks and Banks 1995, Bernak et al. 2005). They argue that schools are too much geared towards teaching Caucasian middle-class students and, so, there is no bridging of gaps relating to diversity. Although these authors are referring to American schools, English schools have also undergone significant demographic changes, with newcomers and immigrants of varying ethnicities, as well as socio-economic backgrounds. As Hargreaves (2006) and Hargreaves and Shirley (2009) argue, the English school system remains rooted in a nineteenth-century model of schooling for an industrialising society. Thus, the English school system needs to adapt its approaches to learning in order to recognise changes within and differences amongst its student population.

Approach 3: school-based, individual or system solutions

The issue as to whether attainment gaps are a system, school or an individual problem is key to this approach. Proponents of school-based solutions point to the fact that it is important for schools to reach as many students as possible in their attempt to reduce gaps (Gregory et al. 2006, Harvey 2008), while social scientists look for solutions outside of schools to include family (Coleman 1966), faith variables (Mentzer 1988, Miller and Olson 1988, Holman and Harding 1996) and what minority and low-income students are unable to do, compared with those who flourish and are from these groups (Corbett *et al.* 2002) (See Chitpin 2019, p. 6). Jeynes (2015) found that human qualities, including faith- and family-based variables provide insight into how greater numbers of students can be empowered to succeed. Potter (2017b) also found in his case study of an English school leader identifying as a social justice leader that her motivation was, in part, faith based. Notwithstanding this, system determined barriers and supports have been theorised by research undertaken by ISLDN and their network of researchers around the globe. Their work has conceptualised the decision-making of school leaders in terms of a macro-, meso- and micro-conceptual map (Angelle 2017), which has illuminated that, in all contexts, macro-factors affect school leaders in their attempts to achieve greater equity (See Chitpin 2019, p. 6).

Approach 4: professional development strategies

Earl and Katz (2006) are concerned that school leaders may be underprepared to take part in data-based decision-making, due to a pervasive lack of expertise in this area. They are basing their evaluation on research in North America. However, evidence from our research in England finds that school leaders worry that they give agency to the weaponry that big data brings to the judgement of their school leadership. As one leader expressed it, 'The tyranny of the accountability regime leads me to make decisions that may be more about closing perceived attainment gaps than actually doing what is in the students' best interests.' This concern resonates with O'Neil (2016) and her argument that, in 'misguided' hands, data become WMD (Weapons of Math Destruction). It is a worry that the richness of data leads to an industry of analytics and target chasing that 'misses the point.'

The National Professional Qualification of Headship (NQPH) and the more recent National Professional Qualification for Executive Headship (NPQEL) in England have modules connected with data management and interpretation, as does the National Qualification for Subject Leadership (NPQSL). The extent to which these equip school leaders for managing data intelligently is contended because it could be that their greatest effect is to neoliberalise the system still further. Some school leaders who were interviewed were aware of the agency they bring to the neoliberal agenda through the expectation to perpetuate the 'tyranny of data.'

Methodology, methods and data

This paper is informed by empirical evidence collected as a result of a Canadian Social Sciences and Humanities Research Council (SSHRC) three-year grant, of which this article represents results from the first phase of the grant. This English study builds on a similar one carried out in Ontario (Chitpin 2019), identifying the challenges school leaders in England's face and the solutions they propose in making decisions to reduce achievement gaps in their school contexts. The implications this raises for their professional development are also identified and discussed.

As per the Canadian research, the survey design was guided by these three broad questions.

- How do principals use available data in making decisions to reduce achievement gaps?
- What challenges do principals face in making decisions to reduce achievement gaps in contexts of diversity?
- How do principals reflect on the decisions they make with respect to equitable outcomes? (Chitpin 2019, p. 6)

The above questions informed the evaluation of how the participating school leaders have been supported and developed professionally for such decision-making.

In employing the methodology used in Canada, this qualitative case study also served to identify the parameters of the research (Merriam 2000), since case studies are particularistic in nature in that they examine a specific instance but may also illuminate a general problem (Merriam 1998). As in

Canada, this case study is not based on induction for generating generalisations, concepts or hypotheses grounded in systematically obtained data (Abercrombie et al. 1990). Also, as Chitpin has previously argued, it goes beyond the limited notion of context employed in many case studies, as no researcher can go into a situation free from preconceptions but must fit existing perceptions into a pre-existing discourse. This study explores administrators' decisions with regards to increasing the number of students who meet educational expectations and reducing achievement gaps among subgroups of students (See Chitpin 2019, p. 6).

For this English case study, 15 candidates were nominated through the following sources; (1) school leaders who were known to the first author, and (2) word of mouth through the first author's networking. Of those 15 candidates, nine individuals agreed to participate. The schools focused on ranged from junior to post-16 education, including special provision. The participants, five women and four men, were from the Southern Authority (pseudonym), located in Southern England. These participants reflect varying backgrounds – gender, schools and years of leadership experience (ranging from 3 to 19 years). All participants provided written consent and were assured that no individuals would be identified within research dissemination.

This article describes how these nine school leaders make decisions to reduce the achievement gaps within their respective schools. This decision-making process is influenced by considerations such as economic conditions, learning styles, school-based, system-wide or individual solutions and their professional developmental support.

Data collection and analysis

The open-ended, semi-structured interview used to collect data for this study had questions that focused on; (1) the kinds of data school leaders use in order to make decisions, day to day, with respect to bridging gaps among diverse student populations, (2) the challenges they face in making these decisions and (3) how they reflect on the decisions they make with respect to equitable student outcomes. The following are samples of questions used in both the UK and Canadian contexts;

- What is your definition of an achievement gap?
- What is the nature of achievement gaps among diverse student populations in your school?
- What types of data do you have access to with respect to student achievement?
- What specific types of data do you have with respect to student achievement data for newcomers or special needs students?
- What challenges do you face in making decisions related to student achievement for newcomer/special needs students?
- What knowledge, information, data or resources are needed to assist you in making decisions for equitable student outcomes?
- What are the kinds of data-informed decisions you make on a daily basis with respect to student achievement?

These interview questions were validated and field-tested in Canada (Chitpin 2019). Interviews were audiotaped and this article strives to present the authentic voices of the participants insofar as possible. The evidence collected was analysed through collating the interviewees' answers by question, context of school, as well as coding the data in line with the management approaches for reducing achievement gaps, as outlined above. Revisiting this categorisation process, especially through the lens of the fourth approach, exploring professional development strategies, facilitated an interpretation of the data and identification of themes relevant to this special issue. These are discussed and presented in this article. Four themes from the interview data have been identified and are presented now in the Findings.

Findings

Achievement gaps: English government's definition versus school leaders' definition

In England, the government's definition regarding reducing achievement gaps refers mainly to bringing the attainment of disadvantaged students in line with their non-disadvantaged peers. The expectation is for schools to put strategies into place in order to address problems that stand in the way of closing that gap. Educators and leaders are required to account for what is working or not working in their practices.

The government uses the policy lever of premium funding for students it determines as 'disadvantaged economically' and also employs the regulator to examine schools and their leaders' effectiveness in reducing gaps. Matters of leaders' professional development and deeper reflection about the whys and wherefores of closing attainment gaps are not championed by the government in England. This laissez-faire disposition at the centre towards the professional growth of school leaders has implications for professional development of school leaders in education in England.

There was variation in the participants in this study regarding how school leaders defined achievement gaps which, in the main, reflected a difference between perceiving achievement purely in terms of attainment (often in relation to national standardised testing) and having a less quantitative lens for that achievement. Different school leaders used different data to define the gaps, while some used the same data differently to 'construct' the gaps. This was a surprising finding in the context of a government policy lever that standardises and publishes the attainment gap for each school, according to a centrally determined definition of an attainment gap. It is interesting that some school leaders work with a formula at a micro-level that is different from, or in addition to, the formula applied at a macro-level.

> For this school, the achievement gap is, I would suggest, that youngsters underperform against their peers locally and nationally. So there's an achievement gap for outcomes for the youngsters, compared to their peers at any of the local schools and nationally. There's a heightened achievement gap between boys and girls in the context of all being below expectation than average. So, my definition of an achievement gap is youngsters who are underperforming compared to those with the same experience elsewhere. (Leader G)

The evidence suggests that longer-serving leaders are more likely to be less compliant with regards to the national formula. This may imply a greater confidence, the implications of which, for headteacher development, is that early-career school leaders have permission to learn their own supplementary measures of success for enabling greater equity.

There was an evident contrast between leaders who defined gaps as a phenomenon between different groups or cohorts of students and those who saw gaps in terms of what a student achieves in comparison with a national standard. In England, as mentioned above, there are age-related expectations that are standardised nationally. At age 11, it is known as the 'Magic 100,' which is what primary school children learn and what they are expected to achieve in their national standardised tests. At 16, there is a standard pass (Grade 4) and a strong pass (Grade 5), which students know is the benchmark. (NB: remember these are norm referenced and determined through comparable outcomes methods).

Those leaders perceiving gaps between 'categories' of students would generally use the dominant indicator in England of economic disadvantage, although some leaders would also look at gaps relating to gender and ethnic differences, as well as starting points – which would be categorised as low attaining on entry to the school, middle attaining and high attaining. These categories could also be applied to the groupings of gender and ethnicity, where used. In primary schools, the month in the year of birth could also be a data set because it is found that 'summer borns' in the English system appear to relatively underperform compared with children born earlier in the academic year. Furthermore, these leaders might also compare the achievement of chosen 'categories' of children in comparison with national standards/norms.

Boys significantly underperform compared to girls. High attainers on entry significantly underperform against where the national picture expects them to perform. Low attaining on entry are the one group who make "ok" progress. It's still not positive but, compared to their peers, low attaining on entry are those who make better progress than the rest. (Leader D)

Leader D illuminates how granular the application of the data can become in analysing gaps perceived to be existing in a school and how it is influencing the school leader's decision-making. Thus, we have a leader giving agency to the hegemony of the English performativity landscape and his/her use of the data in this way leads to decisions about where leadership attention needs to be addressed. The evidence also illustrates that Leader D is less nuanced in understanding the differences between equity and equality than other leaders in the research sample. This leads us to another finding.

Addressing achievement gaps: equity or equality?

Unlike Leader D, Leader A recognised that the drive for equity was to compensate for the disadvantaged start in life that some of the students had, rather than allocating resources in an equal way. Social justice for this leader was more about positive discrimination towards the disadvantaged to achieve greater equity. This leader went on to explain how this understanding of reacting to deficits in children's lives and intervening to allow them greater equity could be better achieved if led more proactively.

> What's coming more and more to fruition over my leadership journey is we work in a world, which is forever reactive. How can we get to a point where we could be proactive about intervention again? How do you equip professionals with the knowledge to intervene before the crisis has reached? (Leader A)

It is interesting to note that, generally, where leaders felt they and their school were doing well in ensuring equitable student outcomes, they tended not to use academic indicators for perceived gaps, but for measures of equity. Although (s)he used the terms 'equity' and 'equality' differently from the way, these terms are used in this article, leader E said, 'We're about equally differentiating the allocation of resource according to need rather than equity of distribution.' (S)he is noting the difference between using funding to apportion resources equally or dispersing them in a way that positively discriminates towards those with greatest need. Instead of spending the pupil premium in an equally distributed way to all, the money is used to achieve equity of outcome in giving a greater proportion of the resources to the most disadvantaged.

This choice to 'level-up' those representing the greatest gap clearly impacts the decision-making of this school leader. There are also implications for the professional development of school leaders more widely, and these are two-fold. Firstly, it is to improve understanding of the nuanced differences between equity and equality of opportunity. Aligned with this is the earlier argument regarding the contrast between social justice and social mobility. Furthermore, how can school leaders learn to transition from a reactive mode of leadership and management towards a more proactive one, where the anticipation of future achievement gaps leads to strategies earlier on to more effectively predict and, thus, intervene.

Addressing achievement gaps: raising aspiration

Leader G states,

> Probably the major challenge is raising students' expectations of what they can achieve, their parents' expectations of what they can achieve, and some staff expectations. It's not so prevalent, but we did battle and will continue to battle with what more can you expect from these "types" of kids. And the language around our kids of low expectation. And then what is the pedagogy? What is the leadership required to address those low aspirations. (Leader G)

This leader's comment reflects a sentiment common to nearly all those who were interviewed, although perceptions on where the 'locus-of-control' lay in order to address the matter did vary.

One school leader, however, expressed a concern about the tyranny of performativity and the normalising of high expectations being a threat to the well-being of those for whom we should most care for. Leader I says, 'It increases their sense of how unequal things are if you keep expecting for them what cannot be achieved.... I worry that it can increase a sense of alienation.'

Some leaders interviewed had a different view from those who espoused, as Leader G does, that the responsibility lies with the school to raise aspirations. These leaders felt that the causes of low aspiration lay outside the school and the remedy was too great to ask school leaders to reverse the situation. As Leader E expresses it:

> We obviously endeavour to get the best outcomes we possibly can for them. But, for some of our young people it is about addressing, for example, the gap around their social, emotional and mental health needs which, then, in turn, leads to better engagement in their English and their maths curriculum, which, in turn, leads to better qualification outcomes....

Such a perspective influences this school leader to make decisions about engaging with elements outside of his/her 'authority.' The 'control' that others can have on that young person becomes the focus of the school's leadership and decision-making:

> We obviously draw upon the government's guidance ... we recognise those. However, in order to get the outcomes that we need for our young people, we have to work "right on the edge" of those expectations because of us bridging that multi-agency challenge..... So, therefore, knowing what social care policies are in place, also health, what capacity they have, and what they can and can't do. (Leader B)

This school leader, in contrast to Leader G, focuses on the locus of control resting with themselves and their school, and thus their staff, to strive for social justice. It is a big task and the evidence implies the preparation for taking on that task comes more from personal conviction and life-narrative than from formal professional development. When talking about when, what or who supported them most to make decisions about how to challenge low expectations and battle cultures of deficit aspiration, leaders identified influences of a personal kind rather than more formal professional development opportunities. For example

> I am a humanistic leader who has little time for government nonsense that we have to conform to. I read a lot and move on when theories become buzz words.... My background gave me the confidence to battle the motivations of others' materialism, work ethic and status. I am who I am and the children are my primary influence on my leadership. (Leader F)

The extent to which formal Continuing Professional Development (CPD) can provide school leaders with instruction about 'being' rather than 'doing' is a key question and one that we should like to research more fully. In the meantime, the findings informing our reflections imply that leaders have drawn more on who they have become from their life-stories to give them the conviction to 'fight' injustice and address inequities. Faith, upbringing and their own schooling experience appear to have a greater influence than formally provided, or accredited, professional input. That input, with respect to them increasing their professional courage, most identified as coming from learning on the job and nearly all referenced the value of networking with other school leaders.

Networking and management of student achievement

> Going beyond the school is really important.... I wasn't sure and no matter what I heard here (my school), I still wasn't sure. I always had somebody else I could call on for a conversation with another school leader, which reveals something else to think about, not necessarily to do, but to think about. (Leader C)

Having other school leaders in a network of some form was important to the school leaders interviewed, in supporting their decision-making. One explained how it helped them think about what they might not be prompted to think about within their own school setting. Clearly, it supports being exposed to ideas and practice in another context that may or may not be applicable in one's own. As Leader I expressed it, 'you learn more about what you are by what you are not.' Another school leader spoke of the value of being linked up with others, which, in this case, was via a consultant her/his school had worked with. As Leader D notes, 'He's linked me with people where it's quite interesting to see what they are doing and how they are doing it. So that's a good example of where networking can be both positive or potentially negative.'

What Leader D argued can be potentially negative is the unthinking way in which (s)he and colleagues may respond. (S)he gave an example of where the school had become too energised in manipulating the data and had missed the point because more time was spent measuring the achievement gaps than improving the learning for the disadvantaged and, thus, not closing any gaps. (S)he described it as

> ... finding themselves bogged down in spending all the time and energy on analyzing how near kids are. How many boys are there? How many pupils are there? What's the cut compared to national average ... but the really, really challenging bit here is the collective working to get the kids to where they can be and where they deserve to be.

Becoming so obsessed by data that it leads to a paralysis of the sort of activity that actually adds value is evidently an implication for leaders making decisions about deployment of teacher and management time; it is a risk that could come from networking, which leads to energy being spent on comparing oneself with other schools/leaders rather than spending the energy applying the learning to one's own context. Therefore, the professional development of school leaders needs to support them in keeping a sense of proportion about being data-driven, data-informed or data-led information. This research has found that the school leaders in England rarely express that they do not have enough data available to them; on the contrary, many say there is too much. The challenge is generally deciding which data is the most pertinent and valuable to use. This is, once more, a significant implication for school leadership professional development.

The most significant benefit from networking is to disrupt school-centric mindsets. It prevents an individual school leader and the site-based team from thinking within their own experience and falling prey to believing that their way of serving young people and, in particular, disadvantaged learners is the 'only way.' The dominance of market ideology in England's educational system perpetuates this risk, as schools become isolated and fragmented from each other due to competition among schools. Markets work in terms of winners and losers and this can increase the sense of isolation the losers feel and, in the context of this article, the schools that are serving the most challenging of young people, who are often the most disadvantaged and disempowered within the English society. Hence, one of the leaders interviewed called for a change in the system.

> ... to solve the problem and meet the needs of the young people, the system has to change. To work in isolation or in silo with these young people, you'll have successes, but you're not going to have it fully close the gap or change things for those families that you're working with, but you might have the capacity to change things if you work on a much larger scale. (Leader A)

This leader espouses the value of being part of a formal network of schools, which in her/his case, in the English landscape, is a multi-academy trust, where state-funded 'independent' schools are networked together through a legal framework.

Conclusion

Making decisions about what evidence is of greatest use to a school leader's decision-making processes for social justice requires considerable reflection. This research has found a need for England's school leaders to consider reflecting more deeply about the whys and wherefores of closing attainment gaps. It is akin to a reflexive activity where the school leader is deciding about what decisions s/he needs to make and how are they going to be made. Reflexivity in school leadership deepens school leaders' evaluation of self and their school (Potter 2017a). The quality of reflection improves and supports the leaders in their decision-making. It can also encourage criticality.

Developing such professional critique early on in a school leader's career is something identified in the findings, alongside attending to the nuances in understanding the difference between equity and equality. A professionally attuned perception of that difference will support school leaders in their decision-making for social justice. It will also develop a more proactive approach to leadership and management when it comes to strategies for enabling greater equity across diverse student needs. Whether the courage to fight for this can come from formal professional development or only from experience (professional and life-experience) was not sufficiently illuminated in the research data, whereas the value of networking certainly was. Networking provides developmental opportunity to avoid the 'dangers of homophily, dominance dynamics and echo chambers' (Syed 2019, p. 205) that potentially exist in their place of work; it can also help ameliorate the negative consequences of the market competition within the English school landscape that leads to winners and losers. It is a landscape that is not conducive to closing gaps and achieving increased equity.

In addition, as the challenge of leading schools increases in complexity (Gronn 2003, Hawkins and James 2016), supporting school leaders in their decision-making becomes all the more crucial. Professional development that supports the leader in their technical proficiency to analyse the data is insufficient on its own. 'Training' in statistical analysis alone does not necessarily develop a deeper consideration of defining what the evidence is illuminating. The gathering, collating and interpretation of the data may not encourage a contemplation of the values and perspectives driving a definition of an achievement gap, which in turn informs an interrogation of notions of equity and equality. Therefore, continuing professional development that recognises problem-solving for social justice is required. It is no easy feat. It is a complicated matter supporting a school leader in making decisions that will not inadvertently widen achievement gaps, further disadvantage the disadvantaged and perpetuate inequality. The findings from this research reveal that a professional able to analyse *why* and *how* they lead, as well as *what* they do, and to generate such knowledge in a networked way, will improve their decision-making. This is because they interrogate the values upon which their decisions are made, through examination of prevailing assumptions, and investigation of the purposes shaping these decisions. Consequently, we argue that professional development for school leadership needs to involve professional growth that comes from developing leaders' use of a framework that assists in eliminating error from their day-to-day decision-making. One such framework is the Objective Knowledge Growth Framework (OKGF), based on Popper's critical rationalism (Chitpin 2016), with which the second phase of our research is concerned.

Disclosure statement

No potential conflict of interest was reported by the authors.

References

Abercrombie, N., Hill, S., and Turner, B.S., 1990. *The Penguin dictionary of sociology*. London, UK: Allen Lane.
Angelle, P., Ed, 2017. *A global perspective of social justice leadership for school principals*. Charlotte, NC: Information Age Publishing.
Angus, L., 2012. Teaching within and against the circle of privilege: reforming teachers, reforming schools. *Journal of Education Policy*, 27 (2), 231–251.
Ball, S.J., 2008. *The education debate*. Bristol, UK: Policy Press.
Ball, S.J., 2012. *Global Education Inc.: new policy networks and the neoliberal imaginary*. Abingdon, UK: Routledge.
Banks, J.A. and Banks, C.A., 1995. *Handbook of research on multicultural education*. New York: Macmillan.
Bernak, F., Chi-Ying, R., and Siroskey-Sabdo, L.A., 2005. Empowerment groups for academic success. *Professional School Counseling*, 8 (5), 377–389.
Bourdieu, P. and Passeron, J.-C., 1977. *Reproduction in education, society and culture*. London, UK: Sage.
Chideya, F., 1995. *Don't believe the hype: fighting the cultural misinformation about African Americans*. New York: Plume.

Chitpin, S., 2016. *Popper's approach to education: A cornerstone of teaching and learning.* New York: Routledge.
Chitpin, S., 2019. Principal's decision-making in bridging the student achievement gap. *International Journal of Leadership in Education.* doi:10.1080/13603124.2019.1613568.
Coleman, J.S., 1966. *Equality of educational opportunity.* Washington, DC: US Department of Health, Education & Welfare.
Corbett, D., Wilson, B., and William, B., 2002. *Effort and excellence in urban classrooms.* New York: Teachers College Press.
Earl, L.M. and Katz, S., 2006. *Leading schools in a data-rich world: harnessing data for school improvement.* Thousand Oaks, CA: Corwin Press.
Fischer, C., et al., 1996. *Inequality By Design.* Princeton, New Jersey: Princeton University Press.
Gregory, A., Nygreen, K., and Moran, D., 2006. The discipline gap and the normalization of failure. In: P.A. Noguera and J.Y. Wing, eds.. *Unfinished business: closing the racial achievement gap in our schools.* San Francisco, CA: Jossey-Bass, 121–150.
Gronn, P., 2003. *The new work of educational leaders: changing leadership practice in an era of school reform.* London, UK: SAGE.
Hargreaves, A. and Shirley, D., 2009. *The fourth way: the inspiring future for educational change.* Thousand Oaks, CA: Corwin.
Hargreaves, D.H., 2006. *A new shape for schooling.* London, UK: Specialist Schools and Academies Trust.
Harvey, W.B., 2008. The weakest link: A commentary on the connections between K-12 and higher education. *American Behavioral Scientist,* 51 (7), 972–983.
Hawkins, M. and James, C. (2016). Theorising schools as organisations: isn't it all about complexity? Paper presented at American Educational Research Association Annual Meeting, Washington, DC, 8-12 April, 2016.
Herrnstein, R. and Murray, C., 1994. *The Bell Curve: intelligence and Class Structure in American Life.* New York: The Free Press.
Holman, T.B. and Harding, J.R., 1996. The teaching of nonmarital sexual abstinence and members' sexual attitudes and behaviors: the case of the Latter-day Saints. *Review of Religious Research,* 38 (1), 51–60.
Jeynes, W., 1999. The effects of religious commitment on the academic achievement of Black and Hispanic children. *Urban Education,* 34 (4), 458–479.
Jeynes, W., 2003. The effects of Black and Hispanic twelfth graders living in intact families and being religious on their academic achievement. *Urban Education,* 38 (1), 35–57.
Jeynes, W., 2015. A meta-analysis on the factors that best reduce the achievement gap. *Education & Urban Society,* 47 (5), 523–554.
Lynch, S., et al., 2017. *Keeping your head: NFER analysis of headteacher retention.* Slough, UK: National Foundation For Educational Research.
Mentzer, M.S., 1988. Religion and achievement motivation in the United States: A structural analysis. *Sociological Focus,* 21 (4), 307–316.
Merriam, S.B., 1998. *Qualitative research and case study applications in education.* San Francisco, CA: Jossey-Bass Publishers.
Merriam, S.B., 2000. *A guide to research for educators and trainers of adults.* Malabar, FL: Krieger Publishing Co.
Miller, B.C. and Olson, T.D., 1988. Sexual attitudes and behavior of high school students' relation to background and contextual factors. *Journal of Sex Research,* 24, 194–200.
O'Neil, C., 2016. *Weapons of math destruction: how big data increases inequality and threatens democracy.* New York: Crown Publishers.
Popper, K., 1979. *Objective knowledge.* Oxford, UK: Oxford University Press.
Potter, I., 2017a. Developing social justice leadership through reflexivity. In: P. Angelle, ed.. *A global perspective of social justice leadership for school principals.* Charlotte, NC: Information Age Publishing, 293–302.
Potter, I., 2017b. Change in Context and Identity: the Case of an English School Leader. In: P. ANGELLE, ed.. *A Global Perspective of Social Justice Leadership for School Principals.* Information Age Publishing. 231–250.
Rothstein, R., 2004. *Class and schools: using social, economic, & educational reform to close the black-white achievement gap.* New York: Columbia University.
Skalski, A.K. and Romero, M., 2011. Data-based decision-making. *Principal Leadership,* 11 (5), 12–16.
Smith, N. (2019). Neoliberalism. *Encyclopedia Britannica.* Retrieved from: https://www.britannicacom/topic/neoliberalism [Accessed 26 January 2020]
Syed, M., 2019. *Rebel ideas: the power of diverse thinking.* London, UK: John Murray.
Thrupp, M. (2007) Education 'inconvenient truth': Part one- persistent middle class advantage New Zealand Journal of Teacher's Work, 4 (2), 77–88

Leading in socially just schools

Promoting socially just schools through professional learning: lessons from four US principals in rural contexts

Pamela S. Angelle, Mary Lynne Derrington and Alex N. Oldham

ABSTRACT
The concept of professional learning, with the principal as lead learner working towards the institutional goal of social justice, is the focus of this descriptive qualitative study. The purpose was to examine the actions and behaviours of US rural principals as they demonstrate professional learning to ensure social justice for marginalised students. Multiple iterations of coding the field notes and interview data resulted in the following themes: Professional Learning in a Social Context; Professional Learning in a Culture of Care; and Professional Learning for Positive Change. This study confirmed that social justice practices for marginalised children may be taught by leading through informal professional learning and is accomplished through learning in a social context for others to observe and hear, development of a culture of care, and focus on positive change in beliefs and attitudes. Professional learning that is embedded in the daily work of schools is the most viable strategy for rural teachers to incorporate social justice practices in their daily work. One implication from these findings is that principals must first become social justice role models and competently practice socially just behaviours themselves. Based on findings from this study, a model for professional learning is offered.

Professional development has been cited throughout the literature as an effective tool for improving teacher practice (Darling-Hammond and McLaughlin 2011; Zepeda 2014). More specifically, professional development that is job embedded (Zepeda, 2015), reflective (Creemers et al. 2013), and engages the principal as the lead learner in the school (Zepeda et al. 2015) is most effective in bringing about school improvement. More recently, research also has examined the concept of professional learning, particularly as it relates to the professional development of leaders. While professional learning and professional development are similar concepts, the distinctions between the two are clear. Professional development is centred in practice and responsibility, is more formal, and is transmitted uni-directionally; that is, from the presenter to the recipient. Furthermore, while professional development is an activity that is short term and passive, Labone and Long (2016) describe professional learning as

> a more internal focus or constructivist approach in which the teacher becomes an active participant who is responsible for his or her own learning, and is instrumental in constructing his or her change within their context. The shift to learning reflects a growth model. (p. 55)

The 'internal focus' implies the need for reflection, thus, describing a process that is 'embedded within the person and the social context of the school' (Veelen et al. 2017, p. 393). Professional learning is centred within the individual (Veelen et al. 2017). Moreover, professional learning is active, looks to move beyond the status quo, challenges negative beliefs, and often involves a change in attitudes (Labone and Long 2016).

The concept of professional learning, with the principal as lead learner working towards the institutional goal of social justice, is the focus of this study. Professional learning that is informal, often unconscious, and focused on changes in attitudes and beliefs is described as 'learning that we are not aware of when it occurs but is acknowledged later on reflection upon incidents, practices, and processes that we have participated in or witnessed' (Mejiuni, Cranton, and Taiwo 2015, as cited in Mejiuni 2019, p. 11). Framed by the social justice work of Theoharis (2009), this research is guided by the following question: How do four rural US principals implement informal professional learning to promote socially just schools for marginalised children?

Challenges of rural schooling

Policy makers and researchers have suggested that one remedy for the problems facing rural communities is to create better rural schools (Huang and Howley 1991, Stern 1994, Kannapel and DeYoung 1999, Schmidt et al. 2002, Gibbs 2005), and better partnerships between rural schools and communities to help initiate more economic success (Muyeed 1982). However, rural schools are faced with many of the same barriers to success that confront rural communities.

Because of geographic isolation (Abel and Sewell 1999) and the lack of professional credentialing of teachers (Malloy and Allen 2007, Burton and Johnson 2010) rural schools have historically faced difficulties in educating students. As more people moved into urban areas, forgotten rural communities and schools fell behind in policy focus, research, and funding (Bassett 2003). As Flora et al. (2015) suggested, 'Our society has become so deeply urbanized that we almost assume urbanization to be natural law' (p. 23). This assertion was reiterated by Lyson and Falk (1993) who suggested,

> Rural programs too often are small versions of urban programs not specially suited to rural needs. Because of the low density and small scale of rural efforts, programs often fail when they are not especially attentive to rural needs. Urban administrative rule often results in high cost for rural programs. (p. 248)

Consequently, national educational policy largely focus on suburban and urban schools when crafting policy. When President Clinton signed Goals 2000 into law, Title I had the responsibility of developing standards and accurate assessments to receive government funds, therefore beginning the standardisation of America's schools regardless of their geography. The new measures, however, had unintended consequences for rural schools because to meet the new standards of equal access, rural schools were forced to consolidate resources (Seal and Harmon 1995). The consolidation of resources, including staff, placed further stress on rural schools to meet the needs of students they were struggling to educate in the first place. Therefore, while one of the major policy goals of Goals 2000 was 'to ensure the needed equitable educational opportunities' (Stedman and Riddle 1998, p. 1), the policy indirectly created further inequity in rural schools, an unintended consequence.

While the standardisation of education took place, research became available to policymakers about the difficulties rural schools might have when implementing broad reforms. A report by the National Rural Development Institute noted that programmes in rural schools designed specifically to help at-risk students were often not available as a result of distance of services, barriers of topography in certain locations, or turnover in trained staff (Helge 1990). Later research on rural schools and the problems they faced when implementing standards-based reforms affirmed the concerns of scholars before the movement began (Darling-Hammond 2010; Rostosky et al. 2003, Peyser and Costrell 2004; Jimerson 2005, Kosciw and Diaz 2008, Ghazali et al. 2009). Nonetheless, the Department of Education, guided by initiatives from the President, continued to move forward with standards-based reforms that largely focused on urban and suburban schools (Baker and Foote 2006), even though 1 in 5 students in America attended a rural school (U.S. Census Bureau 2010).

No Child Left Behind (Act, N.C.L.B., 2002), and *Every Student Succeeds Act* (Act, E.S.S.A., 2015) continued the standards-based reforms started in the early 1990 s. These education policies emphasised creating equitable opportunities for all students (U.S. Department of Education 2014), regardless of the research that underscored that rural schools historically underachieved in educating marginalised student populations. Not surprisingly, research shows that rural schools have continued to fall short of providing equitable opportunities for their students even with the mandates passed as a part of standards-based reforms. As a result, rural schools must manage professional development for teachers with scarce resources and little support. This increases the role of principals as the source of transmission for professional learning. Thus, principal behaviours are often the foundation for learning values, influencing beliefs, and changing culture.

Principal behaviours and teacher learning

Scholars have examined principal behaviours in all community types that are successful at promoting equitable opportunities and positive student outcomes for all students. However, because of the unique nature of rural schools, principal behaviours that help promote positive student outcomes in urban and suburban settings may not apply in rural contexts. Much of the literature that has examined rural schools focused on the lack of rural schools' resources available to address some education issues, including retention of quality staff or the lack of extracurricular activities present for students who attend rural schools. Overall, however, literature concerning effective rural principal behaviours for promoting positive student outcomes is sparse, and even less available when the focus is on social justice and marginalised students.

One strategy to better support marginalised students and raise awareness of equitable issues is through principal provided professional development opportunities that educate teachers about problems faced by marginalised students. Peters (2002) case study of three schools that tried to accelerate their inclusive environment provided professional development on the importance of developing positive teacher-student relationships. Furthermore, Burstein *et al.* (2004) examined how school leadership in southern California moved their schools towards more inclusive practices. The authors noted that professional development effectively 'assisted in teachers change efforts' (Burstein *et al.* 2004, p. 111) and that 'inservices were helpful in establishing a comfort level with inclusive practices' (p. 111).

Hoppey and McLeskey (2013) case study of principal leadership in an effective inclusive school, found that providing high-quality professional development promoted positive student-teacher relationships and helped create a more inclusive environment for the school. Unfortunately, due to a lack of resources, rural principals are often limited in their abilities to offer professional development opportunities, which scholars have opined may contribute to the continued inequitable treatment of marginalised students in rural contexts (Peyser and Costrell 2004). Lacking formal professional development which focuses on the needs of marginalised children, the impact of professional learning from principal's behaviours becomes increasingly important.

We examine professional learning through the same constructivist approach as Veelen *et al.* (2017) and Labone and Long (2016). This lens prioritises professional learning over professional development and views learning as socially constructed by the context where the learning takes place (Labone and Long 2016). Rogers (2014) views this type of learning as informal, including 'unconscious influences' (p. 17) taking place in the 'cultural contexts of life' (p. 29). Moreover:

> through informal learning, we are acquiring a set of values, we are being socialised into a particular culture. This is why informal learning is so important, both for life and also for formal learning. It determines the values, assumptions and expectations we bring to all forms of non-formal and formal learning; it determines our aspirations, our motivations. (p. 17)

Informal professional learning may be acquired through a number of strategies which might include conversation, role modelling, or mentoring (Le Clus 2011). Additional methods of informal learning include observing peers and supervisors, reflection, and reading pertinent materials (Marsick et al. 2006). In all of these instances, knowledge is acquired through some type of interaction with another, takes place in an informal setting, and is shaped by the context in which the learning takes place. Thus, in contexts which are isolated and where funding is scant, professional learning may be an essential component to meeting organisational goals, particularly when those goals focus on enhancing social justice for marginalised students, which may require changes in beliefs and attitudes.

Conceptual frame

Theoharis (2009) social justice leadership framework is a useful lens for examining the social justice practices of principals because it clearly defines what practices of principals are most helpful when creating and maintaining a socially just school culture. While Theoharis (2009) examined the social justice leadership of urban principals, this study will focus on rural principal practices. Specifically, this study will focus on successful socially just practices that advance inclusion, access, and opportunity for all, improve the core learning process, and create a climate of belonging through professional learning.

Other studies have used Theoharis's (2007, 2009) social justice leadership framework to examine the equity practices of urban principals. DeMatthews and Mawhinney (2014) used Theoharis's framework to examine the challenges of two urban principals who worked to create a more inclusive school culture for students with disabilities. Auerbach (2009) turned to Theoharis to examine family and community engagement of principals with Latinos to better promote a more equitable and culturally responsive school. Auerbach (2009) found that principals, like those studied by Theoharis (2007, 2009)), were motivated by an ethical commitment to students.

Albritton et al. (2017) utilised Theoharis' framework to investigate how rural principals who identified themselves as social justice leaders, perceived student diversity, specifically LGBTQ students, and how they maintained an inclusive environment for all students. Further studies found that while rural principals claimed to be socially just, their practices revealed otherwise in Bishop and McClellan (2016) research concerning the lack of social justice leadership for LGBTQ students in rural schools. Their findings highlighted that rural social justice leaders may have a different definition ascribed to social justice than what is found in the social justice literature. These researchers found that LGBTQ students were more successful in rural schools that promoted a sense of belonging. This finding aligned with other research completed about LGBTQ students in other school contexts. Feeling safe and a part of an inclusive environment could lead to more positive student outcomes for LGBTQ students in any educational context (Bishop and McClellan 2016).

Theoharis's (2007, 2009) social justice leadership framework has been used by scholars to explore the supports and barriers principals may face when leading for social justice but also to determine if the leadership practices of principals are socially just. Theoharis's (2007, 2009) study, however, was not inclusive of all marginalised student populations nor geographic areas. His study did not investigate principals in rural settings. Theoharis's (2007) study on social justice leadership theory concluded by stating that, 'areas for future research could involve an expansion of the current study [on social justice leadership] to include rural leaders' (p. 249). Literature underscores the contextual challenges rural principals face when promoting equity for marginalised students in the southern United States. Therefore, this study, framed by Theoharis's (2007, 2009) social justice leadership research will expand social justice literature in two ways by (a) examining rural social justice principals and (b) examining their actions to ensure equity for marginalised students as a whole.

Methods

The descriptive qualitative study examines the actions and behaviours of rural principals as they demonstrate professional learning to ensure social justice for marginalised students. Purposeful sampling was used to select principals who served secondary schools that were located in a rural setting, as described by the US government Johnson Codes 6 and 7, located in a southeastern US state, and who lead schools where at least 15% of students were marginalised (i.e., students of colour, poverty, non-citizens, disabilities, or questioning). A final criterion was to select principals in schools with similar demographics to minimise the impact of extraneous factors. Our final sample of four principals were invited to participate in the study and all agreed. Tables 1 and 2 illustrate the school demographics and the principal characteristics.

For purposes of this study, a semi-structured interview protocol was utilised to support 'discovering and portraying the multiple views of the case' and to focus on the interview as the 'main road to multiple realities' (Stake 1995, p. 64). To ensure reliability, a protocol pilot test was developed, submitted to content experts, and then piloted before official data collection.

The interview questions created were based on Flick's (2013) two types of questions: open and theory-driven. Some questions were designed to be open so that interviewees could speak freely about their leadership and include the contextual factors that could impact their leadership practices, guide their professional learning, and drive decision making. Secondly, theory-driven questions were constructed that addressed principal behaviours and the values underlying those behaviours. In addition, as the interview questions were created, researchers kept in mind the goal 'of building a relationship of trust between the interviewer and interviewee that leads to a more give-and-take in the conversation' (Rubin & Rubin 2011, p. 37).

Principals were provided with an introductory statement of consent before beginning the interview to ensure that they agreed to participate, to confirm that their identity would be kept confidential, and to reiterate that data retrieved from their responses will be used in the study. After the research was explained to respondents, initial interviews commenced and lasted approximately 60 minutes, as did most follow up interviews. The first interview established a baseline for data and follow up interviews were conducted until saturation was reached.

Observations

Merriam (2009) asserted that observations, like interviews, were a primary source of data in qualitative research. Observations require 'practically all of the senses – seeing, hearing, feeling, and smelling.' (Flick 2013. p. 308). Observations were included in this study to allow researchers to observe professional learning that is both unconscious and values driven. Professional learning is embedded in the social context of the school; thus, observations recorded in field notes were determined as the most appropriate method of data collection.

Table 1. School demographics.

Student Ethnicity & Demographics	High School 1	High School 2	High School 3	High School 4
Ethnicity				
European American	77–79%	81–82%	81–82%	74–76%
African American	18–20%	10–11%	1–2%	5–6%
Hispanic or Latino	1%	5–6%	15–16%	19–20%
Asian	>1%	1%	1%	>1%
Demographic				
Economically Disadvantaged	75–80%	45%	30%	60%
Immigrants	1%	>10%	12%	7–10%
LGTBQ	1%	3%	1%	2%
Student enrolment	350–450	850–950	1000–1100	700–800

Table 2. Principal demographic data.

Categories	Gender	Years of Experience	Years of Experience in school
Principal 1	M	17	8
Principal 2	M	26	17
Principal 3	M	24	5
Principal 4	F	29	6

For purposes of this study, researchers utilised non-participant observation. Flick (2014) stated that the non-participant observer 'maintains a distance from the observed events to avoid influencing them' (p. 309). Observations were conducted to immerse researchers in the setting of the study. Observations were set after researchers spent time in the school building and among staff to ensure multiple opportunities to observe professional learning in a variety of school social contexts.

Each principal was observed in various contexts, including staff meetings, student interactions, meetings of professional learning communities (PLCs), parent and staff meetings, and classroom observations. Field notes were recorded using an observation protocol, which was used to guide and focus the observations. This method helped to align field notes with literature and responses from the interviews. Included in the field notes were descriptions, quotations, and observer comments.

Findings

All interview transcripts and all observation field notes were inserted into a qualitative software programme for analysis. The NVivo program organised the codes of interviews and observations of each school. By examining data collected from various sources, findings were corroborated across data sets and potential bias was reduced. Multiple iterations of coding resulted in the following themes: Professional Learning in a Social Context; Professional Learning in a Culture of Care; and Professional Learning for Positive Change. Moreover, coding allowed for trustworthiness which in some cases confirmed the interviews and in other cases quite clearly disconfirmed the words of the principals (Elliott 2005, Riessman, 2008). Following a report of findings, we viewed the findings through the lens of Theoharis' keys as well as considered how these findings may align with socially just leadership.

Professional learning in a social context

While researchers agree that informal, professional learning does not take place in a classroom (Tannebaum, Beard, McNall, & Salas, 2010, Noe et al. 2013), informal learning does takes place within the daily practice of the work setting. Informal learning involves other people and learning activities as part of an interplay between people (Kyndt et al. 2016). As formal professional development was often cost prohibitive with the limited resources of rural schools as well as the distance to cities which might have access to formal learning, professional learning took place through observation, listening, and in groups (Eraut 2004). The principals in this study, likewise, practiced informal learning within the social context of the school.

Observations of Principal 1 found that he knew students by their name and, moreover, also knew about the students' personal lives. While standing in the hallways between classes, Principal 1 was observed asking students about their jobs and family, or commenting about the big play they made in the previous week's sports game or a solo performed for the chorus performance. Principal 1 viewed this simple action, interwoven into his practices as a leader, as creating an inclusive environment: 'the main thing is understanding that every kid that comes through my high school door is valuable and we have to do our best to influence them positively.' The school's environment was created or developed to make all students feel like they belonged.

Principal 2 promoted an inclusive school environment through a social activity with teachers that was not only useful but was entertaining as well. This professional learning activity gave teachers autonomy, while also providing them with resources to help marginalised students, involve the teachers in school activities, and fulfill the professional development requirements of the school district. Principal 2 called it 'DIY PD BINGO.' Each teacher received a sheet of paper that looked like a bingo card, with five columns across and five rows down all filled with professional development activities. To meet requirements from the district, a teacher had to have bingo, or 5 across, up and down, or diagonally, by the end of the year. Choices provided included 'Eat lunch in the cafeteria with students and write a reflection,' 'write and send a positive note to a student or parent,' and 'sponsor a club and write a reflection about your experience.' DIY PD BINGO, though required, was a professional learning experience that required both action and reflection on the part of the teacher. Principal 2 believed he effectively promoted the relationships that could help create more positive student outcomes among marginalised student populations.

In much the same way, Principal 3 understood the importance of a positive school culture for ensuring equity, and used a democratic process to ensure that all staff were 'a part of the effort' when he remarked that 'we want to make sure that every student has every opportunity that any other student may have regardless of SES, race, or whatever your identity may be.' As part of professional learning in a social space, school staff worked as a group to write a technology grant, which was awarded, to improve teaching. Moreover, the implementation of an academic support block was led by a committee of multiple staff members to ensure the process went as smoothly as possible. Administration sat together in the cafeteria for lunch to discuss issues that concerned the school and how to address them collaboratively. With many staff members engaging in leadership decisions, Principal 3 believed he empowered them and was able to more effectively provide positive relationships to students to create the positive school culture he wanted:

> We stress positive relationships with kids for them to be successful, so those are key. I can confidently say that every employee in this building wants kids to be happy when they walk through the door. It's a collaborative effort. It takes everyone pulling in the same direction for the kids to feel safe and happy when they are here. But it also helps create a sense of belonging when they come to school.

Giving the teachers 'ownership' and 'buy-in' for creating a positive environment where teachers worked diligently, implemented high expectations and developed positive teacher-student relationships was also a goal set by Principal 4. By distributing leadership decisions and creating more 'ownership,' Principal 4 created professional learning in a collaborative environment where teachers helped each other solve problems:

> It's more of a team effort now on the high school level. We've done a good job of coming off that island and being team players by making sure those doors are always open for other people to come in, and that's one good thing with our school system as well. Overall, it's a team effort not only in this school but district-wide. Everyone is expected to be better every year.

Professional learning in a social context requires functioning as a team, building knowledge as a group, and working towards the organisational goal of a socially just school together. The social context of professional learning gives everyone, not just the marginalised children, a sense of community in working for something greater than themselves.

Professional learning in a culture of care

Le Clus (2011) noted that learning in everyday settings (also called situated learning) 'focuses on the interactive relationship [between] co-workers and their work environment' (p. 358). When this relationship is minimised, disrespected or in some way one group is privileged over another, social injustice occurs (Mejiuni 2019). Professional learning, as an incidental informal type of learning, may impact learners only after reflection at some point following the learning. One example is promoting socially just school cultures through observations of the leader's modelling of care.

Principal 1 promoted a culture of care through modelling the behaviours he hoped to see. He stressed the importance of effectively modelling to staff and students his expectations and the importance of advancing social justice. Principal 1 had a personal philosophy in which he treated his students and their families like he would his own: 'I go the extra mile for them. That's who I am.' He saw modelling positive relationships as an effective practice for conveying to teachers that they were expected to develop positive student-teacher relationships to create equity for marginalised students regardless of outside factors.

Likewise, Principal 3 believed that positive teacher-student relationships were one of the most effective ways to ensure equity for students. The practice of promoting positive teacher-student relationships started with him. He modelled for his teachers the relationships he wished for them to have as well:

> I get to know my students. I talk to them a lot on a daily basis particularly those that you identify as struggling for whatever reason, whether it's a student who falls into the categories you are talking about today or otherwise, I ask about what's going on in their life and we get to know one another. If nothing else just saying "Hey" to a kid may be exactly what they need. I'm not necessarily going to counsel them about it, but I do want them to know someone here cares about them. It's about creating positive relationships.

He explained his thoughts on creating positive student outcomes, which started with having positive relationships with every student regardless of their background:

> We really emphasize forming positive relationships with kids, and I don't care if you're a different ethnicity, race, low SES, whatever. If you're just an average Joe living here in town from a middle-class household, I expect positive relationships with him in much the same way as anyone else at this school.

In addition to the practice of modelling positive relationships, Principal 3 asserted that high expectations were another practice he used that helped ensure educational opportunities to all students. Holding high expectations was a practice that he believed affected the opportunities of marginalised students the most. Principal 3 emphasised that it was difficult in the past to implement high expectations but with legislated testing, higher expectations had to be the norm:

> It has to be that way [expectations must be high]. Twenty years ago things were so much different, but we have state testing now, and that has changed everything. You know, that hasn't been such a bad thing either, especially for marginalized students.

'It goes back to relationships' concerning creating a climate of belonging, according to Principal 4. She asserted that every school had problems, but ultimately positive relationships help overcome those problems and create a climate of belonging:

> I don't care what school you are at there is a drug problem, a harassment problem or a bullying problem. So, after last year's situation [school shooting] I thought let's try to take a positive approach to things, so that has bled over to so many other things in the school with teachers being able to take that conversation into their classrooms and clubs. There's a sign out there that says just be kind, and those are made by kids and posted everywhere.

Principal 4 insisted that her practices of prioritising positive relationships and high expectations was critical to establishing professional learning in a culture of care:

> I think we've got very committed personnel here that have high expectations and their relationships are the two things that I would say are most important. It's not something you buy as a subscription to some online computer program or just because they have the tech now or anything like that or the type of textbooks we use or anything. It comes down to the expectations and those relationships.

Building relationships as the foundation to a culture of care was paramount to the principals in this study. All principals asserted that a culture of care promoted a sense of belonging in all students, but was particularly essential for nurturing marginalised children.

Professional learning for positive change

As Labone and Long (2016) suggested, professional development is a passive activity where the responsibility for learning is on the transmitter of knowledge. Professional learning, on the other hand, is active, where the learner takes on the responsibility for self-change and change within the context. Marsick and Watkins (2001) posited that informal professional learning, while not structured, is intentional. As the principals in this study sought to encourage staff and students to embrace a socially just school culture, embracing change through professional learning was necessary.

Principal 1 worked to end programs for marginalised children in which students are 'pulled out' of general education classes for additional academic support a move which required change from stakeholders, including teachers, parents, and the student. To help end pullout programs, Principal 1 emphasised to teachers the need to allow high achieving students to help those who struggled with the content: 'I encourage teachers to realize that they can utilize those kids, so to speak, who have already mastered the content to teach those who haven't.' Though he tried to institute peer-to-peer tutoring, teachers were resistant to his strategy because there had been no previous attempts to do so. They were afraid that 'the peer's tutors wouldn't know the information well enough to tutor' and would cause more disruption than help to other students. Principal 1 had to 'try to sell this to the teachers,' but after some time the teachers understood the positive effect on student academic growth. While his implementation of peer-to-peer tutoring was originally met with resistance, he continued to encourage his teachers to embrace change and implement the new strategy. He saw his efforts to promote peer-to-peer tutoring as twofold: helping marginalised students who had not mastered the content while providing additional educational reinforcement to those who had: 'So it's not just helping the marginalized student, but it's also benefiting the higher functioning student by having them teach particular skills. It's benefiting everyone across the board.' As a result, students, especially marginalised students, experienced more academic success. Principal 1, reflecting on this accomplishment stated that, 'we grow our kids here, and it's not me, but the teachers who do it.'

Principal 2 used professional learning to advance relationships among his staff to help ensure positive student outcomes and opportunities for marginalised students. He specifically designed professional learning that centred on creating more positive relationships with students:

> … we are striving hard to make sure that folks understand that the number one way we can affect change in these kids is for someone to be a good positive role model for them. But not just role model but someone that they could develop a positive relationship with because that increases academic performance and outcomes for marginalized students more than anything else in my opinion.

Principal 3 acknowledged that 'there has to be a lot of listening in this position' to be successful, especially if you wish to disrupt the status quo. By practicing leadership in a democratic manner 'everyone now knows that they are a part of the change, and that keeps the process of providing a better education moving forward for everyone, especially marginalized students.' Principal 3 worked to bring about change by promoting a climate of belonging by simply asking the stakeholders what they needed to thrive. He established a bullying hotline at school so that students, parents, or staff could place an anonymous call reporting bullying. 'From some feedback through surveys we found that it may be hard to speak out in public about a bullying situation,' so he responded by creating the bullying hotline because 'people are reluctant to step in or tell us, but they'll call the hotline and say you know I saw this happen today to my friend.' Principal 3 viewed creating change as a direct result of understanding stakeholder needs, then working to meet those needs, to create a safe and positive learning environment for all.

Discussion

This study sought to understand how four rural U.S. principals implemented informal professional learning to promote socially just schools for marginalised children. The distinction between professional development and professional learning is essential to the purpose of this study. Professional development, as a uni-directional exercise, transmits learning from the expert to the learner. As a transmission model, professional development is more formalised and often allows for little learner interaction (see Figure 1). Moreover, cost and a larger location is associated with professional development. While valuable, schools in challenging circumstances, such as rural schools, which are found in more isolated locations with few resources available for professional development, must seek alternatives to professional development training.

Consequently, professional learning, as an informal practice, has replaced regular professional development as an essential tool, particularly when the learning is focused on school wide positive change, such as a change in beliefs and attitudes. Leaders who look to establish a culture of care for marginalised students utilise professional learning in their daily practice, as indicated by the four principals in this study. Through modelling the expected behaviours, words, conversations, and practices which promote a culture of care for marginalised students and by doing so in the social context of the school, leaders serve as an informal transmitter of learning. Those who learn from this model, that is, teachers, other administrators, and staff, may interactively engage in the learning through their own words, conversations, and observations. Even those who do not take in the lessons learned immediately, that which is observed and heard may set the learning upon later reflection. Figure 2 illustrates a professional learning model developed from findings of this study.

Informal professional learning is centred on the individual, is socially constructed, and takes place in the context of the school. Thus, informal professional learning is an achievable, practical, and manageable model for rural school leaders seeking to implement socially just practices. Professional learning for teachers can be a powerful experience simply through witnessing principal's behaviours which demonstrate the value of marginalised students. Teachers who observe socially just behaviours may, through reflection, take on those same behaviours and model social justice for others. Findings from this study add three significant foundational components for understanding the development of social justice informal learning in rural contexts. First, the principal influences informal learning within the school context by

Figure 1. Professional development model.

Figure 2. Professional learning model.

creating social structures and activities to include all students such as in-school social organisations promoting inclusiveness. Seemingly small actions such as conversations can have a large effect especially when these conversations with and about marginalised students are observed by others, including teachers and staff. Second, the principal creates a culture of care by modelling inclusiveness through interactions with students that demonstrate a genuine interest in their lives and a concern for their well-being. The principals in this study placed a high value and prioritised development of a positive relationship with *all* students. In the informal learning model, teachers observe these interactions and follow the principal's example, thus, participating in their own professional learning. In addition to care for students' personal lives, principals actively promoted high academic expectations, believing that all students can achieve at high levels. Third, principals focused on bringing about positive change. The principals in this study were intentional in providing learning opportunities for marginalised students even when encountering staff resistance. Focusing on teamwork and inclusive leadership further influenced teachers to behave similarly. This study confirmed that social justice practices for marginalised children may be contextually developed by leading through informal professional learning and is accomplished through learning in a social context for others to observe and hear, development of a culture of care, and focus on positive change in beliefs and attitudes.

Theoharis (2009) provided guidance in our social justice conceptual framework by identification of three leadership attributes pertinent to this study. The leader: 1) places significant value on diversity and extends cultural respect and understanding of that diversity, 2) builds a welcoming climate and, 3) becomes intertwined with the school's success and school life. While these attributes are widely accepted, how the principal enacts these concepts in a rural setting was demonstrated by the principals in this study.

Rural schools lack resources and geographic connections (Abel and Sewell 1999, Bassett 2003). Moreover, conditions are not likely to change quickly. Thus, professional learning that is embedded in the daily work of schools is the most viable strategy for rural teachers to incorporate social justice practices in their daily work. One implication from these findings is that principals must first become social justice role models and competently practice socially just behaviours themselves. Further research might examine how effective rural socially just principals learn how to enact informal learning as described in this study. Examining how effective principals develop social justice practices will contribute to the development of current and aspiring principals.

Disclosure statement

No potential conflict of interest was reported by the authors.

ORCID

Pamela S. Angelle http://orcid.org/0000-0002-2705-5541

References

Abel, M.H. and Sewell, J., 1999. Stress and burnout in rural and urban secondary school teachers. *The Journal of Educational Research*, 92 (5), 287–293. doi:10.1080/00220679909597608.
Act, E.S.S.A. 2015. *Every student succeeds act of 2015*. Pub. L. No. 114-95.
Act, N.C.L.B. 2002. *No child left behind act of 2001*. Publ. L, 107-110.
Albritton, S., Huffman, S., and McClellan, R., 2017. A study of rural high school principals' perceptions as social justice leaders. *Administrative Issues Journal*, 7 (1), 20–35.
Auerbach, S., 2009. Walking the walk: portraits in leadership for family engagement in urban schools. *School Community Journal*, 19 (1), 9–32.
Baker, M. and Foote, M., 2006. Changing spaces: urban school interrelationships and the impact of standards-based reform. *Educational Administration Quarterly*, 42 (1), 90–123. doi:10.1177/0013161X05278187.
Bassett, D.L., 2003. The politics of the rural vote. *Arizona State Law Journal*, 35 (1), 743–761.
Bishop, H.N. and McClellan, R.L., 2016. Rural school principals' perceptions of LGBTQ Students. *Journal of School Leadership*, 26 (1), 124–153. doi:10.1177/105268461602600105.
Burstein, N., et al., 2004. Moving toward inclusive practices. *Remedial and Special Education*, 25 (2), 104–116. doi:10.1177/07419325040250020501.
Burton, M. and Johnson, A.S., 2010. "Where else would we teach?": portraits of two teachers in the rural south. *Journal of Teacher Education*, 61 (4), 376–386. doi:10.1177/0022487110372362.
Creemers, B.P., Kyriakides, L., and Antoniou, P., 2013. A dynamic approach to school improvement: main features and impact. *School Leadership & Management*, 33 (2), 114–132. doi:10.1080/13632434.2013.773883.
Darling-Hammond, L., 2010. Recruiting and Retaining Teachers: Turning Around the Race to the Bottom in High-Need Schools. *Journal of curriculum and instruction*, 4 (1), 16–32.
Darling-Hammond, L. and McLaughlin, M.W., 2011. Policies that support professional development in an era of reform. *Phi Delta Kappan*, 92 (6), 81–92. doi:10.1177/003172171109200622.
DeMatthews, D. and Mawhinney, H., 2014. Social justice leadership and inclusion: exploring challenges in an urban district struggling to address inequities. *Educational Administration Quarterly*, 50 (5), 844–881. doi:10.1177/0013161X13514440.
Elliott, J., 2005. *Using narrative in social research: qualitative and quantitative approaches*. London: Sage.
Eraut, M., 2004. Informal learning in the workplace. *Studies in continuing education*, 26 (2), 247–273. doi:10.1080/158037042000225245.
Flick, U. (Ed.). (2013). *The SAGE handbook of qualitative data analysis*. Thousand Oaks, CA: Sage.
Flora, C.B., Flora, J.L., and Gasteyer, S.P., 2015. *Rural communities: legacy and change*. Boulder, CO: Westview Press.
Ghazali, S.N., et al., 2009. ESL students' attitude towards texts and teaching methods used in literature classes. *English Language Teaching*, 2 (4), 51–67. doi:10.5539/elt.v2n4p51.
Gibbs, R., 2005. Education as a rural development strategy. *Amber Waves*, 3 (5), 20–26.

Helge, D., 1990. *A national study regarding at-risk students*. Bellingham, WA: National Rural Development Institute.

Hoppey, D. and McLeskey, J., 2013. A case study of principal leadership in an effective inclusive school. *The Journal of Special Education*, 46 (4), 245-256. doi:10.1177/0022466910390507.

Huang, G. and Howley, C., 1991. *Mitigating disadvantage: effects of small-scale schooling on student achievement in Alaska*. Charleston, West Virginia: ERIC Clearinghouse on Rural Education and Development.

Jimerson, L., 2005. Placism in NCLB—How rural children are left behind. *Equity & Excellence in Education*, 38 (3), 211-219. doi:10.1080/10665680591002588.

Kannapel, P.J. and DeYoung, A.J., 1999. The rural school problem in 1999: A review and critique of the literature. *Journal of Research in Rural Education*, 15 (2), 67-79.

Kosciw, J.G. and Diaz, E.M., 2008. *Involved, invisible, ignored: the experiences of lesbian, gay, bisexual and transgender parents and their children in our nation's K-12 schools*. New York, NY: Gay, Lesbian & Straight Education Network.

Kyndt, E., et al., 2016. Teachers' everyday professional development: mapping informal learning activities, antecedents, and learning outcomes. *Review of educational research*, 86 (4), 1111-1150. doi:10.3102/0034654315627864.

Labone, E. and Long, J., 2016. Features of effective professional learning: A case study of the implementation of a system-based professional learning model. *Professional development in education*, 42 (1), 54-77. doi:10.1080/19415257.2014.948689.

Le Clus, M.A., 2011. Informal learning in the workplace: A review of the literature. *Australian Journal of Adult Learning*, 51 (2), 355-373.

Lyson, T.A. and Falk, W.W., 1993. *Forgotten places: uneven development in rural America. Rural America series*. Lawrence, KS: University Press of Kansas.

Malloy, W.W. and Allen, T., 2007. Teacher retention in a teacher resiliency-building rural school. *Rural Educator*, 28 (2), 19-27.

Marsick, V.J., et al. 2006. *Reviewing theory and research on informal and incidental learning*, online submission.

Marsick, V.J. and Watkins, K.E., 2001. Informal and incidental learning. *New directions for adult and continuing education*, 2001 (89), 25-34. doi:10.1002/ace.5.

Mejiuni, O. (Ed.)., 2015. *Measuring and analyzing informal learning in the digital age*. IGI Global.

Mejiuni, O., 2019. Informal learning and the social justice practices of academic leaders as invisible and visible pedagogical inputs in higher education institutions. In Voices in Education, P. Curtis-Tweed and L. Woods, eds.. *Journal of Bermuda College*. Vol. 5. 10-17. Hamilton, Bermuda: Bermuda College

Merriam, S.B., 2009. *Qualitative research: A guide to design and implementation*. Jossey-Bass

Muyeed, I., 1982. Some reflections on education for rural development. *International Review of Education*, 28 (2), 227-238. doi:10.1007/BF00598448.

Noe, R.A., Tews, M.J., and Marand, A.D., 2013. Individual differences and informal learning in the workplace. *Journal of vocational behavior*, 83 (3), 327-335. doi:10.1016/j.jvb.2013.06.009.

Peters, S., 2002. Inclusive education in accelerated and professional development schools: A case-based study of two school reform efforts in the USA. *International Journal of Inclusive Education*, 6 (4), 287-308. doi:10.1080/13603110210143716.

Peyser, J.A. and Costrell, R.M., 2004. Exploring the costs of accountability. *Education Next*, 4 (2), 45-61.

Riessman, C.K., 2008. *Narrative methods for the human sciences*. London: Sage.

Rogers, A., 2014. *The base of the iceberg: informal learning and its impact on formal and non-formal learning*. Toronto: Verlag Barbara Budrich.

Rostosky, S.S., et al., 2003. Associations among sexual attraction status, school belonging, and alcohol and marijuana use in rural high school students. *Journal of Adolescence*, 26 (6), 741-751. doi:10.1016/j.adolescence.2003.09.002.

Rubin, H.J. and Rubin, I.S., 2011. *Qualitative interviewing: The art of hearing data*. sage.

Schmidt, F., et al., 2002. Community change and persistence. *In*: A.E. Luloff and R.S. Krannich, eds. *Persistence and change in rural communities*. Wallingford, CO: CABI Publishing, 95-116.

Seal, K.R. and Harmon, H.L., 1995. Realities of rural school reform. *Phi Delta Kappan*, 77 (2), 119-120.

Stake, R.E., 1995. *The art of case study research*. sage.

Stedman, J. and Riddle, W. 1998. *Goals 2000: educate America act implementation status and issues*. Washington, DC: The Library of Congress. Congressional Research Service Report 95-502.

Stern, J.D., Ed., 1994. *The condition of education in rural schools*. Washington, D.C.: U.S. Department of Education, Office of Educational Research and Improvement.

Tannenbaum, S.I., et al., 2010. Informal learning and development in organizations. In: S. W. Kozlowski and E. Salas, eds., *Learning, training, and development in organizations*. New York: Routlege, 303-332.

Theoharis, G., 2007. Social justice educational leaders and resistance: toward a theory of social justice leadership. *Educational Administration Quarterly*, 43 (2), 221-258. doi:10.1177/0013161X06293717.

Theoharis, G., 2009. *The school leaders our children deserve: seven keys to equity, social justice, and school reform*. New York, NY: Teachers College Press.

U.S. Census Bureau, 2010. *Population distribution and change: 2000 to 2010*. Washington, DC: AUTHOR. Retrieved from: https://www.census.gov/prod/cen2010/briefs/c2010br-01.pdf

U.S. Department of Education, 2014. *For each and every child*. Washington, DC: AUTHOR. Retrieved from: https://www2.ed.gov/about/bdscomm/list/eec/equity-excellence-commission-report.pdf

Veelen, R.V., Sleegers, P.J., and Endedijk, M.D., 2017. Professional learning among school leaders in secondary education: the impact of personal and work context factors. *Educational administration quarterly*, 53 (3), 365–408. doi:10.1177/0013161X16689126.

Zepeda, S.J., 2014. *Job-embedded professional development: Support, collaboration, and learning in schools*. Routledge.

Zepeda, S.J., Jimenez, A.M., and Lanoue, P.D., 2015. New practices for a new day: principal professional development to support performance cultures in schools. *LEARNing Landscapes*, 9 (1), 303–322. doi:10.36510/learnland.v9i1.759.

Critical professional development and the racial justice leadership possibilities of teachers of colour in K-12 schools

Rita Kohli, Marcos Pizarro, Luis-Genaro Garcia, Lisa Kelly, Michael Espinoza and Juan Córdova

ABSTRACT
Research has noted that teachers of Color are disproportionately called upon to address racialized issues in schools serving students of Color. And although many teachers of Color enter the profession wanting to advocate for and with students and their families and are strongly positioned to do so, these responsibilities should not rest entirely on their shoulders. Navigating institutional change as collective work is not something taught within teacher preparation or traditional professional development (PD). But what would happen if critical teachers of Color—those with a structural analysis of oppression and who are committed to social and racial justice—were actually supported and provided leadership development work towards racial justice at their school sites? How might this type of development affect their sustainability in and impact on the field? Using a framework of critical professional development (CPD)—emergent and often grassroots teacher development spaces that frame teachers as politically-aware individuals who have a stake transforming society—this paper will explore the impacts of a racial affinity CPD space, the Institute for Teachers of Color Committed to Racial Justice, designed specifically to promote the retention, growth, and activist leadership of teachers of Color in K-12 schools.

There is a growing body of literature on social justice school leadership that has pointed to teachers as an important resource in rethinking static and hierarchical approaches to change (Lopez 2014, Baker-Doyle 2017, Rojas 2018). Research has also shown that although teachers of Colour are often overlooked for leadership roles, they are needed in this leadership work (Pizarro and Kohli 2018, Kohli 2019, Gist 2019). Unfortunately, navigating institutional change is not something typically taught within teacher preparation or traditional professional development. What would happen, though, if critical teachers of Colour were actually developed and supported as leaders to collectively address racial inequities at their school sites? How might this form of development affect their professional growth, sustainability, and impact?

Using a framework of critical professional development – teacher development spaces that frame educators as 'politically-aware individuals who have a stake in teaching and transforming society' (Kohli et al. 2015, p. 9) – this article explores the possibilities of a racial affinity critical professional development space, the Institute for Teachers of Colour Commited to Racial Justice (ITOC), which is designed to foster the retention, growth, and transformative leadership capacities of teachers of Colour in K-12 schools. Specifically, we share three cases of justice-oriented teachers of Colour who build upon their experiences in ITOC as they work towards social justice in their educational contexts: 1) on a curricular level, developing lessons that are more culturally and community sustaining, 2) on a school-wide level, creating spaces and structures for students and teachers of Colour to thrive, and 3) across the district, organising teachers of Colour to resist policies and practices that foster harmful conditions for communities of Colour. Together, these narratives offer lessons on how critical approaches to professional development can strengthen the social and racial justice leadership capacities of teachers of Colour in their efforts for enduring change.

Context for teachers of colour

Many teachers of Colour choose teaching because they want to serve students of Colour and transform educational conditions for communities of Colour (Irizarry and Donaldson 2012, Gist et al. 2018). Teachers of Colour have been shown to have higher academic expectations for students of Colour (Cherng and Halpin 2016), are more likely to embody culturally sustaining pedagogies (Brown 2009) and, while not all teachers of Colour are politically engaged, because of their positionalities, teachers of Colour are more likely to recognise racial inequities (Dingus 2008; Dixson & Dingus, 2008). However, while students of Colour now comprise more than half of students enrolled in US public schools, teachers of Colour make up just 21% of the teaching force (US Department of Education 2016). Thus, with the assets that they bring to the profession, schools and districts are beginning to focus on their recruitment (U.S. Department of Education, 2016, Haddix 2017).

Within the predominantly White profession, though, teachers of Colour experience racial harm themselves (Dingus 2008, Pizarro and Kohli 2020), and have disproportionately high attrition rates compared to White teachers (Ingersoll and May 2011). While teachers of Colour need support to navigate their racialised realities (Kohli 2019, Mensah and Jackson 2018), it has been noted that typical approaches to teacher learning tend to neglect race, structural inequities, and the knowledge and perspectives of communities of Colour (Cochran-Smith et al. 2015). In addition to primarily centring White teachers, typical models of professional development pay little attention to the racial and socio-political dynamics of schools and neglect the experiences, needs, and agentive capabilities of teachers of Colour. In this article, we bridge research on professional development and on the transformative leadership potential of justice-oriented teachers of Colour to explore how critical professional development can support them in leading justice-centred change at their schools.

Critical professional development

Traditional approaches to teacher professional development (PD) often focus on technical notions of teaching (i.e. grade level planning, literacy growth, classroom management). And while growth along these aspects of teaching is foundational, critical educators rarely have access to professional growth opportunities that centre their political visions. Out of a need for this learning, there has been an increase in critical professional development – development spaces that support the political orientations and critical pedagogical needs of justice-oriented teachers. Built upon models of community organising and teacher inquiry groups (Ritchie and Wilson 2000, Rogers, Kramer & Mosley, 2009), critical professional development centres teachers' roles in transforming schools and society as they are 'designed to provoke cooperative dialogue, build unity, provide shared leadership, and meet the critical needs of teachers' (Kohli et al. 2015, p. 11). Critical professional development ranges in structure and purpose – from regular meetings of a small contingent of teachers to larger annual convenings – but they all afford space for complex reflections about structures, policies and practices that guide social and school based in/equities. In this article, we use the case study of ITOC to explore how teachers of Colour have taken up racial justice leadership in their schools when engaged and supported towards their critical visions.

Institute for teachers of colour committed to racial justice

The Institute for Teachers of Colour Committed to Racial Justice (ITOC) selects participants through an application process that assesses their racial justice leadership capacities and potential. The space is structured to attend to the impact of racism that teachers of Colour experience through models of self- and community-care, to address their racial and ideological isolation by facilitating a sense of collectivity, and to provide opportunities for culturally sustaining professional growth. For three intensive days, teachers of Colour are exposed to theory, models of practice, and leadership tools to strengthen their ability to name and disrupt institutional racism. They are cultivated as a professional community of critical educators poised to challenge policies, practices, and belief systems that marginalise communities of Colour (Kohli and Pizarro 2016). Over the past ten years, approximately half of the attendees have been Latinx, approximately 20% Asian American and Pacific Islander, 20% Black, and 12% of participants have identified as multiracial or other. Reflective of the teaching force, 78% of participants were women, and 22% were men. Approximately half of participants have been novice teachers, having taught less than 5 years, one quarter have taught 6–10 years, and one quarter were veteran teachers having taught more than 10 years. They ranged in age from their early twenties to mid-sixties and have taught subjects across the spectrum, from elementary through high school. In a given year, an average of 30% of ITOC attendees are alumni to the programme.

Methods

In previous studies, we have explored the impact of the three days of ITOC on teachers of Colour, focusing on how feelings of isolation or racial stress are addressed by the convening (Kohli and Pizarro, 2016, Kohli. et al. 2020). Here, we extend this exploration to understand the impact of ITOC on the leadership practices of teachers who attend and, in turn, on their contexts. We are a collective of: 1) two educational researchers who are also former teachers of Colour – one a Chicano former elementary educator and the other a South Asian former middle school teacher – and are co-directors of ITOC, and 2) four teachers of Colour – a bi-racial Afro-Latina middle school teacher, two Latino high school educators (one who was transitioning into the role of a professor/academic), and a Latino elementary educator – who have attended ITOC at least twice. After the 2017 or 2018 convenings, three of the teacher-authors applied and were selected as Racial Justice Teacher Innovation Grant recipients, receiving a small stipend and support to build upon their learnings at ITOC work towards a transformational vision in their classroom, school, or district.

For this article, we engaged in a method of narrative self-study (Clandinin and Connelly 2004). Narrative inquiry builds upon participants' experiences across time, interaction, and location. Narrative self-study allows the data to extend beyond what was experienced and observed by allowing participants to frame their narratives through their personal insight and knowledge. This has been an increasingly utilised method to centre non-dominant teacher experiences in research (Endo, Reece-Miller, Santavicca, 2010), and as a pedagogical tool to raise critical issues with other teachers (Milner 2010). We use this approach so teachers of Colour, through their own standpoint, can be understood as central to the transformational work of schools, and in the knowledge-creation of educational research.

The teacher-authors were tasked in this collaboration to write a short narrative of their professional experiences, guided by the question, 'how has the critical professional development of ITOC supported the racial justice leadership capacities of teachers.' We co-designed the prompt as a written reflection where they were to pay attention to their vision, professional struggles, what they gained from ITOC, and the impact of their leadership work. We also wanted each narrative to include specific moments and details, as they grounded theory in their practice.

The research-authors of the paper read all the drafts, providing feedback to the teachers focused on moments of leadership and themes that cut across the narratives. After several rounds of reading and analysing the narratives through the lens of our question, key themes began to emerge related to the impact of the critical professional development on their efficacy as transformational teacher leaders in schools, and we formed the narratives into three case studies, which we include in the next section. The research-authors then reflected on the collective lessons of the case studies, which is included in the discussion.

Strengthening teacher of colour racial justice leadership

To demonstrate how ITOC serves the agentive possibilities of teachers of Colour, we present three cases. In the first case, we share two narratives – the first written by Luis, an arts educator who taught high school in his own community and worked to affirm and sustain the cultural and linguistic strengths of his students (Paris and Alim 2014, 2017). An experienced critical educator, he shared his pedagogical approach and arts lesson at ITOC in a workshop for other teachers of Colour. The second narrative in the case study was written by Lisa, an educator from an entirely different context and discipline who attended the workshop and was inspired to adapt the curriculum in her classroom to help build community with middle school students in authentic and relational ways. The success she experienced with the lesson then led to her teaching the approach to other educators. In the second case study, Michael, a high school English teacher, narrates his response to the school's alienating school culture by re-centring Latinx students; and in the third case study, Juan, an elementary school teacher, reflects on his leadership work organising with teachers of Colour across the district to challenge racist policies and practices. Overall, we saw that teachers of Colour served as relational and community-engaged knowledge creators, shifters of school culture who demand spaces of belonging for students of Colour, and as collective learners and organisers towards district change. Representing different layers of the work of K-12 teachers – at the curricular, schoolwide, and district levels – the narratives demonstrate how a critical professional development space supported the collaborative leadership development of teachers of Colour as they enact change in schools.

Curricular leadership: developing culturally sustaining classrooms

La Lotería in an arts classroom

While art teachers traditionally are guided to draw on the resources of privileged museums – spaces often irrelevant or disconnected from the lived experiences of students of Colour and their communities – I (Luis) have always understood that some of the most impactful art movements have developed from the political circumstances of communities of Colour. Teaching in the school I once attended, and wanting to provide an education I wish I had as a young person, I aim to use the arts as a way for students to understand their world and explore how historical systems of oppression have affected the well-being of our communities.

My school is in South Central Los Angeles, an Industrial section of the city that before 1948 was the only place in the area where African Americans were allowed to own property, and thus became a cultural and artistic hub that maintained rich African American history. In recent years, with the growth of large im/migrant populations, the region is now a shared Latinx and African American space.

Several years ago, I was teaching a unit on family that included students creating portraits focused on their parents' occupations. On my way to work one day, thinking of different ways that I could extend the unit, I drove past my old home and the bench where my mother would catch the bus for work each morning at 4am. As memories flooded back of my single, working mom and my experiences as the eldest of my siblings, I remembered the time my Spanish teacher used the game of La Lotería in class (a game similar to Bingo often played in Latin America, that displays cultural images with titles and riddles instead of numbers). The rules of the game are explained by Zambrano (2013, v):

> There are fifty-four cards and each comes with a riddle, un dicho. There is a
> traditional set of riddles, but sometimes dealers create their own to trick the

players. After the dealer "sings" the riddle, the players cover the appropriate
spots on their playing boards, their tablas, with either bottle caps, dried
beans, or loose change .... You can win by filling a vertical line, horizontal,
a diagonal, the four corners, the center squares, or blackout.

Seeing La Lotería in school was one of the few times I felt a clear connection to home in school, and I wanted my students to experience that same authentic connection. I knew that teaching students about European artists or centring technical learning was not going to help them navigate the sociopolitical dynamics of their marginalised community. So I decided to build upon the game in my class (Garcia, 2018) in a way that challenged systems of power and reflected their community cultural wealth – forms of 'capital' traditionally unrecognised by school that are the foundation upon which Latina/o/x students and their families successfully navigate hostile systems (Yosso 2005).

As we discussed the history of La Lotería, I prompted students to critically analyse the images, unpacking stereotypical representations of race, class, or gender. I then asked students to re-create a Lotería card in a way that honoured their parents' occupation. By doing this, I was acknowledging their home and communal knowledge as a form of capital and used it to challenge the images in the game.

For example, students made references to El Valiente (see image 1) as someone that is courageous or brave. Others talked about how the image reflected someone that was a macho, critiquing

El Valiente from the game of La Lotería.
By Don Clemente, Inc. (Garcia, 2018) Image: Author's Artifact

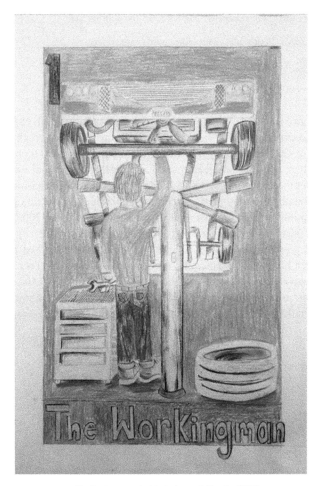

Student re-created Lotería card (Garcia, 2018).

machismo because it reinforces gender stereotypes that some students lamented were reflected in their homes. One student felt that the image of El Valiente was not aligned with his interpretation of being brave. He thought his dad was an authentic Valiente and wanted to challenge this visual narrative of a macho looking man with a knife. He explained:

> In my eyes, my parent – the mechanic – is the *Valiente* for the long hours he works, sometimes with no days off, to make sure we can pay the rent and have something to eat. I titled my card, "The Workingman," because the working man is the tough guy and the only weapon he needs are his mechanic tools.

This family unit allowed students to challenge current stereotypes, gender roles, and issues of race and class that shape their environments, while also enabling them to acknowledge their parents' occupations as a valuable source of capital in their lives. Through this method, we developed an understanding of the socio-economic circumstances and strength of their parents, even when their occupations are often undervalued by society.

I wanted to share this model with other teachers of Colour, so in 2017 (and again in 2018) I facilitated a workshop at ITOC called 'La Lotéria and Art Education as Creative Resistance: Embracing Working Class Occupations in our Classrooms.' While most of the participating teachers were not arts educators, my emphasis was on how the arts could build upon the cultural wealth that students bring into their classrooms to facilitate critical thinking and cultural affirmation. I wanted critical teachers of Colour to experience recreating Lotería cards as essential tools for themselves and their students, so I encouraged them to draw from their students' knowledge to build their own curriculum. This is exactly what we achieved. Several teachers who attended this workshop have adapted this lesson and approach into their own context, sharing a heightened understanding of the vitality of the arts in developing culturally sustaining practices that foster the critical consciousness of students of Colour. Through my own growth as a school leader and by being centred as an expert in ITOC, I was able to support the leadership development of many other teachers of Colour.

La Lotería to build relationships

When I (Lisa) began teaching middle school English and English Language Development three years ago in the Fruitvale neighbourhood of Oakland, I was excited to be teaching a population that reflected my identity. In World War II, African American and Latinx immigrants came to the port town to benefit from war-related work. During a period of 'urban renewal' in which a major freeway was built through the primarily African American portion of West Oakland, East Oakland became Black and Latinx and was a centre of both Black Panther and Chicanx Revolutionary activist group activity in the 1960s and 1970s. The Fruitvale, now primarily Latinx, remains a site of Latinx and Chicanx pride and activism, even as Oakland is increasingly gentrified.

When I started at the school, as a mixed Black and Columbian person, I just *knew* I was going to connect with my Latinx students. I couldn't wait to show off the Spanish I had been bettering through summer trips to Latin America. I knew I needed to learn about my students and their families, but I thought I had a special head start as a Latina. I was shocked to find myself completely disconnected from my students' experiences as recently arrived (or the children of recently arrived) Mexican and Central American immigrants. I was not surprised that students were reluctant to share their migration stories with me, but I was disappointed to see that even in my classroom, students seemed ashamed to speak Spanish despite growing up in a primarily Spanish-speaking area of Oakland.

After that tough first year, I realised that while supporting my students' growth in reading and writing English, I had to change my curriculum to also affirm my students' identities, languages, and experiences. I knew what I wanted: a language-, reading-, and writing-curriculum that valued their experiences as Latinx immigrants. I had no idea how I was going to do that.

That summer, I attended ITOC and participated in a workshop by Luis in which he presented how he had used the traditional Mexican game of chance, La Lotería, to teach high school students to celebrate, critically interrogate, and re-write their culture. I was inspired. After seeing how Luis used La Lotería to teach students about community cultural wealth and funds of knowledge through arts integrated teaching, I realised this is what I was looking for to make my curriculum more culturally sustaining for my students.

I gathered with a group of other educators from my school who were also at ITOC and planned a 3-week unit that would serve as an introduction to my class, to middle school reading and writing, and to identity sharing through Lotería. In this unit, I wanted to purposefully highlight and use Spanish in my classroom. I made sure students were reading grade level texts about the history and cultural significance of Lotería. I engaged students to examine the Lotería cards – which have issues of colourism and sexism prevalent in them – with a critical eye and lens, and write about their analysis of the cards. Lastly, building from Luis' lesson, I asked students to create a brand new Lotería card related to their personal identity and write an essay comparing and contrasting that Lotería card to a traditional Lotería card in the deck.

This unit is now a highlight of the school year. Playing the game with students brings an element of joy and fun to the classroom that is so necessary in building relationships, and it allows for organic moments of students sharing family histories. Supporting them to critically examine a game that was an important part of childhood for some can be eye-opening as they: realise that they do not have to blindly accept the world around them, and reflect deeply on the messages that are contained in seemingly innocuous games and media. Most importantly, this process encourages students to be engaged in reading and writing through topics that are culturally and personally significant to them.

I asked a few current students (two 6th grade boys and one 6th grade girl), how they felt about the Lotería unit. Kathy explained, 'I really liked the curriculum. I wish we could have played black out to take longer, but I feel like the unit connected to my Mexican culture.' Jaime said, 'Oh yeah, I liked it, because that game is from many parts of the world. And since one place was from Mexico and I'm from Mexico, I like it. And my family plays it.' Lastly, Steven, who identifies as Black and is not Latino said that he enjoyed playing the game and learning about a culture different than his own.

After teaching the curriculum for a year, I presented this work at the next ITOC, and my fellow educators of Colour were encouraged and inspired. A colleague asked me to present the curriculum to her graduate class at a nearby university, and I was excited to share my learnings and lead other educators in creating their own Lotería cards. I also heard from a colleague in Southern California who adapted the curriculum for their classroom in Southeast Los Angeles, where they learned about cultural wealth in their community and created Lotería cards to represent that wealth. This teacher stated that the Lotería project was their 'favorite project of the year.' I was grateful to have the opportunity to learn from and with Luis and then, growing as a leader, to be able to apply that learning and pass it on to others in the ITOC community. I am extremely proud of this work and have immense gratitude to ITOC for creating the space that allowed opportunities for leadership development between and among educators of Colour to be the fertile ground for the blossoming and continued nurturing of this work.

Schoolwide leadership: reframing school culture

I (Michael) attended ITOC for four years, the first time being in between my credential programme and my first year teaching. It has been the professional development I needed as it thoughtfully and critically acknowledged race issues I had experienced and continued to witness in education. Although just three days each summer, I have learned far more about racial justice education than I did my entire college career, and ITOC has continued to influence my approach to resist and reimagine a school culture that is responsive to my students.

I am an English teacher at a high school in San José, California that serves predominantly White and middle class students, with little support or spaces for its growing emergent bilingual and Latinx students. In this multi-racial community, students have experienced racism throughout their education. One of my students gave an example,

> My 3rd grade teacher once told me that I needed to be quiet or I'd turn out like them. She was pointing to my friends in the corner. She had separated me from them in order to help me "not go down the wrong path." I knew they weren't bad kids, so it didn't make sense. Eventually, I got in trouble for hanging out with them, and ever since I always just assumed that we were bad. I still feel that way sometimes here at this school, the way they target us.

I struggled to hold back tears of anger as the student shared this story, knowing that this type of behaviour from adults in positions of power was something I too had once endured as a young person. I went to this same school, and as early as my first few weeks on campus, I felt the full weight of the oppressive educational system thrown ruthlessly back upon me. It was traumatising to walk the same halls, enter the same classrooms, and see the same populations of teachers and students that I had 15 years earlier. Although I had changed drastically since then, it seemed as if nothing else had, and thus I felt as I did when I was in 9th grade: marginalised. That feeling was still all too common at our school; many Latinx students on campus have said that they feel disconnected from the school and their peers, expressing that they feel 'alone' on campus and that their teachers 'didn't understand them.'

I was wrestling with how to be a teacher that centres belonging and cariño (love and care) in an environment that is as alienating to Latinx students as my own education was to me. Although a new teacher, knowing that there were few spaces for students of Colour to feel like they belong outside of my classroom, I agreed to advise the Latinx Student Union (LSU). I wanted to grow LSU into a club focused on racial justice, specifically for Latinx students and so I drew from my experiences organising in college and what I learned from ITOC, and the students and I focused on using LSU to shift our campus culture so Latinx students felt welcomed in school.

My first year at ITOC, I attended a workshop that was run by teachers and students together, presenting their work using Youth-led Participatory Action Research (YPAR) strategies. It was inspiring to see what these high school students were able to do, and most importantly the projects all came from the students. One student had done her project on complex post traumatic stress disorder and how it had affected her neighbourhood in Los Angeles. To witness students doing research not for the sake of skill-building, but to understand important aspects of their own lives and their community was amazing. Building upon this learning, I knew I had to include the students as equal stakeholders in the club to make LSU an effective support for Latinx students and myself.

During my second time attending ITOC, I learned about Culturally Sustaining Pedagogy, and in my third summer, I attended a workshop with Luis on La Lotería. With all of the theoretical backing of ITOC, I have been able to shape LSU into a space that serves Latinx students at my school through student-led initiatives, reflection, and consistent growth.

Two years ago I was selected as a Racial Justice Teacher Innovation Grant recipient. With the support of ITOC, LSU developed a district-wide Latinx conference and leadership programme, and we have garnered awards and recognition for helping other Latinx students in the district to build their own LSUs. Most importantly, by creating an active community that has become central to student life and engagement on campus, we have shifted our campus culture so that Latinx students do not feel as invisible as they once did. Teachers have seen and even acknowledged the impacts of LSU, letting us know that it has created a sense of safety for students, and also referring students to us so that they can benefit from the sense of belonging and leadership development LSU provides. Staff have also seen this shift and have sought to become involved in LSU, while also clearly learning from our work. The ASB Leadership advisor, for example, has been making a concerted effort to include more students of Colour, and has on more than one occasion reached out to us to ask for assistance or recommendations. Of all the ways we have shifted the culture on campus, it is the fact that the students themselves tell us they now feel safe and accepted in LSU that matters most. School can oftentimes be hostile towards people of Colour, so I am most proud of the work that has gone in to create this space of belonging. Our numbers have grown each year, and with that so has our presence. With my own cycle of racial justice growth through teaching and ITOC, I have been able to bring back my newfound knowledge to my community and LSU, and together we have grown into a respected club on campus that is built on a foundation of racial justice. This leadership development model continues to grow and benefit an expanding circle of students, staff and teachers.

District leadership: organising sustainable teacher collectives

On the day I (Juan) started my Masters in Teaching, I entered a room packed with mostly white women, which sent me on a flashback to my days as a middle school student just learning to speak English. Once again, I was one of the few students of Colour, yet this time in a teaching preparation programme that boasted a focus on culturally responsive practices and social justice. There were bright spots in my training, like the few instructors that saw our needs as students of Colour and supported us in weekly lunch gatherings where we caucused and shared our experiences. However, we were navigating spaces that were filled with aggressive colleagues, oblivious instructors, and a curriculum that dismissed our value as emerging teachers of Colour. Our literacy instructors used mentor texts that had rich content from Latinx culture, however they focused on teaching the strategy for reading and content without providing context or connection to Latinx authors or characters that reflected Latinx community cultural wealth.

My experience during my teacher training was revealing in the ways that teachers of Colour were sought for the diversity we bring to the classroom, while our actual funds of knowledge were undervalued as we were not provided culturally sustaining practices to develop as teachers of Colour. In addition, there were no spaces or resources that would help us maintain our health in this predominantly White profession. But our commitment was tied to the communities in which we were teaching, and thankfully, we had parents and students who expressed their love and respect for our presence. We brought experiences and identities that reflected their lived experiences and had expertise that could better support the growth and development of their children. And reciprocally, they offered us authentic support by affirming our value in the classroom.

Building on the power of community, when I started teaching, I sought out a network of teachers of Colour that more closely shared my commitment to culturally sustaining teaching and organising for change. I facilitated monthly gatherings where teachers of Colour drank tea, unpacked our experiences, and shared our expertise and resources. Being in community with other like-minded educators invigorated me and gave me the understanding and hope that allowed me to come back to teach the next day. Our time together was validating, and yet, we also struggled to find ways to support each other. As the school year continued, our capacities decreased and priorities shifted. Our gatherings were less frequent and our attendance decreased as well. While I knew these connections were essential to lasting in the profession, I realised how difficult it was going to be to have a group of teachers of Colour who were available to support each other consistently. This pattern continued for a few years, with educators of Colour appreciating the space but finding it hard to commit. I was looking for support and models for coordinating this work.

The first time I heard about ITOC was from a professor that I met during my teaching preparation programme, after I shared with him the ways in which I wanted to organise with racially reflective peers. He said, 'You should apply for this conference in California, dedicated to supporting teachers of Colour.' I was fortunate to be accepted in the summer of 2015. The professional development I experienced at ITOC was unexpected. Up to that point in my career I had normalised sitting and listening to speakers talk about everything teachers had to do to be successful. This was the first time I felt that the presenters, concepts, and language were giving voice to what I was feeling and had not previously been able to name. Learning about the secondary trauma teachers of Colour endure, and how we feel greater exhaustion and hurt because we more closely empathise with our students' experiences was validating and helped me make sense of what I was experiencing as a teacher. I was learning the concepts, framing and tools that I had been missing. I left ITOC that year feeling energised, seen, and knowing that my feelings and experiences were valid. I felt that I could speak up and push for change. When I returned to ITOC two summers later with a small group of colleagues, we were inspired as a group by the power of a space filled with teachers of Colour who were developing critical consciousness. We engaged in conversations with other teachers of Colour who had developed workshops for colleagues that encouraged critical thinking in welcoming spaces, and we committed to working together to mirror that work in our own community. That summer we applied for the Racial Justice Teacher Innovation grant with the goal of setting up meetings for teachers of Colour to come together and build a community and grow as critically conscious educators. Our goal was to create a space where we could feel the same ways we felt at ITOC, building on the ITOC tools and leadership development strategies. We felt that replicating this space would be invigorating to our work.

ITOC provided a template through its comprehensive model of developing teacher-leaders of Colour, including culturally sustaining community building, tiered professional development, focused growth, and a working group model of building racial justice action plans. Through support from the leadership team and the network of educators, we designed and facilitated monthly home meetings where we shared food, stories, engaged in scholarly readings, increased our capacity, and left with validation and new knowledge and skills to combat racism and hostility in our workplaces. The personal/professional connections we built at ITOC helped us maintain our collective passion in the different projects we were leading. As teacher activists, we were all involved in some sort of organising within our schools, unions, and communities. We recognised the urgency of taking action in making sure our students, teachers, and families had agency in decision making, learning, and teaching. We knew the power of the system and so we also knew we had to take action, even if it meant longer days and shorter weekends; and ITOC provided us a model and the tools to grow as leaders who could support each other.

Having a space where we can share the work we are doing and get feedback and support has been tremendously valuable and we continue to seek each other out. The resources and space we shared have helped us become stronger advocates in our individual projects and we have networked to make connections across schools and districts. We find each other in union gatherings and hold space together to learn collectively. We lean on each other to advocate for resources and call out injustices within our teaching spaces. There are barriers to achieving our goals in this work: we are in different districts, our priorities vary, and our differences (such as years of experience, as well as shifting and distinct emotional, psychological, and professional needs) limit our organising and ability to provide mutual support. Still, our work is evolving as we use our monthly gatherings to continually reflect the needs and wants of the participants, just as ITOC taught us. We are now planning activities that re-energise us and help us connect with our humanity. We have organised gatherings to: make art in collaboration with a local art museum, participate in restorative circles, practice yoga together, and continue home get togethers. Building on what we learned and how we were supported through ITOC over multiple years, we are developing authentic relationships based on a shared racial justice vision and the need to be in community with each other so that we can continue the work individually and collectively for the rest of our professional lives.

Discussion

These four teachers had racial justice visions for education that built upon the assets of students and their families and were culturally sustaining. Unfortunately, their leadership skills, as is the case for so many other teachers of Colour, are often neglected by limited definitions of school leadership and change work (Kohli & Pizarro, 2016). At ITOC, however, they were able to engage in models of collaborative leadership development that valued their insights, knowledge, skills and creativity in building transformative schooling for students of Colour.

Because they rarely have like-minded colleagues, critical teachers of Colour are often left to develop curriculum in isolation (Martinez 2017). Building upon his childhood experiences, memories of the cultural responsiveness of his own teacher, and his own critical approach to arts education, Luis developed curriculum attending to his students' critical consciousness (Friere, 1970) – something uncommon in high school Arts education. When he was provided an opportunity to present his work at ITOC, he was excited that the transformative impact of the curriculum could be seen and adapted by like-minded peers. Lisa, who attended his session, saw power in Luis' work – not as a 'best practice' to be implemented 'as is' for student achievement (Patel 2020), but instead as an approach that could strengthen the humanisation, joy, and cultural sustainment of her pedagogy. Through contextually responsive coaching, Luis supported Lisa as she adapted the unit to her middle school English class and to her students' needs. Similar as it had been for Luis, the success of the curriculum and the opportunity to then present on her process developed her confidence not just as a teacher, but as a leader and expert among her peers. ITOC provided space for racial justice leadership through collective peer learning/teaching.

Critical scholars have argued that a teacher's role is political and agentive, and the reach of racial justice teacher leadership can extend across and even beyond schools (Giroux, 2012 2010). ITOC offered a community of support, tools for racial justice leadership, and space for critical teachers of

Colour to dream. Although isolated at his institution, Michael met educators at ITOC who not only shared his vision for education, but had engaged in justice work through YPAR and culturally sustaining pedagogies. He learned of the transformative possibilities of working alongside students to create systemic change (Cammarota and Fine 2010). This exposure influenced what he believed was possible on his campus, and fuelled his leadership to build a space of belonging and activism with Latinx students that quickly shifted the culture of his school. Seeking a similar approach with teachers in his district, after attending alone, Juan invited other colleagues to attend ITOC. By returning together, they developed shared racial literacies and leadership tools to combat their isolation and numerous racialised obstacles as they built a collective and enduring vision for activism across their district.

Conclusion

School leadership is often narrowly defined and prescribed, and is typically understood as individualised or hierarchical work. Additionally, teachers of Colour are profoundly undervalued in a predominantly White profession and schools steeped in institutionalised racism. This can limit their ability to create the cultural shifts they know are needed at their school sites. The leadership-efficacies of teachers of Colour flourish, however, when their culture, language, and epistemologies are valued, and they are supported to collectively reimagine the boundaries and possibilities of education. While each teacher-author in this article embodied racial justice in distinct ways, together, their narratives show the transformative power of critical professional development for teachers of Colour when collaborative approaches to learning and visioning racial justice are at the heart of school change. When community-oriented teachers of Colour are centred as leaders, they support other teachers of Colour in developing as leaders, and there is great power in collectively reimagining what schools can look like – in the curriculum, in school culture, and through teacher organising. ITOC demonstrates how critical professional development can be designed to circumvent the isolating and silencing of critical teachers of Colour, and can both re-inspire and support them to work together towards racial justice in their classrooms, schools, and across their districts.

Disclosure statement

No potential conflict of interest was reported by the authors.

References

Baker-Doyle, K.J., 2017. *Transformative teachers: teacher leadership and learning in a connected world*. Cambridge, MA 02138: Harvard Education Press. 8 Story Street First Floor.
Brown, A.L., 2009. 'O brotha where art thou?'Examining the ideological discourses of African American male teachers working with African American male students. *Race ethnicity and education*, 12 (4), 473–493. doi:10.1080/13613320903364432.
Cammarota, J. and Fine, M., Eds. 2010. *Revolutionizing education: youth participatory action research in motion*. Routledge.
Cherng, H.Y.S. and Halpin, P.F., 2016. The importance of minority teachers' student perceptions of minority versus White teachers. *Educational researcher*, 45 (7), 407–420. ahead of print. doi:10.3102/0013189X16671718.
Clandinin, D.J. and Connelly, F.M., 2004. Knowledge, narrative and self-study. In: J.J. Loughran, et al., eds. *International handbook of self-study of teaching and teacher education practices*. Dordrecht: Kluwer, 575–600.
Cochran-Smith, M., et al., 2015. Critiquing teacher preparation research: An overview of the field, Part II. *Journal of teacher education*, 66 (2), 109–121. doi:10.1177/0022487114558268.
Dingus, J.E., 2008. "I'm learning the trade" mentoring networks of black women teachers. *Urban education*, 43 (3), 361–377. doi:10.1177/0042085907311794.
Dixson, A. and Dingus, J.E., 2008. In search of our mothers' gardens: Black women teachers and professional socialization. *Teachers college record*, 110 (4), 805–837.

Endo, H., Reece-Miller, P.C., and Santavicca, N., 2010. Surviving in the trenches: A narrative inquiry into queer teachers' experiences and identity. *Teaching and teacher education*, 26 (4), 1023–1030. doi:10.1016/j.tate.2009.10.045.
Freire, P. 1970. Pedagogy of the oppressed (MB Ramos, Trans.). New York: Continuum, 2007
Garcia, L. G. (2018). La Lotería as creative resistance: The funds of knowledge, critical pedagogy, and critical race theory in art education. In J. M. Kiyama & C. Rios-Aguilar (Eds.), Funds of knowledge in higher education: Honoring students' cultural experiences and resources as strengths (pp. 66–84). Routledge.
Giroux, H., 2010. Teachers as transformative intellectuals. *Kaleidoscope: contemporary and classic readings in education*, 35–40.
Gist, C.D., 2019. The teacher testimony project: A research, pedagogical, and advocacy vehicle for teachers of color. *Multicultural perspectives*, 21 (1), 33–40. doi:10.1080/15210960.2019.1573064.
Gist, C.D., White, T., and Bianco, M., 2018. Pushed to teach: Pedagogies and policies for a black women educator pipeline. *Education and urban society*, 50 (1), 56–86. doi:10.1177/0013124517727584.
Haddix, M.M., 2017. Diversifying teaching and teacher education: Beyond rhetoric and toward real change. *Journal of literacy research*, 49 (1), 141–149. doi:10.1177/1086296X16683422.
Ingersoll, R. and May, H., 2011. *Recruitment, retention and the minority teacher shortage*. Santa Cruz, CA: The Consortium for Policy Research in Education.
Irizarry, J. and Donaldson, M.L., 2012. Teach for America: The latinization of US schools and the critical shortage of Latina/o teachers. *American educational research journal*, 49 (1), 155–194. doi:10.3102/0002831211434764.
Kohli, R., et al., 2015. Critical professional development: Centering the social justice needs of teachers. *International journal of critical pedagogy*, 6 (2).
Kohli, R. (2019). Lessons for Teacher Education: The Role of Critical Professional Development in Teacher of Color Retention.Journal of Teacher Education,70(1), 39–50 doi:10.1177/0022487118767645
Kohli., R., Burciaga, R., and Pizarro, M., 2020. Beyond the technical: Critical professional development supporting the holistic needs teachers of color. *In*: C. Gist and T. Bristol, eds. *Handbook on teachers of color*. To be published Fall. Funded by the American Educational Research Association.
Kohli, R. and Pizarro, M., 2016. Fighting to educate our own: Teachers of color, relational accountability and the struggle for racial justice. *Equity and excellence in education*, 49 (1), 72–84. doi:10.1080/10665684.2015.1121457.
Lopez, A.E., 2014. Re-conceptualising teacher leadership through curriculum inquiry in pursuit of social justice: Case study from the Canadian context. *In*: *In International handbook of educational leadership and social (in) justice*. Springer: Dordrecht, 465–484.
Martinez, A.N., 2017. 18 A people's education model to develop and support critical educators. *In*: Picower and Kohli eds. *Confronting racism in teacher education: counternarratives of critical practice*, 139–144.
Mensah, F.M. and Jackson, I., 2018. Whiteness as property in science teacher education. *Teachers college record*, 120 (1), 1–38.
Milner, H.R., 2010. Race, narrative inquiry, and self-study in curriculum and teacher education. *In*: *In Culture, curriculum, and identity in education*. Palgrave Macmillan: New York, 181–206.
National Center for Educational Statistics (2020). Characteristics of Public School Teachers. Accessed on August 25, 2020 at https://nces.ed.gov/programs/coe/indicator_clr.asp
Paris, D. and Alim, H.S., 2014. What are we seeking to sustain through culturally sustaining pedagogy? A loving critique forward. *Harvard educational review*, 84 (1), 85–100. doi:10.17763/haer.84.1.982l873k2ht16m77.
Paris, D. and Alim, H.S., Eds. 2017. *Culturally sustaining pedagogies: teaching and learning for justice in a changing world*. Teachers College Press.
Patel, L. (2020). Stepping through the portal: We are the one's we have been waiting for. *Keynote for the Institute for Teachers of Color Committed to Racial Justice*. [accessed 11 June 2020].
Pizarro, M. and Kohli, R., 2018. "I stopped sleeping:" Teachers of color and the impact of racial battle fatigue. *Urban education*.
Ritchie, J.S. and Wilson, D.E., 2000. *Teacher narrative as critical inquiry: rewriting the script*. Teachers College Press.
Rogers, R., Kramer, M.A., and Mosley, M., Literacy for Social Justice Teacher Research Group, 2009. *Designing socially just learning communities: critical literacy education across the lifespan*. Routledge.
Rojas, L., 2018. Transforming education for students of color: Reenvisioning teacher leadership for educational justice. *SoJo journal: educational foundations and social justice education*, 4 (2), 25–40.
US Department of Education. (2016). The state of racial diversity in the educator workforce. https://www2.ed.gov/rschstat/eval/highered/racial-diversity/state-racial-diversity-workforce.pdf.
Yosso, T.J., 2005. Whose culture has capital? A critical race theory discussion of community cultural wealth. *Race ethnicity and education*, 8 (1), 69–91. doi:10.1080/1361332052000341006.
Zambrano, M.A., 2013. *Loteria: a novel*. Harper Perennial.

The role of trade union provision for critical professional learning in supporting member teachers' social justice leadership practice

Halil Buyruk

ABSTRACT
This study examines the role of critical professional learning in leading socially just schools. The study investigated the experiences of teachers who are the members of Egitim-Sen, an active teacher union in Turkey. The article first focuses on the relationship between professional development and teacher unions followed by the definition of the roles of teachers as social justice leaders in constructing socially just schools. Then, it presents findings from a qualitative study of 12 Egitim-Sen member teachers with different experiences. The data were analysed using the phenomenological research design and presented under the themes of 'critical professional learning experiences', 'injustice in schools', and 'union member teachers as social justice leaders'. The findings indicate that the union member teachers take part in union training in various forms and that these experiences contribute to raising teachers' awareness of injustices in their schools with their critical professional learning experiences. Union member teachers play active roles in constructing socially just schools both individually and as organised union members.

Introduction

Many studies emphasise that teachers play key roles in the effectiveness of education reforms, in promoting the quality of education and in students' developing skills specific to today's society (OECD 2005, Barber and Mourshed 2007, WB 2018). Teachers are expected to adapt to changes in education and to be the actors of the change process. However, it is a matter of controversy whether teachers have the qualities necessary for fulfiling the tasks expected of them (Connell 2009). Therefore, the need for professional development in accordance with new goals is often emphasised (Ginsburg and Yeom 2007, Sorensen and Robertson 2017). Based on such an approach, many countries use more professional development activities to improve the quality of teachers.

Teachers' gaining skills consistent with the requirements of the time is mostly considered as an important step for professionalism. The definition of teacher professionalism changes according to historical and social conditions and power relations (Whitty 2006). This makes it difficult to determine the activities to promote teacher quality. Defining teachers' professional needs, just like defining professionalism, is a political process; and the approaches of various actors in the field of education about how to secure teachers' professional development can also differ. Global organisations such as OECD and WB- which would like to shape the education on the basis of economic priorities- attach importance to teachers' ability to inculcate twenty-first-century skills into students (Ananiadou and Claro 2009, Vegas et al. 2012). In addition to that, teachers are expected to gain new values and a new worldview in parallel to the changes (Sorensen and

Robertson 2017). The aim is to achieve all these skills through a lifelong learning process that covers teacher training (Villegas-Reimers 2003). On the other hand, economic and social changes, migration waves, the multi-cultural structure of schools and classrooms, and increasing social and economic inequalities require school administrators and teachers to develop a social justice-based approach. Teacher unions also get involved in developing democratic values and social justice-based policies, as well as industrial and professional issues (Stevenson and Gilliand 2017). All these developments result in including critical and social justice-related issues in programmes for teachers' professional development.

The roles of professional organisations in the formation and development of professions are important. Unions, on the other hand, are the structures in which generally workers are organised. Teachers mostly have been organised within unions unlike other professional groups, and they have acted like workers in this sense. However, the fact that teaching is a public service and that it has a professional ideology has caused it to be in conflict with the union model (Torres *et al.* 2000). While teacher unions have fulfilled union functions on the one hand, they have also struggled to develop educational policies and to protect professional rights on the other hand (Carter *et al.* 2010). Additionally, the approaches claiming that unions should spread their activities into all areas of social, economic, and political life instead of restricting to professions and workplaces have started to guide union policies over time (Waterman 1993, Weiner 2013). Unions' interest in economic and professional issues and their search for solutions to social and political problems enable their members to learn about and improve in those issues. Thus, unions' professional development activities can perform important roles in supporting member teachers' social justice leadership practice. In this context, this paper aims to analyse the role of union-supported critical professional learning in leading socially just schools by setting out from the experiences of union member teachers.

Professional development and teacher unions

Professional development can have different meanings because of the lack of consensus in the definition of professionalism in the literature (Gewirtz *et al.* 2009). Evans (2008) defines professional development as a development in the status of the profession as a whole and also as an improvement in knowledge, skills, and practices. In addition to promoting teachers' performance by improving their knowledge and practice, their attitudes towards their profession can also be improved. Research has shown that professional development is also effective in enhancing teachers' beliefs and behaviours (Villegas-Reimers 2003). Hence, it encourages them to acquire new values in parallel to the changes in education (Little 1993). Yet, the determination of the new values and the scope of professional activities are closely related to the meaning teachers give to professional development.

When considered in terms of teachers, professional development can either involve strengthening and developing an individual teacher's professionalism and practice or it can be used as an umbrella term that includes all learning programmes teachers join to raise the quality of education and to develop teaching (Ben-Peretz *et al.* 2010). Thus, professional development can be considered as all formal, informal and non-formal learning experiences from pre-service teacher education to retirement independently of who provides it (Desimone 2009). Professional development models for teachers can be classified into two groups on the basis of scale (Villegas-Reimers 2003). One of them is the smaller scale work in schools and classroom and the other type are programmes that are conducted in cooperation with certain organisations or institutions. Work that unions do in professional issues can be considered in the second group. Teacher unions' interest in professional issues, holding workshops for their members, forming discussion groups, and offering training in professional issues have a long history (Bascia 2000, Osmond-Johnson *et al.* 2019). Moreover, their interest in such issues has increased with the popularisation of professional development.

In the last quarter of the 20th century especially, issues related to social justice were defined within unions' area of struggle (Weiner 2013). Thus, the professional development activities of teacher unions were not kept restricted to professional issues but expanded to include policies to address social issues and social justice. All these developments caused unions to follow policies to support their members in professional issues and to establish social justice and equity in education (Osmond-Johnson et al. 2019). In addition to their indirect functions, teacher unions also have direct activities to support their members' professional development, to be their voice in the workplace, and to strengthen the union (Bangs and MacBeath 2012, Stevenson et al. 2018). Teacher organisations have various traditions in professional development, which can vary according to local dynamics (Bascia 2000). For instance, while local organisations decide on the professional development activities of teacher unions in the USA and in Canada, national or state offices provide speakers, finance and the materials necessary. Bascia (2000) describes teacher training offered by another organisation or institution as one of the second-generation professional development strategies. Professional development activities held by teacher unions which led to the securing of the involvement of women and minority groups in management positions in schools can be considered in this group. Apart from those organised and systematic educational activities, teachers can also organise different professional learning processes through their unions. These may be in the form of informal discussion and reading groups or working groups. Teacher unions can also take on a more active part in identifying and meeting needs in professional development, in providing professional learning opportunities and in building alliances with a wide range of governmental and non-governmental bodies (Stevenson et al. 2018).

Socially just schools and teachers as social justice leaders

Social inequalities affect the field of education, and educational processes play a role in reproducing and legitimising existing inequalities. Zanten (2005) states that one of the most consistent results of educational research has been the patterns of educational inequalities since the first large scale studies carried out in the 1960s. Although there is a significant increase in access to education in many parts of the world, inequalities and injustices due to class, race, religion, gender and ethnicity are still persistent. The latest data on PISA, which OECD uses to measure and compare the knowledge and skills of students in different countries, reveal that there are still major educational inequalities worldwide (OECD 2019).

Three fundamental approaches of social justice can be mentioned in building socially just schools to reduce inequalities. One of these is the distributive justice approach- which recommends allocating extra funds and resources to students on the basis of economic needs to support school participation and student success (Gewirtz 1998). This approach, which was applied especially in Western countries during the social state period, was criticised for focusing only on economic justice, without taking into account how cultural disadvantage affected students' educational outcomes (West and Nikolai 2013). It was claimed that race and ethnicity could also be the reasons for low performance in education where indigenous students or students from minority ethnicities performed lower than their peers with race and class privileges (Williams 1986, McWhirter 1997, Wang 2004). Reflecting the histories, cultures, perspectives, and contributions to society of disadvantaged groups in school practices and curricula is one of the educational applications which can support recognition for marginalised students (Keddie 2012). Fraser (2008), who stated that these two approaches of justice could sometimes conflict, emphasised that there should also be political justice and described a three-dimensional theory of justice. The third dimension of justice is the policy of representation. Most schools around the world privilege white, western and middle-class ways of knowing and being (Keddie 2012). In this context, the fair representation of the minority and marginalised groups in decision-making processes provides a political space in which they can have a voice in describing their educational needs. Representation is necessary for the actualisation of distributive and recognition justice.

Teachers have important duties in building socially just schools and in developing a worldview based on social justice among students. However, there are conflicts and struggles on how to shape educational policies and how to form the curricula available in education. In this process, which can be defined as a struggle for hegemony with a Gramscian approach, teachers as social justice leaders, have the potential to play a role in eliminating injustices based on social class, gender, and race. In this way, critical consciousness necessary for a world shaped by social justice can be raised by using the materials of disadvantaged groups in schools and by including them in representation processes (McLaren 2003, Darder et al. 2009).

The roles of teachers as social justice leaders are not limited to developing a way of critical thinking. They can also play roles in implementing the policies enabling disadvantaged students to access qualified education and supporting the development of students who are in this group (McKenzie and Scheurich 2004, Bell 2007, Furman 2012). Thus, steps can be taken to secure social justice in schools with dimensions of distribution, recognition, and representation. It is important for teachers to carry out their work as an autonomous activity so that they can perform such an intellectual function (Giroux 1988). However, on looking at the recent developments, we see that teachers' autonomy has decreased with the centralised management and curricula, and the increasing role of standardised tests (Sahlberg 2016). Further, teachers' fulfiling such an intellectual function is related to their ability to develop critical consciousness. However, teacher-training programmes are getting away from building intellectual skills and a critical consciousness (Sleeter 2008, Potelli and Oladi 2018) and so there are problems in implementing social justice leadership. In this context, teacher unions can contribute to teachers' gaining critical and intellectual consciousness and to their development as social justice leaders through professional development programmes. In this way, it can be possible to build schools on the basis of social justice and to lead accordingly.

Education in Turkey and Egitim-Sen

In the Turkish Education System, the Ministry of National Education (MoNE) carries out the planning, implementation, and monitoring of national policies and strategies for all levels of education and training centrally. Primary and secondary education is compulsory in the 4 + 4 + 4 format for twelve years for all citizens. The total number of students in the formal education system in Turkey is 18,108,860 according to 2018/19 National Education statistics (MoNE 2019a). Approximately 8% of the students attend private schools whereas 9% of them attend open education institutions. The number of teachers is 1,077,307 and 15% of them work in private schools. Education is largely publicly funded in Turkey, but schools can receive contributions from parents through their school–parent associations because of insufficient funding. Private organisations can also donate to the schools. The lack of sufficient resources for schools, especially at the primary level, causes each school to create their own resources. Such a situation has increased inequalities between schools and caused social segregation. There are important success differences between high schools of various types and levels. According to PISA 2018 data, the difference in reading skills among some high school types is about 200 points. This is directly related to the separation of high schools according to the academic success of the students. Socio-economically advantaged students are 76 points ahead of the disadvantaged students (MoNE 2019b). Similar patterns are evident in the transition into higher education. Students' socio-economic level, the types of schools they graduate from, the educational status of their families, the geographical region they live in all can impact on their achievement in the higher education entrance examination (Cetingül and Dülger 2006, Atac 2017).

The Turkish education system has a mono-cultural structure largely ignoring the religious, cultural, and ethnic differences (Baysu and Agirdag 2019). Although reforms such as elective courses are available for ethnic groups, the reforms are inadequate in terms of their access to educational rights (Kaya 2009). Moreover, a sect of Islam is in a hegemonic position in terms of religious education and thus, other beliefs and cultural groups may be subject to discrimination

(Baysu and Agirdag 2019). On the other hand, the number of refugees in Turkey has rapidly increased due to the civil war in Syria. There were 3,687,244 refugees in Turkey on November 21st, 2019 according to the records of the UN Refugees Agency and almost 30% of them were children at school age (UNHCR 2019). A number of problems are encountered in integrating those children- almost half of whom are not enrolled in an official educational institution (ERG 2017).

Teacher organisation in Turkey has a long history and an established tradition (Altunya 1998). Egitim-Sen was founded in the 1990s as the inheritor of this tradition, but it gained its legal status in the 2000s. The union came to the fore with its effective opposition to the loss of rights in education as a result of neo-liberal policies applied globally in those years. As Turkey's third-largest teacher union, Egitim-Sen develops policies about social and professional issues- mainly about the above-mentioned educational inequalities and injustices- and carries out actions (Egitim-Sen 2014a). These policies include preparing and publishing booklets against education inequalities and neo-liberal policies, creating campaigns, training union representatives, organising conferences, and congresses. Union members faced pressure and punishment for their effective opposition. In addition, it can be said that the authoritarian atmosphere that emerged after the failed coup attempt on July 15 was reflected in the unions and a significant decline was experienced in union activities.

Research design and methodology

This qualitative study sought to examine and interpret union member teachers' experiences of the role of critical professional learning in building socially just schools. The qualitative approach was the best way to reveal the experiences of teachers and to understand in what ways they could act as social justice leaders (Patton 2014). A phenomenological design was employed to fully comprehend and describe in-depth the range of experiences reported by teachers (Creswell 2007). Phenomenological studies focus on understanding the phenomenon from the views of participants who have experienced it (Christensen et al. 2014, Patton 2014).

The participants of this study were selected using snowball sampling among K-12 teachers (Patton 2014). They are all union members half of whom are female. They are aged between 27 and 62 and they have teaching experience between 5 and 38 years. Since the phenomenological approach aims to reach the experiences of the participants and to obtain in-depth information, it is appropriate to work with a small number of participants (Gray 2004). The interviews were limited to 12 teachers because the responses that started to be similar were interpreted as reaching the interview saturation point (Gentles et al. 2015). Since interviews are the main data sources in phenomenological researches, I preferred semi-structured, in-depth interviews that were not pre-scriptive and did not limit the information that participants stated (Smith and Osborn 2004). The interview form included questions on teachers' relationship with the union, their experiences on the inequalities and injustices in the school, their individual and organised practices against those inequalities, and the contribution of the union activities/training to overcome these injustices. In each interview, I encouraged the participants' freedom of expression and shaped the questions according to the context of the participants (Knapik 2006). The interviews were held sometimes in the teachers' room and sometimes in the branch offices of the union. We preferred the branch offices mostly because the participants felt more comfortable there. The scope of the interviews was explained to the participants and the interviews were audio-recorded after receiving their consent. All interviews were transcribed before being translated into English.

Data analysis

In performing a phenomenological analysis of the interview data, a set of stages was conducted. First, the collected data were coded by examining, comparing, reducing, conceptualising and categorising (Creswell 2007, Patton 2014). The next step was to define themes by clustering common expressions. The experiences were described by using the themes and the textural and structural explanations containing the meanings and essence of the experiences were formed (Moustakas 1994). In reporting the findings, I tried to describe the role of critical professional learning in leading socially just schools and of the practices emerging on this axis by setting out from the teachers' experiences. The themes were not selected a priori, but also emerged from the theoretical discussions. I reported the findings through narrative presentation gleaned from the interviews, using pseudonyms to ensure participants' anonymity. Thus, the meanings the teachers assigned to their roles in schools and to their practices in educational processes were defined with similarities and differences on the basis of their descriptions and interpreted.

The role of the researcher

In qualitative research, interviews refer to a process based on collecting data as a result of the relationship and collaboration between the researcher and the participant, rather than being a technique in which the researcher collects information about a phenomenon. The researcher is part of the knowledge production process and it is important to be aware of his/her approach to the phenomenon (Creswell 2007). The researcher's explanation of his/her own assumptions and tendencies paves the way for the reader to better understand the research (Merriam and Tisdell 2016). In this context, my previous experiences as a union member teacher was the starting point for the study, doing research on a subject related to my experiences. During my teaching experience, what I experienced and saw in schools made me think about the role of the teacher in the formation of just schools. Being a union member teacher helped me focus on the role that the union can play in this regard.

Findings

This paper, aiming to reveal the role of critical professional learning in building socially just schools, is based on the experiences of 12 union member teachers. The findings were presented under the themes of critical professional learning experiences, injustices in schools, and union member teachers as social justice leaders.

Critical professional learning experiences

It is possible for teachers to be social justice leaders by developing critical consciousness against current injustices. The training programmes of teacher unions, which offer a critical learning experience, may contribute significantly to developing such consciousness. Egitim-Sen carries out these programmes for four different groups of members- namely, for administrators, workplace representatives, young staff, and union educators. Although the content differs according to the target groups, the training programmes mainly include topics such as economic and social conditions, unions, changes in education, employment, organisation and gender (Egitim-Sen 2014b). Engin, who is the workplace representative of his school where he had been teaching for a long time said the following in relation to joining the training programme and to his experiences:

> A training programme that I had joined for the first time. (...) It was a nice atmosphere with other colleagues. It was a two-day programme. Presentations were made on education, communication and being organised. Meeting were held about the history of unions and teachers' organisation, changes in education and their reflections into schools and gender.

One of the main goals in those training programmes in which mostly active union members called 'staff' join is to offer training and organisation within the framework of principles and values advocated by the union thereby building union consciousness and culture. Other goals include expanding the union in quantity and in quality and inculcating democratic values such as equality, liberty, and social justice in members (Egitim-Sen 2014b).

Manager or educator training is also offered to spread the training at the bottom and to enable more members to benefit from the training. Saying that she attended a training session on gender organised by the head office, Nergis stated that this training given by academic staff specialised in various fields was offered to the trainers of the branches that will train other members. Canay, in her statement 'I made sense of the situations I experienced and witnessed every day with those training sessions' meant that she gained awareness of the situations she experienced. Thus, it may be said that the head office training mostly aims to raise union consciousness and that it also creates learning environments in which knowledge about education and teaching is shared.

Egitim-Sen member teachers can participate in various commissions in the head office or branches, create working groups, and participate in congresses, panels, and conferences organised by the union. Sinan, who took part in a conference, which was a form of critical professional learning, conveyed his experiences as follows:

> Those conferences are like a school for teachers. You can both join the discussion groups in branch offices and thus contribute to organising the discussions from the bottom to the top and you can also be chosen and included in work groups of the head office if have more interest in such issues. We had in-depth work under the pre-determined headings with those groups.

Mahir, who as Sinan had, described the process of preparation for a conference and reported his experiences as:

> Our commission was related to the right to education. We had long discussions about the history of education, the concept of right, the development of educational rights and how to consider them. I can say that is was like a school for me.

Teachers create reading groups and organise workshops on education and learning in the branch offices or in places called cultural centres even though such activities are not considered as a training programme. Another learning process is to share daily experiences. Member teachers who unofficially gather at the branch offices or at the cultural centres talk and discuss their experiences in school, education, and learning. Such a process of sharing enables especially young teachers to develop an approach to education and teaching.

Interviews reveal that union training activities and informal learning experiences create environments in which teachers develop their education, school, and teaching perspectives, gain critical consciousness, and have the opportunity for self-development.

Injustices in schools

The union member teachers interviewed mentioned various injustices in schools. One of the fundamental injustices in education in Turkey is social segregation between and within schools. Parents' economic status and educational level can determine the schools that their children will attend. Quality differences emerge among public schools due to parents' contributions to schools. All this leads to injustice in schools.

> Of course, some schools have their money. How? School-parent association raises the money. In other schools, parents don't have the money to give. (…) A school is well equipped because parents help. Teachers are chosen accordingly. On the other hand, the school management gives students whose financial position is not good to a teacher who is not preferred much (Eylem).

Academic high schools and vocational high schools accept students from different segments of society. Children of families with low socio-economic level and with a low level of education usually go to vocational high schools.

> Generally, those who were eliminated, those who have no other alternatives and children of families who want their children to have a job go to vocational high schools. (…). There are poor, slum dwellers' children in our school. Because these schools cannot prepare children for examinations. They cannot send those students to university. They probably become intermediate staff in the industry (Taylan).

The emergence of such differences between high schools and the distribution of students in those schools according to their socio-economic conditions takes place through a competitive testing system because the type of high school in which students attend almost determines the higher education programme that they are to attend. The students' standardised test scores determine the type of schools they are to go to, and the socio-economic and cultural characteristics of the parents can be said to be effective in the formation of this score.

> What do parents do? They choose the school where their children can pass exams (…). Students are in pursuit of passing exams. Rich students having a goal have gone to private schools. Those who receive high scores from exams go to good state schools. The remaining goes to either religious schools or vocational high schools (Sevil)

The curricula are prepared centrally in Turkey and are implemented all over the country as a standard. Therefore, they fail to meet the needs arising from ethnicity and belief differences. Although ethnic languages are widely used in some regions, they are not used as the language of education. The creeds of only one sect of Islam come into prominence in classes teaching religious values. Stating that it is a conservative environment and minority children cannot express themselves, Elif explained the situation as follows:

> The number of elective courses in religion has increased. But you see that all of them are taught on the basis of a sect. (…) The Ministry of National Education makes an agreement with religious foundations, religious officials come to school for teaching and then what happens? Other belief groups are ignored.

There is also gender inequality in education. The number of girls attending school has been increasing more and more. However, differences between regions, rural and urban areas, and socioeconomic levels to the disadvantage of girls arise in access to education. On the other hand, LGBTI students can be exposed to discrimination in schools. In addition, the number of refugee students in schools has increased considerably in recent years due to refugee migration. It caused various problems in schools and teachers having no previous experience with such a situation. Nergis, who worked with refugee children, described her experiences as in the following:

> I observed that there were discriminating attitudes towards foreign students. Teachers display discriminating attitudes even though they do not state directly. There are teachers who say, 'why do you teach them?' 'Teach our kids'. 'They should go to their country.' Or 'Why are they here?'. They say, 'why should we care them while our kids are here?'

There is a great deal of injustice for students in schools, but there are also problems in teachers' involvement in the decision-making process and in their self-expression. Teachers who are critical of policy and practice and look for change can be isolated when the centrally set policies are implemented in schools.

> You are isolated when you have a critical attitude. They make you feel that there is an environment of tranquillity and that you disturb it. It in fact has to do with having only a small number of us. You can face punishment when you have an objection. Almost all of the school managers are the members of unions supporting the government (Sinan).

It can be said in general that social inequalities are also reflected in schools and that the disadvantaged students have problems in access to the right to education due to existing inequalities.

Union member teachers as social justice leaders

Although there are structural reasons for injustices in schools, it is possible to reduce inequalities by empowering disadvantaged groups and implementing social justice policies. Union-member teachers interviewed mentioned their individual and organised efforts for their schools to operate on the basis of social justice. They emphasised that it was necessary to become aware of inequalities experienced in schools and then to think about ways of solutions to overcome these inequalities and injustices. Most of the teachers interviewed said that the union and training programmes played important roles in raising their awareness and they claimed that they developed a collective consciousness as union members where they had developed similar ideas about what could be done in schools.

> Union training, the reports published by the union, and conversations with our friends enable us to have an idea about what is at issue. I mean it is possible for us to see the big picture in this way (Sinan).

Some teachers emphasised that the attitudes of the Egitim-Sen member teachers towards the problems and injustices that might arise in schools would be similar although they were not pre-determined, and thus that it could be possible to talk of Egitim-Sen member identity.

> An Egitim-Sen member teacher is egalitarian, he or she opposes injustice and discrimination. He or she has clear reactions to harassment, he or she is libertarian. He or she uses solidarity-based, integrative language (Deniz).

The union member teachers I interviewed were trying to build a culture based on social justice in school and in their own classes based on what they saw as their identity as an Egitim-Sen member. Nergis, for instance, describing her approach in the classroom, said 'I try not to use discriminating, isolating language; I try to make my students feel that differences are something nice.' In a similar way, Deniz also emphasised that he tried to create a democratic culture based on participation. The teachers interviewed stressed that they looked to reach a certain number of like-minded teachers in school so that their individual attitudes could come together as organised behaviour. Intervening in school culture requires a certain amount of power and so working with other teachers is vital.

> You can determine school culture if you are powerful in school. Then the management is obliged to consider you when they do something. (…) It becomes easier to have democratic processes in the teachers' council, to bring up the topics you wish to discuss and to make the decisions you wish (Sinan).

Organised interventions in school policies occur mostly in a case of crisis and when there is an incident. Union member teachers come together and try to find a solution when there is a problem rather than acting in a planned manner.

> They wanted to plan their schedule according to Friday Prayer. You can say what is wrong with it. There can be teachers and students who want to join Friday Prayer. At first, it seems so but there will be pressure in the classrooms about joining Friday Prayer. The circumstances cause it. People are becoming more and more conservative. We had a meeting with colleagues, brought up the issue, and made them take their step backward (Taylan).

It became apparent in schools where the union was powerful that teachers were more effective in building socially just schools, that they could act together, that they could find solutions to problems, and that they could do more to build a democratic culture. An authoritarian management approach was reflected in schools. For example, the system of student representation – which Deniz saw as playing an important role in the formation of democratic culture – was abolished by a regulation. Similarly, the names of clubs through which gender activities could take place were also changed with a regulation. Despite these regulations, Deniz reported on what had been achieved:

> We secure that clubs in which students can work actively be founded, we hold conferences, panels, or we help students to do such activities. We brought up those issues in the teachers' council so that such clubs could be started, and conferences and panels could be held. Of course, we first come together with colleagues and make sure they are approved by the council.

Organised activities of teachers play an important role in establishing democratic functioning. Deniz said that they tried to make more room for anti-discrimination activities that emphasise brotherhood, solidarity, and peace. I asked him whether they did all those according to a plan. He said that they, as Egitim-Sen member teachers, did not meet specifically but that they continuously created an environment of discussion and sharing in the staff room. The increase in the number of teacher union members and the environment where the school is located also prepares the ground for democratic culture and for collective work. Deniz stated that the teachers acted in a more union organised manner and established a workplace council in the past. However, he emphasised that the political climate in the country was reflected in the school and therefore they could no longer do such activities. Many teachers stated that an authoritarian and a fear culture had been created in the country in recent years. People, including the union member teachers, prefer to stay in the background or at least to remain silent due to fear of being dismissed after the failed coup attempt.

> Dismissals and the environment of pressure created especially after the failed coup attempt and the punishments given weakened the effectiveness of unions in schools. We now cannot do the activities which we could easily do previously. The school manager who has close relations with the government can give punishment more easily (Engin).

The dominant culture cannot be said as the only reason why union member teachers are now more passive in schools than in the past because many teachers interviewed stated that the union's approach also accelerated this process and that the members lost their faith in the union.

> The union is now inadequate in determining attitudes towards current policies. It has to do with the political atmosphere in the country, but no ties can be set up with schools. We cannot feel the power and support of the head office (Taylan).

> Internal discussions hinder us from acting together. Sometimes we discuss who from which group will join a union activity. The functioning of democratic processes has been weakened. The atmosphere in the country has also affected it (Deniz).

Teachers interviewed said that being a union member, joining training sessions, attending panels and conferences contributed significantly to their work. Features such as 'self-expression', 'setting up relations', 'collective action', 'self-confidence', 'empathy', 'leadership', and 'sharing' can be listed among these contributions. On the other hand, the members also emphasised that the union could not contribute enough to the professional development of teachers. Although the union was aware of the changes put into practice in the education and teaching profession under the influence of global organisations, it failed to display an integrative stance against policies implemented. The union gives little space to activities aimed at professional development and improving education quality.

Discussion and conclusion

Inequality in income distribution, racial, religious, ethnic, and gender-based discrimination policies and practices cause injustice in schools and create various obstacles to different segments of society in terms of exercising the right to education. Leading socially just schools can make it possible to reduce such injustice relatively, to raise the consciousness of disadvantaged individuals, and to reach better quality education. Teachers as social justice leaders who have developed critical consciousness can play active roles in building socially just schools. It is important that teacher unions contribute to teachers' professional development through training programmes so that teachers can develop such consciousness and can take on responsibilities in leading socially just schools. Egitim-Sen is a teacher union that organises many actions on industrial, professional, and social issues. This study analysed the role of trade union provision for critical professional learning in supporting member teachers' social justice leadership practice by focussing on the micro-processes in schools.

Egitim-Sen organises training programmes at various levels for its members (Egitim-Sen 2014b). Those programmes mostly aim to raise the awareness of active members called 'staff' in relation to comprehending economic and social functioning and to developing consciousness. As Stevenson et al. (2018) emphasise, unions can be strengthened, teachers' professional development can be supported and their voice in the workplace can be heard in this way. However, professional learning experiences are not restricted to the training programmes offered by the union. The union holds congresses and symposiums on various subjects (they were more often in the past), invites speakers from universities, organises conventions, and issues a journal enabling academic sharing. In addition, branch offices also function as informal learning environments. As many unions have done for years (Bascia 2000, Osmond-Johnson et al. 2019), Egitim-Sen contributes significantly to the professional development of its members as social justice leaders even though these opportunities are limited.

Inequities are evident at various levels of education in Turkey. Although the causes of inequities stem from wider societal structural issues, there is also injustice stemming from practices in schools, school management, and teachers' attitudes. Those practices in schools include discrimination based on ethnicity, religious beliefs, and sexual orientation. The bureaucratic and centrally administered education system cannot deal adequately with social differences. As Baysu and Agirdag (2019) stated, religious, cultural, and ethnic differences are largely ignored in the education system which largely reflects the dominant culture. School administrators and teachers who cannot develop critical consciousness cannot contribute to the construction of socially just schools. The research revealed that teachers who have a critical professional learning experience can contribute to the development of socially just schools. Union member teachers intervene in school culture both individually and as organised union members and display practices aiming to develop social justice and opposing discrimination in schools. These practices contribute to the establishment of a more democratic environment in the school by increasing participation in decision-making processes, empowering the organisation of student clubs, panels, and conferences. The findings demonstrated that Egitim-Sen member teachers tended to build an identity of 'egalitarian', 'democratic', and 'libertarian' teacher. The authoritarian atmosphere, conservative environment, and oppressive school administration create obstacles for union member teachers to act as social justice leaders. Even though it can be said that they are more passive now than in the past, it is apparent that teachers having critical professional learning experiences continue to work to build socially just schools in several ways.

Disclosure statement

No potential conflict of interest was reported by the author.

ORCID

Halil Buyruk http://orcid.org/0000-0003-4817-3798

References

Altunya, N., 1998. *Türkiye'de ögretmen örgütlenmesi (1908–2008)*. [Teacher organisation in Turkey]. Ankara: Ürün Yayınları.

Ananiadou, K. and Claro, M., 2009. *21st Century skills and competences for new millennium learners in OECD countries*. OECD Education Working Papers, No. 41. Available from: www.oecdilibrary.org [Accessed 4 December 2019].

Atac, E., 2017. Reading educational inequalities in Turkey: statistics and geographic distributions. *Education and Science*, 42 (192), 59–86.

Bangs, J. and MacBeath, J., 2012. Collective leadership: the role of teacher unions in encouraging teachers to take the lead in their own learning and in teacher policy. *Professional Development in Education*, 38 (2), 331–343. doi:10.1080/19415257.2012.657879.

Barber, M. and Mourshed, M., 2007. *How the world's best-performing schools come out on top*. London: McKinsey & Company. Available from: https://www.mckinsey.com [Accessed 10 December 2019].

Bascia, N., 2000. The other side of the equation: professional development and the organizational capacity of teacher unions. *Educational Policy*, 14 (3), 385–404. doi:10.1177/0895904800014003003.

Baysu, G. and Agirdag, O., 2019. Turkey: silencing ethnic inequalities under a carpet of nationalism shifting between secular and religious poles. *In*: P. Stevens and G. Dworkin, eds. *The Palgrave handbook of race and ethnic inequalities in education*. Switzerland: Palgrave Macmillan, 1075–1098.

Bell, L.A., 2007. Theoretical foundations for social justice education. *In*: M. Adams, L.A. Bell, and P. Griffin, eds. *Teaching for diversity and social justice*. New York, NY: Routledge, 1–14.

Ben-Peretz, M., et al. 2010. Educators of educators: their goals, perceptions and practices. *Professional Development in Education*, 36 (1–2), 111–129. doi:10.1080/19415250903454908.

Carter, B., Stevenson, H., and Passy, R., 2010. *Industrial relations in education: transforming the school workforce*. London: Routledge.

Cetingül, P.I.T. and Dülger, I., 2006. Analysis of the ÖSS results according to school types, cities and regions in Turkey. *Education and Science*, 31 (142), 45–55.

Christensen, L.B., Johnson, R.B., and Turner, L.A., 2014. *Research methods, design, and analysis*. Boston, MA: Allyn & Bacon.

Connell, R., 2009. Good teachers on dangerous ground: towards a new view of teacher quality and professionalism. *Critical Studies in Education*, 50 (3), 213–229. doi:10.1080/17508480902998421.

Creswell, J.W., 2007. *Qualitative inquiry & research design*. Thousand Oaks, CA: Sage.

Darder, A., Baltodano, M.P., and Torres, R.D., 2009. Critical pedagogy: an introduction. *In*: A. Darder, M. P. Baltodano, and R.D. Torres, eds. *The critical pedagogy reader*. New York: Routledge, 1–26.

Desimone, L.M., 2009. Improving impact studies of teachers' professional development: toward better conceptualizations and measures. *Educational Researcher*, 38 (3), 181–199. doi:10.3102/0013189X08331140.

Egitim-Sen, 2014a. *Egitim-Sen tüzük*. [Rules]. Ankara: Eğitim Sen.

Egitim-Sen, 2014b. *Egitim-Sen çalışma programı (2011–2014)*. [Work Programme]. Ankara: Egitim-Sen.

ERG, 2017. *Bir arada yaşamı ve geleceği kapsayıcı egitimle inşa etmek*. [Building life and future together with inclusive education] Available from: https://indd.adobe.com/view/6066c857-843a-4d49-b7e9-77f635a950cf [Accessed 3 November 2019].

Evans, L., 2008. Professionalism, professionality and the development of education professionals. *British Journal of Educational Studies*, 56 (1), 20–38. doi:10.1111/j.1467-8527.2007.00392.x.

Fraser, N., 2008. Reframing justice in a globalising world. *In*: K. Olson, ed. *Adding insult to injury: Nancy Fraser debates her critics*. London: Verso, 273–294.

Furman, G., 2012. Social justice leadership as praxis: developing capacities through preparation programs. *Educational Administration Quarterly*, 48 (2), 191–229. doi:10.1177/0013161X11427394.

Gentles, S.J., et al., 2015. Sampling in qualitative research: insights from an overview of the methods literature. *The Qualitative Report*, 20 (11), 1772–1789.

Gewirtz, S., 1998. Conceptualizing social justice in education: mapping the territory. *Journal of Education Policy*, 13 (4), 469–484. doi:10.1080/0268093980130402.

Gewirtz, S., et al., 2009. Policy, professionalism and practice: understanding and enhancing teachers' work. *In*: S. Gewirtz, et al., ed. *Changing Teacher Professionalism*. USA and Canada: Routledge, 3–16.

Ginsburg, M. and Yeom, M., 2007. Professionalism and the reform of teachers and teacher education in the Republic of Korea & The United States of America. *Asia Pacific Education Review*, 8 (2), 298–310. doi:10.1007/BF03029264.

Giroux, H.A., 1988. *Teachers as Intellectuals*. USA: Bergin and Garvey Publishers.

Gray, D.E., 2004. *Doing research in the real world*. London: Sage.

Kaya, N., 2009. *Forgotten or assimilated? Minorities in the education system of Turkey*. Istanbul: Tarih Vakfı.

Keddie, A., 2012. Schooling and social justice through the lenses of Nancy Fraser. *Critical Studies in Education*, 53 (3), 263–279. doi:10.1080/17508487.2012.709185.

Knapik, M., 2006. The qualitative research interview: participants' responsive participation in knowledge making. *International Journal of Qualitative Methods*, 5 (3), 1–13. doi:10.1177/160940690600500308.

Little, J.W., 1993. Teachers' professional development in a climate of education reform. *Educational Evaluation and Policy Analysis*, 15, 129–151.

McKenzie, K.B. and Scheurich, J.J., 2004. Equity traps: a useful construct for preparing principals to lead schools that are successful with racially diverse students. *Educational Administration Quarterly*, 40 (5), 606–632. doi:10.1177/0013161X04268839.

McLaren, P., 2003. Critical pedagogy: a look at the major concepts. *In*: A. Darder, M. Baltodano, and R.D. Torres, eds. *Critical pedagogy reader*. New York: Routledge Falmer, 69–96.

McWhirter, E.H., 1997. Perceived barriers to education and career: ethnic and gender differences. *Journal of Vocational Behavior*, 50 (1), 124–140. doi:10.1006/jvbe.1995.1536.

Merriam, S.B. and Tisdell, E.J., 2016. *Qualitative research: a guide to design and implementation*. San Francisco, CA: Jossey-Bass.

MoNE, 2019a. *National education statistics: Formal education*. Ankara: MoNE.

MoNE, 2019b. *PISA 2018 Turkey preliminary report*. Available from: http://www.meb.gov.tr [Accessed 20 December 2019].

Moustakas, C., 1994. *Phenomenological research methods*. USA: Sage Publications.

OECD, 2005. *Teachers matter: attracting, developing and retaining effective teachers, education and training policy*. Paris: OECD Publishing.

OECD, 2019. *PISA 2018 results (volume II): where all students can succeed*. Paris: OECD Publishing.

Osmond-Johnson, P., Campbell, C., and Faubert, B., 2019. Supporting professional learning: the work of Canadian teachers' organizations. *Professional Development in Education*, 45 (1), 17–32. doi:10.1080/19415257.2018.1486877.

Patton, M.Q., 2014. *Qualitative research and evaluation methods*. USA: Sage.

Potelli, J.P. and Oladi, S., 2018. Neoliberal elements in Canadian teacher education: challenges and possibilities. *Alberta Journal of Educational Research*, 64 (4), 1–15.

Sahlberg, P., 2016. The global educational reform movement and its impact on schooling. *In*: K. Mundy, *et al*., eds. *The handbook of global education policy*. West Sussex: Wiley-Blackwell, 128–144.

Sleeter, C., 2008. Equity, democracy, and neoliberal assaults on teacher education. *Teaching and Teacher Education*, 24 (8), 1947–1957. doi:10.1016/j.tate.2008.04.003.

Smith, J. and Osborn, M., 2004. Interpretative phenomenological analysis. *In*: G. Breakwell, ed. *Doing social psychology*. Oxford, UK: Blackwell, 229–254.

Sorensen, T.B. and Robertson, S.L., 2017. The OECD program TALIS and framing, measuring and selling quality teacher". *In*: M. Akiba and G.K. LeTendre, eds. *International handbook of teacher quality and policy*. Abingdon, UK: Routledge, 117–131.

Stevenson, H. and Gilliand, A., 2017. The teachers' voice: teacher unions at the heart of a new democratic professionalism. *In*: J. Evers and E. Kneyber, eds. *Flip the system: changing education from the ground up*. London: Routledge, 108–119.

Stevenson, H., Milner, A., and Winchip, E., 2018. *Education trade unions for the teaching profession: strengthening the capacity of education trade unions to represent teachers' professional needs in social dialogue*. European Brussels: European Trade Union Committee for Education..

Torres, C.A., *et al.*, 2000. *Political capital, teachers' unions and the state: value conflicts and collaborative strategies in educational reform in the United States, Canada, Japan, Korea, Mexico and Argentina*. Los Angeles: Pacific Rim Center, University of California..

UNHCR, 2019. *Syria regional refugee response. Inter-agency information sharing portal*. Available from: https://data2.unhcr.org/en/situations/syria [Accessed 13 December 2019].

Vegas, E., *et al.*, 2012. *What matters most in teacher policies? Framework for building a more effective teaching profession*. Washington, DC: World Bank.

Villegas-Reimers, E., 2003. *Teacher professional development: an international review of the literature*. Paris: UNESCO International Institute for Educational Planning.

Wang, D.B., 2004. Family background factors and mathematics success: a comparison of Chinese and U.S. students. *International Journal of Educational Research*, 41 (1), 40–54. doi:10.1016/j.ijer.2005.04.013.

Waterman, P., 1993. Social movement unionism: a new model for a new world. *Review*, 16 (3), 245–278.

Weiner, L., 2013. Social justice teacher activism and social movement unionism: tensions, synergies and space. *Multidisciplinary Journal of Educational Research*, 3 (3), 264–295.

West, A. and Nikolai, R., 2013. Welfare regimes and education regimes: equality of opportunity and expenditure in the EU (and US). *Journal of Social Policy*, 42 (3), 469–493. doi:10.1017/S0047279412001043.

Whitty, G., 2006. Teacher professionalism in a new era. *Paper presented at first general teaching council for Northern Ireland Annual Lecture*, March, Belfast.

Williams, J., 1986. Education and race: the racialisation of class inequalities? *British Journal of Sociology of Education*, 7 (2), 135–154. doi:10.1080/0142569860070203.

World Bank, 2018. *World Development Report 2018: Learning to realize education's promise*. Washington, DC: World Bank.

Zanten, V.A., 2005. New modes of reproducing social inequality in education: the changing role of parents, teachers, schools and educational policies. *European Educational Research Journal*, 4 (3), 155–159. doi:10.2304/eerj.2005.4.3.1.

Teacher development to build practice in socially just schools

Promoting professional growth to build a socially just school through participation in ethnographic research

Begoña Vigo-Arrazola and Dennis Beach

ABSTRACT
We have used the concept of ethnography as explanatory critique in earlier research in three projects in Spain relating to teacher professional development and leadership for socially just schools. This research involved participant observations, interviews, informal conversations, document analysis and virtual ethnography. However, we have also conducted a meta- ethnographic analysis on research products from the projects. Our intention was to try to identify any potentially common themes and ideas concerning how interaction between researchers and participants may have influenced the research and the contexts they were part of as a means to generate useful knowledge for leadership and professional development for educational change and social justice. We describe and analyse these themes in the present article and conclude by highlighting key aspects and possible implications.

Introduction

Education justice relates to how societies protect and recognise the means and qualities individuals require through and in their education by which to live a good life: i.e. to fulfil personal and interpersonal ambitions and be satisfied and virtuous in terms of one's intellectual reasoning and making decisions in life. Education justice is thus both a process and a goal that demands an equally fulfiling participation of all groups in an education. Yet currently education systems do not provide this, not even in globally highly regarded democracies such as those of the Nordic welfare states (Beach 2018). Identifying and developing models of professional learning for social justice leadership and professional development could therefore be of value. But if learning, leadership and development for and towards social justice in and through education systems and the schools in them is an aim (Forde and Torrance 2017), sensitivity towards social contexts and their particular material conditions and cultural history is also important (Jones 2010, Bolívar 2011, Hamilton et al. 2018).

Ethnographic research can play a significant role here, not only in developing sensitive contextual knowledge for professional development and education leadership for social justice, but also in creating just changes within schools, their curricula and their leadership ideologies and practices as well (Harris 2011, Murillo and Hernández 2014, Beach 2017, 2018). Where there are needs of change in participants' lives there are always also possibilities for change as well (Mansfield 2013, 2014, Bogotch and Reyes-Guerra 2014) and there is a value in ethnographic research when it comes to identifying and contributing to these developments. Interaction between researchers and participants can influence the practices researched, the perspectives held by actors on these practices, their knowledge, and the ways they put this knowledge to work in schools and classrooms (Carr and Kemmis 1986, Parsons et al. 2018).

In this article, we will attempt to illustrate how ethnography can be useful for supporting leadership and/for professional development for social justice in the respects presented in the above paragraph and explicated in the research writings of Carr and Kemmis (1986) and Parsons et al. (2018). We will point to several key functions identified in earlier research. The first concerns providing concepts for the development of professional knowledge from reflection on action. The second involves opening up spaces and opportunities for reflection between practical experience and theorised discourse. The third concerns collectively deconstructing and reshaping taken for granted world-views and practices as part of a professional development process. Working collectively is important as it overcomes the division of labour that has developed in expert societies with a strong division of knowledge and differentiation between research/science and practice and researchers/scientists and others. These conventional distinctions between researchers and their practices and others and their obstruct emancipatory theory-building (Harding 1995, Beach 2005). Collective ethnography in the interests of justice has the capacity to generate a sense of community between researchers and researched that can overcome the lure of performativity and the reproduction of dominant class interests in research (Beach 2005).

The first point of reference for this article concerns these principle aims of collective intellectual labour through ethnography against performativity and for education justice. The second is three studies conducted in Spain where researchers had tried to live out these principles through their research designs and in their research practices. Spain is a country whose national political–economic relationships have been internally transformed in a neo-liberal direction recently, with this bringing about significant changes in relation to education policy and the management and organisation of schools and teachers' work (Verger et al. 2016). There has been a shift in ideology away from State governance and goals of equivalence towards goals of freedom of choice and parental influence but the outcomes of reform seem to have rarely led to more socially just and equitable institutions and outputs (ibid). Rather the reverse is the case and this provides us with our research problem: how do researchers successfully engage with teachers and education leaders in/for professional development for social justice in adverse conditions and education markets.

When addressing this research problem, we have reanalysed publications from the three projects[1] from the perspective of social justice and with respect to implications for the work of education leaders and leadership groups. The two first projects ran from 2008 to 2011 in three small rural schools. The third ran from 2012 to 2015 in eight rural and urban primary and secondary schools. Together they comprised 2000 hours of participant observation, over 200 interviews with school inspectors, education leaders, teachers and parents, some informal conversations and document analysis and, in the third project, some virtual ethnography using Face-book, blogs and web sites (Hine 2004, Shumar and Madison 2013).

There were two main research objectives in this research. The first objective was to understand the production of creative teaching practices in the interests of inclusion in mixed age non-selective classrooms. The second was to gain information about interactions between family and school and the strategies used by teachers to encourage family involvement. Encouraging family involvement was important to successful and productive learning and professional development for social justice according to the three projects. In the present article, we have applied a meta-ethnographic analysis in an attempt to develop an ethnographic synthesis around these findings that can connect them to professional development and education leadership. Three professional development research questions have guided this analysis:

What kind of professional learning did the projects generate?

How was it communicated?

What implications are there for professional development initiatives, for educational leaders and leadership strategies for social justice?

As stated in the first paragraph of the article, education justice is both a process and a goal for full and equal participation of all groups in an education, and this makes professional development for educational change and social justice ethically imperative given current conditions of inequality, injustice and marginalisation in schools, educations systems and society (Beach 2017, 2018).

Initial method: ethnography as explanatory critique

Ethnography as explanatory critique was the research method in the three research projects. Formed within critical ethnography, ethnography as explanatory critique involves exploring the co-incidences that materialise within the empirical reality of education and investigating how they are lived, experienced, challenged, and changed from within by subjects themselves (Beach 2017). The method credits subjects with agency therefore, but not in a simplistic way, as it also emphasises the dialectics and complexity of the social world. Relationships to participants are different therefore to those common in traditional intellectual research (Beach 2017). Guided by the metaphor of the Theatre of oppressed (Denzin 2018), participants are co-enquirers and co-producers of valuable knowledge that can stimulate and focus individual and collective awareness on new action. Using ethnography as explanatory critique in education research is therefore not just a way to generate a more progressive contextually sensitive research-based knowledge for and about leadership and professional development. The method also counters tendencies towards audience pacification in traditional qualitative research (Denzin 2018).

The tendency towards pacification is a flaw in conventional science and leads it to not only fail to recognise the possibility of collective (counter hegemonic) intellectualism against the dominant class interest (Gramsci 1971), but to also critique such work as unscientific (Hammersley 2006). The argument is that science should strive for neutrality and objectivity and should therefore not become involved in politics or take sides as this represents a form of partisanship and is not a legitimate research position (ibid; Hammersley 1993).

We see things differently. In line with Gramsci (1971) and Harding (1995) our position is that when acting ethically in the interests of marginalised groups, researchers should strive for deep familiarity with the researched and their life-situation in order to generate deep/strong forms of objectivity in relation the social and material conditions and interests of research contexts and those in them (Harding 1995). Deep familiarity and strong (committed) objectivity form a basis from which to criticise and challenge processes of class rule and power in ways and their foundations (Beach 2017). Researchers should strive to make a difference through commitments to activism against domination, exploitation, and the power of the dominant class hegemony and by establishing and sustaining more rational and socially just research circumstances and relationships (Harding 1995, Madison 2011) and the production of knowledge for political purposes. The misconceived idea of personal/subjective/political neutrality and (false/weak) objectivity needs to be overcome (Harding 1995) as a step towards building impetus for social transformation towards a more just education and a fairer socio-political economy and culture (Madison 2011).

Researching family participation as an act of social justice

Educational policies have long recognised the importance of family participation and involvement in schools to facilitate school success for all students, and ethnographers have provided rich and evocative descriptive and narrative accounts of this participation. Examples include writings such as those by Cerletti (2013), Lea *et al.* (2011), Mansfield (2013, 2014)), Parsons *et al.* (2018), Posey-Maddox *et al.* (2014), Symeou (2008) and Theodorou (2008). These articles recognise the possible influence of research results through professional development on the participants and on their reflection on their practices, and the subsequent reconstruction of these practices. However, they can also tend to describe in a sense a selfish research process that confirms the clarity of the research, its validity, and the creativity and skills of the researcher/s but does not explain how contributions to just forms of social change take form, or what may support or hinder them (Mansfield 2013, 2014).

Work by Bergnehr (2015), Boivin and Cohen-Miller (2018), Crozier and Davies (2007), Crozier (2005), Schecter and Sherri (2009) or Bouakaz (2007) are some exceptions. In line with Freire's (1970) notion of conscientisation, their research treats practical actions and common sense knowledge as a subject for critical appraisal. Relationships to the mode of production form a starting point for social transformation and potentially (if at times only locally) revolutionary practice (Vigo-Arrazola 2020) as a pre-requisite to creating the possibility for effective action against the dominant class and capitalist hegemony. We have therefore also used meta-ethnography for the present article to try to identify, analyse, and produce a narrative account of value to educational leadership and professional development for social justice from studying in detail individual ethnographies that attended to action and change against hegemony.

Using meta-ethnography

Noblit and Hare (1988) introduced the method of meta-ethnography into educational research in an attempt to systematically identify patterns that they felt had begun to emerge from individual ethnographic writings when they were compared and as a way to expand the horizon of analysis and its comparative base (Eisenhart 2017). We used three sorts of data to these ends. They were:

(1) Original data from our own research projects
(2) The published outputs from these studies
(3) Other research literature from (a) projects that we were familiar with or (b) systematic searches in Scopus, Eric, Google Scholar and Sciencedirect using search items such as ethnography OR ethnographic AND family OR parents and education OR school AND equity OR inclusion.

Steps 2 and 3 (above) are the meta-ethnographic parts of the analysis. We followed a stepwise process to select the literature that was most relevant. This involved:

(A) Reading the abstracts of the list of identified works to select a research sample of articles considering 'ethnography' and 'parental involvement', and strategies for developing this involvement in school, for further closer detail analysis.
(B) We made a complete reading on these selected articles to identify the details relating to interaction between researcher and research subjects
(C) Coding and indexing the material using coding practices inherited from grounded theory methodology

What we were aiming to do here was identify and catalogue key concepts in the research, which we then examined for similarities and overlap. We then explored the relevance of each concept within the individual studies and set out to find and describe any possible common grounds from which to form a general claims narrative from them about professional development for educational leadership for social justice.

Knowledge for educational leadership and professional development

Research about parental participation in school was the kernel of analysis in the three original projects and had been an important aspect of educational politics recognised by international organisations of education for several decades (OECD 2019). Article 27 of the 1978 Spanish

Constitution relating to the right to education, grounded this aim politically in Spain. Article 27 noted that public authorities must guarantee the right to education and that parents, teachers and students should be able to influence the control and management of all institutions funded by the public Administration (art. 27.5, 7, CE). The participation of families in schools was a prime example and the exchange and coordination of information in teaching and research were important aspects. From having been a recommended practice, parental involvement had become a politically emphasised requirement in national policy of paramount importance for school quality and for changing the nature of education in schools.

Parental involvement had become an aspect of national democracy and educational research had the task of contributing knowledge about the conditions of development for the realisation of these aims. In the coming pages, we will try to elucidate on this in relation to knowledge for and about professional development and educational leadership for educational change and social transformation. We will begin by drawing attention to the following distinct points that emerged in the research concerning which kinds of research contexts had according to the meta-ethnographic analyses led to the strongest and most sustainable forms of parental engagement:

(1) Research that had been able to transform research situations into horizontal communities of learning where ethnographers and teachers challenged and changed understandings of their role in research by opposing traditional intellectualism and its divisions between active seekers and producers of knowledge versus passive objects and recipients. These conditions are necessary for the development of strong objectivity (Harding 1995)
(2) Research where thus, teachers and parents were recognised as creative agents in the research who were attributed consciousness and an ability to enter into the research process as responsible researcher-reporters of their own history who were capable of taking action in their own interests
(3) Research that engaged research subjects in acts of empowerment in which researchers and researched melded as co-inquirers who were collectively engaged in the transformation of research and/through acts of public intellectualism

The identification and analysis of research that illustrates these different points is useful in its own right in relation to research as praxis and social emancipation (Lather 1986). However, for the present article, we need not consider what implications the findings might have for the development of knowledge for education leadership and professional development for social justice. We found two further dimensions or themes in these respects. One related to research conditions in which a partial transformation of conventional research and educational social relations had taken place. The other involved a deeper and more explicitly voiced and materialised challenge to traditional intellectualism and its social relations of production. They represent in a sense, the main research results. We will present them in the coming pages under the headings of (a) *Research as dialogue around the development and communication of scientific knowledge for education justice* and (b) *Deconstruction and reconstruction processes for social transformation and transformative learning and development*.

Research as dialogue around the development and communication

The research examples organised into this category all recognise the value of representing participant's voices and promoting reflection and transformation in researched situations:

> We have tried to enable participants to be active by turning the ethnography into a dialogical collaboration project to confront history as opposed to just reacting to it ... We listened to teachers and parents as conscious and reflective agents who are seeking to understand the why of their situation and not just the what and how aspects. We dialogued with teachers and with the families. We shared our experiences and our background tried to share thoughts about our common lives and experiences. (Researcher Fieldnotes)

These aspects of listening to teachers and parents, narrating experiences and giving voice and feedback resulted in the production of a research report from researchers for each school and meetings were created for presenting the report to the participants. There were meetings both with individual schools and with representatives from all schools. This was organised centrally by researchers using the facilities available at the university:

> In order to present the analysis of the information from different schools we organised a meeting in the Faculty ... Families and teachers and researchers are there together. We are presenting how each school is carrying out different ways of parental' participation and some teachers are reflecting about their practices when they now know about also other ways of working. One teacher says 'We could do other things in order to facilitate the participation of the families in the school'. We want teachers and families to feel recognised. Another adds "families appreciate that the research had acknowledged teachers". We say 'recognising and representing voices and trying to engage in theoretical reflection on observed practices and to contrast different models of action is one of our aims'. (Fieldnotes)

As in the first example, there is recognition here of the voices of informants and their perspectives. However, giving voice can work in different ways. Researchers and research subjects can voice to present points of view on experiences of ingrained forms of oppression and marginalisation in education or alternatively, words may disguise/disfigure and misrepresent injustices as primarily linked to individual causes. Changing discourses and changing social practices are thus dialectically inter-related and networked together and voices are thus possible to rearticulate in the interests and goals of greater educational justice. The research adopted critical theory to problematise the contradictions underlying daily practices to these ends:

> Through the sessions at the university I began to rethink, where are we? Exchanging experiences and knowing the knowledge behind our practices is a perspective that you do not realize when you are working ... Sitting makes you think and reflect on what you are doing. You have an opportunity to contrast your ideas with others and organize your ideas about how to work (with family participation) in the school. (Small Rural School Teacher)

> You think about other possible references. You get to know each other's ways of thinking. In general, there is no time for this normally. This session has been a way of creating space for dialogue and thinking (about) a diversity of approaches when (encouraging) the participation of families in the school ... Knowing other practices enriches the different ways in which these practices can be carried out. (Secondary School Teacher)

When commenting on statements like these researchers generally referred to two principles. The first was the importance and value of creating a space for reflective conversations. These conversations were about how teachers used their experiences of family participation in the school in a collective debate (Cerletti 2013). The second was for promoting reflection that aimed to connect teachers' connections with the life of children and their families and to enliven these connections within the curriculum.

Deconstruction and reconstruction processes during the research

Recognising and representing participant's voices as a way of promoting reflection in researched situations is discussed in the previous section and the possibility of evidence in some cases also of the development of a critical consciousness during the research as part of a natural interaction process between researcher and research subjects as co-analysts, data-producers and producers of practical knowledge. *Yet giving voice in these circumstances* was not just about letting people express themselves, however deeply. In addition, it was also a culturally and historically constructed metaphor and practice for agency, representation, identity, and power (Harding 1995).

In the present section, we will show further examples of ways of this political act of giving voice as political agency. These examples relate to the second level of results. They relate to ways of constructing spaces to promote and engage in social transformation in a material sense, beyond just talk and reflection, in circumstances where researchers, teachers and parents not only came together to discuss their practices but also to recognise the value of their practices and develop and test strategies of change. Working collectively in the interests of social justice and equity came to involve both a collective deconstruction and collective reconstruction of research practices in these circumstances.

> Today we are in a school. Researchers, teachers and families are commenting on the analyses we have been doing during the research process. Teachers are highlighting their changes, how they are thinking of their teaching practices in a more aware way and they are looking for more possibilities to consider the children's life in the classroom. They are asking too about possibilities to change the ethnography into a dialogical collaboration project incorporating on-line resources as well as a way to confront history as opposed to just reacting to it. (Field-notes from the meeting at the school)

The value of ethnographic research towards educational leadership and professional development is not directly obvious here but relates to empowerment processes where teachers and families have extended their actions in the research, to both point out and point to development options in the research context. This situation, where research leadership and professional development for social justice seem to develop a progressive turn is described further in Vigo et al. (2015), 2016), in Vigo and Dieste (2017) and Vigo-Arrazola (2020). Researchers learnt from their engagements with teachers and parents about the critical skills and knowledge of these people. They then transformed their grasp of own reality in accordance and reconceptualised themselves as people and as professionals. They were no longer uniquely special privileged possessors of expert knowledge with automatic rights to determine courses of action in research about others. They had become co-learners and co-constructors of knowledge not individual solution makers.

> The interaction between the experience of the teacher and the experience of the researcher has motivated teachers to create a free text project in their school, promoting that the lives of children and families enter the school. Their experiences and those of their families are heard and discussed among all. These experiences are then connected to the curriculum of the class through topics such as cohesion, coherence, syntax or morphology ... Progressive relationships between reflection and action appear inside dialogue that involved confronting contradictions of practice from a dialectical perspective similar to Freire's idea of conscientization ... (Field notes in Suburban School)

> Performativity demands, such as requirements to publish and answering the questions of governments and financiers, had blocked more far-reaching developments previously. It was as if we simply had to be in control somehow .... Performativity demands had to come second to engagements in change. We knew this of course from Gramsci's writings. Yet it had taken us some time to see what the practical obstacles were and how to overcome them. We did this thanks to dialogical activity with teachers and parents first. Then by connecting theory back to practice to regenerate experiences and understandings about how to enhance family participation and influence. We had to go beyond and challenge the common sense of our own practices in ways that resulted in cognitive conflict followed by change. (Field notes in Suburban School)

Considerably more equality in terms of interactional rights emerge here. Research roles have successively become more horizontal. They ultimately finish up with a redefined contract for university academics. At this point, research collaboration has not only opened up a space for reflection between practical experience and theorised discourse, it has also led to people collectively deconstructing and reshaping taken for granted views and practices. New ideas about how a research project might take shape emerge. They are presented as a way to establish useful knowledge and promote actions that are recognised as valid by the community first, and then only afterwards, almost as a secondary value feature, by educational authorities and university employers.

> The project aim is to systematize well-founded experience to create new and scientifically informed foundations for an educational practice and enhanced critical awareness. It will draw on researchers to support the process and feedback sessions will be set up collaboratively as part of this ... The interaction between the participants and researchers will form a space where teachers and families generate a critical dialogue as a basis for rethinking and re-forming lived social relations .... and as a means to create solutions. In this way, the project will go beyond the description of what happens in a space and time, favouring a process of transformation and professional development from within. Changes in action will be based on new knowledge

generated in context from participant perspectives and experiences based on their meanings and their interpretations. (School Project)

These project aims describe a process of a progressive intellectualisation of practice for a project that lasted one year. However, after this the teachers, supported by the head teacher, then created a further project with a larger group of teachers and parents entitled 'Textos en libertad. Inclusión del texto libre en las aulas' [Texts from freedom. Inclusion of free text in classrooms]. Once again they asked for collaboration with university researchers (see also Vig-Arrazola et al. 2016).

> The aim of this project is to improve the learning of Language through writing as an act of freedom … An important part of is the creation of a working group in which readings, experiences, perspectives are exchanged in feedback sessions. The central axis is the inclusion of the free text and, therefore, the inclusion of students. Feedback sessions will create conversational contexts between teachers, other stakeholders and researchers in a horizontal way in two- or even three-way dialogue. There will be collective meeting sessions between the researchers, families and teachers to try to encourage, share and by this enrich individual and group reflections. The project will generate spaces for making comparisons and engendering further thinking about future actions. Actions will be established, developed and assessed scientifically. Committed agents will do this in context. (Project of the school)

This project description was written by teachers, the head-teacher and parent representatives at one of the research sites. The centrality of the concept of strong objectivity is obvious in the description, though not named as such but perhaps more important is how description also illustrates how research had become part of day-to-day praxis. The project established a praxis circle as a foundation for/of educational leadership and professional development and as a way to discover, deconstruct, explore, learn, contribute to and shape reflection and action upon the world in order to transform it (Bouakaz 2007; Vigo et al. 2015). Informed by critical praxis theory, the research from which this project developed had been able to develop feedback to research subjects. These ideas that then played a role in transforming the research situation as part of a professional development process of collaborative, interactive, research-based teaching and educational leadership as professional praxis and public intellectualism.

The research thus went as far as transforming the research production relations and overcoming the differentiation of theory and practice in common sense and as a conditioner of behaviour and relations between researchers and others (Boivin and Cohen-Miller, 2018). The traditional researcher–participant relationship had shifted from researcher-led to co-constructed research, which is significantly different from merely seeking to describe, observe, report on, discuss and analyse the content of action in specific researched places and spaces. It connects to a quest for a professional development that is actually based on (and is not just for) social transformation.

Discussion

This article has aimed to render an account of the meaning of professional development in/as and for social transformation using ethnographic research as/for explanatory critique and meta-ethnography. It has progressed by describing and analysing how interaction between researchers and participants influenced both the unfolding research process, the practices researched, and the perspectives held by practitioners on these practices and the contexts of which they were part. Different examples show how the contribution to knowledge development and professional development was driven and contributed to leadership education and professional development for social justice, as processes that build on respect, care, recognition, and empathy that lead to social transformations.

Ethnography worked in different ways to promote this development in different types of school. These different developments from the methodology are quite normal for ethnography. Ethnographic research is contextual and socially, spatially and temporally located. So as a result, the schools developed different participation strategies for parents in relation to the characteristics of the students and their families. However, there were consistencies as well: particularly in relation to the development of deep and sustained parental participation. The most consistent and important was overcoming the research divide in the social transformation of the researched situations, which seems to be a difficult challenge that is far from easy to overcome (Denzin 2018).

We have identified two points for consideration in these respects. They are related to (1) *Research as dialogue around the development and communication of scientific knowledge*; (2) *Deconstruction and reconstruction processes during the research*. They attend to key concepts of horizontality in the research, the role of the researcher and the research subjects, the empowerment during the research process, and the transformation in researched situations, respectively. They corresponded to evidence about:

- Overcoming the division of labour that has developed in expert societies with a strong division of knowledge and a strong differentiation between research and practice (Beach 2005) to contribute to emancipatory theory-building and to empower researchers and researched to change their actions together
- A common struggle to demystify and denaturalise what is normally taken for granted and to challenge the structures and divisions of labour in research that normally differentiate and privilege researchers from and over the researched
- Recognising performativity demands and the (sometimes self-imposed) requirements to get the highest citation rating, satisfy a funding agency or shake another grant of the funding tree for what they are and making these demands secondary demands to the development of change. It means putting progressive change first in research for leadership and professional development for social justice, before the accumulation of external credits and funding

The basic commodification of research is a great problem in these circumstances. Giving time to research so the aims of social change and justice can be attained is another important requirement. As Jeffrey and Troman (2004) point out, without time to engage with participants as informants the possibilities for ethnography are seriously challenged in the original sense of the concept. Yet the original forms of ethnography along these lines have actually usually done very little to contribute to social transformation in these respects. Time is important therefore but also other demands too, such as the demands of context sensitivity, deep familiarity and strong objectivity (Harding 1995). The key may be we suggest, to put these other demands first and to acknowledge that fulfiling them will take a significant amount of time and effort.

The work of Bergnehr (2015), Bouakaz (2007), Cerletti (2013), Schecter and Sherri (2009), and to a lesser extent perhaps Crozier and Davies (2007) and Crozier (2005) may be examples. The research they have done seems to have consciously developed spaces for interaction and a horizontal dialogue that is driven by and in the interests of participants and not only researchers. There is also an attempt to contribute to a logic of reflection that focusses on the reconstruction and not only deconstruction of researched situations and the changes necessary to educational situations for successive social improvement to take place as part of the cyclic processes of critical research. These changes involve the role-content and role-relations between researchers and other participants. They form when the research process provides an opportunity for respondents to grow through and change related to thoughtful assessments of their experiences (Lather 1986, p. 70). Their value is expressed in terms of catalytic validity (value for change) based on conscientisation by responding to the challenges the research offers to the metaphors of conventional theatre in research activities and as social relations of conventional research production (Denzin 2018).

The struggle for conscientisation and catalytic validity reaches back to the opening paragraph of the article about the means and qualities individuals require through and in their education to live a good life as being both a process and a goal. Discrimination, marginalisation and segregation are serious global problems in schools today however, and there is therefore a serious need to assist policy makers and educational leaders in creating more equitable educational systems and experiences for all pupils (Verger *et al.* 2016, Forde and Torrance

2017, McMahon and Forde 2019). There is, in other words, a serious practical and ethical need for educational leadership and/for professional development for social justice and though this may happen rarely, hopefully our research will help to contribute to some basic guidelines as to how it could be encouraged.

Exclusion and marginalisation are often based on differences related to social class, gender, sexuality, ethnicity, disability, locality, and language, but additionally, market-based and privatisation reforms have had significantly detrimental consequences (Beach 2017, 2018). Education systems may be said to operate without class/colour/disability/gender and race bias, but aggregated performances clearly show that class, gender, colour/whiteness and positions on various ability-spectra remain significant in relation to education differentiation as challenges for progressive leadership and future professional development (Forde and Torrance 2017, McMahon and Forde 2019). Justice and inclusion are still very limited, even in countries that have leading positions on OECD justice barometers (Jones 2010, Pihl et al. 2018, King 2019).

Almost all OECD countries have national policies for common comprehensive education and teacher education and school leadership and management projects that should produce intellectually and ideologically prepared teachers and managers to work in these schools (ibid). Yet in normal use, these policies nevertheless produce exclusion, hierarchy and injustice more obviously than they do inclusion, equality and justice (Forde and Torrance 2017). Policies remain ineffective it seems, perhaps because they avoid acknowledging and confronting marginalisation and injustices head on (Jones 2010). Yet doing so may be beneficial (ibid). The present research suggests this at least.

What we are implying here is that the turn to neoliberalism and increased educational performativity may have worsened the problem of education inclusion, justice, and equality, but they did not cause the problem in the first place. The problem preceded neo-liberal marketisation, as a proposed but deeply flawed solution (Jones 2010). There are of course however also variations here too. These variations range from *extreme neoliberalism* with unregulated markets, minimal welfare states, extensive income differentials and gross social inequalities to *regulated neoliberal states* with regulated markets as part of a dominant class project that is run and has been designed in the interests of dominant global elites as a means to restore and consolidate class power (Beach 2018). Neoliberal states do not auger well for the struggles for education justice equality and inclusion in the future or for the preparation of teachers and educational leaders who are committed to take on these educational challenges (Jones 2010, Forde and Torrance 2017). Teachers and education leaders who are able to work as researchers and drivers of their own professional history, as organic intellectuals within that history acting together with other stakeholders in the interests of education and social justice might be a step in the right direction.

Madison (2011) set up five questions to consider in relation to critical engagement for change in these respects. The article attends to three of them. They involve asking:

(1) How we reflect upon and evaluate our own purpose, intentions, and frames of analysis as researchers and education professionals
(2) How a dialogue of collaboration between ourselves and others becomes established and is maintained in practice
(3) How the specificity of the local story relevant to the broader meanings and operations of the human condition is identified, constructed and interpreted into future political action

The point here is, as we interpret it, that both critical ethnography and education for social change begin with an ethical responsibility to address processes of unfairness or injustice within a particular *lived* domain (Jones 2010). This is the first step. The next one involves recognising that lived conditions of existence are not always (or are indeed in some cases of structural oppression and exploitation are never) as they *could* be (Madison 2011), and that as a result, there is an obligation to make a contribution towards changing these conditions (ibid; Beach 2018). This recognition has also been our point of departure and our insistence.

Conclusions

Research projects using critical ethnography as explanatory critique played a vital role in the process of development for educational leadership and professional development for social justice in two ways. These two ways involved firstly digging at (in order to penetrate beneath) surface appearances of the *status quo* and to unsettle neutrality and taken-for-granted assumptions. They involved secondly, accomplishing these acts in active partnership with other social actors. They were not things than could be accomplished by academics acting alone on behalf of others to stimulate 'their' reflection. Bringing to light the underlying and obscure operations of power and control was important, but changing them was the key to social transformation and this was not possible when acts of studying and researching can and do deteriorate into acts of domination.

Beyond the sense of the ethnography as a research method to describe and to produce knowledge to be communicated in professional education for professional development, we thus always have to try to overcome the risk of a traditional intellectualism that reproduces structures and relations of hierarchy and subordination that obstruct professional empowerment. Instead, we argue for the necessity for a researcher commitment towards engagement, empathy, critique and feedback in the interests of social change, including the transformation of the social relations of production of education and of research as well for a more emancipatory education leadership and professional development for social justice. We do this for the following reason.

The creation of new history follows from emergent dialectical processes of mediation and negation that comprise a complex totality of dynamics and antecedent socio-cultural forms manifesting in ideas about what is possible and feasible (Gramsci 1971, Maisuria 2018). However, as well as this there is also the efficacious capacities held by all human beings in terms of their abilities through their consciousness, (material) labour, and intellectual power to challenge dominant ideas and institutional forms and practices of the ruling class of their historical epoch (Freire 1970, Gramsci 1971, Beach 2017). Ethnography for educational leadership and professional development for social justice can play a critical role in this process of the making of history. However, in order to do so, like all useful social science, it has to both produce knowledge for social change and political purposes and also accomplish this and contribute to such changes as well, within teaching communities for progressive leadership and professional development.

Note

1. *Evaluation and methodology: Bases to improve teaching in an inclusive rural school* [grant number 262–101]; *the improvement of teaching and learning in a rural school from a creative perspective inclusive* [grant number 262–103]. *Families and schools. Discourses and everyday practices on the participation in compulsory education* (EDU2012-32657). Fundamental Research Projects MEC. (2012–2015).

Disclosure statement

No potential conflict of interest was reported by the authors.

ORCID

Begoña Vigo-Arrazola http://orcid.org/0000-0001-9734-8596

References

Beach, D., 2005. The problem of how learning should be socially organized: relations between reflection and transformative action. *Reflective practice*, 6 (4), 473–489. doi:10.1080/14623940500300541.

Beach, D., 2017. Whose justice is this! Capitalism, class and education justice and inclusion in the Nordic countries: race, space and class history. *Educational review*, 69 (5), 620–637. doi:10.1080/00131911.2017.1288609.

Beach, D., 2018. *Structural injustices in Swedish education: academic selection and education inequalities*. Singapore: Palgrave MacMillan.

Bergnehr, D., 2015. Advancing home–school relations through parent support? *Ethnography and education*, 10 (2), 170–184. doi:10.1080/17457823.2014.985240.

Bogotch, I. and Reyes-Guerra, D., 2014. Leadership for social justice: social justice pedagogies. *Revista Internacional de Educación para la Justicia Social*, 3 (2), 33–58.

Boivin, N. and Cohen-Miller, A., 2018. Breaking the "Fourth Wall" in qualitative research: participant-led digital data construction. *The qualitative report*, 23 (3), 581–592.

Bolívar, A., 2011. Aprender a liderar líderes. Competencias para un liderazgo directivo que promueva el liderazgo docente [Learn to lead leaders: leadership competencies to promote teacher leadership]. *Educar*, 47 (2), 253–275. doi:10.5565/rev/educar.50.

Bouakaz, L., 2007. *Parental involvement in school: what promotes and what hinders parental involvement in an urban school*. Lärarutbildningen: Malmö University.

Carr, W. and Kemmis, S., 1986. *Becoming critical: education, knowledge and action research*. Philadelphia: Falmer Press.

Cerletti, L., 2013. Enfoque etnográfico y formación docente: aportes para el trabajo de enseñanza [Ethnographic approach and teachers' training: contributions to the work of teaching]. *Pro-Posições 24*, 2 (71), 81–93. doi:10.1590/S0103-73072013000200007.

Crozier, G., 2005. Is ethnography just another form of surveillance? *In*: G. Troman, B. Jeffrey, and G. Walford, eds. *Methodological issues and practices in ethnography (Studies in educational ethnography*. Oxford: Elsevier, Vol. 11, 95–110.

Crozier, G. and Davies, J., 2007. Hard to reach parents or hard to reach schools? A discussion of home–school relations, with particular reference to Bangladeshi and Pakistani parents. *British educational research journal*, 33 (3), 295–313. doi:10.1080/01411920701243578.

Denzin, N.K., 2018. Staging resistance: theatres of the oppressed. *In*: D. Beach, C. Bagley, and S. Marquez da Silva, eds. *The handbook of ethnography of education*. London and New York: Wiley, 375–402.

Eisenhart, M., 2017. A matter of scale: multi-scale ethnographic research on education in the United States. *Ethnography and education*, 12 (2), 134–147. doi:10.1080/17457823.2016.1257947.

Forde, C. and Torrance, D., 2017. Social justice and leadership development. *Professional development in education*, 43 (1), 106–120. doi:10.1080/19415257.2015.1131733.

Freire, P., 1970. *Pedagogy of the oppressed*. New York: Continuum. 2007 edition.

Gramsci, A., 1971. *Selections from the prison notebooks*. Edited by: Hoare, Q. and Now ELL-Smith. London: Lawrence and Wishart.

Hamilton, G., Forde, C., and McMahon, M., 2018. Developing a coherent strategy to build leadership capacity in Scottish education. *Management in education*, 32 (2), 72–78. doi:10.1177/0892020618762715.

Hammersley, M., 1993. Research and 'anti-racism': the case of Peter Foster and his critics. *British journal of sociology*, 44 (3), 429–448. doi:10.2307/591811.

Hammersley, M., 2006. Ethnography: problems and prospects. *Ethnography and education*, 1 (1), 3–14. doi:10.1080/17457820500512697.

Harding, S., 1995. "Strong objectivity": A response to the new objectivity question. *Synthese*, 104, 331–349. doi:10.1007/BF01064504

Harris, A., 2011. System improvement through collective capacity building. *Journal of educational administration*, 49 (6), 624–636. doi:10.1108/09578231111174785.

Hine, C., 2004. *Etnografía virtual [Virtual Ethnography]l*. Barcelona: UOC.

Jeffrey, B. and Troman, G., 2004. Time for ethnography. *British educational research journal*, 30 (4), 535–548. doi:10.1080/0141192042000237220.

Jones, K., 2010. Central, local and individual Continuing Professional Development (CPD) priorities: changing policies of CPD in Wales. *Professional development in education*, 37, 759–776. doi:10.1080/19415257.2011.616089

King, F., 2019. Professional learning: empowering teachers? *Professional development in education*, 45 (2), 169–172. doi:10.1080/19415257.2019.1580849.

Lather, P., 1986. Research as praxis. *Harvard educational review*, 56 (3), 257–278. doi:10.17763/haer.56.3.bj2h231877069482.

Lea, T., et al., 2011. Problematising school space for Indigenous education: teachers' and parents' perspectives. *Ethnography and education*, 6 (3), 265–280. doi:10.1080/17457823.2011.610579.

Madison, D.S., 2011. *Critical ethnography: method, ethics, and performance*. London and New York: Sage.
Maisuria, A., 2018. *Class consciousness and education in Sweden: a Marxist analysis for revolutionary strategy in a social democracy*. New York: Routledge.
Mansfield, K.C., 2013. The growth of single-sex schools: federal policy meets local needs and interests. *Educational policy analysis archives*, 21 (78), 1–30. doi:10.14507/epaa.v21n87.2013.
Mansfield, K.C., 2014. How listening to student voices informs and strengthens social justice research and practice. *Educational administration quarterly*, 50 (3), 392–430. doi:10.1177/0013161X13505288.
McMahon, M. and Forde, C., 2019. *Teacher quality, professional learning and policy: recognising, rewarding and developing teacher expertise*. London: Palgrave Macmillan.
Murillo, F.J. and Hernández, R., 2014. Liderando escuelas justas para la justicia social [Leading Fair Schools for Social Justice]. *Revista Internacional de Educación para la Justicia Social (RIEJS)*, 3 (2), 13–32.
Noblit, G.W. and Hare, R.D., 1988. *Meta-ethnography: synthesizing qualitative studies*. Newbury Park: Sage.
OECD, 2019. *PISA2018 results (Volume III): what school life means for students' lives*. Paris: PISA, OECD Publishing. doi:10.1787/acd78851-en.
Parsons, A.A., et al., 2018. Parental involvement: rhetoric of inclusion in an environment of exclusion. *Journal of contemporary ethnography*, 47 (1), 113–139. doi:10.1177/0891241616676874.
Pihl, J., et al., 2018. Nordic discourses on marginalisation through education. *Education Inquiry*, 9 (1), 22–39. doi:10.1080/20004508.2018.1428032.
Posey-Maddox, L., Kimelberg, S.M., and Cucchiara, M., 2014. Middle-class parents and urban public schools: current research and future directions. *Sociology compass*, 8 (4), 446–456. doi:10.1111/soc4.12148.
Schecter, S.R. and Sherri, D.L., 2009. Value added? Teachers' investments in and orientations toward parent involvement in education. *Urban education*, 44 (1), 59–87. doi:10.1177/0042085908317676.
Shumar, W. and Madison, N., 2013. Ethnography in a virtual world. *Ethnography and education*, 8 (2), 255–272. doi:10.1080/17457823.2013.792513.
Symeou, L., 2008. From school–family links to social capital urban and rural distinctions in teacher and parent networks in cyprus. *Urban education*, 43 (6), 696–722. doi:10.1177/0042085907311825.
Theodorou, E., 2008. Just how involved is 'involved'? Re-thinking parental involvement through exploring teachers' perceptions of immigrant families' school involvement in Cyprus. *Ethnography and Education*, 3 (3), 253–269. doi:10.1080/17457820802305493.
Verger, A., Lubienski, C., and Steiner-Khamsi, G., 2016. The emergence and structure of the global education industry: towards and analytical framework. *In*: A. Verger, C. Lubienski, and G. Steiner-Khamsi, eds.. *World yearbook of education 2016 The global education industry*. London: Routledge.
Vigo, B. and Dieste, B., 2017. Contradicciones en la educación inclusiva a través de un estudio multiescalar [Contradictions in inclusive education through a multi-scalar study]. *Aula Abierta*, 46, 25–32. doi:10.17811/rifie.46.2017.25-32
Vigo, B., Dieste, B., and Julve, C., 2015. Construcción de la participación de las familias en la escuela. Un estudio etnográfico. *Fo´rum Europeo de Administradores de la Educacio´n de Arago´n Revista digital de FEAE-Arago´n sobre organizacio´n y gestio´n educativa*, 15 (V), 23–26.
Vigo, B., Dieste, B., and Thurtson, A., 2016. Aportaciones de un estudio etnográfico sobre la participación de las familias a la formación crítica del profesorado en una escuela inclusiva. *Revista Electrónica Interuniversitaria de Formación del Profesorado*, 19 (1), 1–14.
Vigo-Arrazola, B., 2020. Research feedback as a strategy for educational transformation. *In*: G.W. Noblit, ed.. *Oxford research encyclopedia of education*. London, UK, New York, USA: Oxford University Press.

'Every single student counts': leadership of professional development underpinned by social justice for sessional staff in a South Australian university

Sarah K Hattam and Tanya Weiler

ABSTRACT
This paper reports on continuing professional development (CPD) innovations in an Australian university to address challenges commonly faced by sessional academics teaching progressively diverse student cohorts. With the impact of Widening Participation (WP) policy increasing university participation of students in recognised equity groups, equipping educators with structured CPD highlighting the strengths of pedagogies underpinned by social justice is essential. Through interviews with teaching staff, our study examines the impact of CPD in our enabling programme at the University of South Australia. This paper outlines how the development and implementation of CPD initiatives focused on social justice have increased educator confidence to engage with and support students from under-represented groups. Our paper demonstrates leadership of these initiatives has both led to the coordination of this approach to CPD and the development of a Community of Practice (CoP). We have built a CoP dedicated to developing social justice leaders in classrooms, positively contributing to changing the hegemonic approaches commonly found in teaching in higher education (HE) due to the increasing influence of neo-liberalism on both universities and educators.

Introduction

> Because again, it's just helped me to realise the fact that there is a multitude of reasons why people might not be quite ready for university (Tutor #2).

While a neo-liberal logic centred around increased development of higher education (HE) as an industry rather than a public good is increasingly shaping the university sector, Australia has also identified targets for widening educational participation and many universities have commenced delivery of pre-degree enabling programmes. Enabling programmes are defined as award programmes of instruction that incorporate enabling subjects or modules designed to develop academic skills to facilitate the transition of students into higher level award programmes (National Association of Enabling Educators in Australia, 2019). Although embedded within HE institutions, the enabling space is different to traditional HE because of the diversity of the student cohort (Bennett et al. 2016). While the average equity representation in undergraduate programmes at our university is approximately 30%, we have 70% identifying with one (or more) of the equity categories. The equity group categories often intersect, and our students are likely to experience 'insersectional' marginalisation (Zipin 2017).

Our enabling programme is delivered at UniSA College (of University of South Australia) which is closely aligned with Australia's widening participation (WP) targets, specifically that '20% of undergraduate enrolments in higher education should be students from low socio-economic backgrounds' (Bradley et al. 2008, p. xiv). In Australia, 26% of young people do not complete secondary school by age 19 with 40% of low SES young people not completing secondary school by age 19 (Lamb et al. 2015). Between 2008 and 2105, there was an increase of 50.4% of student enrolments from lower-socioeconomic groups into university programmes (National Centre for Student Equity in Higher Education (NCSEHE) 2017) across Australia, with a significant number entering via enabling pathways.

Students who join enabling programmes have often exited school early or attained limited success in their final years of secondary education. Sociological explanations of early school leaving describe the gatekeeping practices of some schools (Smyth et al. 2004) contributing to the social reproduction of inequality (Bourdieu and Passeron 1977). Our pre-degree programmes have the potential to act as an 'intervention' in this cycle by providing equity groups with a 'second chance' to access the economic and social benefits produced from attaining tertiary qualifications. Our programme provides a supported university transition where students develop academic literacies and competencies to succeed in a tertiary environment and on successful completion, earn a score for undergraduate application.

Geographically, South Australia is large and sparsely populated. It is more than seven times the size of England (almost 1 million square kilometres), with only 1.7 million people, of which 1.34 million live in its capital, Adelaide. UniSA College programmes are based in Adelaide, but also delivered in four regional centres of the State, the furthest being 775 kilometres from Adelaide. Classes are delivered face to face at all sites, some regional students travelling more than 1000 kilometres to attend. As Programme Directors responsible for ensuring teaching excellence in each of our respective programmes we have witnessed how being unaware of inclusive practice models of teaching, specifically when transitioning from traditional undergraduate programmes to teaching in WP can disempower otherwise excellent educators unfamiliar with enabling pedagogies.

As reported on in this paper, our study investigates if CPD initiatives informed by social justice discourses impacted on how sessional academic staff described their teaching practices and philosophy to align with an equity agenda. This paper outlines how the development and implementation of such initiatives influenced how sessional staff engaged with and supported students from under-represented groups. Through capturing the voices of sessional staff and their experiences of the introduced CPD, we seek to outline the connection between these initiatives and increased confidence to be socially just educators leading within university teaching spaces. To provide context for our participants experiences of teaching at our university, the paper first outlines the impact of neo-liberalism on Australian universities. This is followed by a brief description of enabling education and pedagogies as they have developed over the last fifteen years in Australia.

Literature review: CPD in HE

Our review of literature on CPD found that while Australia has a national standards framework for quality learning and teaching as well as support and sustainability of sessional staff in HE (Commonwealth Government 2014), implementation of the framework across institutions is haphazard and patchy (Pennington 1993, Donnelly and McSweeney 2011, Turner et al. 2016). Development of the framework was motivated by the RED Resource (Percy et al. 2008), a large-scale study that argued for attention into how professional development is delivered to sessional tutors. This research found that across the 16 Australian universities examined, few had a cohesive strategy to support and train their casual staff. Rather, 'paid participation in compulsory professional development for sessional teachers is atypical; and despite various national and institutional recognition and reward initiatives, many sessional teachers continue to feel their contribution is undervalued' (Percy et al. 2008, p. 1).

Since publication of these findings, significant work has been conducted more broadly on both the importance of professional development of casual staff teaching in Bachelor and Post-Graduate programmes (Crimmins *et al.* 2017, Heath *et al.* 2018), alongside the leadership of this development by subject coordinators (Lefoe *et al.* 2011). In this paper, we draw on Burke *et al.*'s (2017, p. 141) important work on changing pedagogical spaces for WP in HE where they recommend that 'senior leaders in higher education must take seriously the responsibility to provide a structured framework to tackle issues of pedagogical exclusions and inequalities'. Burke *et al.* (2017) apply a critical lens to WP approaches due to the focus of WP on providing increased access to HE, without paying attention to what happens for students from equity backgrounds as suggested here, 'higher education pedagogies might also be complicit in the reproduction of inequalities even after entry to higher education has been achieved' (Burke *et al.* 2017, p. 1–2). Our experience of teaching in enabling education has led us to recognise pedagogical problems in secondary schools and universities that enabling education has an opportunity to disrupt which can transform access to and participation in HE with a commitment to social justice by enabling educators through adoption of critical 'enabling' pedagogies (Hattam and Stokes 2019).

Despite clear understanding amongst WP practitioners and researchers that a difference in approach and academic identity is required to work in this space, CPD within enabling education is an under researched area. Of particular importance to teaching within WP programmes is a common practice that educators 'cited their own experiences of being a student as sources of guidance for their own practice. Several saw this as a potential trap, for their own experience of HE was often significantly different from that of their students' (Blackmore & Wilson 1995, p. 232). Rather, CPD should involve 'promoting critical awareness of one's and other's assumptions to lead to a change in attitudes' (Teräs 2016, p. 261) that may require multiple and diverse development strategies by the institution.

The CPD needs of academic staff go well beyond pedagogical skills, and those opportunities which run over an extended time period and include initiatives such as action research or development projects are more likely to result in sustained changes in classroom practice (Teräs 2016). Workshops or pragmatically focussed CPD events which emphasise the need to change lecturer's practice or technique can be lacking in a strong theoretical framework which inevitably leaves them falling short in enhancing pedagogical understanding (Gibbs 1995, cited in Teräs 2016). Recognition of this gap provided a leadership opportunity in which we could address potential discourses of deficit and improve outcomes for both staff and students.

Background: widening participation context in Neo-liberal Australia

While Australia's social-liberal roots have created fertile ground for the WP agenda, universities have undergone significant changes with the slow but steady influence of neo-liberalism on the tertiary education sector (Olssen and Peters 2012). This has led to a greater focus on retention rates, completion numbers and the rationalisation of almost every aspect of what we do within the university today (Connell 2011). The strategies of neo-liberalism encourage individual responsibility and deny the inequalities that specific groups such as women, low-SES, Indigenous, gay and lesbian, and non-Anglo experience in Australia. Instead, it is assumed that the market will provide 'equal' choices and freedom for all. The consequence of such logic is a rejection of claims by 'special interest' groups and a focus on the interests of the 'mainstream' (Johnson 2000).

Within the Australian context, the neo-liberalising of tertiary education has negative impacts for educators and students with the constitution of dominant discourses of *success, achievement, benchmarks, excellence, innovation, class privilege, status,* and *intelligence* asserting themselves in institutional systems, structures, processes, practices and culture. According to McKay and Devlin (2014, p. 954), these discourses are also 'inherently middle class, dominant and subordinate other discourses' producing a struggle for students from low-SES or equity groups to make sense of the alienating space of universities'. The dominant discourses also undermine educators' efforts to adopt a holistic approach to their jobs that encompasses emotional and effective domains. Educators' efforts to make positive contributions to students' lives are being 'devalued in a systemic context which prioritises a narrow range of measurable outputs and scores' (Acton and Glasgow 2015, p. 109).

In Australia, the neo-liberal discourses often compete with a socialist understanding of the important role tertiary education can play in social mobility, acting as an equaliser of the disparities of the social class system in discourses of equality of opportunity (Sawer 2003). In comparison with other developed nations, such as the United States, Australia's Federal Government has historically prioritised funding for the tertiary education sector as a public good, and implemented necessary regulations to ensure the sector provides genuine pathways for mobility through the class strata, such as those advocated in the Review of Australian HE (Bradley et al. 2008).

Such Pathway programmes exist within the structures and hierarchies of the broader university; therefore, the efforts for *equity* must be balanced alongside an institutional emphasis on *excellence* (Burke et al. 2017). From the inception of the enabling programme, tensions were identified with traditional HE pedagogy. Many of the challenges faced by equity students do not align with the traditional challenges of the middle classes, which the institution has been designed to engage and support. The WP agenda has also sparked some criticism within HE about the reduction in standards (Burke et al. 2017, p. 433). Problems with HE pedagogy are not just symptomatic of the power dynamic between teacher and students but also the way that universities define who belongs. The *legitimate* or *hegemonic* university student is constructed along class, ethnic and gendered lines, and according to these qualities is more likely to be white, middle class and male (Burke et al. 2017).

What this means for a diverse cohort of students is that some HE teachers value specific behaviours or traits of a 'good' university student, without deconstructing how those traits or behaviours are more easily performed by a student who attends university with a certain level of economic, social or cultural privilege. Burke et al.'s (2016) work on deconstructing deficit views of students from equity groups define the traits of the 'good' student as exhibiting a 'love of learning', time management, 'right' attitude, following instructions, prioritising study, its value and worth, willing to work hard and do what is expected and being smart/intelligent. Failure to deconstruct our own assumptions about 'capability' to succeed at university then lends itself to shaping our pedagogical practice to support the 'legitimate' university student and not the one that appears uncommitted but has a multitude of barriers to education preventing them from performing as a 'good' student. Re-defining the framework of who belongs at university is central to enabling education and can be applied across mainstream HE to ensure student engagement and completion of degrees for an increasingly diverse cohort contributing to social mobility in Australia. A lack of commitment to socially just pedagogy maintains the hegemony of education privilege of the middle-classes, in direct opposition to the policy aims of WP.

Literature review: enabling education & pedagogy

Since the establishment of UniSA College, the enabling sector has flourished across Australia and enabling practitioners and educators began to define a distinctive approach to teaching students in preparatory programmes and courses taught in universities that encompassed inclusive approaches (Hockings 2010); transition pedagogy (Kift et al. 2010); pedagogies of care (Motta and Bennett 2018); and critical pedagogy (Bourdieu and Passeron 1977; Shor 1992, Freire 1994; Gonzalez et al. 2013). This approach is now commonly defined as 'enabling pedagogy' and borrows heavily from critical pedagogy (Bennett et al. 2016, 2016, Bunn 2019, Jones et al. 2019, Willans 2019). It is useful to have a set of agreed practices, theories and research nationally to describe what we do and how we do it.

The rapid growth in our programme saw our teaching team increase from 8 to 34 casual tutors as student enrolments have grown from 300 to over 1200 over the past nine years. As Programme

Directors with oversight of our respective programmes, we identified some sessional staff were struggling with the demands of teaching a diverse cohort of non-traditional students, or approached teaching enabling students from a deficit view. Approaching teaching of enabling students with the same expectations or pedagogy found in undergraduate teaching can lead to increased attrition, reduced student satisfaction and negative experiences of HE (Bennett et al. 2016). While all sessional staff employed at the College have undergraduate teaching experience in their respective disciplines, only a minority had experience teaching enabling students prior to the growth of the enabling sector and none had any formalised training in enabling pedagogy.

Enabling pedagogy contrasts with the 'monological banking-style of HE that positions the teacher as expert and the students as an empty vessel, lacking knowledge' (Burke et al. 2016). Instead, there is an emphasis on adopting a dialogic approach to teaching that sets out the 'teacher does not talk knowledge *at* students but talks *with* them' (Shor 1992). Affirmation and validity of the learner is encouraged with a strong emphasis across the curriculum about demystifying the university experience and avoiding a deficit approach, rather looking for ways to draw on resources students bring with them (Hattam and Stokes 2019; Gonzales et al. 2013). We recognise the importance of scaffolding assessment to enable students to demonstrate skill development across the semester and that the affective elements (Ahmed 2004, Motta and Bennett 2018) of being a new student are often key to transition and a sense of belonging and can be a determining factor in whether students complete the programme.

With increasingly diverse cohorts within many schools and universities more broadly, there is an argument for a wider adoption of enabling pedagogies to promote further inclusion and socially just education. Enabling pedagogy or 'critical teaching approaches' (Shor 1992) can have a transformative effect for people who are power marginalised (Hattam and Bilic 2019) thereby countering the otherwise dominant neoliberal approach. Our contribution to the discussion on CPD strategies specifically addresses the necessity to distinguish between traditional HE pedagogies and enabling pedagogies with casual teaching staff in an enabling programme for social justice. Further to this is how this translates into tutors becoming leaders in enabling pedagogy within their HE classrooms, providing a more socially just and inclusive space.

CPD innovations for social justice

A series of innovations were implemented to provide Tutors with multiple ways to engage with CPD and to ensure that regional tutors located at a geographical distance were not excluded from accessing CPD and were included in the process of building a CoP. We adopt Wenger's definition of CoPs (Wenger et al. 2002) as 'groups of people who share a concern, a set of problems, or a passion about a topic, and who deepen their knowledge and expertise in this area by interacting on an ongoing basis'. The establishment of CoP's which de-privatise the teaching space and foster collaboration between teaching staff has found positive links between student achievement and Professional Learning Communities (Vescio et al. 2008). This is supported by Wenger et al. (2002, p. 3) as they suggest:

> however they accumulate knowledge, they become informally bound by the value that they find in learning together. This value is not merely instrumental for their work. It also accrues in the personal satisfaction of knowing colleagues who understand each other's perspectives and of belonging to an interesting group of people. Over time, they develop a unique perspective on their topic as well as a body of common knowledge, practices and approaches.

Our specific CPD initiatives included tutor induction, inclusive and enabling pedagogy workshops, teaching squares, action research projects and a reading group. For the purposes of this paper, the findings relate specifically to the impact of the 'Inclusive and Enabling Pedagogy Workshops' and the monthly 'Reading Group'. The Workshops aimed to develop awareness of pedagogical approaches specific to enabling education with a focus on countering deficit views, building relationships and encouraging inclusive practice approaches. The monthly Reading Group facilitated discussion and reflection on scholarly articles on enabling and critical pedagogies.

Research methods

This study was conducted within an Australian university in 2020 by employing qualitative research methods through semi-structured interviews. A semi-structured interview can be defined as 'a research approach whereby the researcher plans to ask questions about a given topic but allows the data-gathering conversation to determine how the information is obtained' (Graham 1984, p. 112). We adopt Wenger et al.'s (2002) conceptualisation of CoP being the fusion of the characteristics of 'community' – the shared engagement of the group and practice the shared collection of resources, artefacts and ideas and domain – the knowledge or expertise area. Further, CoPs foster the possibility of peer learning opportunities within the domain, which have the potential for meaningful exchange flowing on to improvements in student outcomes. Further outlined by Lave and Wenger (1991), narrative is a central tenet within CoPs. For this reason, the 'narrative interview' (Riessman 2002) was a suitable method to importantly capture the reflective elements of the CPD that participants were involved in. As Burchell et al. (2002) claim, HE course providers 'need to be willing and able to listen to individual stories of the experience of CPD'. Interviewees were asked specifically to reflect on their experience and tell their story of participating within these various CPD initiatives with specific focus on their practice and their teaching philosophy.

The research team invited all sessional staff who had attended at least one Tutor training workshop to participate. While Tutors may also have been involved in additional CPD initiatives, attendance at a minimum of one workshop was mandatory for eligibility in order to allow participants to reflect specifically on the theoretical aspects of enabling pedagogy. A total of nine sessional staff participated in the study, representing 26% of the total sessional team, and 31% of those sessional staff who have participated in tutor CPD.

Tutors were invited via email to an interview either via telephone or in person. This ensured tutors from regional areas could participate. Three participants are regional tutors. Considering the nature of sessional employment within universities and the authors responsibilities including employing sessional staff, all invitations and interviews were managed by a Research Coordinator to limit possibilities for feelings of coercion to participate. As stated by Ryan et al. (2013, p. 162) within the sessional workforce 'Job insecurity is high and there is absolute discretion afforded to course coordinators around employment and re-employment'. After each interview, these were transcribed by a third party and deidentified. Ethics approval for this project was received from the University prior to the commencement of the research and the researchers observed ethical considerations throughout the research process.

Each interview was roughly 45 minutes in duration and consisted of questions grouped into the following broad categories: the perceived benefits of CPD for sessional academics on their teaching practice; for their students; educator understanding of their own pedagogy and practice as a result of their participation; any perceived changes in teaching now or into the future. Interview transcripts were analysed individually by each author and then again collaboratively. Analysis was iterative where we sought to identify and analyse common themes or recurring patterns within the transcripts for either neo-liberal or equity discourses. The data analysis tools outlined in the followed section were employed in the analysis of the interviews.

Research methodology

The research methodology utilised in the study is a discourse analysis. The conceptual tools provide insight to how the casual academics make meaning of their teaching practice as they navigate the competition of neo-liberal discourses evident in HE pedagogy and discourses of social justice constituted in enabling pedagogy. There are various versions of discourse analysis that encompass a range of methods. As Gillen and Petersen (2005) suggest:

> At one end of a continuum one might put the algorithmic approach to language processing that informs computer software such as voice recognition and translation software. At another end one might put the poststructuralist disruptions of belief in any notion of 'transparency' in language. (p. 146).

The approach we utilise in this study belongs at the poststructuralist end of the continuum through the adoption of the work of Foucault. According to Foucault (1972, p. 49), we can no longer continue to treat: 'discourses as groups of signs (signifying elements referring to contents or representations) but as practices that systematically form the objects of which they speak. Discourse is more, or larger, than language, or words: 'it is useful to talk about discourses as frames, since they provide frameworks or ways of viewing issues' (Bacchi 1999, p. 40).

Foucault's theory of discourse offers us a way of thinking about the way that the meaning-making system works through language, but also has broader implications for what a society or culture defines as the 'truth' through competing systems or 'knowledges'. To quote Foucault (Foucault 1972): 'each society has its regime of truth ... that is, the types of discourses which it accepts and makes function as true' and which is 'centred on the form of scientific discourse and the institutions which produce it' (pp. 72–73). What regime of truth exists in HE institutions about who belongs at university, who is a 'good' student and what does 'success' look like? As suggested earlier, intelligence – (as a scientific and measurable indicator of belonging and success at university) is a regime of truth that has more recently competed with sociological accounts of the social reproduction of inequality in education that has proposed success in education is more strongly connected to socio-economic status than IQ scores (Bourdieu and Passeron 1977). For this research, a discourse analysis of the responses provides insight to how the casual academics make meaning of their teaching practice as they navigate the competition of neo-liberal discourses evident in HE pedagogy and discourses of social justice constituted in enabling pedagogy.

A Foucauldian shift from the fixed individual to the socially constructed subject supports the contextual nature of the subject and is inscribed in the concept of subjectivity, which is the 'conscious and unconscious thoughts and emotions of the individual, her sense of herself and her ways of understanding her relation to the world' (Weedon 1987, p. 32). Discourse itself produces subjects as figures who embody the specific forms of knowledge that the discourses produce (Hall 1997), which subsequently underpins what we do. Through the neo-liberalising of tertiary education in Australia, the dominant discourses of *success, achievement, benchmarks, excellence, innovation, class privilege, status, and intelligence* have influenced pedagogical practice. Social justice discourses of education, on the other hand, are *equity, diversity, inclusive, empowering, transformative, culturally responsive* that have historically competed in Australia and gained traction because of the WP agenda post 2008.

Analysis of findings: seeing themselves as contributing to a social justice project through education

Interviews with casual academic staff demonstrate the impact of the CPD initiatives we implemented in our programme. The findings show that the professional development workshops provided space for sessional teachers to consider the social justice discourses constituted in the enabling pedagogies. Perhaps more significantly, they also show how this has shaped their teaching practice to achieve positive outcomes for students. The most pertinent common themes we found in the interviews relate to changes in attitude towards the students; changes in teaching practice; feelings of connection for regional tutors; desire for greater autonomy over curriculum development and concern with the insecure nature of academic work that produces an invisibility and vulnerability for the staff. Due to space limitations, we do not include a discussion of all of these themes but instead focus on the data that relates to how their teaching philosophy has shifted as a result of engaging in the professional development on inclusive and enabling pedagogies.

A central aim of the enabling and inclusive pedagogy workshops has been to deconstruct preconceived assumptions held about students from equity groups that could be harmful to the environment and culture of the teaching space, specifically how the tutors provide a sense of belonging for the students. The assumptions may be constituted as a result of the neo-liberal discursive fields of the university that define success or a 'good' student in specific ways that reflect social class and privilege. This connects with Teräs (2016, p. 261) suggestion that CPD should not just focus on building teaching strategies, but also addresses the need for 'attitude shifts', or in Foucauldian terms, a shift in 'subjectivity'. A key message of the workshops centres on the importance of avoiding a deficit approach (Burke *et al.* 2017) in communication with the students as well as providing greater insight to the specific sociological challenges of the students. One of the tutors (#3) reflected on how her attitude towards the students shifted as a result of the earlier workshops:

> 'They ran a session talking about the different demographics of the students, explaining their social demographic background so that is obviously a lot of students from lower socioeconomic backgrounds. A lot of students where they're first in family. She talked about the mental health challenges, [and] she talked about students from refugee backgrounds and I think that was a lot of information that I wasn't given when I started. And that was really eye-opening for me and really changed how I thought about the students and how I thought about my work'. T3

Another tutor (#6) shared how they found it especially useful to be presented with the complexities that students from equity groups face in engaging with HE for the first time and the connection made between educational disadvantage and teaching approaches, as expressed here:

> 'I think it was good in saying, "Look, here are the reasons." In other words, a lot of it might be confidence. There's nobody in their family that's been to college or university, they feel out of place, et cetera. Understanding that and how that relates to pedagogy, and enabling people as well, I think was really helpful. It's one of things at the time you don't realize, but then it kind of percolates'. T2

The comment made that it 'percolates' signifies how the tutor also has potentially undergone an attitude change and shift to their subjectivity as the presentation of social justice discourses within the workshop had been impactful enough to remain with them over time and shape their view of their role as an enabling educator and their subsequent approach towards the students. Another tutor (#6) details how they were unaware of the term or concept of 'enabling pedagogy' prior to attending the workshops and although they had observed that their teaching practice needed to be refined for their student cohort, they were unfamiliar that our specific type of education programme has its own pedagogical approaches:

> 'Back then, the term enabling pedagogy was something that had only been introduced to me. I never used that term, I never knew about that term. It was only me going in and really thinking, "Well, this is how the teaching space I'm in is ... this is what it is." So there was papers that were sent to me, some reading which I really got into. That kind of really helped ... [to gain insights that] this is the audience, this is the challenges potentially'. T6

Connecting strongly with Gibbs (1995, cited in Teräs 2016) emphasis on the need to underpin CPD with strong theoretical frameworks, the value of the provision of electronic literature on enabling pedagogy on a dedicated teaching and learning resource site and the influence this has had on shifts in attitude is reflected in this comment by Tutor #7:

> 'And some of the readings were reassuring to go, no, slow down, take it slowly, be guided by the students as well. It's okay. There's no single right and wrong [approach]. This is what the research was of adult learners, not necessarily the research of the delivery. It was going, these are the needs of the adult learners. And I think for me that made sense in the context of the people we work with in our learning center. That it's like you can't come in with a rule book and not be guided by what the students are telling you. You can't come in with a rule

book to lecture and tutor and it'd be that black and white in the way you do it. You need to be guided with the way what people are giving you as well'. T7

Tutor #7 is a regional sessional tutor who has attended the workshops face-to-face; however, this comment highlights the importance of sharing pedagogical knowledge across different platforms for all tutors to access. Tutor #7 echoes other tutors' comments with reference to the importance of understanding the needs of the individual learner and to 'develop a unique perspective on their topic as well as a body of common knowledge, practices and approaches' (Wenger et al. 2002, p. 3) as they have a shared understanding of the experiences, challenges and strengths of our students from equity groups from engaging with the CPD. From these comments, the influence of social justice discourses is shown in their views towards the students as they demonstrate a sensitivity and interest in wanting to connect and understand the individual student's life circumstances and barriers to education.

The centrepiece of the research regarding 'if' and 'how' the constitution of social justice discourses in the CPD has influenced the sessional tutors teaching practice and their identity as an enabling educator resonated throughout the interviews with strong and affirmative examples.

Tutor #2 identified how their teaching practice now heavily focuses on how they build relationships with the students, to be '*super positive and super encouraging*' and show that they care:

> 'Yes, I think it changed our relationships and I think it just gave me so much more patience and so much more understanding. And I think if there's a student struggling, it helped me more to try to understand what perhaps is going on for them, what support they need, how I can build a relationship with that student to also whatever negative experiences they had in the past with education to hopefully help them overcome that and feel supported and feel valued and have some faith in themselves, and see that they can make a new start and that they have the support at the college to make that new start'. T3

Tutor #2 reflected on how the CPD encouraged a greater sense of purpose and autonomy over their role as tutor, inspiring them to show leadership through investing greater effort and time in their teaching to achieve positive outcomes for the students, as featured in this comment: 'for me, it showed that first of all you can take some ownership of the teaching that you do in some way. And secondly, that I think there is a direct correlation between the time that is invested in students, and the outcome, in terms of their grades and whatever'. The interview excerpts included here demonstrate the increased confidence gained to teach diverse student cohorts. The shifts in teaching philosophy for some of the tutors have also been profound as the enabling and inclusive workshops have encouraged them to reflect on their conception of who belongs at university and modify this to be more inclusive. Tutor #5 attributes her shift in thinking as being heavily influenced by the CPD as she describes the shift in these terms:

> 'I was brought up with, "Okay, if you do well at school, you deserve to go to uni," with that mindset. I'm in my 50s, so this goes back a long way. And that's how everybody thought, going to university was a privilege. And also having my own kids, you realize that everybody has a different skillset, [it] doesn't mean that it's better or worse than anybody else's skillset. And everybody now, I believe, should have the opportunity to further that skillset regardless what it is, and how they express those skills'. T5

The shift towards a philosophy of equal opportunity and inclusivity to education appears to be the most common demonstration of the influence of the discourses of social justice in the tutor's responses. Tutor #3's response that all students have a right to tertiary education and the university should invest time and resources into ensuring the success of each student cuts through the neoliberal logic that it is the student's responsibility for their success or failure at university:

> Well, what I'm thinking, I think the main thing, what I see here at the college is that there's an approach that every single student counts and every single student deserves an opportunity. And I think that's probably not so much the case in other parts of the university where it's more about numbers. You either keep up or you drop out, tough luck for you, and there isn't that focus on the individual persons. (T3)

Tutor #3 candidly captures the hegemonic teaching approaches traditionally experienced across HE that they themselves observed as a student as well as being indoctrinated in upon taking up teaching roles in undergraduate programmes.

Conclusion: future platforms

In the assessment of the impact of our initiatives to build a CoP applying Burke *et al.*'s (2017) earlier proposition, the most significant insight of this investigation is that there is a marked deviation from hegemonic HE pedagogies as a result of the inclusive and enabling pedagogy CPD that we have developed and facilitated as leaders within our university. This leadership has then continued through the adoption of these approaches within the classroom space, contributing to tutors becoming leaders in socially just education spaces. With the increase in numbers of non-traditional students entering university across our nation and in similar industrialised nations, we propose that all universities need to review their teaching practice and consider how they can also ensure that teaching staff are inclusive of all students, no matter their background, to have a sense of 'belonging' (Burke et al. 2017) in university spaces. Completion numbers according to socio-economic band reveal a disparity where 68.9% of students from lower-SES backgrounds complete their university degree compared with 77.7% of students in the higher-SES band (Edwards and McMillan 2015, p. 6). While a deficit explanation would attribute the lower completion number on working-class students lack of resilience or low aspirations, the problems with HE pedagogy are well documented.

While our research questions focussed on the sessional teachers account of the CPD initiatives implemented within an enabling programme at a university, there are parallels to draw here between other educational establishments. Through the leadership role held by Sarah Hattam and Tanya Weiler, both Program Directors, it was possible to instigate the formal elements of the CPD initiatives outlined here, including workshops, teaching squares and established mentoring. It is noted however that the CoP that emerged from these initiatives did not require this formal leadership role, and provides a platform for ongoing conversations regarding enabling pedagogies and connections between teaching staff. It is these crucial conversations and opportunities that formal CPD have created to foster the informal CoP conversations which can be applied in other educational settings.

We have had opportunities to lead the development and facilitation of CPD within our academic unit, and in addition, advocated for it to be expanded across other programmes and teaching spaces. This was expressed by one of the tutors who had not been teaching for a very long time in the enabling programme but felt strongly about the impact of the enabling pedagogies in stating they 'do understand about other areas of the Uni and that this approach should be shared' (Tutor #1).

We are aware that our attempts to build a CoP are actions of individuals within a larger institution with its dominant discourses, processes, structures and conditions for the sessional staff that our initiatives cannot fully address or eliminate. While senior leaders of Australian universities need to prioritise and adequately resource professional development for its growing body of sessional teaching staff, there are many other elements of a sessional Tutors working conditions that also need attention to ensure the well-being and security of its staff.

Further, this paper sheds light on the possibilities which exist to foster CoPs in other educational institutions. The work that we have done in this area has received recognition at an institutional level and more recently through a national citation with the Australian Awards for University Teaching. We hope this will provide a platform for broader conversations about the importance of building CoPs to support sessional staff as well as the implementation of inclusive pedagogies in the pursuit of social justice interests for access and inclusion in higher education.

Acknowledgement

The authors would like to acknowledge and thank Myfanwy Tilley for her time, expertise and support in the data collection process. Thank you to our willing participants who generously provided their time and insights to their experiences of sessional teaching in our enabling program. We are incredibly grateful and hope your insights will provide a platform for future discussions across our sector.

Disclosure statement

No potential conflict of interest was reported by the authors.

ORCID

Sarah K Hattam http://orcid.org/0000-0002-3667-6753
Tanya Weiler http://orcid.org/0000-0003-0477-5279

References

Acton, R. and Glasgow, P., 2015. Teacher wellbeing in Neoliberal contexts: A review of the literature. *Australian journal of teacher education*, 40 (8), 99–114.

Ahmed, S., 2004. *The cultural politics of emotion*. Scotland: Edinburgh University Press.

Australian Government, 2014. Higher Education Standards Framework, Australian Government, viewed 10 March 2019, https://docs.education.gov.au/system/files/doc/other/finalproposedhesframework-advicetominister.pdf

Bacchi, C., 1999. *Women, policy and politics: the construction of policy problems*. London: Sage Publications.

Bennett, A., et al., 2016. *Enabling Pedagogies: A participatory conceptual mapping of practices at the University of Newcastle*. Australia, Australia: University of Newcastle.

Blackmore, P. & Wilson, S. 1995. Learning to Work in Higher Education: some staff perceptions. Journal of In-Service Education. 21(2), 223–234

Bourdieu, P. and Passeron, C., 1977. *Reproduction in education, society and culture*. London: Sage.

Bradley, D., et al., 2008. *Review of Australian higher education*. Canberra, Australia: Department of Education, Employment and Workplace Relations.

Bunn, R., 2019. We need to help students discover themselves and see into the life of things: advice from open foundations lecturers in philosophy. *In*: A. Jones, A. Olds, and J. Lisciandro, eds.. *Pedagogy and practice engaging students in transitional educational spaces*. London: Taylor and Francis Group.

Burchell, H., Dyson, J., and Rees, M., 2002. Making a difference: a study of the impact of continuing professional development on professional practice. *Journal of in-service education*, 28 (2), 219–230.

Burke, P., et al., 2016. *Capability, belonging and equity in higher education: developing inclusive approaches*. University of Newcastle: Australia.

Burke, P., Crozier, G., and Misiaszek, L., 2017. *changing pedagogical spaces in higher education: diversities, inequalities and misrecognition*. London: Routledge.

Connell, R., 2011. *My university: notes on neoliberalism and knowledge for the consideration of the academic board* (unpublished paper). Sydney: University of Sydney.

Crimmins, G., Oprescu, F., and Nash, G., 2017. Three pathways to support the professional and career development of casual academics. *international journal for academic development*, 22 (2), 144–156.

Donnelly, R. and McSweeney, F., 2011. From humble beginnings: evolving mentoring within professional development for academic staff. *Professional development in education*, 37 (2), 259–274.

Edwards, D. and McMillan, J., 2015. Completing university in Australia A cohort analysis exploring equity group outcomes. *Australian council for educational research*, 3 (3).

Foucault, M., 1972. *the archaeology of knowledge*. London: Routledge.

Freire, P., 1994. *Pedagogy of hope: reliving pedagogy of the oppressed*. Translated by Robert B Barr. London: Continuum.

Gibbs, G., 1995. Changing lecturers' conceptions of teaching and learning through action research. (ed.) Brew, A. Directions in staff development. Buckingham Open University Press, 21–35

Gillen, J. & Petersen, A., 2005. 'Discourse analysis', (eds) Somekh, B. & Lewin, C., Research methods in the social sciences. Sage Publications. New York, 146–153

Gonzalez, N., Moll, L., and Amanti, C., 2013. *Funds of knowledge*. Hoboken: Taylor & Francis.
Graham, H., 1984. Surveying Through Stories. In: C. Bell and H. Roberts, eds.. *Social researching: politics, problems, practice*. London: Routledge & Kegan Paul.
Green, W., et al., 2017. Enabling stories: narrative leadership, learning and identity in a faculty-based teaching community of practice. In: J. McDonald and A. Cater-Steel, eds.. Implementing Communities of Practice. Singapore: Springer Nature, 159-181.
Hall, S., 1997. *Representation: cultural representations and signifying practices*. Milton Keynes: The Open University.
Hattam, S. and Stokes, J., 2019. Liberation and Connection: fostering critical students who are active agents of their own learning. In: A. Jones, A. Olds, and J. Lisciandro, eds.. *Philosophy, pedagogy and practice engaging students in transitional educational spaces*. London: Taylor and Francis Group.
Hattam, S. and Bilic, S., 2019. 'I can be powerful as an individual agent': experiences of recently homeless women in an enabling program, transformative pedagogies and spaces of empowerment in higher education. *Journal of international studies in widening participation*, 6 (1), 65-79.
Hattam, S., Stokes, J., and Ulpen, T., 2018. Should I stay or should I go? Understanding student subjectivity, institutional discourse and the role enabling academics can play in empowering students within the system. *International journal of educational organisation and leadership*, 25 (1-2), 1-14.
Heath, M., et al., 2018. *Smart casual towards excellence in sessional teaching in law*. Canberra: Australian Government Department of Education and Training.
Hockings, C., 2010. *inclusive learning and teaching: research synthesis*. York: Higher Education Academy.
Johnson, C., 2000. *Governing change: from Keating to Howard*. University of Queensland Press: Queensland.
Jones, A., Olds, A., and Lisciandro, J., 2019. *Transitioning students into higher education: philosophies, pedagogies and practice*. London: Routledge.
Kift, S., Nelson, K., and Clarke, J., 2010. Transition pedagogy: A third generation approach to FYE-A case study of policy and practice for the higher education sector. *The international journal of the first year in higher education*, 1, 1-20.
Lamb, S., et al., 2015. *Educational opportunity in Australia 2015: who succeeds and who misses out*. Melbourne: Centre for International Research on Education Systems, Victoria University, for the Mitchell Institute.
Lave, J. and Wenger, 1991. *Situated learning: legitimate peripheral participation*. Cambridge: Cambridge University Press.
LeFoe, G., Parrish, D., Malfroy, J., McKenzie, J., & Ryan, Y. 2011. Subject coordinators: Leading professional development for sessional staff. Sydney: Australian Learning and Teaching Council
McKay, J. and Devlin, M., 2014. Uni has a different language to the real world: demystifying academic culture and discourse for students from low socioeconomic backgrounds. *Higher education research and development*, 33 (5), 949-961.
Motta, S. and Bennett, A., 2018. Pedagogies of care, care-full epistemological practice and 'other' caring subjectivities in enabling education. *Teaching in higher education*, 235, 631-646.
National Centre for Student Equity in Higher Education (NCSEHE). 2017. *Successful outcomes for low-SES students in Australian higher education*. Curtin University: Western Australia.
Ober, R. and Bat, M., 2007. Paper 1: both-ways: the philosophy. *Ngoonjook: a journal of australian indigenous issues*, 31, 64-86.
Olssen, M. and Peters, M.A., 2012. Neoliberalism, higher education and the knowledge economy: from free market to knowledge capitalism. *Journal of education policy*, 20, 313-345.
Pennington, A., 1993. Induction support from higher education. *Journal of in-service education*, 19 (2), 8-13.
Percy, A., et al., 2008. *The RED report, recognition - enhancement - development: the contribution of sessional teachers to higher education*. Sydney: Australian Learning and Teaching Council.
Riessman, C.K., 2002. Analysis of personal narratives. In: J.F. Gubrium and J.A. Holstein, eds. *Handbook of interview research: context and method*. Thousand Oaks, CA: Sage, 695-710.
Ryan, S., et al., 2013. Casual academic staff in an Australian University: marginalised and excluded. *Tertiary education and Management*, 19 (2), 161-175.
Sawer, M., 2003. *The ethical state? Social Liberalism in Australia*. Victoria: Melbourne University Publishing.
Shor, I., 1992. *empowering education: critical teaching for social change*. Chicago: University of Chicago Press.
Shor, I. and Freire, P., 1987. *A pedagogy for liberation: dialogues on transforming education*. London: Bergin & Garvey.
Smyth, J., et al., 2004. *"Dropping out," drifting off, being excluded: becoming somebody without school*. Peter Lang: New York.
Teräs, H. 2016. Collaborative online professional development for teachers in higher education. Professional Development in Education, 42(2), 258-275 doi:10.1080/19415257.2014.961094
Turner, R., et al., 2016. What role do teaching mentors play in supporting new university lecturers to develop their teaching practices? *Professional developing in education*, 42 (4), 647-665.

Vescio, V., Ross, D., and Adams, A., 2008. A review of research on the impact of professional learning communities on teaching practice and student learning. *Teaching and teacher education*, 24, 80–91.

Weedon, C., 1987. *Feminist practice and poststructuralist theory*. London: Blackwell Publishers.

Wenger, E., 2001. Communities of practice. *In*: N.J. Smelser and P.B. Baltes, eds.. *International encyclopedia of the social & behavioral sciences*. Pergamon.

Wenger, E., McDermott, R., and Snyder, W.M., 2002. *Cultivating communities of practice: a guide to managing knowledge*. Boston Massachusetts: Harvard Business School Press.

Willans, J., 2019. Tales from the borderland: enabling students' experiences of preparation for higher education. *International studies in widening participation*, 6 (1), 48–64.

Zipin, L., 2017. Pursuing a problematic-based curriculum approach for the sake of social justice. *Journal of education*, 69, 67–92.

A cross-school PLC: how could teacher professional development of robot-based pedagogies for all students build a social-justice school?

Elson Szeto, Kenneth Sin and George Leung

ABSTRACT
This paper aims at extending the understanding of principal leadership in support of teachers' development of robot-based pedagogy for students in a cross-school professional learning community (PLC) of Hong Kong's special education. Sixty representative teachers from over 30 special schools, that is 50% of the total number of special schools, participated in the community over the past 2 years. The teachers not only developed the pedagogy but also observed and collaborated in the schools regarding their technological, pedagogical and content knowledge. The development of robot-based learning for individual students' different special educational needs is an innovative differentiated approach to fostering socially just learning in schools. The key research question is: How could teacher professional development of robot-based pedagogies for all students build a social-justice school? We adopted a qualitative cross-case study of four schools participating in the PLC. Although the professional development did not aim at principals' and teachers' social-justice practices for all students, the case study demonstrated the principals' leadership support and the teachers' enthusiasm for learning to change their pedagogies with the use of new robotic technology for socially just differentiated teaching. Implications of the cross-school PLC for building social-justice school communities are also discussed.

In the international trend of pursuing quality education, enhancement of teachers' professional learning and development is an important component of school improvement practice across societies (Schleicher 2016). Teachers play a leading role of helping students, not only with their academic performance but also with their whole-person development, in the frontline practices in ordinary schools (Morris and Patterson 2013). However, academic achievement is still prioritised in standardised measures of school performance and social-justice issues remain unattended in different types of school. In contrast, special schools are taken for granted as social-justice schools for all students with various special educational needs (SEN) (Ainscow et al. 2013). Principals and teachers seem to be the practitioners of developing socially just learning and teaching for all students with various educational needs in the schools. Principals' support plays an important role as leadership for learning (Cheng 2017). Concomitantly, technological knowledge plays a salient role of changing pedagogy for all students (Darling-Hammond et al. 2017, Koh 2019).

Teachers need to pay attention to new technological, pedagogical and content knowledge (TPACK) (Huang et al. 2020). Teacher professional learning of new knowledge to innovate differentiated pedagogies for every student is the core of the development. Whether or not the professional learning reflects teachers' conceptions of building social-justice schools with the innovative pedagogy for all students is yet to be studied.

This paper is framed with the key question: How could teacher professional development of robot-based pedagogies for all students build a social-justice school through a cross-school professional learning community (PLC)? We have studied 60 representative teachers from 30 special schools, constituting 50% of all special schools in Hong Kong, through their professional development of robot-based pedagogy in the PLC. The pedagogy refers to the use of programmable robots for differentiation of teaching various SEN, engagement of students in the learning process, mediation of social interaction between teachers and students and among students (Hughes-Roberts et al. 2019). This was a pioneering professional development of innovative pedagogies for specific characteristics of every student with various levels of SEN in the school community of Hong Kong's special education. The key question is elaborated as three research questions:

(1) What principal leadership support was provided for teacher professional learning in the cross-school PLC?
(2) How could this cross-school PLC enrich the teachers' practice in building a social-justice school for different student populations in individual special schools?
(3) What insights into building of a social-justice school can be derived from the leadership practices of teachers in the cross-school PLC with the principals' support?

Literature review

Policymakers have initiated systematic professional development programmes for teachers in K-12 education through ministries of education, universities and teacher training agencies (Schleicher 2016). This is widely recognised as an important part of quality practices in schools towards innovation in education (Barrera-Pedemonte 2016, Vincent-Lancrin et al. 2019). International policy development of equal education for all has been also advocated over the past decades (UNESCO 2015, OECD 2017). Thus, multi-level support of teacher professional development for student learning is imperative in education systems. At the school level, school leaders have fostered teacher professional development in professional learning communities (Thoonen et al. 2011, Stevenson et al. 2016). Concomitantly, teachers face increasing diversity of student populations and stakeholders' overemphasis on standardised school performance and deeply rooted stratification of students' academic outcomes (Echazarra et al. 2016, Admiraal et al. 2019). Thus, principals and teachers face various social-justice dilemmas in practice, for example, a dilemma between students' academic achievements and equal and equitable opportunities for every student's whole-person development of non-academic intelligences (Francis et al. 2017, DeMatthews 2018, Szeto & Cheng 2018). The dilemma reflects the argument of how a social-justice school can be built through teacher professional development in a socially just education system.

Teacher professional development, TPACK and PLC

In frontline teaching, whether teachers' continuing professional development merely aims at fostering student academic achievements for the central administration or alternative goals is yet to be studied. There are different indicators, methods or theoretical frameworks of teachers' knowledge and professional teaching competencies in different educational contexts (OECD 2014, Darling-Hammond et al. 2017). Among these, the classical framework has referred to teachers' knowledge vis-à-vis content and professional growth in teaching competencies in the classroom proposed by Shulman (1986) since the 1980 s. He argued that teachers should be able to integrate pedagogy and content knowledge as professional critical knowledge through which a framework of Pedagogical Content Knowledge (PCK) was conceptualised for teacher education and professional development in education reforms (Shulman 1987). The concept has further evolved alongside the waves of new and innovative technologies used in education. While widely accepting the salience of using technology for teaching and learning, Niess (2005) advocated enhancing the PCK framework by integrating technology as the fourth component. Then, expecting to help teachers enhance student learning development, Thompson and Mishra (2007) further revised the concept as TPACK.

TPACK is one of the classical frameworks adopted for pre-teacher education programmes and in-service teachers' professional development of new pedagogies with technologies (Voogt et al. 2013, Szeto & Cheng 2017). In fact, new technologies such as robots have become inseparable tools for teaching and learning in different social contexts (Blanchard et al. 2016, Szeto et al. 2016). Teachers need to extend their pedagogical and content knowledge to gain new technological knowledge for differentiated teaching strategies (Huang et al. 2020). They are often required to be innovative by integrating new technology into their teaching (Chen et al. 2011, Koh 2019). It is believed that the integration of TPACK can align diverse students' learning needs and improve their development in the policy of inclusive education (Koehler and Mishra 2005, Mittler 2013, Szeto et al. 2020). When adopting TPACK for the development of innovative pedagogy, however, school leaders need to support teacher learning of new knowledge for the change in formats such as seminars/workshops and PLCs (Admiraal et al. 2019). For individual teachers, PLCs organised inside and outside of school are a popular means of teacher professional dialogue about new knowledge such as technological knowledge for new ways of teaching (Stoll 2010). A PLC provides the space for professional learning and development. TPACK is considered a timely framework for teachers' professional learning to change their teaching (Koh et al. 2017). It can also be adopted as a theoretical lens to explore what and how teachers transform new technological knowledge as innovative pedagogy in a PLC.

Teacher learning for all students: a means to build social-justice schools

With this theoretical lens, teachers can explore new technological knowledge with their peers for reflective orchestration of pedagogies in a PLC (Koh 2019). Innovative teaching may be developed for the needs of the increasingly diverse student populations and those with various levels of SEN. The goal is to help teachers adapt students' competencies with new knowledge for positive outcomes other than academic performance (Darling-Hammond et al. 2017). Some PLCs emphasise teachers' ability and capacity for students' academic performance as the outcomes of teacher professional development (e.g. Koh et al. 2017). Others may promote systemic improvement of schools (e.g. Harris and Jones 2010). Particularly, the framework is adapted in teacher professional development of new pedagogies with the use of new technologies based on the characteristics of student populations in the school (Huang et al. 2020). Teacher learning in PLCs guided by the TPACK framework seems to be widely adopted and an appropriate mode of professional development in school communities of individual social contexts (Curriculum Development Council [CDC], 2017, Chai 2019, Szeto & Cheng 2017). This trend is different from those studies with a narrow focus on student academic performance in specific contexts (Hairon and Dimmock 2012, Qiao et al. 2018). Thus, teacher professional learning of new technological knowledge for the different needs of all students can reflect a notion of developing social-justice teaching, if not of building a social-justice school.

Different principals and teachers interpret social-justice schools differently in individual education contexts. These differing interpretations have led to continuing arguments and debates about the issues of social justice in teaching, learning and school community improvement (DeMatthews and Mawhinney 2014; Szeto & Cheng 2018, Wang 2018). The core meanings are social equality, equitability, marginalisation of the minority groups of difference and difficulty in the diverse context of a society (Cribb and Gewirtz 2003, Theoharis 2010). Thus, if teachers can change their pedagogies for all students via the PLC, part of the objective will be interpreted in relation to social-justice teaching and learning in schools, if not all. In response to the debate, this research investigates teacher learning of new technology to innovate robot-based pedagogies for individual students' difference and difficulty of SEN. We follow the argument of fostering socially just teaching in the special education context of this Asian Chinese society.

Teacher professional development in Hong Kong

The policy of teacher professional development aims at encouraging an official target of 50 hours per teacher annually over a 3-year cycle in Hong Kong, starting from the 2003/2004 school year (Committee on Professional Development of Teachers and Principals [COTAP], 2015). At the system/community level, the Education Bureau (EDB) guides, manages and provides structured continuous professional development seminars and workshops for the school community. Related development activities have been listed on the EDB training calendar webpage (https://tcs.edb.gov.hk/tcs/publicCalendar/start.htm) followed by updated information. Concomitantly, COTAP advises the Government of Hong Kong Special Administration Region on policies and measures, and provides relevant activities related to the qualifications and development of teachers and principals. The EDB and COTAP collaboratively strengthen teachers' competencies and capacities through continuing professional development with necessary support. This collaboration is also extended to universities, schools and other external funding sources wherein teachers could enrol in structured development with multi-level support from the school. The more successful teachers we have in the classroom, the more students who will succeed in schools, and then our education could soon become excellent (Chetty et al. 2011, Bardach and Klassen 2020). Thus, the modes of teacher learning range from short-term educational courses to post-graduate diploma/degree programmes or self-initiated professional activities in PLCs.

The different modes of teacher professional development have been recognised as an effective strategy for improving teaching in Hong Kong schools (COTAP 2015). Particularly, PLC and TPACK are highly recommended for achieving such improvement. A PLC is a collective and collaborative platform for teacher professional learning and exchange of knowledge and experience, while the four major themes of TPACK are highlighted: 'Curriculum and Assessment', 'Learning', 'Teaching' and 'Access' (e.g. Niess 2005, Thompson and Mishra 2007). In the Secondary Education Curriculum Guide, for example, the TPACK framework is adopted as an indicator of teacher professional development and collaboration in terms of integrated knowledge of new technology, innovative pedagogy and content development of the curriculum (Book 11, CDC 2017, p. 9 & p. 22). Such peer activity has already occupied a significant portion of teachers' time during working and non-working hours, even though they may not need to prepare any activities for their participation. In fact, schools are not required to report their teachers' continuing professional development (CPD) activities to the EDB as 'Schools and teachers exercise autonomy on, and take responsibility for, their own CPD' (COTAP, https://www.cotap.hk). Despite this, the curriculum has framed a model of professional development for teachers in Hong Kong.

Methodology

With the aforementioned policy in Hong Kong, we identified a valuable opportunity for investigation into a pioneering, large-scale cross-school PLC. In the education system, special schools are classified by the type of SEN including intellectual disabilities (ID), hearing impairment, hospital, physical disability (PD), social development, and visual impairment. The students with ID are arranged in the school for ID-mild, ID-medium, ID-mild and medium, or ID-serious subject to the diagnosis. Besides, the students may have other SEN symptoms such as autistic spectrum disorders (ASD), attention deficit/hyperactivity (ADHD) and/or emotion difficulties. Those studying in a special school of social development may be ordinary students, while a PD school enrols both ordinary students with PD and those with SEN and PD. Teachers from 30 special schools ($n = 30$) had been engaged in the development of robot-based pedagogy with two robots from 2017 to 2019. Two teachers per school assigned by the principals participated in the PLC involving a total of 60 teachers ($n = 60$). They learnt robotic programming as a means of robot-based pedagogy with specific lesson plans. The PLC aimed at developing teachers' competencies of using robots for teaching students with different levels of special educational needs in the schools (Huang et al. 2020). In the PLC, they conducted peer-observation, sharing and dialogue as a collaborative community with a clear focus on the robot-based pedagogy. Furthermore, they followed their own vision of developing the pedagogy for enhancement of every student's learning development in the special schools.

The robot-based pedagogy is a new approach to differentiated teaching and support of individual students with various SEN difficulties. With the use of programmable robots, the students are not only engaged in learning but also in social interaction and sensory development for quality of living in the school community (Hughes-Roberts 2019). Whether or not this reflects the concept of fostering socially just teaching for all students is yet to be investigated. We adopted a qualitative approach to conducting a cross-case study of four special schools (Creswell 2012). TPACK was the theoretical framework adopted to explore the ways the teachers developed the robot-based pedagogies as inspired by the literature review. This research design involved the research team participating in the PLC over the past 2 years (Cohen et al. 2018). We had informed the teachers that the research team would sit in the PLC and develop the robot-based pedagogy together. In return, we shared the findings of a previous research study related to teachers' technological, pedagogical, and content knowledge as a guiding principle of professional development in Hong Kong (Szeto & Cheng 2017). Not only were the details of teacher professional learning observed, but also their experiences of broadening the students' learning opportunities with the pedagogy in the school were shared in the cross-school context. In so doing, we built up a rapport and mutual understanding with the teachers over the past 2 years (Yin 2014). Thus, we were able to adopt purposive sampling for the cross-case study.

Participants

When developing the robot-based pedagogy, we could invite specific schools to participate in the cross-case study. We identified the schools for students with mild and medium intellectual disabilities (School A), serious intellectual disability with various physical disabilities (School B), and medium intellectual disability (Schools C & D). See Table 1. It is worth noting that the same type of ID school enrols diverse student populations including ID of mild and/or medium levels combined with other SEN symptoms, and serious ID with various physical disabilities. The principals and teachers of the schools accepted the invitation. The semi-structured interview method was used to capture the principals' leadership support of teachers' participation in the PLC over the past 2 years.

Notions of building social-justice schools are expected in the exploration of teacher learning and development in the PLC. An information sheet about the study was sent to the principals and teachers of the participating schools. After receiving the signed consent forms, we then conducted

Table 1. The four special schools and participants of the cross-case study.

Ranking	School A	School B	School C	School D	Total
School leader	Principal A	Principal B	Principal C	Principal D	4
Senior teacher (Middle leader)	Teacher A1	Teacher B1	-	-	2
Subject teacher	-	Teacher B2	Teachers C1 & C2	Teacher D1	4
Type of SEN	ID: mild & medium	ID: serious with PD	ID: medium	ID: medium	3

Note. ID = intellectual disability with the level from mild and medium to serious; PD = Physical disability.

the interviews in the four schools in the final phase of the development in the PLC (Creswell 2012). The interview content was recorded on digital audio devices and anonymously transcribed verbatim. As each interview lasted for 1 to 2 hours, the transcripts provided rich data for further analysis. Instead of pseudo names, we use coded names for the principals and teachers of the four participating schools. Table 1 lists the schools with the principals' and teachers' coded names, their position, and type of SEN of the school.

As there is only a small number of special schools in Hong Kong, we cannot provide the school profiles in details, to avoid disclosure of the participating schools. Principal A of School A has a passion for pursuing effective pedagogy for improvement of individual students' learning, especially those with ASD, while Principal B explores various forms of educational innovations for enhancement of students' intellectual and physical capacity for meaningful living in School B and beyond. Principal C expects to use robots to build a positive learning atmosphere in School C. Similar to Schools A and B, Principal D looks for effective and innovative pedagogies for raising students' learning development beyond the walls of School D. Thus, the four principals ($n = 4$) encouraged two teachers from each school to develop the robot-based pedagogies for the students through the cross-school PLC. For different reasons, we only received six teachers' ($n = 6$) acceptance of the invitation. Two teachers, Teacher A1 and Teacher B1, are middle leaders of the schools, while the other four are subject teachers. The teachers supported and motivated by the principals were the core members representing their schools in the PLC. We captured if there were any embedded notions of socially just teaching for the students with the robot-based pedagogy in the schools.

Data collection and analysis

Due to the different student populations and contexts in the schools, analysis of the cross-case study was conducted in two phases as a procedure to ensure the internal validity of the qualitative analysis (Cohen et al. 2018). In the first phase, two researchers separately coded and categorised emerging themes from the interview data in NVivo 12. We individually discussed with the researcher the themes they identified after the individual coding. We then combined the two sets of analysis where Cohen's (1960) kappa was calculated to measure the inter-rater reliability, and a figure of 0.79 was obtained. This suggested a high level of consistency between the two researchers' individual analysis. In the second phase, we further discussed to resolve any disagreements of the themes (Glaser 1992). Consent was reached on three themes, namely: (1) the principal's leadership practices in support of the cross-school PLC; (2) the teachers' sharing of experiencing and developing robot-based pedagogy with teachers from different types of special schools in the PLC; and (3) any emergent conception of socially just pedagogies for individual students' learning with the use of robots also identified across the four special schools. It is worth noting that new insights into the cultivation of social-justice schools may be derived from the teachers learning to program a robot for individual students' difficulties in learning in the PLC. We proceed to report the findings in answer to the research questions followed by discussion of the insights attained.

Findings

The cross-case study of this professional learning of robot-based pedagogy shows the findings of the principals' leadership support and teachers' enthusiasm for improving the opportunity for individual students' learning development. With the integration of robots into the schools, the teachers explored the robot as the students' learning partner or school helper. The exploration reflected innovative teacher learning beyond newly differentiated pedagogy for student learning. A notion of building social-justice schooling for all students among the principals and teachers consistently drove the professional development in the cross-school PLC. Thus, we further compared the four schools' rationales of participating in the PLC with the principals and teachers' responses. Their visions of cross-school professional development for all students are similar. We can then identify the details of their responses in answer to the questions: the principal leadership support for the teachers' participation in the PLC, the effects of the teachers' development of robot-based pedagogy, and the insights into the building of a social-justice school.

Vision for all students: teacher professional learning across schools

We have integrated an overall vision of the four participating schools' development of student-centred innovative pedagogies with the use of robots in the PLC. The teachers supported the principals' leadership for the collaborative learning of robot-based pedagogy for different student populations with various SEN in the special schools. Particularly, the six teachers treasured the opportunity for cross-school and cross-subject collaboration. They could participate in a pioneering PLC for developing robot-based pedagogy for 2 years and gain more knowledge of other special schools in the city. Teachers B1 & B2 enjoyed being able *'to learn new technology of developing different pedagogies for our students that make us so nervous'* in a cross-school setting. *'The principal recommended that I join the PLC'*, Teacher A1 recalled. For Schools C and D, the three teachers were happy to learn new things in the PLC for improvement of students' learning. As teaching professionals, the six teachers were very clear of their identity and role in developing innovative pedagogy for all students' learning needs and their personal development in their schools instead of being robotic developers.

Similarly, the principals emphasised the importance of using different pedagogic innovations for all students with the use of technology. Principal B responded, *'the PLC should be an effective approach to exploring new knowledge for helping students, and teachers could adopt action research for the exploration'*. For School D, Principal D welcomed the PLC *'as a means of professional dialogue and sharing among teachers from different special schools for educational innovations through which students can benefit'*. Principal C had three expectations of participation in the PLC, namely *'integration of the robot with all the technologies in the school [School C]'*, *'highlighting teachers' role as teaching professionals'*, and *'sufficient support of the teachers' development in the PLC'*. Principal A focused on *'the need for strong leadership for teachers' collaboration across the schools through the PLC'*. Thus, the four principals provided sufficient support for the teachers' development of robot-based pedagogy for the student populations in the schools.

It is worth noting that the four schools infused an overall vision of exploring potential robot-based pedagogic innovations. The principals and teachers intended to broaden the learning opportunities for every student with different levels and types of SEN. They focused on every student's needs for and challenges in learning and quality living in their school communities. Their coherent vision contextualises the characteristics of a social-justice school in the context of special education. The cross-school PLC may be a collective means of infusing the embedded concept of building a social-justice school. In fact, the development of robot-based pedagogy for every student's needs via the cross-school PLC is more effective than an in-school PLC.

School leadership support for teacher professional learning in the PLC

We have further captured both the principals' and teachers' perceptions of the leadership support of developing robot-based pedagogy through the cross-school PLC. In general, the participating schools looked forward to experiencing the innovative process and subsequent outcomes for the students in need. They agreed that the PLC was a large-scale and unusual professional learning, development and sharing in the school community involving approximately 50% of the special schools in Hong Kong. The principals and teachers also agreed on the importance of school leaders' support and extra resources for teachers' participation in the PLC. Without such support, teachers could not have the opportunity during working hours, while the financial resources were used to recruit part-time teachers to take over their teaching loads. We specifically explored the principals' and teachers'

Table 2. School leadership support for teacher professional learning in the PLC.

Leadership Support	School A	School B	School C	School D
Direction	- Envision teacher learning in the PLC for all students' benefit - Expect strong and effective leadership - Support the PLC for school improvement	- Learn and explore new knowledge to stimulate every student with love - Generate new ideas to help students with hope	- Support the use of new technology for every student based on their learning ability and capacity. - Understand the challenges of teaching with robots	- Aim at using big data instead of programming - Simplify the difficulty of using robots in teaching - Collaborate with other professionals
Innovations	- Focus on motion and interaction as the core of robot-based pedagogy - Integrate technologic and pedagogic knowledge for the diverse students' needs - develop crossover of robot and pedagogy for individual differences	- Need more time for the innovation - Promote a work-life balance for the teachers - Develop collaboration between the subject and IT teams - Interact with the robot to stimulate students' thinking	- Able to adapt and differentiate robot-based pedagogy for the levels of ID - Expect sustainable innovation of developing robot-based pedagogy	- Able to stimulate every student with different SEN and backgrounds from every school - Think out of the box for differentiated teaching of the same topic
School Network	- Understand diverse school contexts - Expand school collaboration to broaden student learning as a win-win network	- Share with colleagues what is learnt in the PLC for students' benefit - Connect with the community beyond the walls of the school	- Build a culture of PLC as a means of professional collaboration within and beyond the school	- Connect the 30 schools via the PLC - Build a promising and supportive network for learning.

responses to find out the details of school leadership support for pedagogic development in the PLC through which notions of building social-justice schools might be identified. Table 2 summarises the leadership support of the schools.

The leadership support of the four schools is very strong and welcomes pedagogic innovations with the use of robots in connection to a broader school network. Thus, the first key support is the leadership direction of broadening teachers' learning opportunities for exploring and developing robot-based pedagogy for every student with various learning abilities, capacities, and limitations. The teachers from different special schools can collaborate towards the direction. Principal B asserted, '*Helping students with the new robot-based pedagogies must be rooted in trust, hope, and love*'. Teacher C2 agreed that '*the principal supports our use of the robot and points out the importance of innovative pedagogies, although it is challenging and difficult*'. Thus, the leadership reflects a clear supportive direction of the participation, and every student's learning needs are the core of developing robot-based pedagogy. Principal A and Teacher A1 emphasised '*a win-win situation for both the teachers and students that the former can learn, explore and develop their professional capacity, while the latter can benefit from the innovative pedagogy with the use of robots*'. The direction should not only cover the school improvement as a whole, but also stimulate the senses and abilities of students with different SEN and characteristics. Indeed, the student population of each school from the same type of SEN is very diverse.

With this diversity of SEN in mind, innovations or new pedagogic knowledge can be a means of broadening learning opportunities for individual students' differences and difficulties. Innovation is another key leadership support for teacher learning in the PLC. In School D, both the principal and teacher shared the same vision of stimulating every student with different SEN from each school. Teacher D1 emphasised that '*we need to think out of the box in the design of instructional plans for every subject. Collaborative and innovative development is a great experience we have got from the PLC, although programming is not our profession*'. Teacher B1 also treasured the collaborative experience. '*I lead the subject team and he [Teacher B2] is from the IT team*', Teacher B1 recalled and continued, '*Our collaboration can facilitate adaptive robot-based pedagogy for different students in the classroom*'. For the teachers, '*this is a new exploration to broaden their perspective and the students, in return, will benefit from the innovative teaching*', Principal B expected. In fact, we observed the opportunity and challenge of developing robot-based pedagogy for the students over the past 2 years. Similar to Principal A's reflection, '*This seems to implement a kind of social responsibility for the students as expected by the donor who wants to change practices of learning and teaching with the robot in special schools*'. So, the innovation of robot-based pedagogy and related knowledge can be adaptive and differentiated in individual subjects for the diverse student population in different schools.

We have further identified the next key leadership support of building a collaborative school network. Although there were 30 schools joining the PLC, this might or might not facilitate a school network that can sustain the pedagogic development or other explorations for the student populations beyond the individual school contexts. This echoes Principal B's strategy of '*turning the school into a local community by inviting partnership with parents and other stakeholders of the society to organize community carnivals as public education of special education the school has offered over the years*'. The two teachers of School B would like '*to share the knowledge of robot-based pedagogy for the students of School B with other teachers from different schools, and all teachers could know different ways of using the robots for all students*'. The principal and teacher of School D also shared the idea of building a supportive school network for the innovative pedagogy. In contrast, Schools A and C shared the knowledge and experience with their teaching colleagues in an in-school PLC. Regardless of in-school or cross-school PLC, the principals expected to enhance their teaching teams if the outcomes were valuable for school improvement. Principal A emphasised, '*We learn different students' characteristics from different school contexts that can strengthen our teachers*'. Teacher A also said, '*We welcome collaboration with other colleagues if they are interested in the knowledge and practices learnt in the cross-school PLC*'. Both Principal C and the two teachers shared that they had already built a PLC culture in the school as a means of teachers' professional learning if not connecting to other schools.

In short, the supportive role of school leadership we have reported highlights three important supportive elements: the leadership direction, innovations and school network. To facilitate professional learning, development, and practice, these supportive elements from a perspective of school leadership can provide different opportunities for not only the teachers but also students, who can benefit from the outcomes of innovative robot-based pedagogies. This is adaptive and differentiated teaching for the diverse SEN of every student's learning in different school contexts. The most important mindset shared by the principals and teachers demonstrates the built-in notion of building a social-justice (special) school as the students and parents may face unequal or helpless experience in the society.

Teachers' robot-based pedagogies for different students across the schools

The four principals provided strong support for the professional learning and development of robot-based pedagogy. Thus, the teachers can enrich their understandings of the needs of different students with various SEN across the schools, and experienced three phases of the developmental process in the PLC. The first phase was a learning process of programming the robot based on their new lesson plan and differentiated approaches to teaching. Teacher A1 recalled, '*We need to go through the learning first and the next is development of the pedagogy with the robot*'. The second phase was a rethinking process of the students' limitations of SEN in relation to the differentiated characteristics of potential robot-based pedagogies. At this point, we also shared the empirical research of teacher professional learning, challenges and preferences through the TPACK framework as indicated in the curriculum guide and COTAP's website (COTAP 2015, CDC 2017). Teacher C2 reflected that '*teachers' focus should be teaching instead of programming*'. The teacher expected to have a pre-programmed robot as a teaching assistant for a specific type of SEN such as ASD due to the technical challenges. The third phase was the application of developed robot-based pedagogies in the schools. '*The technology can compensate for the limitations or difficulties of the students in the learning process*', Teacher B1 responded, and continued, '*We hope to create an accessible learning environment for the students*'. With this in mind, we further explored the data to contextualise the key components of the three developmental phases in the PLC: continuing professional learning, cross-subject collaboration, and robot-based pedagogies for all students across the schools. Table 3 contextualises the professional development of robot-based pedagogies for all students in the PLC.

The table seems to reconfigure the practice of a cross-school PLC through which teachers from individual schools learn new technological knowledge to integrate with pedagogical change and content for all students. In this case, teachers learnt robotic programming in the first year and then integrated the robot they had chosen into their teaching in the second year. Then, they needed to design new or revised lesson plans of the subject they taught as the complete development of robot-based pedagogy in the PLC. The outcomes were 30 innovative lesson plans and video recordings of implementing the plans in the schools for cross-school sharing and comments in the PLC.

We have reported the findings of the cross-case study. The principals' and teachers' commitment to building a social-justice school are contextualised in the coherent school vision for all students, the school leadership support for teacher professional learning via the cross-school PLC, and the robot-based pedagogies for different students across the schools. To integrate the answers, we first discuss the findings related to the first two questions and then the insights into the building of a social-justice school through the cross-school professional development in the next section.

Discussion

The four participating schools' visions for teacher professional learning for all students with various characteristics of SEN and difficulties are coherent and salient in the cross-case study. The vision anchors the ideology of building social-justice schools in teachers' exploration of innovative robot-based pedagogies for all students in the past two years. The intention of addressing any social-justice issue in learning and teaching due to students' SEN characteristics and difficulties has been embedded in the vision (Szeto et al. 2019). This responds to the key question. Then, we have contextualised the ideology from the teacher professional learning enriched in the PLC. Any insights derived from the contextualisation are further discussed in the following themes.

TPACK as a theoretical lens of the PLC: the shared mission for all students

The important role of school leadership support should be able to provide a clear leadership direction, welcome pedagogic innovations and change, and build relevant school networks for the specific teacher professional development via the PLC. The supportive role answers the first question and echoes school leaders' dedicated commitment in support of the schools and communities (Thoonen et al. 2011, DeMatthews 2018). It is argued that the quality and effect of teacher professional development are questionable (Darling-Hammond et al. 2017). Despite this, the four principals may have various emphases in the professional development on the three aspects of support in this cross-case study. However, they have a common focus on the benefit for all students through the teachers' robot-based pedagogies. This study has identified the shared mindset of the principals and teachers about the core of the professional development. Teachers had to be flexible and keep searching for appropriate teaching methods with the use of the robots for the students in the context of special schools (Huang et al. 2020). The leadership support should focus on students' benefits from new ways of stimulating capacities and differentiating teaching intervention of different abilities.

Table 3. Professional development of robot-based pedagogies for all students in the PLC.

Component	Teacher A (School A)	Teachers B1 &B2 (School B)	Teachers C1 & C2 (School C)	Teacher D School D
Professional Learning	- Learn beyond the individual schools - Compare different student populations' needs of the schools - Discuss and share the experiences for school improvement	- Learn new knowledge from experience sharing - Reflect on students' responses to teaching for professional growth - Benefit all student learning via new technologic pedagogy	- Learn new knowledge - Apply robot-based pedagogy in classrooms - Share new teaching methods by the robot chosen for the school	- Work hard on new lesson plans with the use of the robot - Unlearn the new knowledge with professional dialogue - Think out of the box for diverse students with SEN
Cross-subject Collaboration	- Start with the core subjects for the in-school collaboration loop for using robots - Hope to refine robot programming for each subject in the school - Free teachers' thinking about new ways of teaching for the students' needs	- Broaden teachers' perspectives by sharing their robotic-based pedagogy - Think of different teaching methods with the use of robots if supported by the technical team	- Learn with other subject teachers to facilitate teachers' growth - Explore teaching different subjects in individual schools - Build a cross-subject collaboration loop in and out of the school	- Increase teachers' professional learning, sharing and programming through the PLC - Learn robotic programming as an extra challenge to teachers' loading
Robot-based Pedagogies for All Students across the Schools	- Aim for one student one robot - Program the robot for adaptive teaching according to students' unique difficulties in schools - Make crossover between pedagogy and robot with the use of AI - Cater for students' individual needs to enhance the learning atmosphere with the big data	- Build new teams for playing, experiencing and exploring robot-based pedagogy - Use robots to build students' touching and cognitive senses - Write simple games for the students to raise their self-confidence, ability and social sense - Program the robot as a teaching assistant to draw students' attention and/or a helper for the students in everyday living	- Make use of the robot for higher learning effects of the students - Connect robots with ASD students - Adapt robots in teaching, a challenge to pedagogic innovations - Need effective in-school technical support - Select the right robot for the students, an important decision	- Spend a long time completing the programming for differentiated teaching of specific subjects - Make use of the robot's repetitiveness for students with attention deficit disorder and other SEN. - Help teachers assist students' learning in the classroom - Build a new learning platform for students and teachers according to specific SEN contexts - Help students become independent

Note. AI = artificial intelligence; ASD = autistic spectrum disorder

The professional learning and development via the PLC in the past 2 years stimulated teachers' solving of technical challenges, and maximised their commitment to the specific target for the students. This answers the second question. The PLC has enriched and broadened the teacher professional knowledge and experiences in a sharing community of 30 special schools. This PLC effect is similar to the argument of Admiraal *et al.*'s (2019) findings of studying individual schools'

PLCs. We further argue that a cross-school PLC with clear and specific goals, content design for the targeted beneficiaries (students), and an appropriate theoretical framework such as TPACK adopted in this study, should be more powerful for teachers' innovation of their pedagogies with new technological knowledge over a longer period of time. Integration of new technologies in teaching and learning becomes a means to facilitate new pedagogy in schools (Blanchard *et al.* 2016). However, Koh's (2019) study addressed the challenge of integrating technology with teachers' pedagogy with the TPACK design scaffolds, while we adopted TPACK as a theoretical lens for identifying enrichment of the teacher learning, development and sharing in the PLC. Despite this, TPACK focuses on teachers' integration of technology with pedagogical and content knowledge and their instructional approaches instead of students. Further research is thus needed.

A pattern of the teacher professional development in the cross-school PLC

For the last question about any insights derived from the teacher learning, we further interpret the three components contextualised from the development process over the past 2 years. See Table 3. The components seem to interweave a pattern of teacher professional development in the cross-school PLC. The first component, professional learning, interweaves the length of professional development scheduled for a continuous period such as 1 or 2 years. So, the teachers from each school start the development with a clear and specific goal as a small group in the PLC (Admiraal *et al.* 2019). The two teachers of School C agreed, '*Robotic programming is not some simple skills and that's why we needed to work together for technical and pedagogical solutions in the beginning.*' The second component, cross-subject collaboration, reflects rapport or trust that naturally emerged among the teachers over the lengthy period of the PLC. As indicated by Schleicher (2016), stakeholders' trust empowers teacher professional learning towards change. The rapport emerged in the PLC relaxes the teachers' out of the box thinking about the different ways of integrating robots into teaching a single subject. Sharing with other teachers from different schools inspires them to generate new teaching ideas. '*The sharing and collaboration let us explore new pedagogies for the student needs in individual schools*', Teacher B2 rejoiced about the PLC experience. Because of this rapport, they could move beyond the comfort zone of a subject to collaborate on various differentiations across subjects for different students with various levels of ID in the same school. Teacher B1 argued, '*There is neither a standardized teaching method nor the best one depending on students' characteristics and needs.*' In return, the teachers gained better understandings of students' SEN characteristics and learning needs across the schools.

The last component, robot-based pedagogies for all students across the schools, highlights the students as the main concern of what and how they can benefit from the robot-based pedagogies in the classroom. The participating teachers recalled their experiences at the final sharing meeting and celebration of the 2-year cross-school PLC. They realised the focus on practice of their robot-based pedagogies for different learning needs of individual students or groups of students in their schools. Indeed, the students are the ultimate beneficiaries of the continuing professional development in the past 2 years. From the first day we met in the PLC, the teachers always emphasised that teaching should be their priority in any form of teacher professional development. They also mentioned what students' characteristics and learning needs are and how the teacher professional development fits students' personal growth. It is worth noting that the teachers' participation initially shapes the pattern of teacher professional development in the cross-school PLC contextualised by the three components.

Conclusion

This cross-case study has unveiled the teacher professional development of innovative robot-based pedagogies through the cross-school PLC over the past 2 years in Hong Kong. The ideology of socially just teaching for students as the centre of the learning and development is contextualised to reflect the salience of socially just schooling (Francis *et al.* 2017, DeMatthews 2018, Szeto *et al.* 2019). Thus, we make no claim of generalising the findings identified from the study in the context of an Asian Chinese society. The findings are indicative of a cross-school PLC. The principals' support and teachers' commitment reflect the shared vision of the professional learning and development of new technologies for any innovative approaches to adapting and differentiating teaching for all students facing various levels of SEN difficulties in the school. This marks a pioneer pattern of the development in the PLC that little research has been conducted (Huang *et al.* 2020). Indeed, students are the core of teacher development, be the PLC inside, outside or across the school.

Development of the robot-based pedagogy was a shared mission of the teachers participating in the PLC. Thus, we have been able to contextualise the pattern of teacher professional development in the cross-school PLC over the past 2 years. The contextualisation shows the professional dialogue with the principals and teachers, challenges, and outcomes. More importantly, the insights derived from the pattern reflect the significant role of school leadership with a clear shared vision and support resources, rapport for sharing and collaboration among teachers, and students who are the beneficiaries of teacher professional learning and development across the schools. These can affect the strength and contribution of sustainable teacher professional learning in a cross-school PLC. Further research is needed: How the pattern interwoven by the three components are well connected to foster socially just professional development towards building social-justice schools in various socio-cultural contexts warrants further exploration.

Acknowledgement

We would like to thank Dr. Rick Lui, Centre for Special Educational Needs and Inclusive Education from The Education University of Hong Kong, for his expert advice. As a professional consultant, he raised critical questions on school-based teacher professional learning and principal leadership practices for school development in this study.

Disclosure statement

No potential conflict of interest was reported by the authors.

References

Admiraal, W., *et al.*, 2019. Schools as professional learning communities: what can schools do to support professional development of their teachers? *Professional development in education*, 1–15. doi:10.1080/19415257.2019.1665573

Ainscow, M., Dyson, A., and Weiner, S., 2013. From exclusion to inclusion: A review of international literature on ways of responding to students with special educational needs in schools. *En-clave Pedagógica*, 13 (2013/14), 13–30.

Bardach, L. and Klassen, R., 2020. Smart teachers, successful students? A systematic review of the literature on teachers' cognitive abilities and teacher effectiveness. *Educational research review*, 30, 100312. doi:10.1016/j.edurev.2020.100312

Barrera-Pedemonte, F. (2016). High-quality teacher professional development and classroom teaching practices: evidence from talis 2013. *OECD Education Working Papers, No. 141*. Paris: OECD Publishing. doi: 10.1787/5jlpszw26rvd-en

Blanchard, M.R., *et al.*, 2016. Investigating technology-enhanced teacher professional development in rural, high-poverty middle schools. *Educational researcher*, 45 (3), 207–220. doi:10.3102/0013189X16644602

CDC, 2017. *The secondary education curriculum guide*. Hong Kong: Education Bureau, the Government of Hong Kong Special Administrative Region.

Chai, C.S., 2019. Teacher professional development for science, technology, engineering and mathematics (STEM) education: a review from the perspectives of technological pedagogical content (TPACK). *The Asia-Pacific Education Researcher*, 28 (1), 5–13. doi:10.1007/s40299-018-0400-7

Chen, C.H., *et al.*, 2011. The integration of synchronous communication technology into service learning for pre-service teachers' online tutoring of middle school students. *Internet and higher education*, 14 (1), 27–33. doi:10.1016/j.iheduc.2010.02.003

Cheng, E.C.K., 2017. Managing school-based professional development activities. *International journal of educational management*, 31 (4), 445–454.

Chetty, R., Friedman, J.N., and Rockoff, J.E., 2011. The long-term impacts of teachers: teacher value-added and student outcomes in adulthood (Working Paper No. w17699, p. 1–94). Cambridge, MA: National Bureau of Economic Research.

Cohen, J., 1960. A coefficient of agreement for nominal scales. *Educational and psychological measurement*, 20 (1), 37–46. doi:10.1177/001316446002000104

Cohen, L., Manion, L., and Morrison, K., 2018. *Research methods in education, 8th ed.* Abingdon, Oxon: Routledge.

COTAP, 2015. *Odyssey to excellence ...: progress report.* Hong Kong: Committee on Professional Development of Teachers and Principals.

Creswell, J.W., 2012. *Educational research: planning, conducting, and evaluating quantitative and qualitative research.* Boston, MA: Pearson.

Cribb, A. and Gewirtz, S., 2003. Towards a sociology of just practices: an analysis of plural conceptions of justice. *In*: C. Vincent, ed.. *Social justice education and identity.* London, UK: RoutledgeFalmer, 15–29.

Darling-Hammond, L., Hyler, M.E., and Gardner, M., 2017. *Effective teacher professional development.* Palo Alto, CA: Learning Policy Institute.

DeMatthews, D., 2018. Social justice dilemmas: evidence on the successes and shortcomings of three principals trying to make a difference. *International journal of leadership in education*, 21 (5), 545–559.

DeMatthews, D. and Mawhinney, H., 2014. Social justice leadership and inclusion: exploring challenges in an urban district struggling to address inequities. *Educational administration quarterly*, 50 (5), 844–881. doi:10.1177/0013161X13514440

Echazarra, A., et al. (2016). How teachers teach and students learn: successful strategies for school. *OECD Education Working Papers*, No. 130, Paris, France: OECD Publishing. doi: 10.1787/5jm29kpt0xxx-en

Francis, B., Mills, M., and Lupton, R., 2017. Towards social justice in education: contradictions and dilemmas. *Journal of education policy*, 32 (4), 414–431. doi:10.1080/02680939.2016.1276218

Glaser, B.G., 1992. *Basics of grounded theory analysis: emergency vs forcing.* Mill Valley, CA: Sociology Press.

Harris, A. and Jones, M. 2010. Professional learning communities and system improvement. *Improving Schools*, 13 (2), 172–187.

Hairon, S. and Dimmock, C., 2012. Singapore schools and professional learning communities: teacher professional development and school leadership in an Asian hierarchical system. *Educational review*, 64 (4), 405–424. doi:10.1080/00131911.2011.625111

Huang, K.-Y., Chen, Y.-H., and Jang, S.-J., 2020. TPACK in special education schools for SVI: A comparative study between Taiwanese and Chinese in-service teachers. *International journal of disability, development and education*, 1–16. doi:10.1080/1034912X.2020.1717450

Hughes-Roberts, T., et al., 2019. Examining engagement and achievement in learners with individual needs through robotic-based teaching sessions. *British journal of educational technology*, 50 (5), 2736–2750. doi:10.1111/bjet.12722

Koehler, M.J. and Mishra, P., 2005. What happens when teachers design educational technology? The development of technological pedagogical content knowledge. *Journal of educational computing research*, 32 (2), 131–152. doi:10.2190/0EW7-01WB-BKHL-QDYV

Koh, J.H.L., 2019. TPACK design scaffolds for supporting teacher pedagogical change. *Educational technology research and development*, 67 (3), 577–595. doi:10.1007/s11423-018-9627-5

Koh, J.H.L., Chai, C.S., and Lim, W.Y., 2017. Teacher professional development for TPACK-21CL: effects on teacher ICT integration and student outcomes. *Journal of educational computing research*, 55 (2), 172–196. doi:10.1177/0735633116656848

Mittler, P.J., 2013. *Overcoming exclusion: social justice through education.* New York, NY: Routledge.

Morris, J. and Patterson, R. (2013). World class education? Why New Zealand must strengthen its teaching profession. Available from: https://nzinitiative.org.nz/on Accessed 19 December 2019.

Niess, M.L., 2005. Preparing teachers to teach science and mathematics with technology: developing a technology pedagogical content knowledge. *Teaching and teacher education*, 21 (5), 509–523. doi:10.1016/j.tate.2005.03.006

OECD, 2014. *TALIS 2013 results: an international perspective on teaching and learning, TALIS.* Paris: OECD Publishing. doi:10.1787/9789264196261-en

OECD, 2017. *Educational opportunity for all: overcoming inequality throughout the life course.* Paris: OECD.

Qiao, X., Yu, S., and Zhang, L., 2018. A review of research on professional learning communities in mainland China (2006–2015): key findings and emerging themes. *Educational management administration & leadership*, 46 (5), 713–728. doi:10.1177/1741143217707523

Schleicher, A. (2016). Teaching excellence through professional learning and policy reform: lessons from around the world. *International Summit on the Teaching Profession.* Paris: OECD Publishing. doi: 10.1787/9789264252059-en

Shulman, L.S., 1986. Those who understand: knowledge growth in teaching. *Educational researcher*, 15 (2), 4–14. doi:10.3102/0013189X015002004

Shulman, L.S., 1987. Knowledge and teaching: foundations of the new reform. *Harvard educational review*, 57 (1), 1–22. doi:10.17763/haer.57.1.j463w79r56455411

Stevenson, M., et al., 2016. Leading learning: the role of school leaders in supporting continuous professional development. *Professional development in education*, 42 (5), 818–835. doi:10.1080/19415257.2015.1114507

Stoll, L., 2010. Professional learning community. *In*: P.Peterson, E.Baker, and B.McGaw eds.. *International encyclopedia of education*, 3rd., 151–157. England: Elsevier.

Szeto, E. and Cheng, A Y N. 2017. Pedagogies across subjects: What are preservice teachers' TPACK patterns of integrating technology in practice? *Journal of Educational Computing Research*, 55 (3), 346–373.

Szeto, E. and Cheng, A Y N. 2018. How do principals practise leadership for social justice indiverse school settings? A Hong Kong case study. *Journal of Educational Administration*, 56 (1), 50 – 68.

Szeto, E., Cheng, A Y. N., and Sin, K K. F. 2020. Still not inclusive? A critical analysis of changing the SENCO policy in a Chinese school community. *International Journal of Inclusive Education*, 24 (8), 828–848.

Szeto, E., Cheng, A. Y. N., and Sin, K. K. F. 2019. Challenges of difference and difficulty: How do principals enact different leadership for diverse student population in a changing Chinese school context?*International Journal of Leadership in Education*, 22 (5), 519–535.

Szeto, E., Cheng, A. Y. N., and Hong, J. C. 2016. Learning with Social Media: How do Preservice Teachers Integrate YouTube and Social Media in Teaching? *The Asia-Pacific Education Researcher*, 25 (1), 35–44.

Theoharis, G., 2010. Disrupting injustice: principals narrate the strategies they use to improve their schools and advance social justice. *Teachers College record*, 112 (1), 331–373.

Thompson, A. and Mishra, P., 2007. Breaking news. TPCK becomes TPACK! *Journal of computing in teacher education*, 24, 38–39.

Thoonen, E.E.J., et al., 2011. Teaching practices: the role of teacher motivation, organizational factors, and leadership practices. *Educational administration quarterly*, 47 (3), 496–536. doi:10.1177/0013161X11400185

UNESCO, 2015. *EFA global monitoring report: education for all 2000-2015: achievements and challenges*. Paris, France: UNESCO.

Vincent-Lancrin, S., et al. (2019). Measuring innovation in education 2019: what has changed in the classroom? *Educational Research and Innovation*. Paris: OECD Publishing. doi: 10.1787/9789264311671-en

Voogt, J., et al., 2013. Technological pedagogical content knowledge: A review of the literature. *Journal of computer assisted learning*, 29 (2), 109–121. doi:10.1111/j.1365-2729.2012.00487.x

Wang, F., 2018. Social justice leadership – theory and practice: a case of Ontario. *Educational administration quarterly*, 54 (3), 470–498. doi:10.1177/0013161X18761341

Yin, R.K., 2014. *Case study research: design and methods*, 5th ed. Los Angeles, CA: Sage.

Supporting gender-inclusive schools: educators' beliefs about gender diversity training and implementation plans

Mollie T. McQuillan and Jennifer Leininger

ABSTRACT
Transgender and gender-expansive students are disproportionately at risk for a host of negative academic and health outcomes; yet, few educators receive training on gender-inclusive school practices. This descriptive study used evaluation survey data from employees ($N = 1,425$) across 80 schools participating in gender-inclusivity professional development sessions. Using a mixed-methods approach, we assessed educators' beliefs about the need and relevance of the training, capacity to improve learning environments, intended implementation of strategies, and suggestions for future trainings. We examined outcomes using descriptive statistics and assessed the educators' roles using regression analyses with- and without school fixed-effects. Our results showed educators wanted even more training on gender diversity and believed the professional development provided was useful and relevant. They reported having increased capacity to create a safe educational environment and discuss gender issues with others in their school environment. We found differences by educators' roles in schools and across schools in how capable educators felt in engaging parents, relevance to self, and usefulness. Future trainings and research should address these differences. The findings from this study provide a description of educators' responses to gender-diversity trainings from 80 schools, highlighting the broad relevance of and need for educator gender-diversity professional development.

Gender-inclusivity trainings are one important tool in providing equal learning opportunities for transgender and gender-expansive youth, who are disproportionately at risk for a host of negative academic and health outcomes (Institute of Medicine 2011, Reisner et al. 2016); yet, it is unclear what educators think about this training and what, if any, plans they have to implement specific practices from the training. The term *gender-expansive* covers a wide range of identities. It refers to an even broader spectrum of people who do not conform to societal ideals of femininity and masculinity, including transgender youth. The term gender-expansive is often used interchangeably with *gender nonconforming, gender-variant*, and *gender-creative*. Gender identities reflect a personal sense of self as male, female, some combination of the two, or something else. Similar to gender-expansive, *transgender* is an umbrella term used to describe people with gender identities that do not match their sex assigned at birth; whereas, *cisgender* refers to individuals whose gender identity matches their sex assigned at birth (Adelson 2012). Both cisgender and transgender identities are types of *gender identities*, which typically begin to emerge around age 3 or 4. School practices and social interactions that are *gender-affirming* will recognise and support individuals' gender identities and how they express their gender, such as their appearance and behaviours (Sevelius 2013).

Understanding educators' beliefs about gender-inclusivity training may be increasingly important as school practices concerning transgender students have come to the forefront of policy conversations in districts across the United States in the last decade (Philips 2017, Lewis and Kern 2018). Identifying whether teachers and staff want professional development training concerning gender-diversity and what kind of professional development training they believe they need provides school leaders with important information about pressing concerns of their employees. This study examined how educators from an array of American Midwestern schools responded to gender-diversity professional development, which aims to create more gender-inclusive schools. Our cross-sectional, descriptive study took a mixed-methods approach using post-training evaluation survey data from school employees ($N = 1,425$) across 80 participating schools and districts. We assessed educators' beliefs about their capacity to improve learning environments, and the need and relevance of the training through a quantitative analysis of survey ratings. The authors analysed this data using descriptive statistics overall, followed regression analyses by educator role, and regression analyses by educator role with school fixed effects. We also explored qualitative, open-ended survey responses to describe the intended implementation of strategies and suggestions for future training.

Background

Gender-expansive youth in U.S. schools

Many transgender and gender-expansive people experience high rates of discrimination, victimisation, and other forms of violence compared to their cisgender and gender-conforming peers (Institute of Medicine 2011, Reisner *et al.* 2014, 2016, White Hughto *et al.* 2015). As outlined in the minority stress theory, these chronic, adverse, social processes may happen at multiple societal levels for minorities and are theorised to be the fundamental cause of some diseases. The daily and common use of gender-based insults and bullying in American schools has been well-documented across many institutions and subcultures, especially among male students and in institutions that emphasise traditional gender roles (Pascoe 2005, Ispa-Landa 2013, Reigeluth and Addis 2015). In the United States, many young people and adults 'police' variation in gender norms to establish their own social status and justify harassment of individuals who do not conform to gender stereotypes (Heinze and Horn 2014). Governmental and educational institutions contribute to these social stressors through unjust policies and the discriminatory implementation of social policies (Hatzenbuehler 2016).

Stressful social interactions among students are associated with educational and health risks. When compared to their cisgender peers, transgender people are less likely to attend college (Crissman *et al.* 2017) and several studies have shown positive associations between the discrimination and violence transgender students experience in school and academic outcomes, such as dropping out, less school engagement, and skipping school (Sausa 2005, Greytak *et al.* 2009, Grossman *et al.* 2011). One likely cause of these disproportionately negative outcomes among transgender youth are the high rates of bullying that transgender students experience. In a representative sample of Californian young people, transgender students had almost three times the odds of considering suicide and 2.5 to 4 times the odds of engaging in substance abuse compared to cisgender youth (Day *et al.* 2017, Perez-Brumer *et al.* 2017). The authors of these studies found the increased risk behaviours in transgender youth were, at least partially, explained by a higher incidence of bullying in schools (Day *et al.* 2017, Perez-Brumer *et al.* 2017). This type of bullying intensifies over time if an adolescent's peer group reinforces this behaviour. In a network analysis study, Birkett and Espelage (2014) showed if a students' peers in school engaged in more name-calling and bullying behaviour related to gender than the individual students engaged in this more of this behaviour over time.

Rather than alleviating these social and health risks, some educational practitioners contribute to the high rates of victimisation and marginalisation that transgender and gender-expansive students face by reinforcing gender stereotypes, making transphobic comments, misgendering transgender students, overtly harassing gender-expansive students, and their discriminatory implementation of policies (Grossman and D'augelli 2006, McGuire et al. 2010, Pascoe 2011, Snapp and Russell 2016). Dessel et al. (2017) found that gender-expansive students' positive relationships with their teachers influenced student's grades and confidence. Furthermore, poor teacher-student relationships disproportionately influenced transgender students' grades and self-confidence. Conversely, there was a correlation between teachers who had positive responses to diverse gender expressions with gender-expansive students reporting greater motivation to do well in school, academic self-concept, school connectedness, school morale, and school safety (Ullman 2017). The relationships between teachers and gender-expansive students have important implications for school success.

In addition to educator-student relationships, other indicators of positive school climate relate to gender-diverse students' beliefs about their school. For instance, studies surveying lesbian, gay, bisexual, transgender, and queer (LGBTQ) students indicate transgender students who identified gender-inclusive practices (i.e. the presence of gender-inclusive lessons, comprehensive resources for transgender students, and LGBTQ student support groups, and supportive teachers) in their school reported higher levels of safety and engagement in school (McGuire et al. 2010, Greytak et al. 2013). Transgender students have also pointed to the lack of gender-inclusive supports as a major contributor in their decisions to drop out of school (Grossman and D'augelli 2006). There is growing evidence that improving school climate, and, specifically, relationships with both educators and peers, may have far-reaching positive effects for gender-expansive and transgender students.

Educator knowledge of gender-inclusive practices

Educator training is one way that schools are attempting to build educators' understanding of the connection between gender and schools. In addition to delivering content, professional development has the potential to influence teachers' beliefs (Clark and Peterson 1984, Kagan 1992, Fives and Gill 2014). Familiarity around issues related to gender, including factors such as greater awareness of anti-LGBTQ bullying and harassment, knowing people who identify as LGBTQ, and self-efficacy, relate to whether educators will intervene when in gender-based bullying (Greytak and Kosciw 2014). Teachers' beliefs about gender-expansive students have real consequences in their behaviours towards gender-expansive youth.

Developing affirming practices related to gender-inclusivity and gender-diverse students is an area where teachers have reported they are woefully unprepared to deal with complex issues revolving around gender, at least in part because they have not received much, if any, training or pre-service education on the topic (Szalacha 2004, Sherwin and Jennings 2006, Macgillivray and Jennings 2008). This means educational practitioners often do not have the confidence or resources needed to develop lessons and, relatedly, may not able to facilitate inclusive conversations with their students around gender.

Comprehensive gender-inclusivity trainings are offered in a number of cities across the United States and many provide similar basic components (Szalacha 2004, Greytak et al. 2013, Ryan et al. 2013, Case and Meier 2014, Payne and Smith 2014, Meyer and Leonardi 2018). First, facilitators provide definitions for key terms to provide a shared language for school staff to discuss gender identity and expression in meaningful ways. This aspect of diversity training is often not included in educational leadership programmes, teachers' pre-service training, or in education textbooks. O'Malley and Capper (2014) found that even when educational leadership programs centered around social justice, only 50% of programmes discussed gender. There qualitative findings suggest discussions about gender occurred because individual professors embedded these discussion into their courses, not because gender was a core concept in the entire social justice curriculum. A study of 77 teacher education programmes indicated at least 40% did not provide this basic vocabulary to its pre-service educators (Sherwin and Jennings 2006). Similarly, most pre-service texts exclude definitions of gender identity and neglect to offer methods to proactively support transgender and gender-expansive students (Macgillivray and Jennings 2008).

Second, gender-inclusivity trainings provide strategies to engage gender-expansive students, their peers, and other educational stakeholders such as parents. These strategies encourage teacher confidence and greater self-efficacy (i.e. a greater belief in their ability to perform a task) when navigating conversations around gender. In one interview study of educators with transgender students at their school, elementary school teachers reported they lacked self-assuredness in addressing questions related to gender and sex in their classes (Payne and Smith 2014). The educators' expressed anxiety and fear about facilitating conversations about gender with students and the larger community within their interviews. These educators stated they needed relevant vocabulary and acknowledged a lack of understanding about the school structures that disproportionately affect gender-expansive students. They also reported being unaware of the unique experiences and needs of transgender students in comparison to cisgender students. Educators in this interview study requested training, policies, and procedures to help them respond more confidently. Relatedly, in a multi-site, observational study of teachers receiving gender-inclusivity trainings, Ryan *et al.* (2013) found trainings contributed to teacher confidence about developing more gender-inclusive lessons. The researchers concluded these lessons encouraged positive changes in student behaviour, even among young elementary students. The lessons encouraged inclusive language and tactics to become an ally to students who had been bullied based on their gender expression.

It is unclear how the educators receiving these trainings were responding to them at a larger scale, which was beyond the scope of the qualitative studies reviewed. This paper addresses whether educators and school staff who received a gender-inclusivity training from a large children's hospital in the Midwestern United States believed the training was useful, relevant, provided tools for them to respond effectively to questions and challenges related to gender identity, and whether they intend to implement the lessons from the training in their classroom. In addition to describing overall differences in teacher belief ratings and implementation, we examined if there were differences based on educators' roles in the school district and between school districts using hierarchical regression analysis and hierarchical analysis with district fixed effects. Testing differences between educator roles and between districts provides insight into how the participant's position within a school district and the larger school context may influence their ratings of the training.

Similar to other gender-inclusivity trainings documented in the research literature (Szalacha 2004, Greytak *et al.* 2013, Ryan *et al.* 2013, Case and Meier 2014, Payne and Smith 2014, Meyer and Leonardi 2018), the training programmes evaluated herein aimed to improve attendees understanding of gender inclusivity in school and provide tools to create affirming environments. This included establishing key terms and concepts related to gender, outlining specific tactics for school staff to use in their classroom or administrative work, and providing examples of model school policies for gender support and inclusion. Educators were encouraged to reflect on their own gender identity and their beliefs about gender (Rands 2009). The facilitator also led a discussion with educators on ways to discuss gender diversity with students, parents, and the other members of the school community.

Evaluating educators' beliefs about the training is an important initial step towards understanding how they will engage with gender-diverse students and create gender-inclusive environments. Without training on the topic, educators rely on their personal constructs of gender based on their own experiences and socialisation (Fives and Gill 2014). These personal beliefs about gender may then influence how educators interpret what is socially acceptable gendered behaviour, and respond to new situations related to gender diversity within their schools For instance, educators disproportionately blame and punish gender-diverse students for being bullied, attributing other students' bullying behaviour to the bullied students' gender expression, and educators enforce gender-diverse expression as dress code violations (Sausa 2005, Snapp et al. 2015). Whereas, educators report taking on supportive roles for LGBTQ students and perceive doing so to be of greater importance when they have had inclusivity training (Swanson and Gettinger 2016). Greater insight into what educators believe about training' and their own ability to engage with gender diverse students provides a better understanding of how receptive and motivated teachers may be to embedding practices that challenge a gender binary into their own work.

Understanding teachers' beliefs about gender-inclusivity training are also necessary to inform school administrators, the individuals ultimately responsible for implementing inclusive policies and changing educators' practices. In a study of New York administrators, Payne and Smith (2018) find administrators cited a lack of teacher interest in inclusivity training and irrelevance to their school context when explaining why they did not employ this kind of training. Administrators are making predictions about how their teachers and staff will respond to this training without the benefit of an analysis showing how educators actually do respond, as this study provides. This mixed-methods study contributes to the existing literature by describing educators' beliefs and plans following gender-diversity professional development sessions.

Methods

This cross-sectional, descriptive study examined post-training survey data from administrators, teachers, and staff who received the gender-inclusivity training ($N = 1,425$) in 80 schools. Surveys were distributed and collected at the end of the trainings by the facilitator, the second author on this paper. Data collection took place over a three-year period between October 2013 to December 2016. The Institutional Review Boards at Ann & Robert H. Lurie Children's Hospital and Northwestern University determined the study did not meet the human research criteria and was therefore exempt from review because we used deidentified, pre-existing evaluation data.

The professional development program conducted an average of three trainings a month with audiences ranging from seven to 200 people. It was designed and facilitated by the second author. Trainings were held in diverse school settings, including private and public institutions, from elementary to four-year colleges. Most participants were from urban and suburban locations, with only 1.5% of the sample from small towns or rural areas.

The facilitator adapted the training to the needs of the schools, so the length of time for each session (90 minutes to a two-day session), the location, and suggestions provided by the facilitator varied. Additionally, some participants' attendance at the training was compulsory while other participants chose to attend, and participants could have attended multiple sessions in districts that offered more than one session.

The first author of this paper was a graduate research intern at the same time within the children's hospital, who designed the research study and used both quantitative and qualitative analyses of an evaluation survey. These analyses included both numerical ratings and open-ended responses, to address the study goals. The first author was not involved in the design or facilitation of the professional development trainings.

Procedure

The surveys, included in Appendix A, were collected following the training sessions. Participants completed hard copies of the evaluation, i.e. paper-and-pencil, which included a multiple-choice question about their role in the school and a self-report scale to assess agreement with statements about the training. The survey also included open-ended questions regarding personal implementation and suggestions for future training. The survey did not collect identifying information. The training itself was composed of a PowerPoint presentation with breaks for discussion. While the length of time and overall content of the presentation varied, all presentations included the following: important terms, the role of schools in socialising gender roles, the educational and mental health risks gender-expansive/transgender students face, how to meet the needs of all students, specific supports necessary for gender-expansive/transgender students (including best practices to create inclusive schools), supporting parents in discussions about gender identity, and additional resources for educators.

Measures

As described below, the evaluation survey included a variety of questions about educator's role at their school, their assessment of the relevance and fit of the training, their plans to implement new strategies as a result of the training, and other related questions. Appendix A containes the complete survey used in this study.

Roles
Respondents were asked, 'What is your role at your school?' and were provided the following selections: 'Teacher,' 'Administrator,' or 'Other.' The 'Other' category included non-faculty school staff, social workers, school psychologists, and parents of transgender students at the school.

Schools
Participants responded to the open-ended question, 'What school do you work for?' A research assistant then used the written school names and coded each school using the school's state-assigned number provided by the Illinois State Board of Education so that differences across school districts could be tested.

Usefulness, relevance, and fit of the training
Participants rated the following statements: 'This training will be useful in my work,' 'The topics covered were relevant to me,' 'The topics covered were relevant to my school,' 'The suggestions and examples provided by the facilitator felt practical and fit the needs of my school,' and 'The training addressed the questions that I had regarding transgender and gender non-conforming youth.' Participants self-reported agreement using a 5-point Likert scale ranging from '1 = Strongly Agree' to '5 = Strongly Disagree' ratings. We found high internal consistency among these items ($\alpha = .88$).

Capability
We asked participants to report how much they agreed with the following statements: 'I feel more capable of discussing concepts of gender non-conforming and transgender students with parents,' 'I feel more capable of discussing concepts of gender non-conforming and transgender students with other faculty and staff,' and 'After the training, I now feel more equipped to create a safe school environment for transgender and gender non-conforming students.' Participants indicated agreement by responding to a 5-point Likert scale ranging from 'Strongly Agree' to 'Strongly Disagree' ratings. There was a high degree of reliability among the capability items ($\alpha = .88$).

Appropriateness of time for the training
There was one question about the timing of the training. Participants used the same 5-point Likert scale described above to rate their agreement with the statement: 'The time allotted for the training was sufficient.'

Plans to implement new strategies
Participants responded to the following open-ended prompt, specifying implementation plans at six months and 12 months: 'What changes do you see yourself and your school implementing in regard to gender nonconforming and transgender students?'

Suggestions for future trainings
Researchers used an open-ended question requesting participants' suggestions for future trainings to assess future needs and possible areas for improvement in the training, 'What suggestions would you make for this training in the future?'

Analysis

We utilised a mixed-methods analysis of the belief ratings and open-ended response questions. First, we described the percent of participants in each educational role category for the sample. Next, we provided frequencies for the entire sample to describe the level of overall agreement there was for each statement.

Following these general descriptions, we used ordinary least squares (OLS) regression to assess the relationship between different educational roles and the nine belief statements. We created dichotomous variables for school roles (reference category: teacher). We used mean imputation for the level of agreements to each item, in order to account for missing data (n ≤ 5%), and used the scaled items as continuous variables. We used OLS regression models over ANOVA to examine variation across roles so the results could be compared to our school fixed effects model.

Next, we examined if belief ratings differed across schools by using the same OLS models with fixed effects for the 80 school groups. The fixed-effects model accounted for the fact that multiple responses from educators in the same school are more similar than responses from educators in other schools and allowed us to assess if there were significant differences between the school groups.

We used a content analysis to analyse the data from open-ended responses to prompts about implementation plans and training suggestions (Corbin and Strauss 2008, Charmaz 2014). We developed the coding scheme by first open-coding the responses for important ideas and themes. Using the main themes that emerged during selective coding, we developed a coding scheme for the content analysis. With this coding theme, we categorised all responses and were able to provide descriptive statistics in the form of frequencies.

Results

Quantitative results

Descriptive results
Roles. The largest percentage of participants, 50%, described themselves as teachers (*n* = 711). The 'other' option was the second most frequent selection with 39% of participants (*n* = 558). Respondents who selected this category included food service workers, legal counsel, parents, athletic coaches, social workers, school psychologists, and other non-teachers or non-administrators connected with the schools. The remaining 11% of participants identified as administrators (*n* = 159).

Beliefs about usefulness, relevance, capability, and time. There was a high agreement with the usefulness of the training, with 95% of participants reporting they agreed or strongly agreed that the training was useful, and 94% and 96% responding that they strongly agreed or agreed that the training was relevant to the participant and the participant's school, respectively (see Chart 1). Ninety-three percent of participants reported similar strong agreement/agreement with the statement that the trainer's suggestions were practical and fit the needs of the school. Finally, 89% of respondents marked that they agreed that the facilitator addressed questions they had about gender-expansive and transgender youth.

Educators also responded favourably to feeling capable of discussing concepts related to gender-expansive students with other faculty and staff, with 92% agreeing or strongly agreeing.

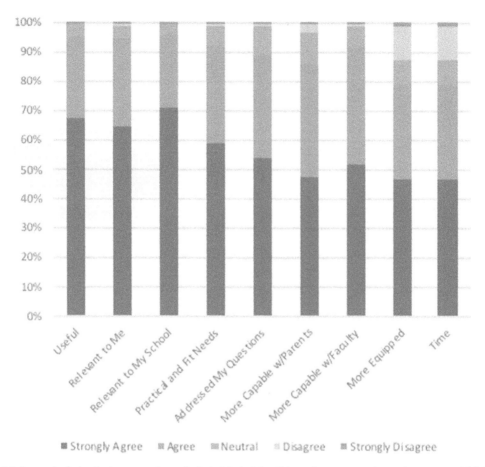

Chart 1. Bar graph of educators' responses to gender inclusivity training. This graph represents educators' agreement with belief statements in a survey following the gender-inclusivity training.

Fewer participants indicated confidence about their ability to discuss these issues with parents (86%), but 92% responded positively indicating that they felt equipped to deal with issues related to gender in their school after the training.

As shown in Chart 1, the item with the least amount of agreement was regarding the appropriateness of the allotted time, with 79% of participants indicating they strongly agreed or agreed with the sufficiency of time allotted ($M_{time} = 1.88$, $SD = 1.02$).

OLS regression results

Roles and ratings. We found several differences in how educators in different roles rated the training; most of the significant differences were between teachers and participants who selected 'other.' As shown in Table 1, when compared to teachers, administrators ($\beta = -0.111, p = 0.055$) and 'others' ($\beta = -0.112, p = 0.003$) did not rate the training as relevant to themselves, although for administrators there was only a marginally significant statistical difference. Participants who selected 'Other' found the training slightly less useful compared to teachers ($\beta = -0.099$, $p = 0.004$). They reported that the suggestions of the facilitator were less practical and not in line with the needs of the school as well ($\beta = -0.118, p = 0.002$) and they reported less support for the statement that their questions were addressed ($\beta = -0.120, p = 0.004$). Regarding capability, the participants who said they were not teachers or administrators reported that they felt less capable of talking about transgender and gender-expansive issues ($\beta = -0.202, p = 0.000$). They also reported

Table 1. OLS regression models for educator roles and agreement with statements.

	Useful	Relevant to Me	Relevant to My School	Suggestions Practical and Fit	Addressed Questions I Had	Capable of Discussing w/Parents	Capable of Discussing w/Other Staff	Equipped to Create Inclusive Environment	Appropriate Amount of Time
Constant	1.424	1.480	1.332	1.546	1.641	1.795	1.578	1.615	1.902
	(0.023)	(0.025)	(0.021)	(0.025)	(0.027)	(0.030)	(0.026)	(0.026)	(0.039)
Administrator	0.044	−0.111	0.033	−0.027	−0.022	−0.068	0.082	0.016	−0.044
	(0.053)	(0.058)	(0.050)	(0.058)	(0.064)	(0.071)	(0.061)	(0.062)	(0.091)
Other	−0.099	−0.112	−0.009	−0.118	−0.120	−0.202	−0.036	−0.110	−0.033
	(0.034)	(0.037)	(0.032)	(0.038)	(0.041)	(0.045)	(0.039)	(0.040)	(0.059)
Overall R-squared	0.016	0.007	0.001	0.007	0.006	0.014	0.003	0.006	0.000

All models use teachers as the indicator variable. Standard errors in parentheses.

not feeling fully equipped to create a safe school environment for gender-expansive and transgender students ($\beta = -0.110$, $p = 0.006$). As shown on Table 1, all the effect sizes were small.

OLS regression with school fixed effects results
Differences between schools. Next, we tested the influence of school differences on our model by including school fixed-effects, as shown in Table 2. Between-school differences accounted for 30% of the variation in the usefulness rating ($R^2 = .006$ $R^2 = .38$, $F(2, 1343) = 2.96$, $p < .05$), 18% in the rating about relevance of the training to the participant ($R^2 = .100$, $F(2, 1343) = 5.53$, $p < .030$), and 31% of the differences in feeling capable of discussing gender-expansive issues with parents ($R^2 = .062$, $F(2, 1343) = 3.38$, $p < .034$). While none of the models could account for a large change in the overall R^2, school differences significantly contributed to the variation in three of the ratings.

Qualitative results

For the implementation and suggestions survey questions, coders identified the most common themes in the free response after open-coding and then conducted a content analysis. The frequencies below are out of the number of educators who responded to each free response question. Participants were not guided to align their free responses to the belief statements so, although there were overlaps in the themes presented, we did not expect the frequencies in the plans for implementation and suggestions to align with the frequencies from the belief statements.

Plans for implementing new strategies
The inductive coding revealed a number of themes that emerged when analysing respondents open-ended responses about their planned implementation of the training at 6-months and 12-months. Figure 1 shows the common plans for implementing strategies discussed in the training.

We grouped these themes according to the three realms of responsibility referenced in the responses revolving around: the teacher (62%), the school (24%), and shared responsibility for change between the teacher and school (14%). The themes that emerged after examining educators' intended implementation plans included being more self-aware, seeking new classroom resources, pursuing policy changes, and adjusting specific teaching practices and language. One of the most common responses was changing their classroom practices, with almost 30% of educators identifying ways to amend their practices in their open-ended responses about implementation. These classroom changes included asking about preferred names and pronouns and not lining students up by gender. Another 5% of educators noted they would expand their curriculum, either by including specific lessons or by incorporating materials that address gender-expansive identities in their class. Other implementation plans were more general. For example, 22% of educators noted they would be 'more aware' or 'more sensitive,' while 6% of responded they would improve their own communication in some way. We included references to improving communicating with other educators, parents, students, and general statements about communication in this category.

We found that the most common implementation plan at the school-wide level was increasing access to school facilities, such as locker rooms and bathrooms (10%). In addition, educators expressed a desire to change other specific school-wide practices (e.g. changes to forms and name records process) and changing overarching school policies (8%).

Educators discussed general implementation plans that could be shared by individual teachers and by making school-level changes. These included engaging more stakeholders in the school's implementation of the training (4%) and general comments about improving the overall school climate (6%). Only 4% of educators stated they believed the school was doing enough already or they would not do anything to implement what they learned at the training.

Table 2. OLS regression with fixed effects models for educator roles and agreement with statements.

	Useful	Relevant to Me	Relevant to My School	Suggestions Practical and Fit	Addressed Questions I Had	Capable of Discussing w/Parents	Capable of Discussing w/Other Staff	Equipped to Create Inclusive Environment	Appropriate Amount of Time
Constant	1.415	1.478	1.331	1.517	1.613	1.768	1.571	1.609	1.858
	(0.025)	(0.028)	(0.024)	(0.028)	(0.031)	(0.034)	(0.029)	(0.029)	(0.042)
Admin.	0.011	−0.057	0.060	0.027	0.022	−0.041	0.054	0.005	−0.041
	(0.063)	(0.069)	(0.058)	(0.068)	(0.076)	(0.084)	(0.071)	(0.072)	(0.104)
Other	−0.091	−0.121	0.014	−0.060	−0.061	−0.142	−0.010	−0.093	0.077
	(0.042)	(0.046)	(0.039)	(0.045)	(0.050)	(0.056)	(0.048)	(0.048)	(0.069)
School Effects F-Test	0.052	0.030	0.423	0.264	0.345	0.034	0.654	0.106	0.363
ρ	0.297	0.185	0.317	0.291	0.279	0.309	0.362	0.332	0.346
Obs	1425	1425	1425	1425	1425	1425	1425	1425	1425
Schools	80	80	80	80	80	80	80	80	80
Overall R-squared	0.005	0.006	0.001	0.006	0.006	0.014	0.002	0.006	0.000

All models use teachers as the indicator variable. Standard errors in parentheses. Fixed effects OLS regressions labelled with FE in parentheses with standard errors clustered by schools.

Plans for Implementation Themes

Prompt: What changes do you see yourself and your school implementing in regard to gender nonconforming and transgender students? (at 6 and 12 months)?		
Teacher-Level	School-Level	Teacher- and School-Level
Change classroom practices (29%) Change classroom curriculum (5%) Increase awareness/sensitivity (22%) More communication (6%)	Change district/school practices (6%) Change school policy (8%) Change school facilities (10%)	More student, parent, faculty, staff, or community engagement with GNC/T topics (6%) General school climate (8%) Nothing/already doing enough (10%)

Figure 1. Plans for implementation themes.

Suggestions for future trainings

When asked about suggestions for future trainings, our analysis revealed that educators wanted to expand the training options related to gender-inclusivity and provided presentation feedback to the trainer (Figure 2). Among the most common responses were more time for trainings on gender (19%) or to the delivery of the content (e.g. more interactive, more discussion, etc.; 25%). Another 3% of respondents wanted to expand the training to more people and 2% wanted to expand the training to more topics for themselves after they received the training. This included a desire to know the legal implications related to this topic. In addition, 17% of educators wanted more specific resources. Many of these respondents requested specific support related to possible future interactions with parents as well as sample lesson plans and suggested books. About 5% of participants wanted to hear testimonials from students who identified as transgender. About a fifth of respondents said they would not make any changes to the training.

Discussion

Implication for research and practice

This study provides a quantitative description of educators' beliefs and implementation plans following gender-diversity professional development sessions in 80 schools. In the current political climate, there has been an increased discussion about gender diversity in schools and the need, or

Training Suggestions Themes

Prompt: Suggestions for future trainings?	
More time (19%) Expand training to more people (3%) Expand training to cover more topics (2%) Sample lesson plans, curriculum, best practices, resources and specific responses to challenges, situations, or questions (11%)	Provide administrative models (2%) More tailoring content to school or audience (4%) Change presenter technique or materials (25%) More personal stories or testimonies (5%) Misc. (10%) None (19%)

Figure 2. Training suggestions themes.

the lack of a need, to provide schools with more supports to ensure they are promoting the health and safety of all students. One way that schools attempt to address this need is by providing gender-inclusivity training to their employees, but there is little research on the opinions of these practitioners about the training they receive across multiple contexts.

Further, administrators in at least one study questioned the educational relevance of inclusivity training and assumed teachers in their school would not find the inclusivity training useful (Payne and Smith 2018). Feedback from educators in the gender-inclusivity training program we evaluated indicated the vast majority of participants not only want and need this type of training but expressed a desire to have more of it after their initial session, both in breadth and depth. In addition to improving the training of the specific program evaluated, our findings contribute the voices of educators to the policy conversations concerning transgender students in schools more broadly.

Our results suggest that school practitioners wanted more specific training on how to create gender-inclusive classrooms and schools. There are several sources of evidence to support this claim. First, 'appropriateness of time' was the only item to receive less 80% of participants reporting that they strongly agreed or agreed with the statement. Second, there were no significant differences across different roles or across schools in how participants felt about the appropriateness of time statement. Third, we did not see any respondents suggest shortening the training in the qualitative analyses of the open-ended responses; however, 20% of respondents suggested they wanted more time, 17% requested more resources, 2% wanted more training on other topics related to gender-expansiveness not addressed in the training, and 3% recommended training for more people from the school community. A total of 42% recommended the program and reported that it provided them and/or others more information about gender inclusion in school.

We found that educators valued the gender inclusivity training, and believed it was relevant and useful to their work. After the gender-inclusivity training, educators demonstrated a high frequency of agreement (above 90%) that the training was useful, relevant-both to the individual and school, provided practical suggestions fitting their school, and had their questions answered.

As a rough comparison, other general surveys about professional development indicate lower levels of agreement with overall satisfaction with educators' professional development (66%); with available professional development as a good use of time (42%); that their professional development improves educators' practice (49%); professional development fits to educators' context (50%); and professional development provided the necessary skills to implement inclusive practices (48%; (Shady et al. 2013, Bill & Melinda Gates Foundation & Boston Consulting Group (BCG) 2014). Based on the educators' responses to the gender-inclusivity training, we find evidence that educators believed the training was an effective way to begin the conversation about gender in their workplace and perceived usefulness, at least on the part of practitioners, is not a barrier to expanding this type of training. These quantitative results support earlier findings from a few qualitative studies indicating educators desire greater exposure to conversations about gender diversity in order to enhance their practice (Meyer 2008, Meyer et al. 2016, Meyer and Leonardi 2018). This earlier qualitative work provided contextual descriptions of specific gender-diversity training programs afforded by ethnographies and focus groups, while the quantitative component of this study contributes a widespread description of educators' beliefs across 80 schools.

There was also evidence that the training may initiate changes in educators' future behaviour, supporting the findings from interview and observational studies of teachers after gender-inclusivity trainings in other cities that describe changes in teachers' behaviours and more supportive behaviours of students post-training (Szalacha 2004, Ryan et al. 2013, Case and Meier 2014, Taylor et al. 2016). In our study, educators felt equipped to create a safe school environment for gender-expansive and transgender students, felt capable of discussing issues related to gender-expansiveness with other faculty and staff and, to a lesser degree, with parents. Because high self-efficacy in teachers has been linked to greater implementation of training and changes in behaviours in the literature (Bandura 1977, Guskey 1988, Klassen and Tze 2014), these findings are indicative that there may be changes in teacher behaviour after quality inclusivity training. Further supporting this argument, our qualitative findings show that most educators who had implementation plans had specific, small changes to classroom behaviours (30%), such as asking for preferred pronouns. Relatedly, less confidence about working with parents could influence their ability to effectively engage in discussions about gender diversity with other educational stakeholders. Our findings support similar results from studies with fewer participants, suggesting one of the challenges educators perceive in challenging gender norms is their ability to engage parents around topics of gender diversity (Meyer 2008, Schneider and Dimito 2008, Frohard-Dourlent 2016, Malins 2016, Leonardi 2017). Future training with staff and the parent community could address this need.

Our study demonstrates that gender-inclusivity trainings may be an effective way to address some of the needs of educators with some important caveats. One weakness of the training was the failure to tailor it to a broader audience. In particular, we found the training needed to tailor the content and message to participants who did not identify as either teachers or administrators. The 'other' category composed 39% of the sample. Our OLS regression analyses demonstrated there was slightly less agreement from participants reporting 'other' roles for usefulness, relevance to me, practical suggestions, and questions addressed items. Librarians, school psychologists, custodial staff, and parents are all examples of respondents who marked the 'other' category, and who may interact with students daily, playing an important role in students' lives. Notably, we did not find significant differences in how relevant these educators thought the training was for the school. These respondents also had slightly less agreement with statements about feeling capable of discussing these issues related to gender diversity with parents- although between school differences accounted for some of this variation – and believed themselves to be less equipped to create a safe school environment for gender-expansive students. This group reported less agreement in 6 of the 9 statements of interest when compared to teachers. These effects were small but statistically significant. While we were not able to test other demographic differences among participants, these analyses may be capturing participants' differences in how frequently they interact with students, interact with administration, their experiences with gender-expansive people, education levels, and belief systems. Trainers should take care to adapt and tailor trainings to meet the needs of different audiences in schools beyond teachers and administrators. Alternatively, additional trainings could be developed to address the needs of these school employees.

In addition to indicating that many educators need more support, our results show that schools may also need more resources, particularly in engaging parents. We found significant differences across schools with respect to reported usefulness of the training, relevance of the training to the respondent, capability to discuss issues related to transgender and gender-expansive students with parents, and marginal differences to feeling equipped to creating a safe school environment for gender-expansive students. To an extent, this result was expected as some trainings varied in the length of time and, as a result, the depth of the content delivered. Training length depended upon the needs, resources, and capacity of the school district. These findings also signified the importance of capturing demographic information in the schools where the trainings occurred. The length of the training, political and social leanings of the community, the number of gender-expansive students in the school, and the number of related trainings in the district are examples of factors which likely contribute to variation in belief ratings across schools. This should be examined in future research.

Finally, our qualitative findings reveal how attendees envisioned implementing the training content on an individual-level via changes in their classroom, administrative practices, or other work within the school. Additionally, attendees reported an intent to implement school and district-level changes through policy, facilities (e.g. bathrooms and locker rooms), and practices (48%). Participants also indicated a desire for greater engagement of the broader school community, such as parents.

Limitations

There were a number of important limitations of this study. First, this study was not a causal study and we were not able to report on changes in educators' agreement with statements or behaviours without the use of a control group and/or pre-test. Second, the selection into the sample was biased as the participation of the schools or attendees in these trainings were not randomised. Knowledge of the training either was gained through personal recommendations and word-of-mouth or training was offered to the school because of a needs assessment regarding a patient at the children's hospital. Additionally, as noted in the methods, we were not able to retroactively identify which schools allowed educators to self-select into the training to compare to educators whose attendance was mandated. We were also not able to identify which participants received a 90-minute training and which received the two-day training. There may be significant variation in the beliefs and plans of participants self-selecting into a training, and those receiving content covered in a relatively brief 90 minutes compared to a 2-day training with more active involvement of participants. These trainings are not homogenous. However, the authors contend the different conditions in which the trainings were delivered may add to the generalisability of the evaluation of trainings that are taken up by educators in different districts and under different conditions. Other evaluations have offered a more in-depth analysis of one-off trainings and longer workshops (Greytak *et al.* 2013, Smith and Payne 2016). This evaluation offers an overarching picture of educators' responses to the heterogeneous nature of these trainings in the field. Third, there was a single facilitator who provided the training. Therefore, it is impossible to disentangle the effects of the facilitator from the actual training curriculum. Furthermore, the status and authority of the training program may have been challenged less due to the training program's placement within a respected, local hospital and the relationship between the facilitator and key administrators within the district. Past research asserts that these aspects of status and authority play a role in how educators consume professional development (Coburn *et al.* 2008). Fourth, we used pre-existing data and the facilitator did not notice any track variations in the length of time or content adaptations. Fifth, the survey did not assess prior content knowledge or attitudes about gender-expansive people through a baseline pre-test, both of which may have influenced agreement with the belief statements. Sixth, the study was conducted using evaluation data from trainings in mostly urban and suburban Midwestern schools in one state. The results may have limited generalisability based on these geographical constraints and there are documented limitations in using one-time evaluation data to assess long-term changes in behaviours (Guskey 2000, Lawless and Pellegrino 2016).

Future research

Gender-inclusivity training should be seen as a first step towards supporting gender-inclusive schools. Similar to other educational reforms, researchers should continue to investigate other ways district administrators create an infrastructure to guide educators' daily interactions with students towards greater inclusivity. Future research should address several remaining questions. First, future researchers should examine barriers to offering or expanding educators' training on gender inclusivity in their schools. Second, research needs to investigate the content future trainings should include and what institutional supports districts have in place to support the school community (e.g. protective policies). Third, since this study had a limited number of educators from small towns and rural communities, future researchers should broaden the sample to diversify the schools and attendees included. Fourth, researchers should design evaluations with pre- and post-training surveys to capture changes in beliefs/attitudes, behaviours, and content knowledge of educators and their students to assess the impact of the training. Finally, tracking variations in the training content, length, goals, and audience, would enhance our understanding of why educators' beliefs and implementation plans may differ by role and school. These may be important differences contributing to educators' beliefs and behaviours (Lawless and Pellegrino 2016). More research is needed to understand what types of trainings and how much is needed for different districts.

Conclusions

Professional development for school practitioners regarding gender identity and creating gender-inclusive environments is a crucial step towards educating adults in schools about the needs of gender-expansive and transgender students (Rands 2009). Our study contributes to the existing literature by examining local educators' beliefs about the usefulness and relevance of training specific to gender identity using data from 1,425 school employees across a diverse array of schools (80). We found that educators believed the gender-inclusivity professional development that they received was useful and relevant. The majority of educational professionals agreed that they had improved their capacity to create a safe, educational environment for students and of discussing gender issues with parents, students, and their school community after the training. Using regression analyses with and without school fixed effects, we evaluate quantitative trends in these beliefs across educators' roles within schools and across schools. The results suggest that trainings should attempt to incorporate the needs of non-teaching and non-administrative attendees, as these staff members also contribute to schools' climate and culture.

Our results provide quantitative and qualitative support for trends described in the existing research literature indicating that there is a need for more training related to gender for educational professionals (Szalacha 2004, Macgillivray and Jennings 2008, Ryan et al. 2013). In our sample, we found school practitioners were interested in additional, in-depth training on gender inclusivity, including practical tactics for implementing affirming practices. Moreover, this evaluation informs ongoing policy conversations in districts nationwide about how institutions can and should support their staff in addressing the needs of transgender and gender-expansive students more broadly. This study highlights the need for trainings to address gender-diversity and gender-inclusivity in schools, which may be an important step towards closing the health and educational gaps between gender-expansive youth and to their peers.

Acknowledgments

This research was supported by Ann & Robert H. Lurie Children's Hospital of Chicago's Gender & Sex Development Program, the National Academy of Education/Spencer Dissertation Fellowship, and the Sexualities Project at Northwestern University. We are grateful to Drs. Lisa Kuhns, Robert Garofalo, James Spillane, and Diane Whitmore Schanzenbach for providing comments and additional insights contributing to this paper.

Disclosure Statement

No potential conflict of interest was reported by the authors.

Funding

This work was supported by the Ann & Robert H. Lurie Children's Hospital of Chicago's Gender & Sex Development Program; Northwestern University Institute of Policy Research; Sexualities Project at Northwestern University; National Academy of Education/Spencer Dissertation Fellowship.

ORCID

Mollie T. McQuillan http://orcid.org/0000-0002-2522-3871

References

Adelson, S.L., 2012. Practice parameter on gay, lesbian, or bisexual sexual orientation, gender nonconformity, and gender discordance in children and adolescents. *Journal of the American academy of child & adolescent psychiatry*, 51 (9), 957–974. doi:10.1016/j.jaac.2012.07.004.

Bandura, A., 1977. Self-efficacy: toward a unifying theory of behavioral change. *Psychological review*, 84 (2), 191–215. doi:10.1037/0033-295X.84.2.191.

Bill & Melinda Gates Foundation., Bill & Melinda Gates Foundation., & Boston Consulting Group (BCG). 2014. *Teachers know best: teachers' views on professional development*. Available from: /z-wcorg/

Birkett, M. and Espelage, D.L., 2014. Homophobic name-calling, peer-groups, and masculinity: the socialization of homophobic behavior in adolescents. *Social development*, 184–205. doi:10.1111/sode.12085.

Case, K.A. and Meier, S.C., 2014. Developing allies to transgender and gender-nonconforming youth: training for counselors and educators. *Journal of LGBT youth*, 11 (1), 62–82. doi:10.1080/19361653.2014.840764.

Charmaz, K., 2014. *Constructing grounded theory*. Sage.

Clark, C.M. and Peterson, P.L. 1984. Teachers' thought processes. *Occasional Paper No. 72*. Available from: https://eric.ed.gov/?id=ED251449

Coburn, C.E., Bae, S., and Turner, E.O., 2008. Authority, status, and the dynamics of insider–outsider partnerships at the district level. *Peabody Journal of education*, 83 (3), 364–399. doi:10.1080/01619560802222350.

Corbin, J., and Strauss, A., 2008. *Strategies for qualitative data analysis*. Basics of Qualitative Research. Techniques and procedures for developing grounded theory, 3.

Crissman, H.P., et al., 2017. Transgender demographics: a household probability sample of US adults, 2014. *American journal of public health*; Washington, 107 (2), 213–215. doi:10.2105/AJPH.2016.303571.

Day, J.K., et al., 2017. Transgender youth substance use disparities: results from a population-based sample. *Journal of adolescent health*, 61 (6), 729–735. doi:10.1016/j.jadohealth.2017.06.024.

Dessel, A.B., et al., 2017. The importance of teacher support: differential impacts by gender and sexuality. *Journal of adolescence*, 56, 136–144. doi:10.1016/j.adolescence.2017.02.002

Fives, H. and Gill, M.G., 2014. *International handbook of research on teachers' beliefs*. New York: Routledge.

Frohard-Dourlent, H., 2016. 'I don't care what's under your clothes': the discursive positioning of educators working with trans and gender-nonconforming students. *Sex education*, 16 (1), 63–76. doi:10.1080/14681811.2015.1022819.

Greytak, E.A., Kosciw, J.G., and Diaz, E.M. 2009. *Harsh realities: the experiences of transgender youth in our nation's schools*. Gay, Lesbian and Straight Education Network. Available from: http://www.glsen.org/sites/default/files/Harsh%20Realities.pdf

Greytak, E.A. and Kosciw, J.G., 2014. Predictors of US teachers' intervention in anti-lesbian, gay, bisexual, and transgender bullying and harassment. *Teaching education*, 25 (4), 410–426. doi:10.1080/10476210.2014.920000.

Greytak, E.A., Kosciw, J.G., and Boesen, M.J., 2013. Educating the educator: creating supportive school personnel through professional development. *Journal of school violence*, 12 (1), 80–97. doi:10.1080/15388220.2012.731586.

Grossman, A.H. and D'augelli, A.R., 2006. Transgender youth. *Journal of homosexuality*, 51 (1), 111–128. doi:10.1300/J082v51n01_06.

Grossman, A.H., D'augelli, A.R., and Frank, J.A., 2011. Aspects of psychological resilience among transgender youth. *Journal of LGBT youth*, 8 (2), 103–115. doi:10.1080/19361653.2011.541347.

Guskey, T.R., 1988. Teacher efficacy, self-concept, and attitudes toward the implementation of instructional innovation. *Teaching and teacher education*, 4 (1), 63–69. doi:10.1016/0742-051X(88)90025-X.

Guskey, T.R., 2000. *Evaluating professional development*. Thousand Oaks: Corwin Press.

Hatzenbuehler, M.L., 2016. Structural stigma and health inequalities: research evidence and implications for psychological science. *The American psychologist*, 71 (8), 742–751. doi:10.1037/amp0000068.

Heinze, J.E. and Horn, S.S., 2014. Do adolescents' evaluations of exclusion differ based on gender expression and sexual orientation? *Journal of social issues*, 70 (1), 63–80. doi:10.1111/josi.12047.

Institute of Medicine. 2011. *The health of lesbian, gay, bisexual, and transgender people: building a foundation for better understanding*. Washington D.C.: The National Academies Press. https://www.iom.edu:443/Reports/2011/The-Health-of-Lesbian-Gay-Bisexual-and-Transgender-People.aspx

Ispa-Landa, S., 2013. Gender, race, and justifications for group exclusion urban black students bussed to affluent suburban schools. *Sociology of education*, 0038040712472912. doi:10.1177/0038040712472912.

Kagan, D.M., 1992. Implication of research on teacher belief. *Educational psychologist*, 27 (1), 65. doi:10.1207/s15326985ep2701_6.

Klassen, R.M. and Tze, V.M.C., 2014. Teachers' self-efficacy, personality, and teaching effectiveness: a meta-analysis. *Educational research review*, 12 (SupplementC), 59–76. doi:10.1016/j.edurev.2014.06.001.

Lawless, K.A. and Pellegrino, J.W., 2016. Professional development in integrating technology into teaching and learning: knowns, unknowns, and ways to pursue better questions and answers. *Review of educational research*. doi:10.3102/0034654307309921.

Leonardi, B., 2017. Navigating the relationship between policy and practice: competing discourses of fear and care in teachers' sense-making about the FAIR education act. *Journal of education policy*, 32 (5), 694–716. doi:10.1080/02680939.2017.1320730.

Lewis, M.M. and Kern, S., 2018. Using education law as a tool to empower social justice leaders to promote LGBTQ inclusion. *Educational administration quarterly*, 54 (5), 723–746. doi:10.1177/0013161X18769045.

Macgillivray, I.K. and Jennings, T., 2008. A content analysis exploring lesbian, gay, bisexual, and transgender topics in foundations of education textbooks. *Journal of teacher education*, 59 (2), 170–188. doi:10.1177/0022487107313160.

Malins, P., 2016. How inclusive is "inclusive education" in the Ontario elementary classroom?: Teachers talk about addressing diverse gender and sexual identities. *Teaching and teacher education*, 54, 128–138. doi:10.1016/j.tate.2015.11.004

McGuire, J.K., et al., 2010. School climate for transgender youth: a mixed method investigation of student experiences and school responses. *Journal of youth and adolescence*, 39 (10), 1175–1188. doi:10.1007/s10964-010-9540-7.

Meyer, E.J., 2008. Gendered harassment in secondary schools: understanding teachers' (non) interventions. *Gender and education*, 20 (6), 555–570. doi:10.1080/09540250802213115.

Meyer, E.J. and Leonardi, B., 2018. Teachers' professional learning to affirm transgender, non-binary, and gender-creative youth: experiences and recommendations from the field. *Sex education*, 18 (4), 449–463. doi:10.1080/14681811.2017.1411254.

Meyer, E.J., Tilland-Stafford, A., and Airton, L., 2016. Transgender and gender-creative students in pk-12 schools: what we can learn from their teachers. *Teachers College record*, 118 (8), 1–50.

Pascoe, C.J., 2005. 'Dude, you're a fag': adolescent masculinity and the fag discourse. *Sexualities*, 8 (3), 329–346. doi:10.1177/1363460705053337.

Pascoe, C.J., 2011. *Dude, you're a fag: masculinity and sexuality in high school, with a new preface*. Berkeley: University of California Press.

Payne, E. and Smith, M., 2014. The big freak out: educator fear in response to the presence of transgender elementary school students. *Journal of homosexuality*, 61 (3), 399–418. doi:10.1080/00918369.2013.842430.

Payne, E.C. and Smith, M.J., 2018. Refusing relevance: school administrator resistance to offering professional development addressing LGBTQ issues in schools. *Educational Administration Quarterly*, 54 (2), 183–215. doi:10.1177/0013161X17723426.

Perez-Brumer, A., et al., 2017. Prevalence and correlates of suicidal ideation among transgender youth in california: findings from a representative, population-based sample of high school students. *Journal of the American academy of child & adolescent psychiatry*, 56 (9), 739–746. doi:10.1016/j.jaac.2017.06.010.

Philips, R.R., 2017. The battle over bathrooms: schools, courts, and transgender rights. *Theory in action*, 10 (4), 100–117. doi:10.3798/tia.1937-0237.1729.

Rands, K.E., 2009. Considering transgender people in education: a gender-complex approach. *Journal of teacher education*, 60 (4), 419–431. doi:10.1177/0022487109341475.

Reigeluth, C.S. and Addis, M.E., 2015. Adolescent boys' experiences with policing of masculinity: forms, functions, and consequences. *Psychology of men & masculinity*. doi:10.1037/a0039342.

Reisner, S.L., et al., 2014. Transgender health disparities: comparing full cohort and nested matched-pair study designs in a community health center. *LGBT Health*, 1 (3), 177–184. doi:10.1089/lgbt.2014.0009.

Reisner, S.L., et al., 2016. Global health burden and needs of transgender populations: a review. *The lancet*, 388 (10042), 412–436. doi:10.1016/S0140-6736(16)00684-X.

Ryan, C.L., Patraw, J.M., and Bednar, M., 2013. Discussing princess boys and pregnant men: teaching about gender diversity and transgender experiences within an elementary school curriculum. *Journal of LGBT youth*, 10 (1–2), 83–105. doi:10.1080/19361653.2012.718540.

Sausa, L.A., 2005. Translating research into practice: trans youth recommendations for improving school systems. *Journal of gay & lesbian issues in education*, 3 (1), 15–28. doi:10.1300/J367v03n01_04.

Schneider, M.S. and Dimito, A., 2008. Educators' beliefs about raising lesbian, gay, bisexual, and transgender issues in the schools: the experience in Ontario, Canada. *Journal of LGBT youth*, 5 (4), 49–71. doi:10.1080/19361650802223003.

Sevelius, J.M., 2013. Gender affirmation: a framework for conceptualizing risk behavior among transgender women of color. *Sex roles*, 68 (11–12), 675–689. doi:10.1007/s11199-012-0216-5.

Shady, S.A., Luther, V.L., and Richman, L.J., 2013. Teaching the teachers: a study of perceived professional development needs of educators to enhance positive attitudes toward inclusive practices. *Education Research and Perspectives*, 40 (1), 169–191.

Sherwin, G. and Jennings, T., 2006. Feared, forgotten, or forbidden: sexual orientation topics in secondary teacher preparation programs in the USA. *Teaching Education*, 17 (3), 207–223. doi:10.1080/10476210600849664.

Smith, M.J. and Payne, E., 2016. Binaries and biology: conversations with elementary education professionals after professional development on supporting transgender students. *The Educational forum*, 80 (1), 34–47. doi:10.1080/00131725.2015.1102367.

Snapp, S.D., et al., 2015. Messy, butch, and queer LGBTQ youth and the school-to-prison pipeline. *Journal of adolescent research*, 30 (1), 57–82. doi:10.1177/0743558414557625.

Snapp, S.D. and Russell, S.T., 2016. Discipline disparities for LGBTQ youth: challenges that perpetuate disparities and strategies to overcome them. *In*: R.J. Skiba, K. Mediratta, and M.K. Rausch, eds. *Inequality in school discipline*. Palgrave Macmillan US, 207–223. doi:10.1057/978-1-137-51257-4_12.
Swanson, K. and Gettinger, M., 2016. Teachers' knowledge, attitudes, and supportive behaviors toward LGBT students: relationship to gay-straight alliances, antibullying policy, and teacher training. *Journal of LGBT youth*, 13 (4), 326–351. doi:10.1080/19361653.2016.1185765.
Szalacha, L.A., 2004. Educating teachers on LGBTQ issues. *Journal of gay & lesbian issues in education*, 1 (4), 67–79. doi:10.1300/J367v01n04_07.
Taylor, C.G., et al., 2016. Gaps between beliefs, perceptions, and practices: the Every teacher project on LGBTQ-inclusive education in Canadian schools. *Journal of LGBT youth*, 13 (1–2), 112–140. doi:10.1080/19361653.2015.1087929.
Ullman, J., 2017. Teacher positivity towards gender diversity: exploring relationships and school outcomes for transgender and gender-diverse students. *Sex education*, 17 (3), 276–289. doi:10.1080/14681811.2016.1273104.
White Hughto, J.M., Reisner, S.L., and Pachankis, J.E., 2015. Transgender stigma and health: A critical review of stigma determinants, mechanisms, and interventions. *Social science & medicine*, 147, 222–231. doi:10.1016/j.socscimed.2015.11.010

APPENDIX A
Gender 101: Training Evaluation

Thank you for participating in this training with the Gender and Sex Development Program at Lurie Children's Hospital. Please complete this short survey regarding your experience. Your feedback is highly valuable to us and your answers will remain anonymous. Thank you!

1. What school do you work for?

2. What is your role at your school?
   ☐ Teacher
   ☐ Administrator
   ☐ Other

3. In the next <u>6 months</u>, what changes do you see yourself and your school implementing in regards to gender non-conforming and transgender students?

4. In the next <u>12 months</u>, what changes do you see yourself and your school implementing in regards to gender non-conforming and transgender students?

5. What did you enjoy most about the training?

6. What suggestions would you make for this training in the future?

7. Are there any additional comments you would like to share regarding the training?

Please indicate your level of agreement with the statements listed below.	Strongly Agree	Agree	Neutral	Disagree	Strongly Disagree
The objectives of the training were clearly defined.	☐	☐	☐	☐	☐
The topics covered were relevant to me.	☐	☐	☐	☐	☐
The topics covered were relevant to my school.	☐	☐	☐	☐	☐
The content was organized and easy to follow.	☐	☐	☐	☐	☐
This training will be useful in my work.	☐	☐	☐	☐	☐
Please indicate your level of agreement with the statements listed below.	**Strongly Agree**	**Agree**	**Neutral**	**Disagree**	**Strongly Disagree**
The facilitator was knowledgeable about the training topic.	☐	☐	☐	☐	☐
The time allotted for the training was sufficient.	☐	☐	☐	☐	☐
I feel more capable of discussing concepts of gender non-conforming and transgender students with parents.	☐	☐	☐	☐	☐
I feel more capable of discussing concepts of gender non-conforming and transgender students with other faculty and staff.	☐	☐	☐	☐	☐
Please indicate your level of agreement with the statements listed below.	**Strongly Agree**	**Agree**	**Neutral**	**Disagree**	**Strongly Disagree**
The suggestions and examples provided by the facilitator felt practical and fit the needs of my school.	☐	☐	☐	☐	☐
The training addressed the questions that I had regarding transgender and gender non-conforming youth.	☐	☐	☐	☐	☐
The question-and-answer portion was useful.	☐	☐	☐	☐	☐
I would feel comfortable reaching out to the facilitator with further questions.	☐	☐	☐	☐	☐
After the training, I now feel more equipped to create a safe school environment for transgender and gender non-conforming students.	☐	☐	☐	☐	☐

Learning about culture together: enhancing educators cultural competence through collaborative teacher study groups

Chrystal S. Johnson, Jennifer Sdunzik, Cornelius Bynum, Nicole Kong and Xiaoyue Qin

ABSTRACT
We describe the impact of an African American history centred collaborative teacher study group (CTSG) professional development experience on the cultural competence of 20 secondary Social Studies and English Language Arts educators. Using mixed methods, baseline data indicated slight movement from the colourblind to the cultural pre-competence level for most. Race, as a fixed category, slightly impacted the increase in participants' cultural competence levels. Gender and teaching experience, however, had little if any impact on cultural competence levels. Selected interviews suggested that participants recognised the importance of teaching with diversity in mind. Yet, many acknowledge lacking the skillset to adequately meet the linguistic and cultural diversity of their students. Overall, participants noted that the professional development experience broadens their cultural competence awareness and would influence their instruction practice.

Global migration flows and socioeconomic segregation have resulted in increasingly culturally and linguistically diverse student bodies in schools around the world. The need for culturally competent educators is critically important due to students' academic achievement, critical consciousness, and social competence being closely related to culturally synchronised learning environments (Gay 2010, Ford 2013, Ladson-Billings 2014, Jett et al. 2016). Collaborative teacher study groups (CTSGs) may offer an effectual professional development experience for preparing culturally competent educators who use culturally relevant pedagogy, are culturally responsive, and address discriminatory practices. CTSGs offer places for educators to entertain divergent perspectives on the influence of race, ethnicity, and culture on educative practices. Through ongoing, dedicated, and well-conceived professional development experiences, educators strengthen their culturally relevant practices through deliberative discussion and problem solving (Stanley 2012). Effective CTSGs include individual follow-up through supportive observation and feedback, dialogues, and mentoring; in fact, beneficial CTSGs provide common, goal-oriented commitments and structure group norms. Researchers agree that core structural features of effectual professional development, such as content focus, duration, active learning, participation, and coherence, are essential to CTSGs. These features matter when it comes to enhancing teachers' knowledge, skills, and classroom practice (e.g. Darling-Hammond and McLaughlin 1995, Guskey and Sparks 1996, Garet et al. 2001, Robinson and Carrington 2002, Guskey 2003).

In this study, the researchers measured the impact of a CTSG that sought to strengthen the cultural competence of 20 secondary Social Studies and English Language Arts educators. This professional development experience, a sustained, intensive, on-site summer institute, focused on incorporating African American history, literature, and culture into classroom curricula while simultaneously emphasising the usefulness of information technology. Prominent scholars of American and African American history and literature led workshops designed to collaborate with participants in thinking about how the diverse narrative of America, especially African Americans' experiences, can be effective in teaching core Social Studies and English Language Arts concepts. Participants read historical documents and literary selections, worked with the geographic information system (GIS), engaged in films, art, and music – all at three African American museums of history located in the Midwest region of the United States (US). Simultaneously, the professional development environment provided a safe space to have conversations about race, racism, and cultural aesthetics.

Despite the power of CTSGs and the need for culturally competent educators, few, if any, investigations explore the cogency of culturally relevant professional development experiences in cultivating secondary educators' cultural competence. Given this dearth of research, this study is timely and relevant. We assert that a CTSG steeped in African American history and culture positively impacts the cultural competence levels of secondary educators. To that end, we posed the following research question:

(1) Does a culturally relevant CTSG professional development experience increase secondary educators' cultural competency levels?

To address the research question, we organised the article into four sections. In the first section, we draw on a transdisciplinary literature base to delineate cultural competence, differentiate it from multicultural education, and share the advantageous nature of CTSGs when it comes to professional development for cultural competence in education. In the second section, we contextualise the professional development experience studied. Specifically, we outline goals, duration, and programming. From there, we describe the research methods employed and present findings. We conclude the article by summarising our argument.

Cultural competence

The research on cultural competence is full-bodied and rooted in the interdisciplinary fields of cross-cultural psychology, nursing, and multicultural counselling (Hammer *et al.* 2003, Sue and Sue 2007, Bustamante *et al.* 2016). This construct is frequently used to measure attitudes, dispositions, values, beliefs, knowledge, and skills of professionals who directly interact with those who differ culturally from themselves. Cultural competence as it relates to teacher education and educator preparation has roots primarily in interdisciplinary research. In the early 2000s, Lindsey *et al.* (2003) used Cross *et al.* (1989) definition and continuum of cultural competence and adapted the continuum to educators, with a focus on culturally proficient educational leadership. Other notions related to the construct of cultural competence have been applied specifically to the field of education to describe how well educators respond to diverse groups of students in K-12 classrooms, including acknowledgement of the cultural knowledge and experiences that students bring to the classroom.

Cultural competence is related to yet distinctly different from multicultural education. Both cultural competence and multicultural education stem from civil rights struggles and confrontations with racism in education. The latter is the phrase chosen by multicultural theorists to describe approaches that promote cultural pluralism and social equality by reforming society, which includes schools, for all to better reflect diversity (Denboba 2005, Diller and Moule 2005). Within schools, multicultural education goals emphasise raising personal awareness about various categories of individual differences, and how these differences enhance or hinder the ways students and teachers generally interact with each other. May and Sleeter (2010) convey schools as cultural sites where students and educators are culturally constructed through membership in multiple cultural communities. To better foster intercultural respect and engagement among both students and educators, an examination of culture should begin with the peeling back of the layers of identity, practice, and existence of all classroom inhabitants.

A culturally competent educator is a product of multicultural education (Banks, 2009). Cultural competence represents one's attitudes towards, knowledge about, and skills in aptly and successfully interacting with culturally diverse populations. Within the field of education, various terms are used to describe the essential dispositions, knowledge, and skills for teaching in a culturally diverse society. Two such terms are culturally relevant pedagogy and culturally responsive teaching. The former was developed by Ladson-Billings (1994). The latter was coined by Gay (2000, 2010) to elucidate culturally based teaching practices. Gay (2000) described culturally responsive teachers as proficient in 'using cultural knowledge, prior experiences, frames of reference, and performance styles of ethnically diverse students to make learning more relevant and effective for them' (p. 29). In other words, culturally responsive teachers are willing and able to interweave students' cultural and linguistic diversities and other distinguishing group characteristics (e.g. disabilities) into classroom instructional practices in ways that meet or exceed students' learning objectives.

Scholars have noted that culturally responsive teachers are culturally competent, and thus these terms are often used interchangeably. Teachers who are effective at teaching students from diverse backgrounds are culturally sensitive, use culturally relevant teaching methods, address discriminatory practices, and often incorporate views and histories of marginalised people into the curriculum. Furthermore, culturally competent teachers are characterised as setting high expectations, using metacognitive strategies, understanding critical literacy, and connecting lessons with students' cultures (Gay 2010).

Despite the various terms that scholars have used to describe teachers' attitudes, knowledge, and skills in accounting for and integrating student cultures into the learning process, the basic elements comprising each concept are similar and are relevant to the development of cultural competence in secondary educators. In this study, we base the construct of cultural competence on Cross' cultural competence model. Cross (1988) asserts that there are delineated levels of responding to cultural differences that define the process of a professional becoming culturally competent.

(a) **Cultural Destructiveness** – The most negative end of the continuum. It describes the organisation or individual's competence as viewing cultural differences as a problem. It demonstrates inflexible behaviours. The culturally diverse individual or group is considered genetically and culturally inferior.
(b) **Cultural Incapacity** – The individual or organisation does not intentionally seek to be culturally destructive, yet they lack the capacity to help culturally diverse individuals or groups. The individual or organisation remains extremely biased. Decisions and actions are guided by ignorance or a sense of superiority. Persons of culturally diverse origins are not valued or acknowledged, and expectations of them are lowered.
(c) **Cultural Blindness** – This is the midpoint of the continuum. The individual or organisation acts with the belief that culture makes no difference. This view reflects good intentions at being unbiased; however, the consequences of this belief can be ignoring or not recognising cultural strengths. In gifted education, this may manifest itself in an organisation's unwillingness to use alternative assessments or change policies and procedures to open doors to diverse students.
(d) **Cultural Pre-Competence** – At this level, the individual or organisation can be viewed as accepting and respectful of cultural differences. An attempt is made to engage in ongoing self-assessment regarding culture. This individual is proactive and seeks knowledge and advice from different cultural groups.

(e) **Advanced Cultural Competence** – This is the most positive and progressive level of Cross' model. Culture at this level is held in the highest regard. The individual or organisation aggressively and proactively develops educational models and approaches based on culture.

We further believe that cultural competence reflects global trends, not just the majoritarian perspectives. As a complex know-act grounded in critical reflection and action, it presents a professional learning experience that is culturally safe, congruent, and effective in partnership with educators and considers the social and political dimensions of schooling. Past knowledge is questioned, and new knowledge is integrated in a dialectical relationship of thinking and action. A person's ability to learn varies depending on the different contexts and situations encountered; learning constitutes a process that changes both the learner and the environment, and it allows the development of competencies.

Collaborative teacher study groups

Designing dedicated professional development experiences to address the complexities of the classroom and diverse student populations can be challenging. The challenge lies in designing and implementing strategies and activities that include conversations on race, ethnicity, and culture. These discussions are sometimes hindered by a lack of readiness to address these difficult topics or contentious issues around race, oppressions, or issues of privilege in the classroom (Abrams and Moio 2009). CTSGs provide a powerful framework for incorporating the features of effective professional development such as providing intensive and ongoing support for application and practice embedded within opportunities for conversation, reflection, feedback, and troubleshooting. The CTSG approach maintains principles of relationship-based professional development, through which teachers benefit from ongoing access to highly qualified facilitators as well as the opportunity to receive feedback, advice, and support from their peers. Collaborative teacher study groups are intended to spark expertise and collective wisdom of thoughtful teachers. Situated in a constructivist view of learning (Hung and Yeh 2013), our CTSG was organised to be a professional development community for educators to foster learning through interaction and sharing ideas.

CTSGs stand in relief to the typical one-way delivery of tips, techniques, or ideas that may or may not have any effect on teaching practice or student achievement. Researchers in collaborative teacher professional development communities have defined characteristics of groups that seem to foster teacher collaborative learning. They provide a place for shared reflective inquiry around problems and issues of teaching. In collaborative groups, teachers can deepen their pedagogical expertise and improve their instruction by sharing specific problems of practice and making the solutions they develop accessible and transferable to various classroom settings (Little 1990, Wenger 1998, Ball and Cohen 1999, Cochran-Smith and Lytle 1999, DuFour 2004, Hammerness *et al.* 2005, McLaughlin and Talbert 2006).

Collaborative teacher study groups for cultural competence

Often times, CTSGs are comprised of educators with varying levels of experience or matters of race, ethnicity, and culture. Culturally relevant CTSGs can help educators 'become more aware of the effects of institutional as well as individual forms of racism and to prepare them to become agents of change by challenging racist practices and policies both in their teaching and in their daily lives' (Lawrence and Tatum 1997, p. 46). A study by DeJaeghere and Zhang (2008) found that a teacher's confidence in their cultural competence improves by participating in meaningful and ongoing professional development. As such, it is vital for educational leaders to create effective, relevant professional development opportunities in which teachers will participate so that they will be able to meet the challenges of teaching in culturally diverse school settings. Banks *et al.* (2001) noted that effective professional development programme should help educators to:

(1) Uncover and identify their personal attitudes towards racial, ethnic, language, and cultural groups;
(2) Acquire knowledge about the histories and cultures of the diverse racial, ethnic, cultural, and language groups within the nation and within their schools;
(3) Become acquainted with the diverse perspectives that exist within different ethnic and cultural communities;
(4) Understand the ways in which institutionalised knowledge within schools, universities, and popular culture can perpetuate stereotypes about racial and ethnic groups; and
(5) Acquire the knowledge and skills needed to develop and implement an equity pedagogy (p. 197).

When educators ignore or reject different cultural expressions of development that are normal and adequate and on which school skills and knowledge can be built, conflicts can occur which may lead to student failure (Nieto and Bode 2012).

This study sought to measure the impact of a CTSG professional development experience that utilised African American history and culture to strengthen the cultural competency of 20 secondary Social Studies and English Language Arts educators. More specifically, the content of our PD experience centred on the long civil rights struggle (1896–1954) and allowed teachers to use dialogue, discussion, and reflection to grapple with themes that elucidate the story of the oppressed. Scholarship on African Americans' freedom struggle has expanded beyond post-*Brown* era examinations of civil rights activism and considers events from the first decades of the twentieth century and the interwar years, which make them an integral philosophical, ideological, and strategic component of teacher development and student success. In the following section, we detail the professional development experience studied.

Background

This PD experience had a combined focus on content, pedagogy and technology. Our interdisciplinary approach afforded participants the opportunity to engage African Americans' rich cultural history and work with subject matter and information technology experts to adapt and develop tools and other curricular materials that met their teaching needs. Participants read historical documents and literary selections, analysed primary sources, viewed films and artwork, and listened to music; they worked with GIS experts to create web-based maps for use in their classroom that incorporated the historical and literary content they engaged with throughout the programme; and central to this experience was access to African American museums. Participants spent 12 hours at three African American history museums collecting and collating spatial data into web-based mapping systems. Taken together, the researchers hypothesised that the PD course content and emphasis on digital humanities and technology adaptations via African American history museums would help participants acquire the knowledge and dynamics to become culturally competent teachers.

Integrating spatial thinking into the study of humanities with topics like civil rights and African American history and literature has come to be recognised as an increasingly important component of effective teaching. In 2006, for instance, the National Academy of Sciences endorsed the implementation of geographic information systems (GIS) at all levels of education. Indeed, this evolving emphasis on spatial thinking has the potential to change humanities teaching in important ways. GIS can profoundly impact students' learning and critical thinking skills and reading comprehension by blending new digital technologies and information literacy to create interactive, visual learning tools that explain things like social injustice in new and different ways. By exposing institute participants to advanced spatial thinking and GIS, this professional development experience fostered collaborative engagements with workshop leaders producing flexible curricular tools that effectively take advantage of digital innovations.

Before arriving at the workshop, participants were encouraged to review supplemental readings and other reference material as well as digital resources demonstrating ways to apply GIS strategies to the humanities. These pre-workshop readings provided a common subject matter background and a preliminary primer on the digital humanities so that the workshop could focus solely on deepening participants' knowledge base and information literacy rather than simply introducing unfamiliar concepts and/or themes.

The workshop started with a welcome reception and orientation. Participants received materials not previously available on the institute's website and other information about the campus and the surrounding community. This first gathering focused on detailing the program's core goals of engaging the humanities to create resources that improve classrooms' cultural and information literacies as well as creating and making widely available innovative online tools utilising information technologies like GIS. Core faculty exemplified topics such as the experiences of African Americans with the New Deal and how they can explain the changing role of the federal government in the nation's economy, and further illustrated how GIS can visually display the enduring political coalitions New Deal programmes helped to produce. This is but one example of how improved information literacy can impact students' critical thinking skills and reading comprehension.

Program days lasted from 9:00 am – 5:00 pm, including field trips to vital African American historical and literary sites in Chicago, Illinois, and Louisville, Kentucky. Throughout this intensive program, participants were given ample-unscheduled time to read and review materials, engage in discussions about program content with peers, and consider how to apply concepts and themes to their particular needs. Upon completion of the program, participants were encouraged to keep in contact with the workshop staff and each other to stay abreast of new research, curricular innovations, and digital resources utilising African American history and literature.

Method

Population and sample

The project invited secondary Social Studies and English Language Arts educators (grades 6–12) nationwide. A committee, comprised of the program co-directors and a local teacher, selected participants on the basis of a written application, which included a résumé of educational background, a three-page statement of purpose, and two letters of recommendation (ideally from a principal, department head, team leader, or a teaching colleague). Due to limited space, 20 participants were chosen. Of the 20 participants, 50% were male (n = 10) and 50% were female (n = 10). Fifty-five per cent (n = 11) of the participants self-identified as African American/Black and 45% (n = 9) as White. The majority (n = 14, 70%) taught Social Studies related courses. The average years of teaching experience stood at 10.

Instrumentation

The researchers utilised a modified Cultural Competence Self-Assessment for Teachers survey because it was developed to help school personnel reflect on their attitudes, beliefs, and practices as related to cultural competence. The instrument originated from the cultural competence continuum presented by Cross et al. (1989). Responses ranged from 1 to 5 ratings with a response of 1 = *rarely*, 2 = *seldom*, 3 = *sometimes*, 4 = *often*, and 5 = *usually*. The survey was slightly modified to reflect the researchers' interest in assessing culture, valuing diversity, and managing the dynamics of difference. Two questions from the categories 'adapts to diversity' and 'institutionalizes cultural knowledge' were removed. Using the Likert scale to respond that they *rarely, seldom, sometimes, often* or *usually* demonstrate a behaviour or perception, teachers could receive a score of 1–5 on each question for a total sum of 150 points. The lowest total of possible points a respondent could receive would be 25.

Data collection

Data collection consisted of data captured from an online survey and standardised, open-ended interview questions that documented teachers' perceptions of the cultural competence levels before and after a CTSG professional development experience. The survey was created using Qualtrics Survey Software and consisted of Lindsey et al.'s (2003) Cultural Competence Self-Assessment for Teachers. Surveys were administered on the second day and the 26th day of the institute, respectively. For the purpose of this study, participants' responses were added together to find a total level of cultural competence and to holistically describe where they may or may not reside on the continuum. The range of survey responses was also used to categorise the participants' self-reported perceptions from low level beliefs to advanced level beliefs along the cultural competence continuum.

Standardised, open-ended interviews were administered to participants at two points in the institute – Week 1 and Week 4. On their second day in the institute, participants individually responded to eleven interview questions that assessed participant knowledge and skills related to cultural competence. On the second to last day of the institute, participants individually responded to four questions that asked them to explain how this experience challenged their conceptions of diversity and teaching with difference in mind.

Data analysis

Survey data were exported into the Statistical Package for Social Sciences (SPSS) ® database for analysis. Cronbach alpha scores were calculated to examine the reliability of the survey instrument. An alpha score was calculated for each of the six survey subscales.

Descriptive statistics entailed mean comparisons, frequency distributions, and standard deviations for the survey subscales. In addition to comparing descriptive statistics, the use of one-way analysis of variance (ANOVA) and cross-tabulations was required in order to analyse the data collected. For the research question, the cultural competence levels of teachers, one total score was calculated for each respondent. This total score included the total sum of each Likert scale scores on questions 1–25. The total score was then divided into the six subscale categories and each respondent received a total rating for each subscale. The subscale values were then calculated to reflect the teachers' scores as either being low, transitioning, or high on the continuum of that subscale. If statistically significant mean differences were determined, further analyses were completed, and then post hoc.

Qualitative analysis generated a comprehensive listing of categories and themes. Using a rigorous process and multiple types of triangulation, important concepts were brought forward from the emic (insider/voices of participants) perspective. Qualitative data were then constantly compared to emerging categories, and those categories and hypotheses were refined and expanded or abandoned in light of new data (Strauss and Corbin 1998). We merged the results of the two data sets. This merging included directly comparing the separate results to facilitate relating the two data types during additional analysis. Finally, we interpreted the combined data to create a better understanding of whether or how a CTSG professional development experience centred on African American history and culture increases secondary educators' cultural competence (Creswell and Plano Clark 2011).

Results

The results presented in this section highlight a combination of quantitative and qualitative results. We delineated findings according to pre-experience cultural competence attitudes, knowledge, and skills and post-experience cultural competence attitudes, knowledge, and skills. For the sake of space, we chose to highlight the interview responses of four participants, Susan, Anna, Carrie, and Micah.

Cultural competency prior to the professional development experience

Attitudes towards culturally diverse populations

Pre-experience participants delineated the scope of diversity accentuating how each promoted respect for diversity in their practice. Listed below are selected definitions of diversity from participants:

Susan: Diversity is differences that include race, gender, sexuality, nationality, class status, etc. … When possible, I try to include the stories and experiences of those traditionally left out of the narrative. I also confront my students about misunderstandings (both theirs) and mine to show that everyone has misconceptions, which we need to address to be better.

Anna: Diversity – wild flowers, not garden flowers. This is an image taken from one of our school's foundresses. I think it is ultimately a matter of unique thoughts, experiences, and it includes biology (ethnicity, gender, gender identity, sexuality, personality) and nurture. I encourage diversity by fostering an environment of safety, growth, & reflection. I utilise the writings (sometimes art & film) of great thinkers.

Carrie: Diversity is multi-cultural, multi-religious, and multi-lingual. Empathy may be the most important aspect of how we teach what we teach. The way to challenge stereotypes is to teach in such a way that students see each other individually and not through a lens of preconceived notions.

Attitudes towards cultural competency

Participants utilised core phrases when asked to define cultural competency. Awareness stood out as a central component of cultural competency. Anna noted that:

> Being aware and active of one's own culture, the school culture, and the diverse (often-nuanced) cultures of our students to know how all cultures at school are affecting each other and to not make any generalizations that might negatively affect the teaching/learning experience.

For the most part, participants remarked that cultural competence is not simply an awareness of other cultures but an understanding of and sensitivity to them. Responses also indicated participants' understanding of cultural competency as comprising skills and knowledge. Expressive individualism was also a theme that emanated from interview responses. Participants were keen to the fact that cultural competency supported students' cultural expression through dress and hairstyles. Love was another important component of cultural competency for some participants. In short, participants not only understood cultural competency as awareness and knowledge of different cultures but also the skill and ability to act in some way. For example, Micah reflected:

> To me, cultural competency is the ability to see cultures, value them, and integrate them in the classroom. Culturally competent teachers know that their students all have unique experiences and voices and they honor them. Culturally competent teachers go out of their way to stay informed and spend time actively trying to understand and learn about new cultures in respectful ways.

Knowledge about interacting with culturally diverse populations

At the beginning of the professional development experience, results indicated that the majority of participants scored close to the cultural blindness stage of the continuum; in fact, the pre-Cultural Competence Self-Assessment for Teachers survey mean (M) was 105.6 with a standard deviation of 12.1. All participants described their experiences working with students from diverse cultural, linguistic, and economic backgrounds as demanding yet meaningful. Anna recognised that her biggest challenge was meeting the learning needs of non-black students in her classroom:

> My classes are 90% African American. We are certainly under-represented in so many ways. I think there is a challenge in serving and teaching them, but I think the bigger challenge is trying to serve and meet the needs of the other students in my classroom.

Carrie, too, noted the challenges encountered in working with diverse student populations:

> I find it very demanding to work in underrepresented communities yet extremely rewarding. The issues you face are quite overwhelming, but you have the opportunity to really make a difference in the lives of a few people.

Susan commented further, explaining the challenges of teaching diverse populations:

> Often schools and programs are underfunded; discipline and community involvement vary. Students often really depend on their teachers and school community. It has been an experience of learning and growth for me.

A few participants mentioned being open to students and communicating with them to gain students' trust and build a close relationship. Micah and Susan both noted that working with diverse or underrepresented communities offered relational win-wins for both teacher and students. Micah articulated that his students knew they could come to him and he would help with any situation, whether this situation was school, family, or community related. Susan too noted:

> The first step is always talking with the student and hearing firsthand what they are experiencing. I build a strong relationship with my students so they trust me enough to share their experiences and struggles with me.

The skillset to aptly interact with culturally diverse populations

Teaching experience, however, did not translate into possessing the skillset needed to work with diverse students. A one-way between-subjects ANOVA was conducted to compare the effect of teaching experience on cultural competency behaviours before and after a professional development experience centred on African American history and culture. Teaching experience categories included 0–5 years, 6–10 years, and 11 years or greater. Of the 20 participants, four self-identified as possessing 0–5 years teaching experience, seven self-identified as possessing 6–10 years teaching experience, and nine indicated having more than 11 years of teaching experience. On the pre-test, the main effect for teaching experience yielded an F ratio of $F(1,19) = 2.150$, $p > .05$, indicating that the effect for teaching experience was not significant. On the post-test, the main effect for teaching experience yielded an F ratio or $F(1,19) = .795$, $p > .05$. Data suggest that teaching experience had no significant effect on participants' cultural competency scores. Power analysis confirms the probability of detecting the impact of teaching experience, if in fact it exists, to be 0.27. Given such low power, it would be worthwhile to revisit this study with a sample size of 104 participants.

Several participants noted their lack of needed competencies to powerfully instruct students from diverse and/or underrepresented communities. Numerous educators mentioned their experiences of teaching students with Limited English Proficiency, including refugees and immigrants, but only a few of them spoke languages other than English. As such, one participant noted language barriers as a primary reason for his experiences having been lukewarm in teaching underrepresented communities. Given their self-identified limited abilities when addressing the learning needs of culturally and linguistically diverse students, most participants described seeking assistance from counsellors or social workers. Carrie noted, 'If the student seemed open,' Carrie noted and continued, 'I would speak with her and try to accommodate her learning needs … I often work with our wonderful student counsellor and support team.' Micah similarly indicated, 'Usually, I start with other teachers who know that student and then involve our counsellors and social workers to see if they have information to share.' It seemed obvious that participants had limited abilities to address cultural issues, though some of them do refer to practice in classrooms.

The power of the CTSG professional development experience

Rethinking diversity

The professional development experience also helped participants reflect on diversity and resulted in a pedagogical shift when thinking about teaching and learning as some participants stated. Participants claimed that they have gained more knowledge, new insights, and deeper understanding of diversity, and they began to reconsider their own biases. Two of them stated that this experience does reaffirm what they already believe in. Here are select descriptions of how this professional development experience helped:

Anna: People can explain things and students can respond with the right answers, but sexism and racism lie deeper than knowledge. Empowerment as well. This institute has shattered off more of the status quo by presenting tools to understand and the richness of images – (visual and narrative) – I hope to fill my teaching with images and tracks to walk when they explode.

Carrie: [I]t does make me glad that we're such a diverse group. I've learned lots of ways to think about history ... I've learned that it is possible to teach a segment of history through the experiences of one person and that is pretty awesome.

Micah: The conversations and discussions have been provocative ... I have a better/renewed belief in the value of multiple stories. I hope to challenge myself to open doors to more cultural perspectives in the discussions, materials, explanations I encourage students to engage in.

Susan: It has helped me reaffirm my belief that education should be accessible for all of our students. It has given me a wide array of content and cultural knowledge that has helped me understand the historical narrative of many of my students. It has also given me time to reflect on my own culture and privileges ... It has encouraged me to teach historical and present day issues of race, gender and identity in a way that creates empathy and understanding with my students.

As these quotes indicate, the CTSG experience provided ample room to grow professionally and personally as well as build community among dedicated teacher colleagues.

Development of cultural competency

We conducted a paired-samples t-test to compare the cultural competency behaviours before and after exposure to an intensive CTSG professional development experience. There was a significant difference in the scores post-professional development experience ($M = 111.90$, $SD = 8.49$) and pre-professional development experience ($M = 105.60$, $SD = 12.1$); $t(19) = 1.965$, $p = 0.064$. These results suggest that extensive CTSG professional development experiences that use African American history, culture, and literature positively impacted participants' level of cultural competency.

The interviews also suggested that this experience helped participants to develop and hone cultural competency and broadened their classroom practice through providing more resources, content knowledge, and pedagogical tools as well as invoking new perspectives. For example, one participant described how this experience has inspired him (or her) to reconsider US history:

> I have listened to individuals in this institute reflect [on] the daily double-consciousness of being African American. I feel that the readings, films, and field trips have inspired me to be a broader listener and developer of lessons. I feel like I've been 'punctured' out of a more academic progressivism and into a rich tapestry of history, filled with suffering, beauty, anger, hope – and things I don't know or understand ... I have more knowledge of the history and the sad transmutation of racism to expose my students to. I have excellent resources to combine personal stories with academic ideas.

Another participant, a white woman growing up in poverty and eager to serve the needs of students in underrepresented communities talked about how the stories she learned could empower herself and her students, most of whom are African Americans:

> I have loved this experience because it has given me numerous examples of Black excellence that I can share with my students to empower and uplift them. I also feel like I have gained deeper insight into historical antecedents so I can better appreciate the modern freedom struggle. When students ask me about what is going on in the world, I will feel more confident with my answers ... I also feel like this experience has validated my desire to use Black history to teach general concepts.

Her statement is powerful given that most white teachers in her school 'have a colourblind approach to diversity' and resist her drive to be culturally responsive. Nevertheless, after this experience, she felt more confident of her ideas. Some participants also described the skills they learn from this experience. One participant noted:

> I have had the opportunity to explore resources I had not, and people and achievements I had not ... New skills – GIS, backward design – will provide new tools upon which to explore questions of diversity.

Gender differences
A factorial analysis of variance tested the effects of gender on cultural competency behaviours. There was not a significant effect of gender on cultural competency behaviours post-CTSG experience at the $p < .05$ level for the condition ($F = 1.78$, $p = .198$). Taken together, these results suggest that gender played a limited to no role in determining changes in cultural competency behaviours after participants underwent the professional development experience.

Racial differences
A factorial analysis of variance tested the effects of race on cultural competency behaviours. Racial types included White, Black or African American, etc. Of the 20 participants, nine self-identified as White and eleven self-identified as Black or African American. On the pre-test, the main effect for self-identified race yielded an F ratio of $F(1,18) = .813$, $p > .05$, indicating that the effect for race was not significant. On the post-test, the main effect for self-identified race yielded an F ratio of $F(1,18) = 2.147$, $p > .05$. Data suggest that race slightly affected participants' cultural competency scores. Power analysis confirms the probability of detecting the impact of race, if in fact it exists, to be 0.39. Given such low power, it would be worthwhile to revisit this study with a sample size of 52 participants.

Discussion

To our knowledge, this is one of a few studies that investigated whether a CTSG professional development experience centred on African American history and culture positively impacted secondary educators' cultural competency levels. We tested one hypothesis: an ethnoculturally CTSG professional development would positively impact the cultural competency levels of secondary educators. Pre-experience, participants described the scope of diversity by emphasising how each promoted respect for diversity in their practice, and utilised core phrases to define cultural competency. Interview responses indicated recognition of cultural competency comprising both skills and knowledge. Post-experience, numerous participants moved from the cultural blindness stage to the cultural pre-competence stage (Cross 1988, Cross et al. 1989). Individuals attempted to engage in ongoing self-assessment regarding culture. Participants proactively sought knowledge and advice on meeting the needs of culturally diverse students during the professional development opportunity. Race, as a fixed category, slightly impacted participants' cultural competency scores. What is less clear is if gender or experience impacted cultural competence levels. To glean a clearer picture of the influence of gender, experience, and race on educators who participate in professional development experiences centred on African American history and culture, it would be worthwhile to revisit this study with a larger sample size. Given that few, if any, funded professional development experiences seek to use African American history to increase the cultural competency of educators, it may seem a daunting task for researchers to gather larger sample sizes than produced by this study.

Secondly, our findings brought into relief the power and purpose of this CTSG professional development experience in how participants conceived of and articulated their cultural competency. Pre-experience, participants exhibited good intentions towards attitudes, knowledge, and possessing the capabilities for aptly interacting with culturally diverse populations. None of the participants described cultural differences as problematic (Cultural Destructiveness). Several noted their lack of knowledge and skillset to deal with cultural differences aptly. Interestingly, participants failed to define themselves as culturally responsive given the documented interchangeability of the terms cultural competence and culturally responsive teaching (Gay 2010). Many described themselves as ineffective at teaching students from diverse backgrounds or using culturally relevant teaching methods.

Post-experience, interviews suggested that this PD experience helped participants developed cultural competency and broadened their practice through providing more resources, content knowledge, and pedagogical tools as well as invoking new perspectives. Moreover, this experience utilised core structural features of effectual professional development such as content focus, duration, active learning, participation, and coherence. It utilised workshops and social media to facilitate dialogue on contentious issues around race, oppression, and privilege (Garet *et al.* 2001). Educators were able to identify their attitudes of diversity and acquire knowledge about African American history and culture as a means for increasing their cultural competence levels (Banks *et al.* 2001).

We recognise that this CTSG professional development experience wanted to first improve teacher knowledge and classroom instruction. The CTSG format was beneficial for our institute as it enabled educators to:

(1) Share their practical knowledge and experiences garnered in their respective teaching careers (and beyond)
(2) Co-design lesson plans, teaching activities, and sectional curricula (unit for some weeks) based on content knowledge shared during the PD experience, and
(3) Gain and/or hone cultural competence through intensive daily interaction and engagements with fellow educators.

Thus, our ethnoculturally CTSG professional development was effective in engaging educators in learning and self-reflection processes, and positively impacted their classroom practices and personal beliefs. Our findings indicated slight movement from the colourblind to the cultural pre-competence level for most of the participants' cultural competence levels. Selected interview responses corroborated the power and purpose of this professional development experience in how participants conceived of and articulated their cultural competency. Our findings support DeJaeghere and Zhang (2008) that participation in meaningful, ongoing professional development improves a teacher's confidence about his or her cultural competence.

Talking about sensitive and difficult topics in teacher study groups can alleviate some of the teachers' concerns and reservations. Learning with and from colleagues might be more effective in self-reflecting about personal beliefs and perceptions. Learning together enables the sharing of experiences and insights, and results in the creation of a shared knowledge base and fosters trust building. Our ethnoculturally CTSG professional development experience enabled participants to learn about cultural groups, including their own, within the broader context of sociocultural history and contemporary society. Such professional experiences allow participants to investigate broader societal structures and reinterpret master narratives of American and global history. Most importantly, these experiences empower educators in the process, eager to break societal chains, and enthusiastic about inculcating to their students a more meaningful way to challenge the status quo.

Recommendations for future research

One of the greatest challenges faced by education today is how to equitably serve all members of our pluralistic society. To provide just education, education scholars argue that all educators should possess cultural competence. Culturally relevant professional development experiences offer a means for increasing the cultural competence level of teachers. This study only begins to reveal the professional development potential – and pitfalls – when using African American history and culture to increase the cultural competency of educators. We recommend, however, that researchers continue to track the value of using African American history and culture as a means for increasing the cultural competency of educators. We further recommend investigations that follow participants into their classrooms once the professional development experience has concluded. Several unanswered questions have been exposed in this endeavour; for example, is there such a thing as a 'too long' professional development experience and whether such professional development fatigue influenced participants' post-test assessments? It is reasonable to infer that all educators desire effectual professional development; however, at what point does being away from family, friends, and communities limit what participants are able to glean from professional development?

Disclosure statement

No potential conflict of interest was reported by the authors.

ORCID

Nicole Kong http://orcid.org/0000-0001-9926-6543

References

Abrams, L.S. and Moio, J.A., 2009. Critical race theory and the cultural competence dilemma in social work education. *Journal of social work education*, 45 (2), 245–261. doi:10.5175/JSWE.2009.200700109

Ball, D.L. and Cohen, D.K., 1999. Developing practice, developing practitioners: toward a practice-based theory of professional education. *In*: L. Darling-Hammond and G. Sykes, eds. *Teaching as the learning profession*. San Francisco, CA: Jossey-Bass, 3–32.

Banks, J., 2009. *The routledge international companion to multicultural education*. New York, N.Y.: Routledge. doi:10.4324/9780203881514

Banks, J.A., et al., 2001. Diversity within unity: essential principles for teaching and learning in a multicultural society. *Phi Delta Kappan*, 83 (3), 196–203. doi:10.1177/003172170108300309

Bustamante, R.M., et al., 2016. Evaluation of a cultural competence assessment for preservice teachers. *The Teacher Educator*, 51 (4), 297–313. doi:10.1080/08878730.2016.1186767

Cochran-Smith, M. and Lytle, S., 1999. Relationships of knowledge and practice: teacher learning in communities. *Review of research in education*, 24, 249–305.

Creswell, J.W. and Plano Clark, V.L., 2011. *Designing and conducting mixed methods research*. Thousand Oaks, CA: SAGE Publications, Inc.

Cross, T., 1988. Services to minority populations: cultural competence continuum. *Focal Points*, 3, 1–9.

Cross, T., et al., 1989. *Towards a culturally competent system of care: A monograph on effective services for minority children who are severely emotionally disturbed*. Washington, D.C.: CASSP Technical Assistance Center, Georgetown University Child Development Center.

Darling-Hammond, L. and McLaughlin, M.W., 1995. Policies that support professional development in an era of reform. *Phi Delta Kappan*, 76 (8), 597.

DeJaeghere, J.G. and Zhang, Y., 2008. Development of intercultural competence among US American teachers: professional development factors that enhance competence. *Intercultural education*, 19 (3), 255–268. doi:10.1080/14675980802078624

Denboba, D., 2005. Cultural competence–what it is, what it's not. *The Alabama Nurse*, 32 (4), 11–12.

Diller, J.V. and Moule, J., 2005. *Cultural competence: A primer for educators*. 1st. Belmont, CA: Thomson Wadsworth.

DuFour, R., 2004. What is a "professional learning community"? *Educational Leadership*, 61 (8), 6–11.

Ford, D.Y., 2013. *Recruiting and retaining culturally different students in gifted education*. Waco, TX: Prufrock Press.

Garet, M.S., et al., 2001. What makes professional development effective? Results from a national sample of teachers. *American educational research journal*, 38 (4), 915–945. doi:10.3102/00028312038004915

Gay, G., 2000. *Culturally responsive teaching: theory, research, and practice*. New York, NY: Teachers College Press.

Gay, G., 2010. *Culturally responsive teaching: theory, research, and practice*. 2nd. New York, NY: Teachers College Press.
Guskey, T.R., 2003. What makes professional development effective? *Phi Delta Kappan*, 84 (10), 748–750. doi:10.1177/003172170308401007
Guskey, T.R. and Sparks, D., 1996. Exploring the relationship between staff development and improvements in student learning. *Journal of staff development*, 17 (4), 34–38.
Hammer, M., Bennett, M.J., and Wiseman, R., 2003. Measuring intercultural sensitivity: the intercultural development inventory. *International journal of intercultural relations*, 27, 421–443. doi:10.1016/S0147-1767(03)00032-4
Hammerness, K., et al., 2005. How teachers learn and develop. *In*: L. Darling-Hammond and J. Bransford, eds.. *Preparing teachers for a changing world*. Washington, DC: The National Academy of Education.
Hung, H.T. and Yeh, H.C., 2013. Forming a change environment to encourage professional development through a teacher study group. *Teaching and teacher education*, 36, 153–165. doi:10.1016/j.tate.2013.07.009
Jett, C.C., McNeal Curry, K., and Vernon-Jackson, S., 2016. Let our students be our guides: mcNair Scholars "guide" three urban teacher educators on meeting the needs of culturally diverse learners. *Urban education*, 51 (5), 514–534. doi:10.1177/0042085914549262
Ladson-Billings, G., 1994. *The dreamkeepers: successful teaching for African American students*. San Francisco, CA: Jossey-Bass.
Ladson-Billings, G., 2014. Culturally relevant pedagogy 2.0: a.k.a the remix. *Harvard educational review*, 84 (1), 74–84. doi:10.17763/haer.84.1.p2rj131485484751
Lawrence, S.M. and Tatum, B.D., 1997. Teachers in transition: the impact of antiracist professional development on classroom practice. *Teachers college record*, 99 (1), 162–178.
Lindsey, R.B., Robins, K.N., and Terrell, R.D., 2003. *Cultural proficiency: A manual for school leaders*. 2nd. Thousand Oaks, CA: Corwin Press.
Little, J.W., 1990. The persistence of privacy: autonomy and initiative in teachers' professional relations. *Teachers college record*, 91 (4), 509–536.
May, S., and Sleeter, C.E., 2010. Introduction. critical multiculturalism: Theory and praxis. In S. May and C. E. Sleeter, eds., Critical multiculturalism: Theory and praxis (1-16). Retrieved from https://ebookcentral.proquest.com
McLaughlin, M.W. and Talbert, J.E., 2006. *Building school-based teacher learning communities: professional strategies to improve student achievement*. New York: Teacher College Press.
Nieto, S. and Bode, P., 2012. *Affirming diversity: the sociopolitical context of multicultural education*. Boston, MA: Pearson Education.
Robinson, R. and Carrington, S., 2002. Professional development for inclusive schooling. *International journal of educational management*, 16 (5), 239–247.
Stanley, A., 2012. The experiences of elementary music teachers in a collaborative teacher study group. *Bulletin of the council for research in music education*, 192, 53–74. doi:10.5406/bulcouresmusedu.192.0053
Strauss, A. and Corbin, J., 1998. *Basics of qualitative research: techniques and procedures for developing grounded theory*. Thousand Oaks, CA: Sage Publications, Inc.
Sue, D.W. and Sue, D., 2007. *Counseling the culturally diverse: theory and practice*. 5th. New York, NY: Wiley.
Wenger, E., 1998. *Communities of practice: learning, meaning, and identity*. Cambridge, UK: Cambridge University Press.

The professional development needs of primary teachers in special classes for children with autism in the Republic of Ireland

Caitríona Finlay, William Kinsella and Paula Prendeville

ABSTRACT
In Irish classrooms, one option for educating children with Autism Spectrum Disorder (ASD) involves placement in a special class co-located in a mainstream primary school. This study surveyed 125 primary school teachers who taught in these classes. An evaluative framework of teachers' professional developmentwas used to analyse primary teachers' perceptions of the specialclass model of provision and the teaching practices that they used. While teachers experienced challenges in these settings that included managing challenging behaviour, perceptions of the special class model were positive. Inclusion of students from special classes to classes in the mainstream context was limited for pupils with greater needs. A wide disparity in the delivery of the curriculum taught in these settings was also identified. Results revealed the need for professional development programmes for teachers to alleviate their experiences of stress and isolation and to improve the outcome of children with ASD.

Introduction

Autism Spectrum Disorder (ASD) is characterised by a range of impairments in social interaction, social communication and language development, combined with restricted, repetitive patterns of activities and interests (American Psychological Association 2013). This condition has lifetime consequences for an individual's learning and independence into adulthood, with up to 60% of individuals unable to live independently (Howlin et al. 2004). The unique characteristics and needs of individuals with ASD pose challenges for teachers in schools (Syriopoulou-Delli and Cassimos 2012). The Department of Education and Skills (DES) in Ireland has developed a special class provision satellite model, co-located in mainstream primary schools specifically for pupils with ASD. These classes have a pupil–teacher ratio of 6:1 and the support of two Special Needs Assistants (SNAs) per class (DES, 2005, Irish National Teachers Organisation 2014). The criteria for establishing a new special class depends on the number of children with ASD seeking a placement, and the level of current provision in the school locality. In 2016, there were 378 special classes for children with ASD in mainstream primary schools in Ireland (Daly et al. 2016). The benefits of special class provision, as outlined in a national survey of schools, included the facilitation of inclusion in a mainstream class for children with ASD, the provision of a 'safe haven' for some learners, a favourable pupil–teacher ratio, accessing an education near their home, and flexibility in the organisation of teaching and curriculum provision (Ware et al. 2009).

While the DES recommends that inclusion of students with ASD in mainstream classes should be the goal of every special class, the findings from a national study of special ASD classes in general indicate that almost half of students remained in their respective special classes for the entire school day (Ware et al. 2009). According to McCoy et al. (2014), the access that children with ASD had to mainstream classes was heavily influenced by informal teacher assessments rather than formal assessments, in conjunction with the advice sought from Special Education Needs Organisers (SENOs) or the National Educational Psychological Services (NEPS). The DES Inspectorate and the National Council for Special Education (NCSE) highlighted a dearth of research exploring the effectiveness of special classes in terms of practices regarding inclusion and the curriculum available to children with ASD (DES, 2006, Parsons et al. 2009). A more recent review of the provision of education for children with ASD in Ireland was commissioned by the NCSE (Daly et al. 2016). In this study, the analysis of primary provision for learners with ASD was gathered from five primary schools nationwide where just two sites analysed had a special class for learners with ASD attached to a mainstream primary school, limiting the generalisation of findings reported. Teachers and principals highlighted the challenges of meeting the needs of these learners that included identifying assessment measures and the difficulties that learners, and those with more complex needs, experienced in accessing the school curriculum. In primary schools with ASD-specific provision, excellent inclusive practices based on curricular activities were recorded (Daly et al. 2016). To address the gaps in the professional needs of these teachers, a more in-depth analysis is required. This paper seeks to address this gap by identifying the professional development (PD) needs of teachers who have taught in special class settings for children with ASD.

Teaching children with autism spectrum disorder

Teaching pupils with ASD presents significant instructional challenges for teachers, as it may lower a teacher's sense of efficacy for working effectively with such students in irish and in international contexts (Klassen et al. 2011, Ruble et al. 2013, Anglim et al. 2018, Rodden et al. 2018). Research also suggests that teaching students with ASD may impose greater stress on teachers than their experiences of teaching other students with SEN (Jennett et al. 2003, Kokkinos and Davazoglou 2009). Ruble et al. (2011) identified significant associations between physiological/affective states and self-efficacy among a group of thirty-five teachers of pupils with ASD. Furthermore, teachers' vulnerability to stress and burnout were also factors associated with attrition amongst special education teachers (Billingsley 2004). A qualitative study completed with irish teachers identified that two-thirds of teachers lacked confidence and were apprehensive about their initial prospect of teaching a child with ASD in their classrooms (Anglim et al. 2018). A review of stakeholders' perspectives of the inclusion of students with ASD revealed that professional learning was required to increase the knowledge and understanding of school staff (Roberts and Simpson 2016).

Research revealed that teachers benefit from induction programmes that allow for supports including liaising with other special education teachers (Kilgore et al. 2003, Gehrke and McCoy 2007). Results from both studies here indicated that having a strong network of support, and a variety of resources, reduced isolation and positively influenced teachers' ability to focus on students' learning and on their intent to remain in their teaching positions. In research exploring the induction needs of special educators, due to concerns regarding teacher attrition rates in the USA (Thornton et al. 2007), responses from 1,153 special education teachers identified that induction programmes should be flexible to consider the context in which teachers worked. Meaningful induction experiences were believed to have lasting effects on teacher quality and retention (Billingsley et al. 2004, as cited in Thornton et al. 2007). Mentoring is also understood to reduce the initial isolation for a beginning special education teacher. It also increases teacher retention and satisfaction levels, as well as strengthening overall school performance (Griffin et al. 2003). While mentoring has been traditionally viewed as a means of supporting beginning teachers, recent research has highlighted its potential benefits when tailored mentoring programmes meet the unique professional needs of experienced teachers (Bressman et al. 2018). Langdon et al. (2014) identified significant gaps in our understanding of induction and mentoring in teaching following a literature review. Additionally, they reported that there were no studies that explored contextual factors of school and the perceptions of induction and mentoring in teaching communities of practice.

Initial teacher education and autism spectrum disorder

On an international scale, it is acknowledged that Initial Teacher Education (ITE) is limited and insufficient in preparing teachers to teach individuals with ASD (McConkey and Bhlirgri 2003, Syriopoulou-Delli and Cassimos 2012, Ravet 2018). Teachers emerging from ITE in Ireland have a range of different experiences and competencies in terms of teaching pupils with SEN (Sugrue 2002, 2011). This has major implications for inclusive practices (Rose et al. 2010). Preliminary findings of a longitudinal study on the components of inclusive education in ITE in Ireland revealed that programmes have not yet developed a 'wholly consistent and coherent approach to inclusive teaching for all learners' (Hick et al. 2018, p. 4). This suggests beginning teachers would struggle to support learners with ASD in their classes. Teacher educators identified that they require further PD to support teachers in ITE to develop teaching competences to meet the needs of learners in inclusive settings. Stoiber et al. (1998) found that more experienced and highly qualified teachers were better equipped, both personally and professionally, to cater for the educational needs of children with ASD. In a UK setting, Ravet (2018) explored teachers' experiences of ITE in addressing the needs of learners with ASD in their classrooms. Participants revealed that there were insufficient inputs on ASD during ITE due to a lack of tutor expertise, concerns regarding medical labelling of children's needs and an overloaded ITE curriculum. There was universal agreement among teachers that in order to make sense of learners' behaviours and needs, a knowledge and understanding of ASD was required.

The education of pupils with ASD typically focuses on addressing the social, developmental, and communicative and life skills of learners, which generally form a more discrete part of the responsibilities of mainstream teachers (DES, 2001). Researchers argue that special education teachers face different obstacles in schools than their mainstream counterparts and, therefore, require support and induction specifically related to teaching children with ASD (Thornton et al. 2007). Access to a formalised induction programme for ASD teaching is not currently available in Ireland (Santoli and Vitulli 2014) and teachers only access additional professional learning once they are in situ in a class for children with ASD (INTO, 2014). However, since 2012, it has been a requirement of all ITE accredited institutions in Ireland to undergo a re-accreditation process that includes mandatory content on inclusive education (Hick et al. 2018). The Task Force on Autism (Department of Education and Science 2001) identified that teachers with only minimal knowledge of, and preparation for, teaching children with ASD, had been faced with setting up new special classes. In 2001, a study exploring the induction needs of teachers of children with ASD in Ireland found that nearly 69% of teachers had little or no knowledge of ASD on appointment to the role (Balfe 2001). Of note is that this research was completed prior to the establishment of the Special Education Support Service (SESS), therefore it is possible that this knowledge gap has reduced in more recent times. The NCSE found that a quarter of a sample of teachers in special classes had 'restricted' recognition and 5% had 'provisional' recognition with the Teaching Council of Ireland (TCI) 2016 (Ware et al. 2009)[1]. Furthermore, Ruble et al. (2011) found no correlation between years of teaching experience and self-efficacy for teaching children with ASD. Teachers in Ireland can work in a special class with their basic teacher qualification only (Clarke and Killeavy 2012). Of concern is that special education teachers perceived themselves as segregated and isolated from the mainstream teaching community (Kilgore et al. 2003). The supportive role of the principal in this regard was specifically mentioned (Thornton et al. 2007). It is acknowledged in the literature that teachers require a wide range of knowledge and skills to teach children with ASD. Recent research in Ireland highlighted that many schools sampled in an evaluation of education provision expressed the need for specific targeted PD to meet the needs of learners with ASD (Daly et al. 2016).

Theoretical framework

Identifying the PD needs of teachers is a challenging endeavour in teacher professionalisation (Merchie et al. 2018) and perhaps more so in the area of special education in Ireland and elsewhere where there are increasing demands placed on teachers (O'Gorman and Drudy 2011). While research has identified that teachers in Ireland engage in PD, they continue to report on their unmet professional needs (McElearney et al. 2019). The school context, and the wider economic, political and educational reforms in Ireland have shaped teachers' professional practice. Furthermore, more recent contextual demands have increased the complexities of teaching and learning that now require teachers to participate in professional learning within a collegial learning space (Conway et al. 2009). Children with ASD have a right to access an inclusive education (United Nations 2006) which may be challenging for children with the greatest need (Roberts and Simpson 2016, Ravet 2018). Inclusion of some children with ASD in Irish primary classrooms remains a challenge for teachers (Anglim et al. 2018). Additionally, with an increase in calls for accountability in education, King (2014) highlighted the need to evaluate the impact of teacher PD on students' outcomes. King (2014) acknowledged a lack of clarity in evaluating PD initiatives. This will become even more pertinent with the proposed implementation of the *Cosán* framework which may seek teachers to engage in professional learning (Broderick 2019) to maintain their Teaching Council membership status. King (2016) proposes that incorporating systemic factors into a PD framework would support teachers' PD planning. Researchers in an Irish context have also called for a systemic approach to include learners with SEN in schools (Kinsella and Senior 2008, Kinsella 2018). However, of concern is that only a slight majority of school principles believed that they had the knowledge and skill to support the inclusion of learners in their schools (Roberts and Simpson 2016), where principals have a central role in managing school systems. Additionally, professional learning and education on ASD and inclusion was prioritised as a need by school staff and should be considered mandatory, or at least a high learning priority, in school systems (Roberts and Simpson 2016).

To identify the PD needs of primary teachers who teach in special class settings for children with ASD, the Teachers' PD framework was adopted (Merchie et al. 2018) for this research. This model was devised based on a synthesis of two prior PD models (as cited in Merchie et al. 2018), outlined below in Figure 1.

Merchie et al. (2018) propose that three complex interactions unfold when identifying student outcomes following PD: Firstly, they propose that it is necessary to review the interconnection between PD and the change in teachers' knowledge, skills and attitude; Secondly, the interplay between the features of PD programmes results in changes in teachers' practice to bring about an improvement in student outcomes; Finally, contextual factors are acknowledged as playing a role where teachers' personal characteristics can impact on student outcomes when implementing and sustaining PD programmes. This model informed an analysis of the survey that was completed to

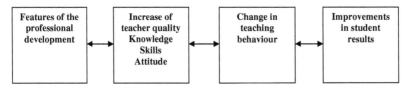

Figure 1. *Teachers' professional development framework* (based on Desmione 2009; Van Veen et al. 2012 as cited in Merchie et al. 2018)

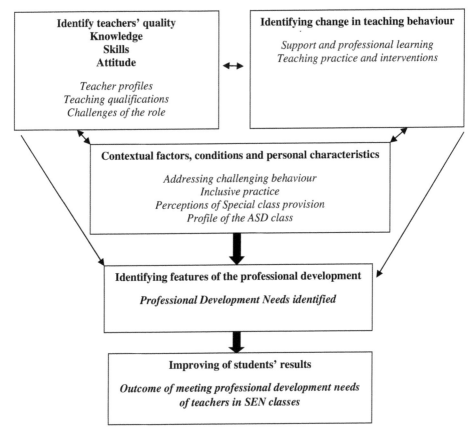

Figure 2. Adopting the *Teachers' professional development framework* (Merchie et al. 2018) to identify the professional needs of teachers who teach in special classes for children with ASD.

identify PD needs of teachers who taught in specialist classes for children with ASD. In Figure 2, three key aspects of this model were explored: Specifically, identifying teachers' quality regarding their knowledge, skills and attitude identifying teachers' changes in teaching behaviour; and the contextual factors, conditions and personal characteristics which inform and impact on teachers who engage with children who have ASD in special class settings. The aim of this research is to explore these areas and to identify the PD needs of teachers who teach children with ASD in specialist class settings to improve the outcomes for autistic children. Research has highlighted that little is known about the outcomes of students with ASD to date in educational systems and they are not doing as well as expected compared to their neurotypical peers (Roberts and Simpson 2016). Additionally, research has identified the poorer lifespan of individuals with ASD that impact on their quality of life (Howlin et al. 2004). This highlights the importance of exploring the PD needs of teachers who teach these children to ensure more positive long-term outcomes for individuals with ASD.

Methodology

The aims of the study were to identify the main challenges Irish teachers experience when teaching in an ASD-specific special class, and to explore teachers' views on what professional learning they perceive as being most beneficial to inform their PD needs. A quantitative design, using a survey method, was employed in this study. Numerical data and participants' comments were collected via an anonymous online survey. The participants in this study were all teachers, who were not deemed a vulnerable group for ethical purposes. Accordingly, an ethical approval was granted by the

Research Ethics Committee of the university to which the researchers are attached. All the researchers had specific experience of working with individuals with ASD and two had previous experience of establishing and teaching in ASD-specific classrooms attached to mainstream primary schools. The researchers initially used a focus group of teachers who taught in these classes for the purpose of exploring context-specific issues which were not specifically identified in the literature review. This was completed to assist in the generation of survey items (Nassar-McMillan and Borders 2002). For the focus group, purposive and convenience sampling was used by selecting four primary teachers known to the researchers. All focus group participants were in their first years of teaching in ASD-specific special classes. All participants completed a process of informed consent granting their permission to use their data for research purposes.

A survey was disseminated to all primary schools in Ireland with ASD-specific special classes, identified from an official list of special classes (NCSE, 2015). This method was to capture as wide a pool as possible to allow for generalisation of results from a large Irish sample. Schools were emailed the link to Qualtrics Survey software and a participant information sheet was also attached. A follow-up phone call was made to each school to ensure the email was received and forwarded to all relevant teachers. In addition, the researchers posted an invitation to partake in the survey on Irish teachers' social media websites, whereby snowballing occurred (Morling 2012). Due to the method of circulation and the anonymity of the survey, the number of teachers who actually received the request to participate is unknown. The total number of teachers in ASD-specific classes was 564 (National Council for Special Education [NCSE] 2015). Former teachers of special classes were also invited to complete the survey, increasing the potential sample. These teachers were also invited as previous research demonstrated that attrition rates were high among teachers with SEN and their experiences (Billingsley 2004, Thornton et al. 2007) could inform the findings particularly to explore what supports teachers need to remain teaching in these classes. One hundred and thirty five responses were received, representing an estimated 24% response rate. Of these responses, ten were considered unusable (final N = 125) as these respondents completed under 33% of the main survey. The survey contained 30 main questions, with seven follow up questions querying specific responses. Participants had the opportunity to provide qualitative comments to open ended question. The questions were generated based on the primary researcher's experiences of working in a special class, together with information gleaned from the literature review and from the focus group. The questionnaire was piloted with a teacher who holds a Master's qualification in ASD Education from an Irish accredited course. The survey data was analysed using the Statistical Package for the Social Sciences (SPSS) Version 20.0.

Results

The PD framework (Merchie et al. 2018) was adopted to analyse the results under three headings. Identifying teachers' quality – knowledge, skills and attitude, Identifying the change in teaching behaviour and the contextual factors, conditions and personal characteristics that impact on those who teach in specialist classes for children with ASD. These items were generated following a comprehensive literature review, consultation with a focus group and the researchers own experiences.

Identifying teachers' quality – knowledge, skills and attitude

Teacher demographics

Seventy participants (56%) reported having three years or less mainstream teaching experience, with one year or less most commonly reported (n = 47; 38%). Seventy-five per cent (n = 94) reported previous teaching experience under the 'other' heading, including the following: special classes for intellectual disabilities, special school teaching, reading school for dyslexia, Montessori classroom, or employment as an SNA. Sixty-five per cent of respondents reported previous teaching experience with a student with ASD, either within mainstream or in specialist settings. Fourteen

Table 1. Demographics of participants (N = 125).

Demographic Characteristic	Category	%	n
Previous experience	Mainstream class	82	103
	SEN	78	98
	Other*	75	94
	Newly Qualified Teacher	<1	1
Previous ASD teaching experience	Yes	65	80
	No	35	44
Length of time teaching in special class	In first year	30	37
	In second year	19	24
	In third year	13	16
	More than three years	28	35
	Not currently in the special class	10	13
Postgraduate qualifications	SEN postgraduate qualification	18	23
	Postgraduate qualification in ASD	14	17
Teaching Council recognition	Full recognition	72	90
	Provisional recognition	4	5
	Restricted recognition	24	30
	Unqualified	0	0
Total			125

*other included the following: special class for intellectual disabilities, special school teaching, reading school for dyslexia, Montessori classroom, SNA.

per cent of participants (n = 17) had an ASD-specific postgraduate qualification. Twenty-eight per cent of participants did not have full teaching recognition with the TCI. See Table 1 for more information.

Challenges of teaching role

Respondents rated 17 aspects of the special class in terms of the level of challenge it presented, with ratings of 0 labelled *'not a challenge'*, 1 labelled *'slightly challenging'*, 2 labelled *'moderately challenging'* and 3 labelled *'extremely challenging'*. The items were totalled to generate a composite score for 'Total Challenge'. Possible scores ranged from 0 to 51. Higher scores denote higher levels of challenge experienced.

Considering the range of scales, the mean score of the participants (M = 26.82, on a scale of 0–51) indicates that they were experiencing the setting as *'challenging'* overall. The alpha level of .84 suggests a good level of internal consistency for the scale (DeVellis 2003), please review Table 2 below for more details. The mean-ratings for various aspects of special class teaching were ranked in order, from most challenging to least challenging. Participants found the *'management of challenging behaviour'* and the *'implementation of an appropriate curriculum'* most challenging and *'interacting with parents'* as being the least challenging aspect of the role, detailed further in Table 3.

A Pearson chi-square (x^2) test for the association found that a weak positive significant relationship existed between how prepared teachers believed they were for the role and whether they had previous ASD teaching experience: x^2 (1) = 7.54, p = .006. Those with previous experience reported being more prepared to teach children with ASD in a special class. Having previous mainstream teaching experience ($x^2(1)$ = 3.455, p = .063), or SEN teaching experience was not significantly associated with how prepared teachers felt for the special class role.

Sixty-two per cent (n = 77) of respondents reported on their experiences of isolation as teachers in the special class. A teacher shared her experiences by utilising the option of expanding on her response in the questionnaire

Table 2. Total challenge scale.

Scale	Variance	Range	M	SD	α	Test of Normality Shapiro-Wilk
Total Challenge Scale	67.846	44	26.82	8.24	.84	.986 (95) p = .397

Table 3. Challenges of special class.

Rating	Aspect of special class teaching	M
1.	Managing challenging behaviour	2.22
2.	Implementing an appropriate curriculum	2.11
3.	Planning	2.11
4.	Assessing the needs of children	2.09
5.	Management of time and organisational issues	1.87
6.	Teaching social skills	1.66
7.	Suitably motivating pupils	1.62
8.	Development and implementation of IEPs	1.55
9.	Differentiation of lessons and activities	1.50
10.	Managing and promoting inclusion	1.48
11.	Implementing specific interventions and teaching methodologies for ASD	1.47
12.	Developing independence and Daily Living Skills	1.47
13.	Obtaining suitable resources	1.45
14.	Collaboration with other teachers and school staff	1.26
15.	Working with SNAs	1.16
16.	Understanding the role of the special class teacher	0.93
17.	Interacting with parents	0.88

As a teacher in my second year within ASD class, it can feel very isolated at times. Every day presents with new challenges and it can feel like you're drowning at times. … To summarise, the pressure and strain an ASD Special Class Teacher can feel is immense and a lot more support needs to happen (Teacher 46).

An independent sample *t*-test identified a statistically significant difference between the level of challenge experienced by teacher and the isolation they reported: $t(105) = 4.508$, $p < .001$ with respondents who reported isolation (M = 29.42, SD = 7.63) reporting higher levels of challenge than those who did not report isolation (M = 22.63, SD = 7.49).

A one-way ANOVA revealed that the level of challenge reported by participants differed significantly between the groups based on their reports of how prepared they perceived they were for special class teaching: $F(2,104) = 12.13$, $p < .001$. As expected, the 'totally unprepared' group (M = 31.26, SD = 7.421) reported a higher level of challenge than the 'well-prepared' group (M = 21.41, SD = 8.441, p = <.001) or the '*somewhat-prepared*' group (M = 25.35, SD = 7.214, p = .001).

Correlations
A number of bivariate correlations were conducted to examine the association between the level of challenge experienced and the profile of students in special classes. See Table 4 for more details.

Qualifications
Figure 3 outlines the satisfaction ratings by respondents regarding the quality of SEN professional learning received as part of ITE and the quality of PD currently available to them.

Eighty-two per cent (n = 102) of respondents were dissatisfied with the preparation level for ASD teaching provided in ITE, as one teacher reported:

> I started teaching in a Junior ASD Class just after I graduated from college. During my three years of training, I received ONE lecture (45mins) on ASD. I hadn't a clue what I was doing when I started teaching (Teacher 123).

Sixty-four per cent (n = 80) agreed that a specialist qualification in ASD should be compulsory for teachers opting to teach in special classes for children with ASD, 19% were unsure of this and 16% of teachers disagreed. The availability of supports were rated by respondents from never (0), sometimes (1) to often (2), and are reported in Table 6. SNAs were the most commonly reported support available to teachers in the ASD special class setting, with systemic supports from the Department of Education and Skills (DES) Inspectorate, Boards of Management and the NCSE reported least frequently.

Table 4. Demographics of special classes.

Number of pupils in each class (n)											
Demographic		0	1	2	3	4	5	6	N	Median	Mean	SD
Number of special classes in the school	0	30	49	25	6	7	7	124	2	2.45	1.364
Number of children in the special class	0	1	1	5	12	44	60	123	5	5.25	.946
Number of non-verbal pupils	38	28	27	13	12	3	1	122	1	1.56	1.466
Number of pupils who exhibit challenging behaviour	10	22	31	24	17	11	8	123	2	2.66	1.633
Number of pupils with comorbid disability	15	19	28	20	18	18	4	122	2	2.63	1.697
Number of pupils full-time in special class	23	15	22	15	21	16	11	123	3	2.72	1.948

Table 5. Pearson product-moment correlations between variables.

Scale	Challenge	Nonverbal	Challenging beh.	Co-morbid disability
1. Challenge	1			
2. Number of non-verbal pupils	.181	1		
3. Number with challenging behaviour	.287**	.214*	1	
4. Number with co-morbid disability	.076	.141	.369**	1
5. Number full time in special class	.194*	.575**	.419**	.214*

*$p < .05$. (2-tailed) ** $p < .01$.

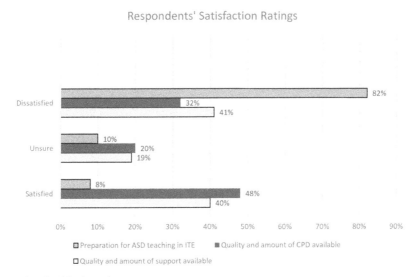

Figure 3. Respondents' satisfaction ratings.

There was a small positive significant relationship between the perceived level of challenge and the number of pupils with challenging behaviour, and also the number of pupils who remain full time in the special class. There was a similar relationship between the number of pupils with challenging behaviour and the number of pupils who were non-verbal. A large positive relationship was found between the number of pupils who did not integrate into mainstream classroom settings and the number of pupils who were non-verbal. The existence of a co-morbid disability was also correlated with challenging behaviour and there was a further correlation between challenging behaviour and pupils remaining full time in the special class. Co-morbidity was also correlated with children who remained full time in the special class (please review Table 5 for pupil demographics). The learners who presented the greatest challenges to teachers were likely to be non-verbal, have co-morbid disabilities, exhibit challenging behaviours in the school setting and were usually located in the special class on a full-time basis.

Table 6. Supports available to respondents.

Rating	Support	M	SD
1.	SNAs	1.74	.501
2.	SESS	1.39	.643
3.	Principal involvement	1.26	.694
4.	Link with other special class teachers	1.17	.657
5.	Colleagues/whole staff	1.16	.652
6.	HSE practitioners- SLT, OT, psychologist	1.09	.574
7.	Middletown Centre for Autism	.71	.689
8.	NEPS	.66	.569
9.	SENO	.56	.619
10.	Local Education Centre	.48	.606
11.	NCSE	.18	.387
12.	Board of Management	.18	.434
13.	Other*	.15	.496
14.	DES Inspectorate	.10	.308

*Support groups, parents, private therapists, college department

Identifying change in teaching behaviour

Comments provided by respondents further illustrate feelings of dissatisfaction (41%, n = 44) regarding their access to supports while working in a special class:

> I had no support and an extremely challenging ASD unit. I left after five months on sick leave for workplace related stress. This was totally out of character for me. I feel the units were added to the school for the extra funding but no support given. School couldn't answer questions about restraint, etc. and there were no policies. Teachers are very vulnerable in this case and children (Teacher 7).

Eighty-nine per cent (n = 111) of respondents reported that the PD and professional learning they completed in the area of ASD led to changes in their practices within the classroom. Figure 4 outlines the reported barriers to completing professional learning including the lack of substitution cover, issue of time and lack of availability of professional learning specific to ASD.

Induction/professional learning

For the purposes of this research, induction is defined within an irish context where it was viewed as critical to teacher educational reform and necessary to support the retention of beginning teachers and

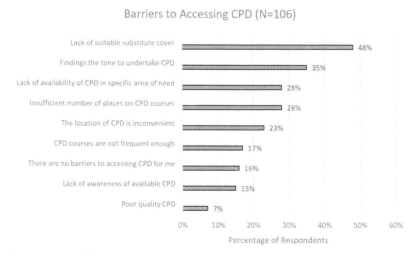

Figure 4. Barriers to accessing CPD.

to assist them to build of their professional learning gained while engaged in ITE (Conway et al. 2009).

Ninety-eight per cent (N = 122) of participants reported that teachers in special classes for children with ASD required induction supports and ongoing mentoring while in the role. A selection of quotes were extracted to illuminate teachers' perspectives:

"Transition for new teachers is equally important for teachers as it is for the students we have" (Teacher 18).

"It can be a huge shock to a teacher who has no experience working with pupils with ASD, they need induction to understand the needs of the pupils, teaching approaches, the huge difference between teaching in a mainstream and a special class" (Teacher 103).

Table 8 illustrates the professional learning activities sought by participants from most requested activities (rating of 1) to the least requested activities (rating of 7).

Teaching practices

Eighty-one per cent (n = 101) of participants reported that they did not teach all the compulsory subjects of the Irish Primary School Curriculum (NCCA, 1999), please review Table 7 for more details. Out of the sample of 125, 84 respondents outlined the subjects that were not taught in the special class (see Figure 5 for more details). There was no indication why the entire sample did not complete this section of the questionnaire. Of these, 96% (n = 81) reported that they do not teach Irish. Of note, just 21% (n = 17) of the 81 respondents not teaching Irish, reported that they were aware that their students had obtained an official Irish exemption. Irish is a compulsory subject in all schools in the Republic of Ireland. Until recently, it was a requirement that all children, including those with ASD, were required to follow the Irish curriculum. Under specific circumstances, such as presenting with a Specific Learning Difficulty (SLD), an exemption from the study of Irish was available. In August 2019, the Minister for Education announced new criteria for schools to grant exemptions to learners

Table 7. Curricular issues.

Question	Response	%	n
Do you have IEPs for all students?	Yes	97	104
	No	3	3
Does each child receive the specified amount of time for each subject?	Yes	15	16
	No	85	88
Do you use the guidelines for teachers of students with GLD?	Yes	74	78
	No	27	26
Would you like a set curriculum for use in the special class for children with ASD?	Yes	73	77
	No	27	28
Are there any subjects on the curriculum that you do not teach in the special class?	Yes	81	85
	No	19	20

Table 8. Induction activities of participants.

Rating	Area	M	SD
1.	Completion of an induction course prior to starting in the class	2.68	1.87
2.	Mentoring: a teacher with experience of teaching in a special class to be a mentor for the teacher in his/her first year	3.09	1.86
3.	CPD delivered throughout the year	3.76	1.79
4.	Observation/placement in other well established classes	3.99	2.17
5.	A support team specifically for teachers in special classes for children with ASD	4.56	1.66
6.	Support group: regular meetings with a group of other teachers working in special classes and a facilitator	4.60	1.55
7.	A visiting teacher/advisory teacher specialising in the area of ASD	5.31	1.81

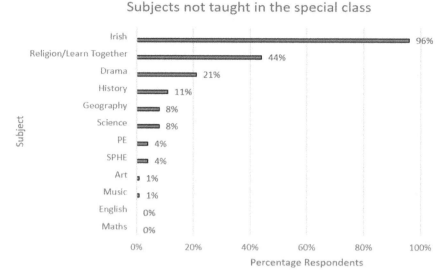

Figure 5. Subjects not taught in the special class (N=84).

(Government of Ireland 2019) who attend special classes for children with ASD. Qualitative responses regarding the reasons why teachers were not spending the specified amount of officially allocated time on each subject, as outlined in the Primary School Curriculum (NCCA 1999), were content-analysed. Ninety-one per cent of the 101 of respondents (n = 92) agreed with the statement that children with ASD required a different teaching approach to that of their mainstream counterparts.

Additionally, teachers reported on general curricular practices in their special classrooms in line with curricular planning of their mainstream counterparts.

Figure 6 illustrates the comprehensive range of teaching methodologies that teachers reported using in the classrooms, with the vast majority of respondents using visual support and TEACCH methodologies, while Picture Exchange Communication System (PECS), Social Stories and physical exercise are also widely reported. Two-thirds of participants reported using Applied Behavioural Analysis (ABA) strategies.

Respondents were asked about their engagement in whole school PD initiatives in the area of ASD, and 45% of 100 responses reported that their staff engaged in whole school PD in the area of ASD, whereas 55% reported no such initiatives.

Contextual factors, conditions and personal characteristics

Perceptions of special class provision

Participants were requested to rate their experiences regarding aspects of special class teaching from Strongly Agree (1) to Strongly Disagree (5). Statements were grouped together to form a scale measuring teachers' perceptions which addressed if a specialist ASD class was an important part of the continuum of provision for pupils with ASD. Three of the items were reverse coded. Potential scores ranged from 8 to 40 with higher scores denoting a more negative perception.

In Table 9, considering the range of this scale, it strongly suggests that the mean score of the participants (M = 18.93, on a scale from 8 to 40) demonstrated positive perceptions. The alpha level of internal consistency is just below .70 and this scale has not been standardised, so caution must be taken when interpreting the results (DeVellis 2003).

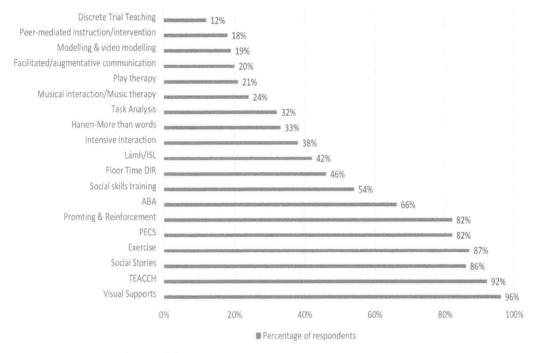

Figure 6. Interventions used in special class.

Table 9. Scale of total perception of special class model.

Scale	Min-max	Variance	M	SD	α	Test of Normality Shapiro -Wilk
Total perception of special class	8–36	23.622	18.93	4.86	.658	.962 (95) p = .007

Discussion

The aim of this research was to identify the main challenges that Irish teachers have experienced in meeting the educational needs of children with ASD who attend a special class. It also explored these teachers' views with regard to the supports that they perceived as most beneficial for their PD needs with the aim of informing further PD programmes to support children with ASD. This section interrogates the results utilising a PD framework (Merchie et al. 2018).

Identifying teachers' quality-knowledge, skills and attitude

Challenges of the role

Teachers reported experiencing challenges in teaching in a special class, where the most challenging aspects were in managing challenging behaviours and implementing an appropriate curriculum, consistent with previous research (Boyer and Lee 2001, Department of Education and Science 2001, Jennett et al. 2003, Scheuermann et al. 2003, Syriopoulou-Delli and Cassimos 2012, Roberts and Simpson 2016, Anglim et al. 2018, Rodden et al. 2018). Approximately two-thirds of special class teachers reported feelings of isolation in this teaching role (Balfe 2001). Balfe identified that teachers who experienced isolation also reported greater challenges when teaching learners with ASD. Research has shown that these challenges lowered a teacher's sense of efficacy, associated with a teacher's physiological/affective state and which, in turn, increased vulnerability to stress and burnout (Billingsley 2004, Klassen et al. 2011, Ruble et al. 2013). These factors have implications for teacher retention and steps should be taken to alleviate this (Anglim et al. 2018).

Results indicate that challenges experienced by teachers were directly affected by the profile of the students in their respective classes. Having pupils who exhibited challenging behaviours, and pupils who remained in the special class full time reported to heighten the level of challenge experienced by teachers consistent with qualitative Irish teachers' experiences of teaching children with ASD in primary and secondary schools (Anglim et al. 2018, Rodden et al. 2018). Specifically, the majority of teachers interviewed from an Irish primary school setting revealed their uncertainty in managing the behaviours of children with ASD due to their lack of pedagogical expertise and teaching experience (Anglim et al. 2018). In an Irish secondary school setting, an analysis of discourses used by secondary school teachers unveiled their feelings of fear and anxiety around the presence of children with ASD in their classes (Rodden et al. 2018). This finding is also consistent with previous research which found that there was little influence on the length of previous experience regarding the challenges that teachers encountered (Balfe 2001). Roberts and Simpson (2016) revealed that teachers' lack of knowledge about ASD and the impact of addressing challenging behaviours in learners was the likely cause of exclusion of these children from inclusive class settings. This has implications for meaningful inclusive practices in schools (Parsons et al. 2009). The support of colleagues and, in particular, school principals, is important for relieving a teacher's sense of isolation and providing a supportive professional environment for special class teachers (Thornton et al. 2007). However, there is a concern when only a slight majority of principals have the knowledge and expertise to support the inclusion of learners in their schools (Roberts and Simpson 2016).

Qualifications and training
Almost two-thirds of teachers reported that a specialist qualification in ASD should be compulsory for special class teaching. Currently, a basic teacher qualification remains the only requirement for teaching in a special class in Ireland. However, the context for this is changing in Ireland with two policy initiatives; firstly, where there will be a requirement on teachers to access PD under the *Cosán* framework (Broderick 2019) and secondly, with the mandatory requirement to include inclusive education in all ITE programmes (Hick et al. 2018). Respondents were largely dissatisfied with the level of input on ASD provided in ITE consistent with research in Ireland and elsewhere (Roberts and Simpson 2016, Anglim et al. 2018, Rodden et al. 2018, Ravet et al. 2018). With the increasing likelihood of teachers interacting with learners with ASD and/or working in ASD special classes at some point during their careers, this research highlights the need to support teachers during their ITE (Ravet 2018, Hick et al. 2018).

Respondents who had previous teaching experience with pupils with ASD reported feeling more prepared for the role of a special class teacher. Therefore, having opportunities to interact with students who have ASD should be incorporated and core to ITE (Hick et al. 2018). Those who reported greater levels of preparation for the role also experienced reduced levels of challenge while in this role. It is suggested that an action-research approach is required where the knowledge and skills that teachers, engaged in ITE, acquire in coursework be put into practice (Brownell et al. 2005). Ravet (2018) also suggests the inclusion of video to bring the reality of ASD to life and to use ASD case studies to stimulate thinking and learning among teachers in ITE programmes. It is important that trainee teachers gain experience with students who present with ASD specifically, and not just students with SEN in general, as, in this study, previous mainstream or SEN experience did not affect how prepared a teacher felt. This suggests that students with ASD present with unique challenges and are potential triggers for increased stress levels of teachers more so than other pupils with SEN (Jennett et al. 2003). This contradicts the current practice that a regular teaching qualification is sufficient to teach in a special class, when teachers with more relevant experience were likely to be better equipped to deal with the challenges that emerged. Hick et al. (2018) suggest the need to strengthen the configuration of school teaching experience and the taught elements of ITE with regard to inclusive education in Ireland.

Identifying change in teaching behaviour

Support and professional learning

Respondents were evenly divided in their satisfaction and dissatisfaction with the support they accessed while teaching in a special class. A third of respondents were dissatisfied with the quality and amount of professional learning available to them. Special Needs Assistants, principal involvement and support from other teachers who taught children with ASD and colleagues were the greatest areas of support identified by participants. However, there was a large variation in the support received from class to class. Interestingly, higher levels of support were reported from Department of Health professionals than from some educational agencies contrary to qualitative findings (Anglim et al. 2018, Rodden et al. 2018). Further professional learning for individuals in these organisations is necessary to allow them to effectively collaborate with, and support, teachers in special classes (Roberts and Simpson 2016).

The majority of teachers reported that the professional learning they completed in the area of ASD led to changes in their practice within the classroom. This finding is somewhat conflicting with findings by Sugrue (2002) who identified that the type of professional learning provided to teachers in Ireland often had an underwhelming impact on classroom practice. In the absence of evidence beyond self-reports, it is an area that requires further study. Teachers experienced many barriers to accessing professional learning that included the lack of suitable substitute cover and difficulties finding the time to complete professional learning. This has major implications for the stress levels of teachers who identified their inability to access the professional learning they required. Beyond enhancing their skills, PD provides teachers with the opportunity to meet other teachers in a similar setting, thus reducing their experiences of isolation and increasing their support networks.

Teacher practices and interventions

One of the factors that can contribute to pupils with ASD underachieving in school is the suitability of the curriculum (Day and Prunty 2015). Currently, there is no 'specialist' curriculum for ASD-specific special classes in Ireland. Three quarters of teachers in this study were utilising the *Guidelines for Teachers of Students with General Learning Disabilities* (NCCA, 2007) for planning. However, the same number of teachers stated that a set curriculum was required to meet the needs of learners in a special class setting. Planning, assessment and the implementation of an appropriate curriculum posed significant challenges to special class teachers in this study. Balfe (2001) also found that teachers experienced challenges in the development and implementation of an appropriate curriculum to meet the needs of learners with ASD. Almost all teachers in this study completed Individual Educational Plans (IEPs) for their pupils, reflecting a commitment to the implementation of best practice guidelines for learners with SEN. Irish research has demonstrated that IEPs are useful for children with ASD in schools (Prunty 2011) including children with ASD from ethnic minorities (Habib et al. 2017).

Most learners in the special classes were accessing a reduced curriculum, with Irish being the most common subject omitted. However, only a quarter of respondents reported that their pupils had been granted an official Irish exemption. Almost half of the special class teachers sampled were not providing religious instruction and several did not teach Drama or Social Environmental and Scientific Education, which are also compulsory subjects in the Primary School Curriculum (National Council for Curriculum and Assessment [NCCA] 1999). A large number of teachers were not teaching subjects for the specified amount of time outlined in the curriculum, as they reported prioritising specific areas of need for their pupils. Language and communication, social interaction and development of adaptive skills were the core areas of need reported by participants. The lack of official guidance was a source confusion for teachers and a considerable variation in the manner in which the curriculum is delivered in ASD-specific special classes. The new directive allowing exceptions from the study of Irish (Government of Ireland 2019) should reduce this confusion for children with ASD in specialist settings.

Participants almost unanimously agreed that children with ASD required a different teaching approach to learners in the mainstream class setting. The main evidence-based interventions and methodologies identified by teachers included visually based supports, TEACCH, Social Stories, Exercise, PECS and ABA. As expected, these interventions reflect the professional learning provided by the SESS. Overall, teachers reported using a variety of ASD interventions (Anglim et al. 2018). This is contrary to Balfe's (2001) earlier findings, in which teachers reported a low level of knowledge about ASD and interventions in ASD. A future study is necessary to determine the fidelity of teachers' implementation of these interventions. In addition, beyond initial training in TEACCH for example, little follow up guidance and support are currently available.

Contextual factors, conditions and personal characteristics

Profile of class and teacher

A special class teacher was identified generally as someone with relatively few years of mainstream teaching experience, who had previous experience teaching a child with ASD and had been teaching in an SEN role. Over one-quarter of participants did not have full teaching recognition with the TCI, as a proportion of teachers came to the role having previously taught in settings such as a special school or in Montessori settings. However, one-third of respondents reported no previous teaching experience with children with ASD prior to obtaining a teaching position in a specialist ASD setting. The number of teachers with postgraduate qualifications specifically relating to ASD was low. Overall, there was a wide disparity in the experience of teachers entering the role. The most common class allocations were two ASD-specific special classes per school, half of which had not reached their full enrolment quota. The profile of pupils identified in this research indicated that each class generally included a pupil who was non-verbal, two pupils who exhibited challenging behaviours and two pupils with a co-morbid disability. Usually, three pupils remained in their special classes' full time, a finding similar to that of the NCSE (McCoy et al. 2014). This profile of the class teacher in a specialist ASD setting is due to change with the *Cosán* framework and the mandatory requirement of inclusive practices for all ITE courses.

Addressing challenging behaviour

Classes with higher numbers of pupils who exhibit challenging behaviours posed a greater level of challenge for teachers. Professional learning in managing challenging behaviour was the most requested area of support by teachers. Challenging behaviour may have a detrimental effect on pupils' opportunities for inclusion, as classes with higher numbers of pupils exhibiting challenging behaviour were correlated with a greater number of students remaining in a special class full time. This has implications also for teacher well-being and their potential vulnerability to burn out (Billingsley 2004). Some teachers reported that the disruption caused as a result of addressing issues around challenging behaviour reduced overall teacher instruction time, thus reducing access time to the curriculum for pupils in the special class. ABA and other behavioural approaches were reportedly used by two-thirds of respondents. This research indicates that teachers should access behavioural support in order to manage challenging behaviour more effectively in their classrooms (Balfe 2001, Roberts and Simpson 2016). Behavioural factors undoubtedly affect outcomes for pupils with ASD, making it imperative that teachers receive increased professional learning and support in managing challenging behaviour. An increase in support and funding is necessary in order for schools to access professionals to guide and promote best practices in behavioural management for learners with ASD and to ensure the safety and dignity of pupils and teachers alike. Possibly, the pupil–teacher ratio may need to be reviewed to factor in the levels of need of pupils enrolled, particularly learners who require extra support, in the form of SNAs or a reduced teacher–pupil ratio (Irish National Teachers Organisation 2014).

Inclusive practice

While the original focus of the special class for ASD was to facilitate inclusion, its remit has changed dramatically. Eighty-one per cent of respondents reported that at least one child remained in the special class for the entire school day and did not access an inclusive setting in school. An analysis of the profile of these students identified that these learners were likely to be non-verbal, have co-morbid disabilities and exhibit challenging behaviours in the school setting. Hence, learners with greater levels of need were less likely to integrate with their peers. This suggests that schools may not be taking full advantage of the special class provision to promote the inclusive practice, as this appears to be strongly dependent on the individual needs and abilities of each child with ASD. The greater the number of pupils who remained in a special class full time, the greater the levels of challenge experienced by teachers. Over half of teachers agreed that the special class should be limited to students who have the potential to be included into the mainstream class, suggesting attitudes towards inclusion were highly dependent on the abilities of the individual child. A more in-depth analysis of teachers' views on what constitutes the 'skills' and 'abilities' is required to support inclusive practice for learners with ASD. Teachers require the support of professionals to manage and promote inclusive practices in schools. This may be a role for the NCSE Inclusion Support Service established in 2015 to assist schools in supporting children with SEN.

Perceptions of special class provision

Notably, this research identified that teachers had positive perceptions of the special class setting as a continuum of educational provision for pupil with ASD, although variations across teachers' reports were also evident. Teachers who reported higher levels of challenge, and experienced a higher number of pupils remaining full time in their respective special classes, also held more negative perceptions of special class provision overall. This finding is not surprising given that access to a mainstream class was viewed as one of the main benefits of having a special class (Ware *et al.* 2009). Teachers who experienced greater levels of challenge and, thus, increased stress and isolation, were more likely to have a more negative perspective of having a special class within their school.

Strengths and limitations

There are strengths and limitations to this research. It comprehensively captures the in-depth experiences of teachers who have taught children with ASD within a specialist school setting in Ireland at a time that has seen rapid changes in the educational provision for this cohort of learners. It captures the experiences of these teachers and identifies their unmet PD needs which are consistent with their international colleagues in similar teaching contexts. The sample of participants in this study constituted almost a quarter of all ASD-specific special class teachers at primary level in Ireland, therefore, allowing for good generalisability of the findings. No study of this type has been completed in Ireland since 2001 and the landscape of educational provision has changed dramatically in the interim, with a significant increase in ASD-specific special classes throughout the Republic of Ireland. This research illustrated how an evaluative framework could support an analysis of teacher's PD needs. However, this research is not without its limitations. This data only captured information from teachers who taught children that attended specialist ASD classes. A comparative analysis that captured the experiences of mainstream class teachers who support these learners in a mainstream classroom context was not explored. The experiences of these teachers would have enhanced this study. In Ireland, there are currently special schools in operation that meet the highly specialist needs of learners with ASD. It would be interesting to explore if the PD needs of teachers in special schools vary from their colleagues based in special ASD classes in mainstream settings. Furthermore, the experiences of SEN teams in schools, including the leadership role of the school principal, were not investigated. Future research would benefit from exploring principals' experiences of meeting the needs of autistic learners in their schools. In the era of inclusive education, the longer term needs and outcomes of learners who attend specialist settings requires examination, particularly to plan and to identify the educational provisions they will need to become active participants in society.

Conclusion

This study revealed the main challenges that Irish teachers experience in meeting the educational needs of children with ASD in special class settings in a mainstream primary school system. This study was timely and provided a vital insight into the PD needs of teachers in this setting, who reported their feelings of being ill-prepared and unsupported in this role. It is necessary to unveil the experiences of teachers in ASD-specific classrooms to inform future planning and delivery of professional learning initiatives to meet teachers' needs. Almost all respondents reported that teachers required professional learning prior to teaching in this setting. This need was further emphasised by qualitative comments, where many teachers commented on the significant challenges they experienced in their initial entry to the special class, many of whom relayed experiences of high levels of stress and burnout. The provision of a formalised compulsory professional learning programme would benefit teachers to tackle the challenges they experience and to provide support to alleviate the isolation and stress they reported. This is set to change with the reconceptualisation of programmes in ITE (Hick *et al.* 2018). Additionally, teachers may opt to avail of professional learning as part of their requirement to retain their teaching status with the TCI from 2020 with the proposed roll out of the Cosán framework to support the PD needs of teachers. In the longer term, this has the potential to lead to better outcomes for pupils with ASD by incorporating systemic factors to support teachers' PD planning (King 2016) particularly in terms of students' curriculum attainment and inclusion, and to safeguard against teacher burnout and attrition. The use of an implementation science approach, currently in its infancy in educational research (Lyon *et al.* (2018), could be a progressive initiative to support the piloting of such initiatives. The use of an implementation scientific approach may perhaps inform the planning and evaluation of student outcomes more systematically. If an educational system is to 'start from the needs felt by the teachers themselves' in designing long-term professional learning plans (UNESCO 2003, p. 25), then perhaps a professional learning programme could include a course for teachers to prepare them to meet the needs of learners with ASD prior to teaching in a special class. In addition, a requirement should be made to ensure the ongoing provision of mentoring, coaching and professional learning for teachers throughout the school year to ensure successful inclusion of children with ASD. The main challenges identified in this study could be addressed to inform ITE and professional learning initiatives to support the PD needs of teachers who work with children with ASD in schools.

Note

1. Teachers who do not possess an appropriate Irish language qualification, are granted a period of provisional recognition to work towards meeting the Irish language requirements. They are eligible for posts as resource teachers and special class teachers in mainstream schools (DES Circular 25/00).

Disclosure statement

No potential conflict of interest was reported by the authors.

ORCID

William Kinsella http://orcid.org/0000-0002-8134-597X
Paula Prendeville http://orcid.org/0000-0002-0830-9817

References

American Psychological Association, 2013. *Diagnostic statistical manual of mental disorders.* 5th ed. Washington DC: APA.
Anglim, J., Prendeville, P., and Kinsella, W., 2018. The self-efficacy of primary school teachers in supporting the inclusion of children with autistic spectrum disorder. *Educational psychology in practice*, 34, 73–88. doi:10.1080/02667363.2017.1391750
Balfe, T., 2001. A study of the induction experiences and the needs of teachers new to autistic spectrum disorders in the Republic of Ireland. *Good Autism Practice*, 2 (2), 75–86.
Billingsley, B.S., 2004. Promoting teacher quality and retention in special education. *Journal of learning disabilities*, 37 (5), 370–376. doi:10.1177/00222194040370050101.
Boyer, L. and Lee, C., 2001. Converting challenge to success supporting a new teacher of students with autism. *The journal of special education*, 33 (2), 75–83. doi:10.1177/002246690103500202.
Bressman, S., Winter, J.S., and Efron, S.E., 2018. Next generation mentoring: supporting teachers beyond induction. *Teaching and teacher education*, 73, 162–170. doi:10.1016/j.tate.2018.04.003
Broderick, N., 2019. From our own correspondent: teachers' professional learning in the republic of Ireland context. *Practice*, 1 (1), 94–97. doi:10.1080/25783858.2019.1591773.
Brownell, M.T., Ross, D.D., and Colón, E.P., 2005. Critical features of special education teacher preparation a comparison with general teacher education. *The journal of special education*, 38 (4), 242–252. doi:10.1177/00224669050380040601.
Clarke, M. and Killeavy, M., 2012. Charting teacher education policy in the republic of Ireland with particular reference to the impact of economic recession. *Educational research*, 54 (2), 125–136. doi:10.1080/00131881.2012.680038.
Conway, P.F., et al., 2009. *Learning to teacher and its implications for the continum of teacher education: a nine-country cross-national study.* Maynooth: The Teaching Council.
Daly, P., et al., 2016. *An evaluation of education provision for children with autism spectrum disorder in Ireland-research report 21.* Trim: National Council for Special Education.
Day, T. and Prunty, A., 2015. Responding to the challenges of inclusion in Irish schools. *European journal of special needs education*, 30, 237–252. doi:10.1080/08856257.2015.1009701.
Department of Education and Science, 2001. *Educational provision and support for persons with autistic spectrum disorders: the report of the task force on autism.* Dublin: The Stationery Office.
Department of Education and Science, 2005. *Circular 02/05: organisation of teaching resources for pupils who need additional support in mainstream primary schools.* Dublin: The Stationery Office.
Department of Education and Science. (DES) Inspectorate, 2006. *An evaluation of educational provision for children with autistic spectrum disorders.* Dublin: Stationery Office.
DeVellis, R., 2003. *Scale development: theory and applications: theory and application.* Thousand Oaks, CA: Sage.
Gehrke, R.S. and McCoy, K., 2007. Sustaining and retaining beginning special educators: it takes a village. *Teaching and teacher education*, 23, 490–500. doi:10.1016/j.tate.2006.12.001
Government of Ireland, 2019. *Minister McHugh announces new criteria for granting exemptions from study of Irish.* Available from: http//www.education.ie/en/Press-Events/Press-Releases/2019-press-releases/PR19-08-12.html [Accessed 28 August 2019].
Griffin, C.C., Winn, J.A., and Otis-Wilborn, A., 2003. *New teacher induction in special education. Center on personnel studies in special education.* Gainesville: University of Florida.
Habib, A., et al., 2017. Pakistani mothers' experiences of parenting a child with autism spectrum disorder in Ireland. *Educational and child psychology*, 34 (2), 67–79.
Hick, P., et al., 2018. *Initial teacher education for inclusion- phase 1 and 2 report.* Trim: NCSE.
Howlin, P., et al., 2004. Adult outcome for children with autism. *Journal of child psychology and psychiatry*, 45 (2), 212–229. doi:10.1111/j.14697610.2004.00215.x.
Irish National Teachers Organisation, 2014. *The education of children with autism.* Available from: http//www.into.ie/ROI/InfoforTeachers/SpecialEducation/ReportsandResources/
Jennett, H.K., Harris, S.L., and Mesibov, G.B., 2003. Commitment to philosophy, teacher efficacy, and burnout among teachers of children with autism. *Journal of autism and developmental disorders*, 33 (6), 583–593. doi:10.1023/B:JADD.0000005996.19417.57.
Kilgore, K., Griffin, C., and Otis-Wilborn, A., 2003. The problems of beginning special education teachers: exploring the contextual factors influencing their work. *Action in teacher education*, 25 (1), 38–47. doi:10.1080/01626620.2003.10463291.
King, F., 2014. Evaluating the impact of teacher professional development:an evidence-based framework. *Professional development in education*, 40 (1), 89–111. doi:10.1080/19415257.2013.823099.
King, F., 2016. Teacher professional development to support teacher professional learning: systemic factors from Irish case studies. *Teacher development*, 20 (4), 574–594. doi:10.1080/13664530.2016.1161661.

Kinsella, W., 2018. Organising inclusive schools. *International journal of inclusive education*, 1–17. doi:10.1080/13603116.2018.1516820.

Kinsella, W. and Senior, J., 2008. Developing inclusive schools: a systemic approach. *International journal of inclusive education*, 12 (5–6), 651–665. doi:10.1080/13603110802377698.

Klassen, R.M., et al., 2011. Teacher efficacy research 1998–2009: signs of progress or unfulfilled promise? *Educational psychology review*, 23, 21–43. doi:10.1007/s10648-010-9141-8

Kokkinos, C.M. and Davazoglou, A.M., 2009. Special education teachers under stress: evidence from a Greek national study. *Educational psychology*, 29 (4), 407–424. doi:10.1080/01443410902971492.

Langdon, F.J., et al., 2014. A national survey of induction and mentoring: how it is perceived within communities of practice. *Teaching and teacher education*, 44, 92–105. doi:10.1016/j.tate.2014.08.004

Lyon, A.R., et al., 2018. Assessing organizational implementation context in the education sector: confirmatory factor analysis of measures of implementation leadership, climate, and citizenship. *Implementation science*, 13 (1), 5.

McConkey, R. and Bhlirgri, S., 2003. Children with autism attending preschool facilities: the experiences and perceptions of staff. *Early child development and care*, 173 (4), 445452. doi:10.1080/0300443032000086926.

McCoy, S., et al., 2014. *Understanding special class provision in Ireland*. Meath: National Council for Special Education.

McElearney, A., Murphy, C., and Radcliffe, D., 2019. Identifying teacher needs and preferences in accessing professional learning and support. *Professional development in education*, 45 (3), 433–445. doi:10.1080/19415257.2018.1557241.

Merchie, E., et al., 2018. Evaluating teachers' professional development initiatives: towards an extended evaluative framework. *Research papers in education*, 33 (2), 143–168. doi:10.1080/02671522.2016.1271003.

Morling, B., 2012. *Research methods in psychology: evaluating a world of psychology*. London: W. W. Norton & Company, Inc.

Nassar-McMillan, S.C. and Borders, D.L., 2002. Use of focus groups in survey item development. *The qualitative report*, 7 (1), 1–12. Available from: http://nsuworks.nova.edu/tqr/vol7/iss1/3/

National Council for Curriculum and Assessment [NCCA], 1999. *Primary school curriculum*. Dublin: National Council for Curriculum and Assessment.

National Council for Curriculum and Assessment [NCCA], 2007. *Guidelines for teachers of students with general learning disabilities*. Dublin: National Council for Curriculum and Assessment.

National Council for Special Education [NCSE], 2015. *Special class list for September 15/16*. Meath: NCSE. Available from: http//ncse.ie/special-classes

O'Gorman, E. and Drudy, S., 2011. Addressing the professional development needs of teaching working in the area of special education/inclusion in mainstream schools in Ireland. *Journal of research in special educational needs*, 10 (1), 157–167. doi:10.1111/j.1471-3802.2010.01161.x.

Parsons, S., et al., 2009. International review of the evidence on best practice in educational provision for children on the autism spectrum. *European journal of special needs education*, 26 (1), 47–63. doi:10.1080/08856257.2011.543532.

Prunty, A., 2011. Implementation of children's rights: what is in "the best interests of the child" in relation to the Individual Education Plan (IEP) process for pupils with autistic spectrum disorders (ASD)? *Irish educational studies*, 30 (1), 23–44. doi:10.1080/03323315.2011.535974.

Ravet, J., 2018. 'But how do I teach them?': autism & initial teacher education (ITE). *International journal of inclusive education*, 22 (7), 714–733. doi:10.1080/13603116.2017.1412505.

Roberts, J. and Simpson, K., 2016. A review of research into stakeholder perspectives on inclusion of students with autism in mainstream schools. *International journal of inclusive education*, 20 (10), 1084–1096. doi:10.1080/13603116.2016.1145267.

Rodden, B., et al., 2018. 'Framing post primary teachers' perspectives on the inclusion of students with autism spectrum disorder using critical discourse analysis'. *Cambridge journal of education*. doi:10.1080/0305764X.2018.1506018.

Rose, R., Shevlin, M., and Winter, E., 2010. Special and inclusive education in the republic of Ireland: reviewing the literature from 2000 to 2009. *European journal of special needs education*, 25 (4), 359–373. doi:10.1080/08856257.2010.513540.

Ruble, L.A., et al., 2013. Preliminary study of the autism self-efficacy scale for teachers (ASSET). *Research in autism spectrum disorders*, 7 (9), 1151–1159. doi:10.1016/j.rasd.2013.06.006.

Ruble, L.A., Usher, E.L., and McGrew, J.H., 2011. Preliminary investigation of the sources of self-efficacy among teachers of students with autism. *Focus on autism and other developmental disabilities*, 26 (2), 67–74. doi:10.1177/1088357610397345.

Santoli, S.P. and Vitulli, P., 2014. Ireland's national induction programme for teachers. *Record*, 50 (2), 89–92. doi:10.1080/00228958.2014.900853.

Scheuermann, B., Webber, J., and Boutot, E.A., 2003. Problems with personnel preparation in autism spectrum disorders. *Focus on autism and other developmental disabilities*, 18 (2), 197–206. doi:10.1177/10883576030180030801.

Stoiber, K.C., Gettinger, M., and Goetz, D., 1998. Exploring factors influencing parents and early childhood practitioners' beliefs about inclusion. *Early childhood research quarterly*, 13 (1), 107–121. doi:10.1016/S0885-2006(99)80028-3.

Sugrue, C., 2002. Irish teachers' experiences of professional learning: implications for policy and practice. *Journal of in-service education*, 28 (2), 311–338. doi:10.1080/13674580200200185.

Sugrue, C., 2011. Irish teachers' experience of professional development: performative or transformative learning? *Professional development in education*, 37 (5), 793–815. doi:10.1080/19415257.2011.614821.

Syriopoulou-Delli, C.K. and Cassimos, D.C., 2012. Teachers' perceptions regarding the management of children with autism spectrum disorders. *Journal of autism and other developmental disorders*, 42, 755–768. doi:10.1007/s10803-011-1309-7

Teaching Council of Ireland, 2016. *Cosán: framework for teachers' learning*. Dublin: TCI.

Thornton, B., Peltier, G., and Medina, R., 2007. Reducing the special education teacher shortage. *The clearing house: a journal of educational strategies, issues and ideas*, 80 (5), 233–238. doi:10.3200/TCHS.80.5.233-238.

United Nations, 2006. *Convention on the right of a persons with a disability*. (UNCRPD). Available from: http//www.un.org/disabilities/convention/conventionfull.shtml

United Nations Educational, Scientific and Cultural Organization (UNESCO), 2003. *Overcoming exclusion through inclusive approaches in education. a challenge & a vision. Conceptual paper (ED2003/WS/63)*. Paris: UNESCO. Available from: http://unesdoc.unesco.org/images/0013/001347/134785e.pdf

Ware, J., *et al.*, 2009. *Research report on the role of special schools and classes in Ireland*. Meath: National Council for Special Education.

Afterword: inserting social justice into professional development

Ira Bogotch

I have spent the last few months thinking about how educators – at all levels of our systems – confuse the words equality, equity, fairness, social justice, inclusion, and excellence. I believe that some of this confusion is deliberate. I will explain later in this Afterword. I have also been thinking about how the intersections of identity politics become barriers to members of marginalised groups in 'seeing themselves' in abstract, philosophical social justice theories. That is, without a vivid representation of a specific marginalised group in the explanation of the theory, then the theory as a whole is problematic, if not irrelevant. And, maybe, that is true. But what that would mean is that not just members of marginalised groups, but every one of us has some initial problem in 'seeing others' who have different pressing real world issues as central to the meaning of social justice. We all begin by thinking that our issue is the most important one. I get it.

In 2002, writing in the *Journal of School* Leadership, before the above thoughts were part of my thinking about social justice, I wrote that because educational reforms are fragile and fleeting, and because there are always demographic and other contextual changes happening within schools and communities, there could be 'no fixed or predictable meanings' of social justice (Bogotch 2002, p. 153). I still think that is true.

I also still believe that theological and legal definitions of the word 'justice' have attempted to solidify constructs around fixed principles. Thus, justice variably assumes (a) morally just outcomes are determined by natural laws; (b) culturally relevant legal practices and outcomes are based upon community standards or majority-held positions; and/or, (c) rule-governed judgements inside institutionalised legal proceedings rely upon legal precedents and traditions. Each of these views of justice has been an attempt to reduce psychological fears of the unknown, and, consequently, attribute leadership to those able to hold onto power: think Thomas Hobbes and his *Leviathan*.

'Social justice,' on the other hand, is through everyday practices whereby the means – the intentions and motivations of human actions – align with the ends, or consequences of those actions, which are professionally/vocationally necessary. In education, the means are our pedagogies, one example being professional development; the ends are our curricula as educational purposes or shared leadership visions. And when we engage through professional learning communities in the actions of critical reflections, we often decide to rethink and re-distribute our (educational) resources, our communicative knowledge-bases. Under all circumstances, the means and ends would be social constructions, followed by reconstructions and decisions to begin again in order to bring about more equitable and socially just outcomes. Education is on-going within and beyond schools.

It is, therefore, with these current and past thoughts in mind – some of which are likely to remain unresolved dilemmas – that I come to the articles in this Special Issue. Happy to say that some of the answers to my open-ended questions were addressed effectively in this Special Issue, which highlights the material realities of professional learning in multiple directions. Nevertheless, deciding where are we today with respect to *social justice and professional development* is always worthy of critical reflections.

In 2012, in *Snapshots of school leadership in the 21st Century: The UCEA[1] Voices from the field project*, I described the status of leadership for social justice as in 'middle passage.' (Bogotch 2012). I saw inserting social justice into educational discourses as

> a long and arduous journey through public school history, a journey that historically has traveled through many real crises in terms of separate and unequal schools for Black and White children, programs to educate impoverished immigrants, the political realities of regional as well as world wars, and the periodic economic downturns that result from unregulated market forces, including unemployment, poverty and homelessness" (p. 193).

And that, like the thirteen articles in this Special Issue, was before we saw the material consequences of the pandemic of 2020, nativist populism, and civil unrest.

As you know, many of those taken into bondage on the middle passage journey across the Atlantic Ocean died; but those who survived to become slaves and then productive US citizens have been able to teach the world many important lessons. Witness Black Lives Matter and what the late Congressman John Lewis called 'good trouble.' In other words, to fully understand meanings of social justice, researchers, following Begoña Vigo-Arrazola & Dennis Beach, in this Special Issue, need to establish close learning relationships with their participants as

> co-enquirers and co-producers of valuable knowledge that can stimulate and focus individual and collective awareness on new action. Using ethnography as explanatory critique in education research is therefore not just a way to generate a more progressive contextually sensitive research-based knowledge for and about leadership and professional development. The method also counters tendencies towards audience pacification in traditional qualitative research (Denzin 2018)" (Vigo-Arrazola & Beach 2020, n.p.).

There is a lot to learn from the thirteen articles: from expanding one's sample (e.g., adding school staff to samples beyond teachers and administrators); deconstructing existing concepts (e.g., teachers as leaders and new research methods); engaging deeply and learning from participants (e.g., critical ethnographies); 'enabling pedagogies (e.g., Freire);' progressing from professional development to professional learning to collaborative learning; clarifying social justice problems (e.g., Foucault); extending leadership for social justice beyond school buildings and educational policies (e.g., collaborations and networks); struggling with deficit mindsets and other inequitable dispositions, especially among aspiring administrative leaders; to always being aware of untended consequences. Some of these themes as lessons were probably helpful reminders to readers, while other themes represented explorations towards new knowledge over time. We may be past the Middle Passage, but we still have a long, long way to go in terms of fully realising leadership for social justice.

Nevertheless, I am more hopeful than disappointed at where we are today. That hopefulness was reinforced again and again by authors who focused initially on individual mindsets in order to better understand *systemic outcomes* (my italics) (Stone-Johnson, Gray, & Wright). Hattam and Weiler tell us that

> [w]e are aware that our attempts to build Communities of Practice (CoP) are actions of individuals within a larger institution with its dominate discourses, processes, structures and conditions ... (n.p.)

Kohli et al. take us from individuals to networks which connect across schools and districts as they also expand upon narrow definitions of school leadership beyond administration.

> Using a framework of critical professional development – teacher development spaces that frame educators as 'politically-aware individuals who have a stake in teaching and transforming society' (Kohli et al. 2015, p. 9) – this article explores the possibilities of a racial affinity critical professional development space, the Institute for Teachers of Colour Commited to Racial Justice (ITOC), which is designed to foster the retention, growth, and transformative leadership capacities of teachers of Colour in K-12 schools (n.p.).

At the same time, however, many researcher-authors confused the terms equality, equity, inclusion, and social justice; others substituted equity as their preferred outcome, rather than social justice (i.e., material changes in people's lives) (Bogotch 2014). In other words, the dependent variables or outcomes were either left unspecified or they stopped short conceptually and materially of societal changes (with respect to hunger, poverty, housing, etc.). To realise the full potential of leadership for social justice, the changes cannot remain inside the boundaries of within-school practices.

With respect to leadership for social justice, we educators have to be more political, more critical in analysing our own terminology, concepts and actions inside the contexts of professional development, professional learning, and professional growth. The pandemic in 2020 gives us no other option. Teaching, learning and leading have been turned inside out and upside down. There are no longer experts who can tell us with any certainty which policies or practices to follow. We are in unprecedented times. And we are in this predicament together. Therefore, we have no choice but to engage with one another in critical reflective practices. We must 'see ourselves' in the problems of others who are different. We should welcome the challenge to shake-up hierarchies and hegemonic (dominant group) thinking. We will be travelling new roads and the journey will be rocky, but at least we don't have to worry that every time we use the term 'social justice' there will be an uproar – as was the case twenty years ago.

In part, that historic backlash was justified because 'social justice' was categorised as a fad. Today, it is easier to see how this misjudgement emerged: most educational reforms come and go. That has been the case since 1904 as noted by John Dewey. So why should 'social justice' (in quotes) as a progressive reform be any different? Well, in 2020, we all can see that not only is social justice (no longer in quotes) relevant and necessary to schooling, it is, in fact, one of the most important issues throughout a democratic society. For this reason, we – educators – have to be political and engage in public discourses. Yet just saying so will not make it happen. As educational researchers, our questions and answers turn on the empirical evidence to confirm or disconfirm our concepts. The evidence must be more than language and communications. It is action and consequences.

Our lives inside a global pandemic are now different. Education as we know it can no longer – for now – be practised face-to-face. Yes, I know that many nations have opened up their schools to teachers and children. I also know that many of these openings have already been aborted. In most instances, our teaching has moved to remote instruction. Likewise, our adult learning, whether it be how to manage new technology platforms or how to manage on-line instruction are both implementation challenges. We are witnessing the revelation that the consequences of the pandemic have exacerbated within-school inequities and beyond-school social injustices. What had remained hidden or ignored is now front and centre. We cannot ignore social, economic, educational and political consequences in order to focus solely on teaching subject matter content, achievement scores, and/or the technical issues of learning. Thus, the first critical reflective practice in any PD would be to ask participants to turn to the person sitting next to them (at the appropriate social distances) and discuss how the pandemic has revealed truths that are becoming evident to parents, teachers, administrators, and staff. To those authors in the Special Issue who identified *awareness* as an important outcome of a PD, the point I am making is that the awareness needs to be shared and then a new plan of action needs to be implemented. As the authors point out, continuous PDs are necessary. What makes this difficult is that educators remain reluctant to engage in public discourses, particularly when viewed as political (Faubert and Bogotch 2019, Bogotch 2019). Collectively, we need to use the pandemic to give educators more courage to engage in public discourses on social injustices

Diversity, equity, equality and inclusion: dance steps towards leadership for social justice

How was 'social justice' used in the conceptual frameworks of professional development, professional learning and collaborative professional learning across contexts in this Special Issue? Is it sufficient to talk about diversity, equity, equality and inclusion, and then conclude that the discourses have been about 'social justice' or 'socially just schools'? To say yes means that we are substituting diversity, equity, equality, and/or inclusion for social justice. Because the interchangeable use of terms is so prevalent among educators, I don't see a clear way forward. We can say that words matter. We can even define each of the above terms, but unless and until we take more care with our use of language, this dance remains a two-step, one step forwards and another back.

In today's 8 to 10 hours a day of required screen time, as our new normal reality, the stakes for PD/PL/PLC/CoP ... have never been higher. But what can we do differently to engage educators, parents, students, community partners, etc.? We know things have changed and that we must change; yet again, it is not enough to assert this need as educational researchers.

Here is my bottom-line: social justice cannot be appended to existing knowledge or skills. Social justice is above and beyond existing knowledge and skills. For those for whom professional development, professional learning and growth have been lifelong scholarly pursuits, the insertion of leadership for social justice requires new learning. Can we reinvent ourselves as educators and citizens to be more actively involved with one another, our parents, our communities, and work collaboratively for social change? Some of us can. But what if that is not what the majority of educators today want to do? To say we/they have a choice is not an option. The pandemic even if it recedes will remain with us for the rest of our lives. That's science-speaking, not politics. We need to build out from the 8 to 10 hour screen days and – following whatever health advice science asserts – to erase inequities and injustices, and make education more inclusive so that one day we can have more socially just schools. The logical conclusion is what we have known for over one hundred years: schools and society are inextricably tied together. We need community/settlement/full service/wrap around schooling which integrates schools with communities. The on-line world is one of staying connected: therefore, let education become the central hub in that societal process. The on-line world will keep blurring the disconnect between school and community, such that this process will encourage educators to engage with dominant societal discourses allowing us – as educators – to make material differences in people's lives. That is my hope for the future.

The open-ended question is how do we as researchers participate in making social justice a reality [for practitioners] sooner rather than later? The answer is always found in our methods. We need to use methods to document material differences as experienced by our research participants. Therefore, we need to listen carefully, document, engage, and then, we analyse, synthesise and interpret, but always as collaborating consultants and learners. As researchers, we learn from engaging with practitioners and documenting their changes.

Conclusions

Social justice, to me, is more than caring and concern on the part of educators. Social justice involves – in its deliberate and explicit use of moral power – disrupting/troubling everyday practices which are inequitable and exclusive. Equity can be addressed with changes of in-school policies and activities; moving towards full inclusion, however, has to be extended to issues found beyond schools inside local communities and societies around the world. Social justice addresses oppressive structures and practices; it is what we are calling today 'systemic' and 'institutionalized.' Whereas the most visible signs of inequity and injustice happen at the individual levels (triggering care and concern), it is the systemic or invisible forces of discrimination, prejudice and exclusion that have to be understood historically and addressed culturally. Social justice is more than addressing the behaviours of one child, one teacher, but rather considering the structural and systemic barriers facing all children and all teachers that prevent changes from happening.

Social justice, therefore, as a public or social construct, involves more than one framework, more than one discipline, more than one issue or problem. Social justice, when internalised – as professional learning (Angelle, Derrington, & Oldham, this volume) and collaborative learning (see e.g., Johnson, Sdunzik, Byrum, Kong, & Qin, this volume; Szeto, Sin & Leung, this volume) -, sees injustices from multiple perspectives challenging structural and institutional barriers. It is not enough to say that problems are complex; one must think across roles, functions, structures, subjects, disciplines, frameworks (e.g., educationally, economically, socially, and politically). And to do so, almost always requires collaboration – on the part of both practitioners and researchers. It involves seeing 'problems' from the perspectives of others, and then going beyond seeing, beyond awareness and taking actions. As human beings, it is often said that even with all of our differences, we have more in common than what separates our thinking and behaviours. However, finding these commonalities has been difficult because of the historical and cultural borders that exist artificially separating us. In this sense, social justice works through differences and disagreements. The realities of social injustices demand that the work take place inside tensions (what Lewin called force-fields). It is what makes some problems seem intractable (e.g., poverty, racism).

Nothing said in this Afterword should indicate that the professional learning processes involved are linear. The interactions of researchers and participants are iterative, but if and only if neither the research design nor the delivery of the professional development be a one-time event. Social justice requires time-series or action research designs (see Vaughan and Mertler 2020) allowing for learning-in-action and then learning anew. One-time, cross-sectional studies provide snapshots. A one-time pre and post data collection provides evidence of learning that is short term. Therefore, understanding the relationship between research on social justice and professional development on social justice is key to advancing our knowledge and skills on this important topic. The challenge is to reveal the contextual social injustices that need to be addressed through actions that subsequently lead researchers to develop theoretical-in-action frameworks. It is a matter of discovering social justice-in-action whether it be through professional or collaborative learning. The validity of the framework is thus *post hoc*, and, at best, a demonstration towards (or away from) social justice which needs to be tested and retested as conditions change.

We now have some broad criteria for analysing the articles in this Special Issue. That criteria would include:

- establishing the necessity of social justice in education,
- viewing the continuity of social justice-in-action,
- assessing the evidence or validity of social justice (based not on intentions, but rather on material differences and consequences),
- extending the meanings of social justice beyond care and concern for individuals and beyond the functions and roles inside school buildings, and lastly,
- being open to reassessing and reconstructing the meanings of social justice from place to place, and from time to time methodologically.

It is not about reporting that social justice was achieved/found; but rather, that progress towards social justice was advanced concretely. This is what the articles in this Special Issue were all aiming to reveal, more or less. Each of the authors here has addressed a range of 'problems' standing in our way of achieving social justice. The more obvious barriers included the inability or unwillingness to clarify the policy differences between equality and equity, that is, between all students versus the individual needs of all students. What we can't do is continue to underestimate the difficulties involved in implementation (see Hutchting & Bickett; McQuillan & Leinger; Potter & Chitpin; Szelie, Tinoca, & Pinho; Torrance, Forde, King & Razzaq). In McQuillan & Leninger, there was a significant difference between how teachers interpreted the PD versus the staff members at the school. What that makes clear is that one size does not fit all with respect to socially just or inclusive schools. This point was made most clear in the article by Buyruk who envisioned trade unions as creating separate political spaces for re-learning.

My last point goes beyond the articles in the Special Issue: that is, unless and until educators communicate and receive a leadership message as part of their education, we will continue to delimit the moral power of educators in society. Educators know more than most policymakers based on every day experiences with students, parents, families, and communities. Our voices for change need to be heard. If educators continue to say and act that change must await until our students take the reins of power, we are doomed. In 2020, the pandemic is a call to educators to engage and speak out now. As educational researchers doing PD, PL, PLC, and CoPs, we can facilitate societal changes. That is our charge.

Note

1. The University Council of Educational Administration is a professional association of doctoral degree granting institutions.

Acknowledgments

I want to acknowledge the contribution of Professor Daniel Reyes-Guerra who read an early draft and made many substantive suggestions.

References

Bogotch, 2019. Towards a socially just system of newcomer school integration: Syrians in Canada and Germany. *In*: R. Papa, *et al.*, eds. *Handbook on promoting social justice in education*. Springer Publishers.

Bogotch, I., 2002. Educational leadership and social justice: practice into theory. *Journal of school leadership*, 12 (2), 138–156. doi:10.1177/105268460201200203

Bogotch, I., 2012. Social justice in middle passage. *In*: M. Acker-Hocevar, *et al.*, eds. *Snapshots of school leadership in the 21st century: the UCEA voices from the field project*. Information Age Publishing, 189–208.

Bogotch, I. 2014. Educational theory: The specific case of social justice as an educational leadership construct. In I. Bogotch & C. Shields (Eds). International Handbook of Educational Leadership and Social (In)Justice. (pp. 51–66). Springer

Denzin, N. (2018). Performance (auto) ethnography: Critical pedagogy and the politics of culture. New York: Taylor & Francis

Faubert, B. and Bogotch, I., (manuscript under review), 2019. Leading with inclusive ideals in Canada and Germany: educators' voices on how to successfully welcome and integrate student refugees into schools and communities. *In*: *Presented at the European Educational Research Association Conference*. Hamburg, Germany, Sept.

Vaughan, M. and Mertler, 2020. Reorienting our thinking away from "professional development for educators" and toward the "development of professional educators". *Journal of school leadership*, 1–16. doi:10.1177/1052684620969926

Index

Page numbers in **bold** refer to tables and those in *italic* refer to figures.

achievement gaps: defined 67, 70; differentiated learning strategies 68; economic/financial solutions 68; English government's *vs.* school leaders' definition 71–2; equity/equality 72; networking and management of 73–4; professional development strategies 69; raising aspiration 72–3; school-based, individual/system solutions 68–9; active learning 54
addressing issues of inequity *45*
adult learning experiences 38
Adult Learning Theory 31
advanced cultural competence 186
affluent schools, defined 52
Agirdag, O. 115
Agosto, V. 27, 29, 30
Albritton, S. 82
Ali, N. 32
Allio, R. J. 17
Anderson, E. 41
Angelle, P. S. 3
anti-racist school leadership: challenges 19, **20**; The Coalition for Equity and Rights 13; 'creating change' and 'making change sustainable' 16; curriculum 16; in England 10–11; and ethnicity 9–10; knowledge 18–19; learning to talk confidently about race/racism 15; professional development opportunities 18; racism/race discrimination 13; recruitment, development, retention and progression of staff 16; school leaders 13–14, 18; student and teacher demographics 15–16; *see also* BAME heritage
Anzaldua, G. 9
Applied Behavioural Analysis (ABA) 208
Arrupe, P. S. J. 57
attention deficit/hyperactivity (ADHD) 150
Auerbach, S. 82
autism spectrum disorder (ASD) 4, 150; challenges of special class **204**, **205**; characteristics 197; correlations 204; curricular activities 198; focus group participants 202; inclusive practice 213; ITE 199–200; Pearson product-moment correlations between variables **205**; qualifications 204; qualifications and training 210–11; respondents' satisfaction ratings *205*; special class provision 197, 208–9, *209*, 213; strengths and limitations 213–14; supports available to respondents **206**; teacher demographics 202–3, **203**; teaching children with 198–9; theoretical framework 200–1, *200–1*; total challenge scale **203**
awareness and reflection 59

Bacchi, C. 24–6, 28
Bacchi's approach: academic researchers 25; systematic content analysis 25; *see also* 'what's the problem represented' (WPR)
Balfe, T. 212
Ball, S. J. 67
BAME heritage: description 11; institutional interaction and students and staff 12–13; students and teachers, England 11–12
Banks, J. A. 187
Bascia, N. 108
Baysu, G. 115
Bednar, M. 165
beliefs of applicants 41
beliefs of aspiring leaders 39
Bellara, A. 27, 29, 30
Bell Curve 67
Bell, D. 11, 20
Bergnehr, D. 124, 129
Bertrand, M. 28
Bickett, J. 31
Birkett, M. 163–4
Bishop, H. N. 82
Blackmore, J. 30
Bogotch, I. E. 4, 24, 53
Boivin, N. 124
Boske, C. 27, 29, 30, 32, 55
Bouakaz, L. 124, 129
British Educational Leadership, Management and Administration Society (BELMAS), 2
Brooks, J. S. 13, 20, 25, 31, 32
Browne-Ferrigno, T. 41
Brown, K. M. 31, 32
Brundrett, M. 33
Burchell, H. 139
Burke, P. 136, 137, 143
Burstein, N. 81

Canadian Social Sciences and Humanities Research Council (SSHRC) 69
candidates' beliefs 39
Capper, C. A. 30, 33
Carpenter, B. W. 30-2, 40
Carr, W. 122
Causton-Theoharis, J. N. 31
Cerletti, L. 123, 129
challenging behaviour 212
Chitpin, S. 65-8, 70
city school district 42
class and teacher, profile of 212
Cohen-Miller, A. 124
Cole, H. A. 33
collaborative teacher study group (CTSG): American and African American history 184; characteristics of groups 186; culturally competent educators 184; data analysis 189; data collection 189; individual follow-up 183; instrumentation 188-9; PD experience 183, 184, 186; population and sample 188; pre- and post-experience 192; rethinking diversity 192; *see also* cultural competence
collective ethnography 122
Committee on Professional Development of Teachers and Principals (COTAP) 150
comprehensive gender-inclusivity trainings 164
continuing professional development (CPD) 73, 150; in HE (*see* higher education (HE)); innovations, social justice 138-9; research methodology 139-40; research methods 139; sessional academic staff 135; social justice project 140-3
Cooper, R. 40
Cosán framework 200
counternarratives 28
critical pedagogy 31, 137
critical professional development: approaches 94; description 93; social and school based in/equities 94; *see also* teachers of colour, K-12 schools
critical self-reflection 55
Critical Social Theory 31
cross-cultural interviews 32
Cross, T. 184, 185, 188
Crozier, G. 124, 129, 136, 143
Cucchiara, M. 123
cultural biographical life histories 32
cultural blindness 185
cultural competence: advanced 186; attitudes towards culturally diverse populations 190-1; blindness 185; civil rights activism 187; description 184; destructiveness 185; development of 192-3; educators 186-7; gender differences 193; incapacity 185; metacognitive strategies 185; and multicultural education 184-5; one's attitudes 185; pre-competence 185; racial differences 193
cultural destructiveness 185
cultural incapacity 185
culturally relevant legal practices and outcomes 218
cultural pre-competence 185

curricular leadership: La Lotería, arts classroom 96-9; La Lotería, build relationships 99-100

Darling-Hammond, L. 17
data-based decision-making 66
data-driven decision-making 66
Davies, J. 124, 129
de Cuevas, R. 33
deficit thinking: educators 40; equity 43-4; equity trap 40; everyone is equal *44*; expectation for student assimilation *45*; expectations for students living in poverty *45*; inequitable structures and systems 44; perceived student deficits 39; positive impact, quality education *44*
DeJaeghere, J. G. 186, 194
DeMatthews, D. 82
Demie, F. 12
Department for Education (DfE) 12
Department of Education and Skills (DES) 197
Dessel, A. B. 164
Devlin, M. 136
Diem, S. 30-2, 40
Dieste, B. 127
Dismantling Racism project (2019) 15
The Dismantling Racism project (2019) 14
district leadership, sustainable teacher collectives 101-3
diversity panels 32
DuFour, R. 54
Dyson, J. 139

Earl, L. M. 65, 69
ecological model, professional development *18*
educational leadership: deconstruction and reconstruction processes 126-8; educational politics 124; parental involvement 125; research examples 125-6
educational plunges 32
educational policy in England: neoliberalism 67; school leaders 66
Education Bureau (EDB) guides 150
education justice 121
educator training 164
Elue, C. 29, 30, 32
enabling pedagogy 137, 138
enabling programmes, defined 134
Endedijk, M. D. 81
England: anti-racist school leadership 10-11; BAME heritage 11-13
English school system 68
Equality Challenge Unit (2011) 13
equity traps 31
Espelage, D. L. 163-4
ethnographic research: collective ethnography 122; defined 121; education leaders and leadership groups 122; functions 122; initial method 123; research objectives 122; *see also* family participation; meta-ethnography
Evans, L. 107
Every Student Succeeds Act (Act, E.S.S.A., 2015) 81

faculty attitudes 29
Falk, W. W. 80
family participation 123–4
Feldman, S. B. 30, 31
Felix, Camacho 12
Fischer, C. 67
Flick, U. 83, 84
Flora, C. B. 80
Flora, J. L. 80
Forde, C. 54, 55, 57
Foucaldian approach 24
Foucault, M. 25, 140
Foucault's theory of discourse 140
Fraser, N. 108
Freire, P. 124
Fullan, M. 17
Furman, G. 31
future school leaders 32

Gasteyer, S. P. 80
Gay, G. 185
gender-expansive youth, U.S. schools 163–4
gender-inclusivity trainings: appropriateness of time for training 167; capability 167; facilitator 166; future research 176–7; future trainings 168, 173; gender-expansive youth, U.S. schools 163–4; limitations 176; new strategies 167, 171, **172**, *173*; policy conversations 163; practices 164–6; procedure 166–7; roles 167, 168; schools 167; training suggestions themes *173*; transgender and gender-expansive youth 162; usefulness, relevance and fit of training 167–9, **169**
geographic information system (GIS) 184, 187–8
Gettinger, M. 199
Gibbs, G. 141
Gillen, J. 140
Goetz, D. 199
Gooden, M. A. 13
Goodman, D. 53
Gramsci, A. 123
Gramscian approach 109
Greene, M. P. 13, 17, 19, 20
Groth, C. 41
Guerra, P. L. 40, 41
Guskey, T. 53

Harding, S. 123
Hare, R. D. 124
Hargreaves, A. 68
Hargreaves, D. H. 68
Harris, S. 31
headteachers 32
hearing impairment 150
Henze, R. C. 13
Hernandez, F. 28, 30, 31, 33
Hick, P. 210–11
higher education (HE) 134; critical 'enabling' pedagogies 136; enabling education & pedagogy 137–8; neo-liberal Australia 136–7; sessional staff 135; workshops 136; WP programmes 136
Hong Kong, teacher professional development 150
Hoppey, D. 81
Huchting, K. 3, 31
Huffman, S. 82
Hynds, A. 55

identity and stance 55
Individual Educational Plans (IEPs) 211
induction/professional learning 206–7
informal learning 81–2
initial teacher education (ITE) 199–200
Institute for Teachers of Colour Commited to Racial Justice (ITOC) 93, 95
institutional racism 10
intellectual disabilities (ID) 150
International School Leadership Development Network (ISLDN) 2, 32–4, 65
interpersonal racism 10

Jean-Marie, G. 13, 20, 25, 30–2
Jeffrey, B. 129
Jeynes, W. 69
Julve, C. 127

Karanxha, Z. 27, 29, 30
Katz, S. 65, 69
Kemmis, S. 122
Kennedy, A. 53
Kimelberg, S. M. 123
King, F. 200
knowledge base 55
Korach, S. 41
K-12 US educational system 43

Labone, E. 79, 81, 87
Ladson-Billings, G. 185
Laible, J. 32
La Lotería, arts classroom 96–9
La Lotería, build relationships 99–100
Langdon, F. J. 199
Latinx Student Union (LSU) 101
Lave, J. 139
leadership experience 41
'Leadership for Professional Learning' 1
leadership preparation: critical consciousness 40–1; defined 40; specific individual programs 40
leadership roles 57
Lea, T. 123
Le Clus, M. A. 85
LGBTQ students 164
Lindsey, R. B. 184
Long, J. 79, 87
López, J. A. 28
Lyson, T. A. 80

Macpherson, W. 9
Madison, D. S. 130
Magdaleno, K. R. 28

Mansfield, K. C. 123
Marshall, J. M. 31, 33
Marsick, V. J. 87
Martin, B. 28, 29
Marzano, R. 54
Mawhinney, H. 82
May, S. 185
McClellan, R. L. 82
McCoy, S. 198
McDermott, R. 138, 139
McGrew, J. H. 198, 199
McKay, J. 136
McKenzie, K. B. 28, 30, 31, 33, 40, 49
McLeskey, J. 81
Mendoza, Y. 32
Merchie, E. 200
Merriam, S. B. 83
meta-ethnography 124
Miller, C. M. 28, 29
Miller, P. 13–15, 20
Milner, A. 115
Ministry of National Education (MoNE) 109
Mishra, P. 149
Misiaszek, L. 136, 143
Mullen, C. A. 31
Murphy, J. 54
Muth, R. 41

National Association of Enabling Educators in Australia, (2019) 134
National Centre for Education Statistics (NCES) 52
National Centre for Student Equity in Higher Education (NCSEHE) 135
National Council for Curriculum and Assessment (NCCA) 211
National Council for Special Education (NCSE) 198, 202
National Curriculum in 1988 67–8
National Educational Psychological Services (NEPS) 198
National Policy Board for Educational Administration (2015) 38
National Professional Qualification for Executive Headship (NPQEL) 69
National Professional Qualification of Headship (NQPH) 69
National Qualification for Subject Leadership (NPQSL) 69
Nelson, S. W. 40, 41
neoliberalism 67
Niess, M. L. 149
Noblit, G. W. 124
No Child Left Behind (Act, N.C.L.B., 2002) 81
No Child Left Behind (NCLB) 27
Normore, A. H. 25, 31, 32
NVivo program 84

Objective Knowledge Growth Framework (OKGF) 66
Office of Standards in Education (Ofsted) 67–8

O'Malley, M. P. 33
O'Neil, C. 69
The Ontario Ministry of Education website 68
ordinary least squares (OLS) regression 168; roles and ratings 169, **170**, 171; school fixed effects 171
Organisation for Economic Co-operation and Development (OECD) indicators 67

Parsons, A. A. 122, 123
Patraw, J. M. 165
Payne, E. C. 166
Pazey, B. L. 33
Pedagogical Content Knowledge (PCK) 149
pedagogies of discomfort 31–2
performativity 67
personal racism 10
Petersen, A. 140
Peters, S. 81
physical disability (PD) 150
Picture Exchange Communication System (PECS) 208
political acumen and advocacy 55
Popper, K. 66
Posey-Maddox, L. 123
Potter, I. 3, 69
Pounder, D. 41
prejudice reduction workshops 32
pre-service leaders' beliefs 41
pre-service texts 165
primary provision schools 66
principal behaviours and teacher learning 81–2
principals' support 147
prior degrees 41
problem definition 29
professional development (PD) 53; defined 107; educational leadership (*see* educational leadership); formal, informal and non-formal learning experiences 107; model *88*; program 166; social justice and equity, education 108; strategies 69; teacher practice improvement 79; teacher unions 108
Professional Development in Education (PDiE) 1
professional learning: in culture of care 85–6; description 79–80; model *89*; observations **83**, 83–4, **84**; open and theory-driven interview questions 83; positive change 87; principal behaviours and teacher learning 81–2; rural schooling, challenges of 80–1; SJL 53–4; social context 84–5; *see also* social justice leadership framework
professional learning communities (PLCs) 84, 148–50, 158
professional preparation programmes 62–3
Public Agenda Report (2008) 17
public schooling systems 33

Race Equity Cycle 20–1
racism 9–10
Ravet, J. 199, 210
readiness, equity-focused leadership 43

readiness to lead 45–7, *45–7*
Rees, M. 139
reflective analysis journals 32
Reis, N. M. 28
researcher, role of 111
resumes 41
Robins, K. N. 184
robot-based pedagogy 151, 155–6
Rodela, K. C. 28
Rodríguez, M. A. 33
Rogers, A. 81
role of programs 43
Rorrer, A. 41
Ruble, L. A. 198, 199
rule-governed judgements 218
rural schooling: national educational policy 80; National Rural Development Institute 80; policy makers 80; standards-based reforms 81
Rusch, E. A. 32
Ryan, C. L. 165
Ryan, S. 139

Schecter, S. R. 124, 129
Scheurich, J. J. 31, 40
school-based, individual/system solutions 68–9
schoolwide leadership, reframing school culture 100–1
Sebastian, J. 30
secondary provision schools 66
selection, composition of programme's cohort 29
selection, importance of 41
Sherri, D. L. 124, 129
Shirley, D. 68
Shulman, L. S. 148–9
sitting leaders' beliefs 41
situated learning 85–6
Sleegers, P. J. 81
Sleeter, C. E. 185
Smith, M. J. 166
Snapshots of school leadership in the 21st Century: The UCEA1 Voices from the field project 219
Snyder, W. M. 138, 139
social development 150
social justice 220–1
social justice leaders: socially just schools and teachers 108–9; union member teachers 113–15
social justice leadership (SJL): awareness and reflection 59; Bacchi's approach 25; defined 82; definition 24; democratic principles and radical egalitarianism 53; development 54; difficult questions 61; economic elite domination 53; educational activist 59–60; educational contexts 52; equity practices, urban principals 82; expressions of justice 53; focus, literature search and analysis 25–6, **26**; Foucaldian approach 24; frameworks 30; identity 58–9; identity and stance 55; issues 28–30; knowledge base 55; knowledge base, context matters 57–8; leadership development 32–3; LGBTQI issues 33; LGBTQ students 82; literature 82–3; magis 60; measures 57; participant demographics **56**; participants 57; picking your battles 61–2; political acumen and advocacy 55; political acumen, being strategic 61; presuppositions/assumptions 28; private and tuition-based 56; procedures 56–7; professional learning 53–4; professional preparation programmes 62–3; school leaders 53; school site professional development programmes 62; supports and barriers principals 82; theories 30; university programs 33; urban principals 82; *see also* leadership preparation; 'what's the problem represented' (WPR)
socially just schools and teachers 108–9
Soyei, S. 17
special educational needs (SEN) 147
Special Education Needs Organisers (SENOs) 198
Special Education Support Service (SESS) 199
Special Needs Assistants (SNAs) 197
special provision schools 66
Specific Learning Difficulty (SLD) 207
Standard Assessment Tests (SATs) 67
Statistical Package for Social Sciences (SPSS) 189, 202
Stephen Lawrence Inquiry Report 9–10
Stevenson, H. 115
Stoiber, K. C. 199
Strand, S. 12
structural racism 10
student and teacher demographics 15
Suarez, K. 19, 20
suburban district 42
Sugrue, C. 211
support and professional learning 211
survey questions 42
Symeou, L. 123

teacher educators 31
teacher practices and interventions 211–12
teacher professionalism: critical professional learning experiences 111–12; defined 106; global organisations 106; injustices in schools 112–13; roles of 107; school administrators and teachers 107; and teacher unions 107–8; *see also* professional development
teachers: classroom contexts 54; data collection and analysis 152; K-12 education 148; learning, social-justice schools 149–50; participants **151**, 151–2; professional development, TPACK and PLC 148–9; professional learning across schools 153; role of 147; school leadership support 153–5, **154**; student populations and stakeholders' 148; TPACK 147–8
teachers of colour, K-12 schools: culturally sustaining pedagogies 94; district leadership 101–3; ITOC 93–4; methods 95–6; schoolwide leadership 100–1; *see also* curricular leadership
Teaching Council of Ireland (TCI) 199
teaching practices 207–8
technological knowledge 147–8

technological, pedagogical and content knowledge (TPACK) 147–50, 156–8, **157**
Teräs, H. 141
Terrell, R. D. 184
Theodorou, E. 123
Theoharis, G. 13, 24, 28, 30, 31, 80, 82, 89
Thompson, A. 149
Thrupp, M. 68
Torrance, D. 3, 54, 55, 57
transcripts 41
transformational learning experiences 31
Transformative Learning Theory 31
transition pedagogy 137
Troman, G. 129
Trujillo, T. 40
Turkey and Egitim-Sen education 109–10
Tyson, K. 30, 31

union member teachers: description 113; Egitim-Sen member teachers 114; organised activities of teachers 114
University Council for Education Administration (UCEA) 2
University of South Australia (UniSA College) 135–7
Usher, E. L. 198, 199

value bilingual education 47
Veelen, R. V. 81

Vigo-Arrazola, B. 3, 127
Vigo, B. 127
visual impairment 150

Watkins, K. E. 87
Watson, T. 13
Weapons of Math Destruction (WMD) 69
Weiner, L. 40
Wenger, E. 138, 139
'what's the problem represented' (WPR): academic researchers 25; achievement gap 27; American public schools 'children 27–8; conventional leadership development 27; definition 25; demographic changes in the US 27; policy 27
Whitmire, T. 17
widening participation (WP) 135
Winchip, E. 115
Winn, K. M 41

Yamato, G. 10
Young, J. K. 31
Young, M. D. 32, 41

Zambrano, M. A. 96
Zanten, V. A. 108
Zarate, M. E. 32
Zhang, Y. 186, 194

Milton Keynes UK
Ingram Content Group UK Ltd.
UKHW051815161024
449570UK00031B/189